CONSIDERING THE GREAT COMMISSION

CONSIDERING THE GREAT COMMISSION

EVANGELISM

AND

MISSION

IN THE

WESLEYAN

SPIRIT

EDITED BY
W. STEPHEN GUNTER
ELAINE A. ROBINSON

Abingdon Press
Nashville

CONSIDERING THE GREAT COMMISSION
EVANGELISM AND MISSION IN THE WESLEYAN SPIRIT

Library of Congress Cataloging-in-Publication Data

Considering the Great Commission : evangelism and mission in the Wesleyan
    spirit / edited by W. Stephen Gunter and Elaine Robinson.
      p. cm.
    Includes bibliographical references.
    ISBN 0-687-49363-3 (pbk. : alk. paper)
    1. Missions—Theory. 2. Evangelistic work. 3. Wesley, John, 1703–1791.
  4. Methodism.   I. Gunter, W. Stephen, 1947–   . II. Robinson, Elaine A.,
  1959–   .
  BV2063.C628 2005
  266'.7—dc22

                                                                        2005014098

05 06 07 08 09 10 11 12 13 14—10 9 8 7 6 5 4 3 2 1

MANUFACTURED IN THE UNITED STATES OF AMERICA

CONTENTS

INTRODUCTION

This collection of essays has its origins in a "Consultation on the Great Commission" held in Atlanta, Georgia, on the campus of Emory University in spring 2002. The more than two hundred delegates represented five continents and multiple constituencies from the denominational bodies that have membership in the World Methodist Council. It was the first event of its kind for United Methodist and Wesleyan denominations, and it was made possible through the joint sponsorship of the Candler School of Theology, the General Board of Discipleship, the General Board of Global Ministries, the Foundation for Evangelism, and the World Methodist Evangelism Institute. A foundational goal for the Consultation was to bring together representative voices from around the globe for three days of intentional conversation about how Methodists and Wesleyans are interpreting and practicing evangelism and mission. The initial support of Dean Russell Richey at the Candler School of Theology and his proactive work to involve the other United Methodist Church and World Methodist Council bodies made the 2002 Consultation a successful venture. The continued support of the Foundation for Evangelism in bringing together United Methodist professors of evangelism annually to continue the conversation and providing stipends for the contributing authors now makes this published volume possible. Here a special word of thanks is due to Paul Ervin, executive director of the Foundation for Evangelism. No less crucial to this entire venture were the leadership of Rev. Dr. Karen Greenwaldt at the General Board of Discipleship and Dr. H. Eddie Fox at World Evangelism and the World Methodist Evangelism Institute, the latter also at Emory University.

The chapters included in this volume are not, for the most part, the papers that were read or the seminars offered in the 2002 Consultation, but a solicited set of essays that fulfill in more formal ways the Consultation's intended goals. In the design of both the Consultation

1

and this anthology, the intention has been to bring concept and practice together. What follow, then, are neither strictly research essays, on the one hand, nor "how to" chapters, on the other. In almost every essay there are components of both. The student looking for conceptual ways to frame issues surrounding mission and evangelism will find constructive theological suggestions, and the district superintendent, pastor, or lay leader looking for ways to engage a mission-minded church or enable an evangelizing congregation will discover resources as well. In both the theoretical and the practical dimensions, the essays seek to engage as well as to move beyond what might be seen as the "traditional" understanding of evangelism and mission to deepen and expand the conversation about their meaning and practice in the twenty-first century.

In the following pages, we divide the essays into three basic parts. In Part One, "Conceptualizing the Great Commission," the essays focus on historical, theological, and other theoretical dimensions of interpreting the Great Commission. This effort at "conceptualizing" concludes with a brief essay by Stephen Gunter intended to set the conversation and provide definitions for the reader. The essays focus on various aspects of the theological and theoretical basis for evangelism and mission: Christology (Gunter), the impact of the rapid growth of Christianity in the Southern Hemisphere (Walls), globalization (Robert), and UMC discipline (Robinson). Part Two, "Contextualizing the Great Commission," addresses the changed and changing contexts for undertaking evangelism and mission. These essays examine the decline and renewal of Christianity in Europe with special reference to megatrends that confront all Western societies (Härtner), the role of women in the past and a challenge to hear them again (Warner), the perspective of Latinos/as in the *barrio* (Recinos), an African approach to church planting (Kurewa), and the context of the means of grace as a Wesleyan way of evangelism that is communal and personal (Knight). Finally, Part Three, "Practicing the Great Commission," provides a variety of essays suggesting ways to practice both evangelism and mission, including such things as faith sharing (Jones), personal witness (Crandall), multimedia communication (Weber), hospitality (Park), Christian education (Blevins), DISCIPLE Bible study (Rankin), the Alpha Course (Meadows), church planting and congregational development (Stone), and "sanctified singing" (Brown).

The concluding essay, "The Future of the Great Commission," is written retrospectively and prospectively—briefly overviewing the content of the volume and looking forward to what future conversations might entail. Indeed, the editors are painfully aware that we have not addressed all the issues that face a mission-oriented and evangelizing church. We are aware that we have written and edited these essays with a specific theological heritage in view, for we are convinced that recognition of theological location is no less pertinent than linguistic, racial, and cultural location. Indeed, theological location might offer a way of connecting the other specific locations. We offer these essays in the hope that they will prove constructive for congregations and denominations that are part of the stream of Christianity called Wesleyan.

PART I

Conceptualizing the Great Commission

CHAPTER 1

The Great Commission 1910–2010

Andrew F. Walls

The Great Migration

Around 1500, a development occurred with more significance for the future of Christianity than the Reformation itself. The Great Maritime Migration began, which was to shape the modern world and have complex effects upon the world's religions. Over the years it was in process, millions of people left Europe to make their homes or seek their fortune in lands that, before 1500, Europeans had not known or had not considered accessible. Whole nations, some with vast populations, came into being as a result of the movement, and the migrants and their descendants established hegemony over much of the world and much of its trade. The movement lasted for four and a half centuries, until the system that it produced imploded during the twentieth century.[1]

When the process began, Europe was more Christian than it had ever previously been. It took many centuries for Europe to become Christian; and by the time the Great Migration began, Christianity had been eclipsed in many other parts of the world where once it had been strong. Western Europeans, holding a form of Christianity heavily acculturated by centuries of interaction with the languages and cultures of Europe, became by default the representative Christians of their time. At first they essayed the crusading mode of propagating their faith, a method developed by long competition with their Muslim neighbors, the only non-Christian people (other than Jews) of whom they had much knowledge. The Spanish Conquest of the Americas was the last of the Crusades. But in much of the rest of the world the crusading method was manifestly out of the question, especially when such a small power as Portugal was the agent. For the most part, the powers of Christendom soon tired of official attempts to promote the spread of Christianity in the non-Western world.

An alternative to the crusading model of evangelization emerged. The initiatives for it came not from official sources, generally, but from radical Christians: those for whom the faith of Christ was more important than the economic, military, and political advantages of overseas activity. The missionary movement was born, based on dedicated people whose function was to offer and persuade without the power to coerce and, unlike the crusader, frequently needing to live on terms set by another society. Born in Catholic Europe and fueled by the new devotion of the Catholic Reformation, the missionary movement had by the seventeenth century entered into genuine interaction with the cultures of China, India, Japan, and Southeast Asia. The Protestant version of the movement took longer to blossom. Beginning in a small way in Puritan North America, it took new forms in the eighteenth century under the influence of German and Central European Pietism. In the wake of the Evangelical Revival, by the early nineteenth century it had set its impression deep on European and American Protestantism as a whole.

The World Missionary Conference

The high point of the Protestant missionary movement was the World Missionary Conference held in Edinburgh in 1910.[2] It was no triumphalist celebration, but a serious attempt at a systematic and businesslike analysis of what Protestant missions had already achieved and what remained to be done. Immense labor went into preparatory documents, notably the *Statistical Atlas of Christian Missions*,[3] designed so that those attending the conference could have all the available data about missions at their fingertips. Representation was carefully balanced to reflect the proportional involvement in missions of the main areas from which missionaries came, i.e., Britain, North America, and Continental

Europe, with a small place reserved for the "colonies," the white populations of Australia, New Zealand, and South Africa. Great pains were bestowed also to cover the entire theological spectrum represented in missions.

No conference was better prepared beforehand. Eight commissions toiled for months to produce book-length reports as a basis of discussion, and discussion itself was kept crisp and pointed by limiting contributors schooled in an age of pulpit eloquence to seven minutes each. The report that has attracted the most attention since then is that of Commission IV, titled *The Missionary Message in Relation to Non-Christian Religions*, with its analysis of replies to a detailed questionnaire sent all over the world.[4] But of all the volumes that together compose the record of the conference, none stands closer to the focus of the meeting than the report of Commission I, published under the title *Carrying the Gospel to all the Non-Christian World*.

The Commission was chaired by John R. Mott,[5] who was the dominating figure at the conference. Its twenty members—eight British, eight North Americans, and four Continental Europeans—included some of the biggest names in the missionary movement at that time. The report conveys its drift in the very title of the first section: "The opportunity and the urgency of carrying the Gospel to all the non-Christian world," and in the opening statement: "It is possible today to a degree far greater than at any time in the past to give the Gospel to all the non-Christian world."[6] The logic is evident. For one thing, the world was now known and explored. For another, it was largely open, not only in the political sense of unimpeded access, but also in the more important sense of the attitudes of its peoples. The decision-making classes in countries such as Japan and Korea, long closed to outside ideas, were now ready to listen. In India, the outcaste and lower caste groups were recognizing the advantages of Western civilization and were taking the Christian message seriously as a result. Africa and the Pacific were at last open to mission enterprise, even if colonial governments still placed obstacles in the way of missions where there was a Muslim presence.

If the Commission was impressed by the opportunities that the contemporary situation offered, it was also insistent that those opportunities might be merely transitory. Certainly, the non-Christian religions were losing their hold on key groups in some countries; but it did not necessarily follow that those classes would become Christian. They might turn elsewhere: the old religions might re-form to meet the challenges of modern thought, or the modern secular education spreading in Asia might create a climate unfavorable to Christianity. Islam, with the aid and protection of European governments, might become the religion of Africa. Western influences were spreading on a global scale, but the net result might be that the worst, not the best, features of Western civilization took root in Asia and Africa. The worst face of the West was already clearly visible among European and American residents in the non-Western world. Behind the present fair winds, the Commission saw unsettled weather coming.

The second and much the largest division of the report is a continent-by-continent survey of the non-Christian world, to which the *Statistical Atlas* is a companion. To the missionary situation in Asia, 142 pages are devoted, with 42 to Africa and 10 to Australasia and the Pacific. The short section "Non-Christians of the Western Hemisphere" is devoted entirely to the native peoples of the Americas, North and South, and to Asian immigrants there. This coverage points to a major lacuna in the World Missionary Conference: the organizers had aimed at theological inclusiveness; the more "catholic" expressions of Anglicanism, though to a significant degree involved in missions, had not been officially represented at earlier mission conferences, and the general theological climate of the time did not make such meeting easy. Although it required great diplomacy, the whole range of Anglican outlook was represented at the Edinburgh conference, and the organizers sought to avoid flash points where traditions might come into conflict. The greatest potential danger lay in discussions of Latin America. The focus of the conference was the unevangelized parts of the world. For many delegates, Latin America as a whole could be considered an unevangelized area; for others, only such mountain and forest peoples as had never been reached by Catholic missions could be so described. The effect was to make all reference to Latin America muted; hence, the marginal place it has in this survey.

Following the section on the Western Hemisphere, the report discusses the Jews throughout the world and then offers a final statement about "Unoccupied Sections of the World," or those areas with no missionary presence. "Unoccupied Sections of the World" first deals with areas of special difficulty of access or sparse population, such as Central Asia, but then resumes the theme of the position of Africa:

> To a far greater degree than even in the case of Asia, the heart of Africa constitutes a vast unoccupied field. . . . There are therefore to be found in Africa . . . more than a third of the population of the entire continent

without any existing agency having plans actually projected for their evangelisation. These figures are overwhelming, and they become more so when it is pointed out that the extent of the effective influence of existing missionary agencies has probably been greatly overestimated. The question can seriously be raised, Has the Church more than made a beginning in the evangelisation of the Dark Continent?[7]

The last division of the report concerns factors to be taken into account in planning for evangelization of the non-Christian world. It includes the substantial chapter "The Church in the Mission Field as an Evangelistic Agency," which includes in its summation the following statement:

> The small native Church, left to itself, is in danger within a generation or two of losing its tone under the influence of monotony, isolation, or ill-success. As a rule it needs the guidance and stimulus of the spiritual ideas, as well as the spiritual aids, which are supplied through contact by means of missionaries with the life of older Churches. While many noble leaders have arisen among the early converts in the field, it will take time to develop a sufficient number of men of knowledge, gifts, and character to enable the Church to stand with advantage, or even with safety, apart from foreign missionaries.[8]

The impression given by this whole division of the report is that the task of evangelization depends largely on Western missionaries. The factors to be taken into account in carrying the gospel to the non-Christian world include these: how missionaries should be deployed, how historical factors have skewed deployment, what methods missionaries should use, and the essential nature of the spiritual disciplines. The thrust of the report is about the responsibility of the Home Church, that is, the church of the fully evangelized world in Europe and North America. There are words addressed to the Home Church on the danger that increasing luxury and growing materialism may enervate it and quench the missionary spirit. Missionaries in the present situation are represented as overstretched physically, mentally, and spiritually, unable to get time for either the intellectual or the spiritual preparation for their demanding task. The Home Church must produce the missionaries and resources needed to tackle the unprecedented opportunities now being offered to evangelize the non-Christian world—before it is too late.

Almost a century later, it is at this point that the greatest difference appears between the conditions under which the older missionary movement sought to fulfill the Great Commission and the conditions of our own day. The best analysts and thinkers of 1910 could take for granted that there was a reasonably homogeneous, fully evangelized world, and a world beyond it that was unevangelized or only partly evangelized. From the fully evangelized world of Europe and North America, the Home Church must send forth its choicest persons to carry the gospel to the non-Christian world, where the Native Church, a tender young plant, stands as earnest of the future. As the report concludes,

> How to multiply the number of Christians who, with truthful lives, and with clear, unshakable faith in the character and ability of God, will, individually and collectively or corporately as a Church, wield this force [intercessory prayer] for the conversion and transformation of men, for the inauguration and energising of spiritual movements, and for the breaking down of all that exalts itself against Christ and His purposes—that is the supreme question of foreign missions.[9]

The analysts and the visionaries of 1910 realized that the hopeful signs they saw in Asia could quickly change to something much less hopeful. They could visualize the church of the West losing missionary zeal under the influence of its rapidly rising standards of living. What they could not glimpse was how soon the West, and Europe in particular, would become part of the non-Christian world. Perhaps the military language of "occupation" helped to disable them from remembering that Christian history, from the first century onward, suggests there are no permanently Christian lands. Christianity is serial in its growth, often decaying in its areas of apparent strength to start anew at or beyond its margins.

The analysts of 1910, living in an age of seaborne communications, held a maritime view of the church and of the world. The carriers of the gospel crossed the seas in order to fulfill their task.[10] Though they lived when the Great European Migration had reached its climax and generally believed that the spread of Western culture was favorable to the gospel, there is little sign in their report of triumphal rejoicing in the Western empires. The principal direct references to the empires are mostly about the ways Western governments obstruct missions, and there is no shortage of reference to the negative impact of certain aspects of Western culture. And while recognizing the difficulties that antiforeign movements in Asia create for missionaries, they have no condemnation for nationalism in claiming:

This national and racial spirit cannot and should not be crushed or checked. It is a matter of profound concern to the Christian Church. It will have much power to hinder or to facilitate the spread of Christ's Kingdom. Christ never by teaching or example resisted or withstood the spirit of true nationalism. Wherever His principles, including those pertaining to the supreme claims of His Kingdom on earth, have had the largest right of way, they have served to strengthen national spirit and not to weaken it.[11]

Even in India, where the national movement gave rise to a strong antimissionary feeling, the movement also denounced and discarded caste, hitherto the main obstacle to Christian preaching.[12] Nationalism should cause missionaries to deepen their work and to have the humility to realize that they must decrease while the Native Church must increase.[13]

On theology, Edinburgh 1910 has little to say. The conference ground rules, of course, precluded the introduction of topics known to be controversial among the participants; even so, it seems remarkable today that so many people, representing such a wide range of theological views, could accept that they were in agreement about what the gospel is. It seems equally remarkable that they could accept that evangelism, translation, education, medicine, literature, industrial training, and "women's work" were simply different methods of conveying it.[14] The most notable questioning voice was that of the German missiologist Gustav Warneck. Warneck was not present at Edinburgh, but sent a long letter to Mott, reproduced as an appendix to the report of Commission I.[15] Edinburgh 1910 reflects a certain confidence that, whatever issues may divide Christendom, there is a consensual theological deposit that is the common heritage of Christians.

The conference was a time of dreams and visions; the excitement of delegates is palpable, even in the staid pages of the official record.[16] The accounts of such participants as W. H. Temple Gairdner show it still more.[17] Not for nothing are the origins of the modern ecumenical movement conventionally dated from this meeting. A mere handful of Asian delegates attended amid hundreds from Europe and North America, and Africa and Latin America were essentially without indigenous representation; yet many who were present caught a first glimpse of what a truly world church might be like. The meeting was not solely visionary; most of it was severely practical, directed to systematic planning and cooperative effort.

Then and Now

The apparatus planned at Edinburgh for international missionary cooperation did come into being, but with much more difficulty than had been anticipated at the conference, and against the background of international events then unforeseen. Within a few years of the meeting came the shock of the Great War that pitted the missionary-sending countries against one another and ushered in the most violent period in modern history that was to last for the rest of the century and beyond it. The whole basis of the secure worldview that underlies the analysis of the world made by Commission I was swept away. Most surprisingly of all, the fundamental assumption on which Edinburgh thinking was founded, and indeed the missionary thinking of the whole previous century, was called into question. The Edinburgh delegates had thought of the Home Church in Europe and North America, the old Christendom, as the base for the evangelization of the rest of the world, and had assumed that it would remain so. But in the course of the twentieth century, perhaps the largest and fastest recession in Christian history (far faster, for instance, than what followed the first rise of Islam in the Middle East) set in. Its most obvious effect was in Europe, but it affected most of the lands newly settled in the Great European Migration. The effect has been slowest in the United States, but not the less clear for that. The old Christendom had lasted many centuries; around 1500, as the West newly engaged with the non-Western world and the Great Migration began, Christianity could be identified with Europe. Five centuries later, Europe could best be described as post-Christian, and Western people were no longer the representative Christians.

All this might seem to invalidate the whole vision and project of the World Missionary Conference were it not for another extraordinary aspect of twentieth-century church history. This is the extent to which the dreams and visions of the conference about the evangelization of the non-Christian world were fulfilled, though not in the way, nor always by the means, nor even in the places that the delegates expected and planned. The fact remains that, by a huge reversal of the position in 1910, the majority of Christians now live in Africa, Asia, Latin America, or the Pacific, and the proportion is rising. Simultaneously, with the retreat from Christianity in the West in the twentieth century—just as the visionaries of Edinburgh hoped—came a massive accession to the Christian faith in the non-Western world. The map of the Christian church, its demographic and cultural makeup, changed more dramatically during the twentieth century than (probably) in any other since the first.

But it happened in ways that the analysts of 1910 could not have predicted. The most favorable signs about the future that were observable to them lay in Asia. They saw multitudes in Japan, in China, in India turning to new ways of thought, and thus, as it seemed, becoming open to Christian ideas as never before. The great Asian cultures had long received the heaviest deployment of missionary personnel and effort. Medical missions (the most financially intensive branch of missions) and other specialties had been developed largely with Asia in mind. Missions were considerably involved in higher education to the university level in Asia, in addition to equipping entire medical faculties there. But the Christian growth that has taken place in Asia has not always followed the patterns of missionary investment. China has indeed seen substantial, if as yet unquantifiable, Christian growth, but it has come in the second half of the twentieth century, in the teeth of official disfavor and often outright hostility. And the growth has been most pronounced in the period after missionaries were excluded from the country. Korea was somewhat cursorily treated in the Edinburgh Commission's report, since Protestant work there was then so new and the country's long period of isolation from foreign contact was so recent. (North Korea's present isolation is in some ways a reversion to tradition.) But the twentieth century—a time of frequent and varied trauma for Korea—saw Korean Christianity becoming a major force in the land, taking shape in the national movement against Japanese colonialism, burgeoning in the times of worst trouble. In recent decades, besides becoming a significant force in North America, Korean Christianity has produced hundreds of missionaries to serve in other parts of the world, including some of the most inhospitable, where Western missionaries never penetrated. If any country can be said to preserve the spirit of 1910, it is South Korea.

A whole chain of churches now stretches across the lands bordering the great mountain ranges from the Himalayas to the Southeast Asian peninsula. Most of these churches were tiny or nonexistent in 1910. Then, and for long after, Nepal was considered a country wholly closed to the Christian message; now it has a thriving church. Vigorous churches have also arisen among the complex of peoples who live in northeast India and southwest China who are neither Indic nor Han Chinese, and these, for the most part, in the twentieth century. There are states in northeast India where Christianity is the majority religious profession. Across the frontier with Myanmar, among peoples of similar ethnic origin, Christian growth has accelerated since the expulsion of missionaries in the 1960s. In each of the countries mentioned—Nepal, India, China, Myanmar—Christians are a minority and often a small one, but taken together (and with the related Christian communities in Thailand) they form a substantial Himalayan-Arakan Christian community of which there was little trace when the conference met in Edinburgh.

Latin America, which diplomacy led the World Missionary Conference to leave aside, has now become a theater of Christian operations, which no one can possibly ignore. The peculiar history of Latin America has given it an unusual Christian trajectory. The conquest was intended to bring it within the existing Christendom; thus, Mexico became New Spain, with the expectation that its laws and customs would be those of old Spain. In the sixteenth century Latin America received the church settlement adopted in southern Europe, a settlement arising out of the conditions and controversies of sixteenth-century Europe. It received the Catholicism of the Council of Trent without going through the processes and experiences that produced the Council of Trent. For several centuries there seemed no reason to doubt the successful incorporation of Latin America within the Christendom framework derived from medieval Europe. But Latin America, though in one sense a European artifact, was no mere extension of Europe; it was a union of diverse peoples with powerful indigenous religious influences. And in the twentieth century, with rapid urbanization and huge social ferment, the lid blew off the religious pressure cooker. A theological upheaval occurred as drastic as those that befell Europe in the sixteenth century, Latin America's delayed Reformation era. As in Europe, there was a pastoral revolution within the established church; as in Europe, reforming zeal took both conservative and radical ecclesiastical forms; as in Europe, popular religious movements burst the bonds of the old church altogether. Protestantism, outside immigrant communities, had traditionally played no significant part in Latin America; at the time of the World Missionary Conference it was hardly visible there. By the end of the twentieth century, however, Protestants formed a significant proportion of the population, in some Central American countries perhaps forming a majority, not of the population, but of the actively practicing Christians in the population. But the movement took an indigenous form: the overwhelming majority of Latin American Protestants are Pentecostal. What in the West has been marginal has in Latin America become the mainstream. Latin America may be an artifact of the West, manifestly carrying the impress of influences from Europe and North America, but its potent mixture of the cultures of three continents has ensured that it has a religious dynamic of its own. Liberation theology and Pentecostal preaching and congregational life are examples of its effect, and the spread of a huge diaspora from Latin America, a further effect of the twentieth century, will ensure that its influences spread far beyond its boundaries.

The analysts of 1910 saw inland Africa as "a great unoccupied field," and questioned whether more than a beginning had been made of the evangelization of the continent. It is perhaps the change in Africa that marks the strongest contrast between the church today and the church as seen by the writers of the report of Commission I. The figure for professing Christians has risen over the period from something like 10 million to something over 300 million. Sub-Saharan Africa has become one of the Christian heartlands, and is quietly slipping into the place in the Christian world that was once occupied by Europe.

A Transformed Church

The twentieth century brought the transformation of the Christian church and opened a new chapter in Christian history. After a Western phase that lasted several centuries, the church has a new shape, a new ethnic composition, and a new cultural orientation. Christianity is again becoming a non-Western religion. There are considerable implications in this for the fulfillment of the Great Commission, making it a different matter from what appeared so plain to the delegates at Edinburgh in 1910. For one thing, North America and Europe will not be presiding at the table. The representative Christians, those by whom the quality of twenty-first-century (and doubtless twenty-second-century) Christianity will be judged, are now Africans, Asians, and Latin Americans; Western Christians are a minority (and if present trends hold, a shrinking minority) in the church. The great theaters of mission are Africa, Asia-Pacific, and Latin America, raising key issues for Christian faith and service and determining the Christian agenda for the whole world that Christ redeemed. Western Christians, so long used to leadership since the time of the Great Migration, will need to learn new skills as assistants and facilitators. The way that globalization works in the world leaves the West in charge. True globalization in the church could put the process into reverse.

The meeting in 1910 envisaged the "Native Church," as the churches of Africa and Asia were then designated, as a tender young plant in need of supervision. It is salutary to remember what many of those churches have encountered since those days. Is there a parallel in Christian history to the story of the church in China over the past fifty years, in terms of what it has endured and how it has emerged? Over the same period, Christian faith in many parts of Africa has been honed on endemic disaster; the normal climate of the life of faith has been war, disruption, dispersion, disease, and disappointment. The churches of South Africa were called to give moral leadership to the nation in ways the Western church has not known for many centuries. Elsewhere churches, often the only functioning forms of civil society when even the state has broken down, have become salt and light to nations in distress. If suffering, persecution, and faithful wrestling with impossible situations are marks of Christian authenticity, then we may assume that God has been training certain churches for leadership in the fulfillment of the Great Commission, imparting to them accumulated knowledge of God's salvation.

Theology is one area in which that leadership may be necessary. Theology is about making Christian decisions. It is the effort to think about faith in a Christian way. The great doctrinal issues of the Trinity and Incarnation were forced on Christians by the need to explore their deepest convictions about Christ by thinking in Greek, using indigenous Greek vocabulary, categories of thought, and methods of debate. It was strenuous and painful—there is no "safe" theology. But it led to discoveries (true discoveries, though not necessarily the final ones) about who Christ is, that never could have been achieved using traditional categories, such as Messiah, alone. The great creeds that resulted can still draw us out in worship and adoration as we recite them. The discoveries came from the process of translation, moving into new intellectual territory by exploring the meaning of Christ in terms of the Greek heritage and identity. And it did not mean abandoning the past; Messiah and the other traditional titles continue to mean what they always did. It did not mean abandoning Scripture; the process made clear things that were in Scripture all the time, but clearly seen only when they were brought out by translation.

Analogous processes have occurred on other occasions as Christian faith has crossed cultural frontiers and required Christians to think in new categories and face issues never faced by Christians before. In our time we could well be entering a period of theological creativity such as the church knew in the third and fourth centuries. That period of creativity arose from the interaction of the gospel with a Hellenistic culture and a firmly established tradition of Greek thought. In our time it could arise from continued Christian interaction with the ancient cultures of Africa and Asia. Issues will arise where events, conditions, and traditions in Africa and Asia force a need for Christian decisions.

The Western theological academy is at present not well placed for leadership in the new situation. It has been too long immersed in its local concerns and often unaware of the transformation that has taken place in the church. It is often hugely ignorant of the world in which the majority of Christians live, their social and religious contexts, and the history and life of their churches. Its intellectual maps are pre-Columbian; there are vast areas of the Christian world of which they take no account. Nor are its products always readily transferable outside the West. Western theology is, in general, too small for Africa; it has been cut down to fit the small-scale universe demanded by the Enlightenment, which set and jealously guarded a frontier between the empirical world and the world of spirit. Most Africans live in a larger, more populated universe in which the frontier is continually being crossed. It is a universe that comprehends what Paul calls the principalities and powers. It requires a theology that brings Christ to bear on every part of that universe, making evident the victory over the principalities that Paul ascribes to Christ's triumphal chariot of the Cross. The new age of the church could bring a theological renaissance with new perspectives, new materials, new light on old problems, and a host of issues never faced before.

In the Epistle to the Ephesians, we have a vivid account of two sharply contrasting Christian lifestyles in the early church. There was the way of life of the first believers, who had never changed their religion and still rejoiced in Torah and circumcision, understanding Jesus wholly in terms of Jewish history and experience. There was also the new Hellenistic way of being Christian that we see in Paul's letters being constructed among former pagans. For them Torah and circumcision had no place; instead, existing Hellenistic social and family life and ways of thinking had to be turned toward Christ. Both ways of life were converted lifestyles; but neither was complete in itself. Each needed the other, for both were building blocks in the New Temple, both were functioning organs in the Body of which Christ was the head. Only as they came together could the Temple be built, the Body function, the full stature of Christ be realized.

When Ephesians was written, there were only two significant cultures and, thus, two converted lifestyles of which to take note. Not so long after the letter was written, one of those, the original Jewish, dropped out of sight. Now the Ephesian moment has returned; however, there are no longer two, but many cultures into which Christ has come by faith. The different converted lifestyles belong together; they are necessary building blocks in the New Temple designed for God's worship. They are all functioning organs in the Body of which Christ is the head. Some of the great tests of Christianity in the new age of the church will be ecumenical. This is no longer a matter of how different confessions and denominational traditions relate to one another. It is rather how our Lord's prayer that all his disciples may be one can be realized in a Body composed of African and Indian and Chinese and Korean and Hispanic and Caribbean and European and North American Christians.

Thus, we return to our starting point. The last phase of the fulfillment of the Great Commission, so well reflected in the World Missionary Conference, took place in the context of the Great Migration. Over a period of four and a half centuries, millions of people of European origin migrated to the non-Western world and, in the process, set up Western hegemony over much of it. The new phase has a different background. From the middle of the twentieth century, the Great Migration went into reverse. Multitudes from the non-Western world have migrated to the West, with the United States as the principal target. The process looks set to continue, as falling population in the developed nations calls for immigration to sustain economic viability and population pressures elsewhere force people to seek new homes. Those coming to the West include multitudes of Christians, who often transplant their churches and congregational life. It is a development that opens the possibility of realizing the Body of Christ in a truly multicultural church, or the terrible indictment of failing to do so. The same development, and the new resources that it brings, sheds new light on one of the supreme evangelistic tasks of the new phase of the Great Commission, the reevangelization of the West.

There are, in fact, several Great Commissions in the New Testament. The most familiar is that in Matthew 28:19-20. Its starting point is the universal authority of Christ; the thrust is the discipling of nations, with baptism and the whole teaching of Jesus shared with the nations. The commission is not to make some disciples in each nation, but to make the nations into disciples. In other words, the commission is about culture, about turning a nation's history and traditions and ways of thought, the things that make it distinctive, the roots of its identity, toward Christ. The outcome—and the process may take many generations—is that glorious diversity of converted lifestyles taken into the building of the New Temple, and pointing in its variety to the full stature of Christ.

There is also the Great Commission of John 20:21: "As the Father has sent me, so I send you." The disciples are commissioned as Jesus was commissioned, with the loving authority of the head of the family. And they are sent for the purposes Jesus was sent for. They are sent to preach and to teach, certainly, but they are also sent to be and to do. They are to feed, heal, and restore people, to confront evil, to suffer, perhaps unjustly, on behalf of others. We cannot set aside either version of the Great Commission. A measure of fulfillment by earlier generations has provided our generation with resources to take up the challenge of both versions in the new age of the church.

CHAPTER 2

The Great Commission in an Age of Globalization

Dana L. Robert

Since 1792, when Baptist shoemaker William Carey wrote his *Enquiry into the Obligation of Christians to Use Means for the Conversion of the Heathen*, the Great Commission has defined what it means to be a Protestant in the broadly evangelical tradition. In his *Enquiry*, Carey argued that Christ's command in Matthew 28:19-20 was not something confined to the time of the disciples, but was a present responsibility for all his followers: "Go therefore and make disciples of all nations, baptizing them in the name of the Father and of the Son and of the Holy Spirit, and teaching them to obey everything that I have commanded you." Within thirty years of Carey's position paper, denominations and groups of like-minded believers in the United Kingdom, Continental Europe, and the United States had founded missionary societies. Although the nineteenth century was designated the "Great Century" of foreign missions by historian K. S. Latourette, the twentieth century saw the greatest geographic expansion of Christianity since the conversion of Europe. At the end of the second millennium since the birth of Jesus, the gospel has spread into every part of the globe and into most of the world's major cultural groupings.

But what are the meaning and the future of the Great Commission in the twenty-first century? Not since the days of William Carey has there been so much dissension among Christians over its meaning. While the Great Commission resonates within the hearts of Protestants as a mark of evangelical identity and faithfulness to the will of God, the context in which it operates has changed drastically over the past few decades. Just as William Carey's context lent itself to the rediscovery of the Great Commission, so today's context is raising questions about its interpretation for Christian mission.

In this essay, I wish to reflect on the meaning of the Great Commission in an age of globalization. While the gospel of Jesus Christ is timeless, the contexts in which mission takes place are always changing. We must exegete the biblical texts and the contexts for Christian mission in the twenty-first century. Christian mission, or witness to the gospel across diverse boundaries, is a process of relating the Christian faith to the ever-changing realities in the world created by God and yearning toward re-creation. Those committed to mission must reflect on it with the Bible in one hand and the newspaper in the other, to paraphrase Karl Barth. As E. Stanley Jones said, when confronted with the inexorable forces of Indian nationalism, "Evangelize the inevitable." In other words, look around the world, see what is going on, and then figure out how the gospel is relevant to that inevitable situation and context.

Is the Great Commission Finished?

The spread of Christianity into nearly every culture in the world by the late twentieth century has raised the issue for many whether the Great Commission should or can retain its centrality for Christian world mission. Has the command "Go into all the world" finally been fulfilled on the part of Jesus' followers? Mission leaders from conservative and liberal perspectives, as well as religious pluralists, are questioning whether the Great Commission is finished. Many evangelical denominations and parachurch agencies worked together during the late twentieth century to reach all the so-called unreached peoples with the gospel message. Called the AD 2000 Movement, this united push concentrated on fulfilling the Great Commission. Central to its energy was a definition of the missionary task that revolved around planting the church in every group of people by the year 2000. Defining the "nations" as ethnic groups of people rather than political entities, in 1974 at the Lausanne Conference on World Evangelization, Dr. Ralph Winter proved with statistics that several billion of the world's people could be reached only by cross-cultural missionaries. Rather than representing the end of the days of cross-cultural mission, as many mainline churches were arguing during the late 1960s and early 1970s, the work of reaching the mosaic of ethnic groups had just begun. Winter launched what became a massive popular movement to reach this mosaic of peoples. The Southern Baptists, Assemblies of God, Wycliffe Bible Translators, Youth With A Mission, the Lausanne Committee on World Evangelization, and virtually every large parachurch missionary agency united to compile databases, conduct educational programs in local churches, and distribute the unreached peoples among mission agencies and evangelical congregations. Their goal was to establish by the year 2000 a church-planting movement within every group of unreached peoples in the world. A series of major conferences emphasized that evangelicals worldwide were committing themselves to the task of finishing the Great Commission in their lifetimes.

Some leaders of the Lausanne Movement and the AD 2000 initiative have questioned whether the Great Commission is, in fact, on the verge of being completed by the successful planting of vital, evangelistic churches among every people group. The AD 2000 Movement closed its doors on March 31, 2001. According to Luis Bush, head of the AD 2000 and Beyond Movement, by the end of 2000, eight out of every ten people had "access to the entire Bible in their own language."[1] Ninety-five percent of the world's population had access to some Scriptures, but also to Christian radio broadcasts and recordings, and to the *Jesus* film. By the end of the year 2000, an estimated 80 percent of the world had heard the gospel.[2] In Bush's mind, the very success of Christian mission led to questions about the interpretation of the Great Commission in the twenty-first century. Ralph Winter, founder of the unreached peoples movement, noted that there are few "traditional mission fields" left.[3]

No less a person than Billy Graham, who has devoted his time and resources to world evangelization for many decades, has suggested that the Great Commission is being fulfilled.[4] On December 8, 2001, during a televised Billy Graham Crusade in Fresno, California, Graham related his message to current events, as he often does, in this case to the worldwide growth of terrorism. He interpreted the events of 9/11 as signs for the second coming of Jesus Christ. One of his main reasons for heralding the imminent return of Christ is that, for the first time in human history, the gospel is being proclaimed worldwide in accordance with Matthew

24:14: "And this gospel of the kingdom will be proclaimed throughout the world, as a testimony to all the nations; and then the end will come." In Graham's millennial vision, international terrorism and the global spread of Christianity are working together as signs of the end of the age.

On the other side of the theological spectrum, a number of missiologists are concluding that the Great Commission should no longer be emphasized as the center of Christian mission because the age of expansion is over. A subtext of this position is that Christian expansion is an embarrassing remnant of colonial history. Robert Schreiter, one of the greatest North American Catholic missiologists today, argues that the paradigm of mission for the twenty-first century should be reconciliation.[5] He is joined by other voices who argue, perhaps in reaction to narrow readings of the Great Commission, that expansion carries with it a connotation of Christian superiority and a history of Western coercion. Schreiter cites 2 Corinthians 5:18-19, "All this is from God, who reconciled us to himself through Christ, and has given us the ministry of reconciliation; that is, in Christ God was reconciling the world to himself, not counting their trespasses against them, and entrusting the message of reconciliation to us." Reconciliation as the twenty-first-century model for mission means the reconciliation of God with humanity through Jesus Christ, of human beings with each other in situations of violence, and of humanity with the cosmos. In this view, the Great Commission is finished not because the task of world evangelization has been completed, but because it proves inadequate in a culturally and theologically pluralistic world.

The New Age spirituality that appeals to our post-Christian Western culture provides a third set of arguments for the irrelevance of the Great Commission. Where Billy Graham sees the globalization of terrorism and of Christianity as signs of the end times, the professional futurist Gerald Celente, author of *Trends 2000*, believes that the quest for spirituality caused by the shock of the events of 9/11 will give rise to what he calls "New Millennium religion." The post-9/11 context reveals that the conditions are right for a "serious attempt to redefine spirituality, for the rise of a worldwide religion that will unite, rather than divide, the peoples of globe."[6] Celente predicts that Christianity and other established religions will disintegrate because of their hypocrisy, as people seek a global religion that supports their individual lifestyles. In Celente's New Age argument, the Great Commission is no longer relevant to human spirituality, which has outgrown the boundaries of any one religion.[7]

Mission as Globalization

Arguments suggesting that the Great Commission is finished have in common the discourse of "globalization." Globalization, according to sociologist of religion Roland Robertson, "refers both to the compression of the world and the intensification of consciousness of the world as a whole."[8] It connotes the "increasing interconnectedness of the world as a single place, and the consequences and dynamics of this growing interconnectedness."[9] Christianity, with its global outreach and expansion, participates in this phenomenon of globalization in the contemporary age. Today, in both the conservative and the progressive discussions, the worldwide spread of Christianity has become *prima facie* evidence for the decreasing importance of the Great Commission in the twenty-first century. These views are problematic for Protestants for whom the Great Commission remains central to their tradition, but who question the relationship between the missionary movement and Western expansionism or imperialism. Unease about the relationship between economic globalization and missionary Christianity is the twenty-first-century version of the twentieth-century concern about the relationship between colonialism and Christian mission. The darker side of economic globalization, with its perceived destruction of local cultures by forces of global capitalism, technologies, and consumerism and the growing imbalance between rich and poor, also raises questions about the Great Commission. Even as we celebrate the worldwide spread of Christianity, critics implicate the Great Commission as the ideological core of a dominant Western socioeconomic system of privilege. What is the relationship of the Great Commission to economic globalization? Should Westerners still go overseas as missionaries when peoples in poor parts of the world associate us with oppressive wealth, political domination, and a culture of materialism?

The events of 9/11 reminded Americans that we live in an interconnected world. Whether international markets, the Internet, or religions, no part of the globe seems beyond the reach of unifying international visions. As world economic integration relentlessly marches forward, groups of people fearful of losing their traditional worldviews deliberately reinforce their own local identities of ethnicity, race, and religion. Yet reinforcing the local aspects of one's identity and then exporting that identity to other parts of the world is, itself, part of the process of globalization. When I was growing up in southern Louisiana, things like barbecued redfish, boiled crawfish, fried okra, and dark-roasted coffee were part of our local culture. Then with the globalization of Cajun food, blackened redfish became a choice item of cuisine all over the world. When I go to remote eateries in Zimbabwe, I can find Tabasco sauce from Avery Island, Louisiana, on the table. Something that was only recently part of a local identity, namely, Cajun food, has been redefined and commodified in the brave new world of global marketing. The local is no longer separate from the global. Rather, the two are intertwined in a process sometimes referred to as "glocalization." The very identity of local culture becomes reified through the process of globalization.

As a historian, I agree with those who argue that world Christianity is one of the chief examples of what we call globalization. It is not enough merely to examine globalization as a *context* in which mission operates. Instead, the Great Commission itself has been an intrinsic part of the globalization process. Roland Robertson argues that religious discourse is where discussions of globalization first emerged. The following analysis suggests some of the ways in which the Protestant missionary movement, as shaped by the Great Commission, is intertwined with globalization in its varied forms.

1. Theological Basis

Today's Christianity can be considered an example of globalization because the vision of the kingdom of God has always provided the central theological framework for the Protestant mission movement.[10] The practical work of cross-cultural mission has been done against the backdrop of God's reign, a vision of humankind united under the lordship of Jesus Christ, with people called from every nation, tongue, and tribe.[11] The good news in Jesus Christ is intended for everyone; that is, the message is a universal one.

In an age when the geographic spread of Christianity is taken for granted, it is hard to recapture how strange it seemed for missionaries to leave forever everything they had known and to venture on tiny ships into foreign lands. Going to places where they did not know the language or the customs, where they lacked medical care, friends, and protection, they went prepared to die. While the early Protestant missionaries were certainly motivated by their desire to save souls from eternal damnation rather than to become martyrs, their writings demonstrate that the great millennial vision of the Kingdom, of the Lamb upon his throne surrounded by believers from all nations, was the inspiration that enabled many of them to sacrifice their lives.

In short, a primary theological warrant for the globalization of the church is the vision of the kingdom of God—the vision hoped for in the Great Commission's command to go to all nations. As believers come from all nations, they enter a universal fellowship. Yet, because the gospel must become part of each culture it enters, the many churches of the world have unique ways of living out the gospel truths in their own cultures. In some ways, then, globalization has been an intrinsic part of the missional vision for the kingdom of God. Indigenous theology within the framework of global church unity has been a self-conscious goal of the Protestant missionary movement, at least since the early twentieth century.[12]

2. Historical Connections

Historians agree that Protestantism as a global phenomenon has accompanied the spread of capitalism. While missionaries have often been the last line of defense for indigenous peoples against exploitation by commercial and political interests, the Western missionary movement and capitalism nevertheless emerged together in human history during the 1700s, and were products of the same forces. The birth of capitalism and the birth of the voluntary missionary agency were part of the same phenomenon of liberating the human being from exploitation by hereditary monarchy, chieftainship, or religious hierarchy. Capitalism and voluntary mission societies replaced the older Christendom model of missions based upon a state-supported church with a more democratizing notion that anyone could choose his or her religion, and even become a missionary to propagate particular points of view.

William Carey was breaking with a state church tradition in advocating that groups of volunteers be sent into the world to offer the Christian religion to the so-called heathen. Carey's theological reinterpretation of the Great Commission broke with the hyper-Calvinism of the eighteenth-century Baptists by arguing that people were capable of choosing to follow Christ if given the chance to do so. In short, God's grace could be appropriated by human cooperation.

Equally significant to Carey's theological formulations was his use of merchant capitalism as one means for the enactment of Christian mission. Carey noted in the *Enquiry* that merchant ships were traversing the world for the sake of material gain. If British merchants were risking their lives halfway around the world, were not devout Christians capable of doing the same for a more noble purpose? The global reach of British trade, along with the British Empire, provided the physical means for the global spread of Protestantism. Carey used the trading company as a model for the voluntaristic missionary society. Merchants founded trading companies in which selling shares raised the cash needed to invest in trade goods and to send agents to the foreign markets. The shareholders shared the profit and losses, depending on the success of the venture. Such voluntary trading companies could be imitated by mission organizations. Members of a denomination, for example, Baptists or Anglicans, could become shareholders by virtue of providing financial support for a missionary. The venture showed a "profit" if the missionary made converts, and it failed if the missionary died or showed no results.[13]

This essentially capitalist model, known as the "voluntary society," became the norm through which Western Protestantism channeled its early missionary zeal. By the 1820s, voluntary mission-sending societies composed of like-minded people existed in the United Kingdom, Continental Europe, and the United States. Since the first task of these voluntary societies was to scout locations where missionaries could flourish, it is no wonder that many of the mission fields of the early 1800s were located in European spheres of influence—for example, India or the Middle East. Missionaries often rode on merchant ships under colonial protection to get to the mission field. Often the only other Europeans with whom they could socialize were colonial officials or merchants stationed in the various mission countries. The early nineteenth-century New England towns, which comprised the heart of American trading networks with the South Pacific and China, also provided America's first foreign missionaries.

In other words, emerging global capitalism was the unwitting midwife of the Protestant missionary movement. Being incarnate in the world of frail humanity meant using the spread of capitalism and colonialism to facilitate church expansion. Even though secular merchants and government officials were often at odds with the ethical stances of the missionaries—for example, early missionary opposition to the slave trade—the missionaries used the emerging capitalist infrastructure to spread the gospel. Antislavery missionaries connected with the Church Missionary Society and the London Missionary Society also believed in introducing Western agriculture and commerce to help African converts improve themselves and to thwart the European colonialists and slavers, a philosophy characterized as the "Three C's" of Christianity, commerce, and cultivation (later civilization). Another important factor in the spread of revivalistic Protestantism around the world was the stationing of evangelical soldiers in British outposts. The spread of Methodism by soldiers and colonists around the world in the early 1800s was the beginning of the globalization of evangelical Christianity. Even as Methodism remained a fairly small movement in Great Britain itself, it exploded among the transient European populations in places like North America, Australia, and India.[14] The expansionism of capitalism and the geographic spread of European colonialism provided contexts in which popular Protestantism became a global phenomenon.

3. The Post–World War II Expansion of the Church

After World War II, Christianity spread throughout the world. In the year 1900, approximately one-third of the world was Christian, and Europeans composed 70.6 percent of the world's Christian population. By the year 2000, approximately one-third of the world was still Christian, but the European percentage of that total had shrunk to 28 percent. Africa and Latin America combined provided 43 percent of the total Christian population. A major demographic shift thus occurred as Christianity grew in the non-Western world, but declined in Europe and remained largely unchanged in North America.

Most missiological writings about globalization refer specifically to this demographic shift in the Christian population: the typical Christian in the twenty-first century is a Latin American or African woman. One of the most interesting factors about this rapid growth is that it largely occurred after the end of European colonialism. Even though colonialism and capitalism provided an infrastructure for the Western missionary movement, indigenous forms of Christianity that explicitly rejected Western control emerged throughout the colonial world in the early twentieth century. On the eve of the Communist takeover in China in 1948, for example, 25 percent of the Christians were already members of indigenous Chinese churches.[15] And when communism drove Christianity underground, church growth continued under indigenous leadership. By the 1920s, a couple of dozen independent denominations had emerged in the Philippines. In Africa, indigenous churches were seen by the colonizers as dangerous, anticolonial movements, and were sometimes met with force.

But with the end of colonialism beginning in the 1960s, groups of Christians in Africa, Asia, and Latin America were free to assert their own identity without being accused of being lackeys of Western interests. So-called mission churches, like Anglicanism, Catholicism, and Presbyterianism, grew exponentially after independence. To take Anglicanism, for example, by the year 2000, there were 17 million baptized Anglicans in Nigeria, compared to only 2.8 million Episcopalians in the United States. At the 1998 Lambeth Conference, which is the highest consultative body of the Anglican Communion, 224 of the 775 bishops were from Africa, compared with only 139 from the United Kingdom and Europe.[16]

For the past twenty years, perhaps the feature of world Christianity attracting the most attention has been the rapid growth of Pentecostalism around the world. Similar to the spread of Methodism in the early 1800s, the growth of Pentecostalism has occurred as people have been displaced from their homes and have begun worshipping with Christians from other language groups and backgrounds. Its attention to healing, signs of the Spirit and a liberating ecstatic worship style provide an appealing alternative to the old-fashioned Western formality of the mainline denominations.

The globalization of world Christianity in terms of its demographic spread shows that the interaction between the global and the local, among other factors, is giving it strength. The universal nature of the gospel is a powerful attraction to Christians who have moved from place to place, are suffering under incompetent governments, and crave the connection with like-minded persons of other races and cultures. In some settings, Christianity has served as a vehicle of modernization and of ideals of individual human rights and democracy. Simultaneously, the ability of the gospel to adapt to local situations gives it vitality and relevance for the people. The interaction between the local and the global is a keen indicator of Christianity's participation in the globalization process in the early twenty-first century.

4. Structures of Mission Today

A fourth way in which mission is a part of the phenomenon of globalization is in the technological base and structural organization of mission itself. Since the first century CE, when Christians used codices, or books, in far greater numbers than members of other religions, to Gutenberg's printing press and the first printed Bible in 1455 and the use of radio and television in the twentieth century, the spread of the gospel has relied on the cutting edge of "information technology." With its computers, databases, statisticians, and Web sites, the Great Commission is riding the wave of technological expansion just as it hitchhiked on the capitalist trading ships and colonial armies of the nineteenth century. Despite Christianity's relative poverty compared to corporate business, evangelical Christianity has one of the most highly developed technological presences of any religious force in the world. The explosion of Web-related mission information in the early twenty-first century is a revolution of information comparable to the expansion of print media on the American frontier of the early 1800s, and in West Africa in the early 1900s. As scholars have frequently demonstrated, access to new sources of information can by themselves facilitate the founding and strengthening of Christian movements in new soil. Historian Andrew Walls makes the point that the infrastructures of many missions in Africa are stronger than those of the countries themselves.[17] Many of these evangelical networks have allied with others to pursue common global strategies; for example, the goal of the AD 2000 and Beyond Movement to plant a church in every people group by the year 2000 and Global Mapping, Inc. (GMI), as a clearinghouse for information about the task of world evangelization.

In The United Methodist Church, the Internet age has facilitated a more entrepreneurial, parachurch approach than the bureaucratic, corporate boardroom model that had become dominant by the 1970s. By the 1980s, it was clear that a more flexible model of mission leadership needed to evolve.[18] Instead of controlling the mission initiatives of the church, the General Board of Global Ministries saw itself trying to facilitate the mission activities of a vast network of churches. With the arrival of the Internet, the board developed an impressive Web site that allows for the democratization of information in a way that was previously impossible.

In the last few years, the board has reorganized itself according to a model that recognizes the emergence of globalization. Instead of having area secretaries running programs according to their specific geographic areas of expertise, the various functions of mission education, mission personnel, local church relations, and so on have been consolidated into units that are supposed to operate globally. This model would have been impossible before the advent of cyberspace. While the jury is still out on whether this model will work or not, the point is that even denominational structures are reflecting the globalization of Christian mission. In the case of the United Methodists, the reorganization may represent a new kind of centralization at the expense of expertise in local cultures, possibly in opposition to the concern for balancing the local and the global. Indeed, the centralization of structures and the democratization of information are aspects of globalization.

5. The Globalization of the Mission Force

The missionary force of the twenty-first century has itself been globalized. Whether within the World Council of Churches or the Lausanne Movement for World Evangelization, in the last twenty-five years, much of the leadership for Protestant missions has been provided by people from the Two-thirds World. Larry Keyes calculated that by the mid-1990s, there were an estimated 88,000 missionaries from the Two-thirds World being sent by 1,600 non-Western agencies. Non-Western missions were growing more than five times faster than Western ones.[19] The Overseas Ministries Study Center in New Haven, Connecticut, probably the most important residential community for missionaries on furlough, has far more Burmese and Korean missionaries than it can accommodate, whereas not long ago, its primary population was Western missionaries. Even though churches in Western countries still control most of the economic resources of the worldwide missionary movement, the missionaries from Brazil, Korea, Ghana, and other non-Western countries are the visible faces of mission in the twenty-first century. These non-Western missionaries have made the old ecumenical slogan come true: "mission to and from all six continents." Devotion to the Great Commission on the part of non-Westerners shows that its expansionary appeal is not confined to Western Christianity.

The Great Commission in a Globalized Future

For the past quarter century, mission scholars have been in agreement that world Christianity has entered an entirely new phase of global mission. The question remains what globalization means for the future of the Great Commission in the twenty-first century. Lutheran missiologist Richard Bliese suggests that, theologically, globalization points to a number of areas that demand our attention, including such things as what is traditionally referred to as "catholicity," a global theological anthropology and reflection on the human condition, Christian mission in relationship to ecumenical and interreligious dialogue, and the global responsibility to struggle against injustices as part of Christian witness, evangelism, and mission.[20]

Given the historical importance of the Great Commission for Protestant missions, The United Methodist Church has more to gain by recontextualizing it for a global age than by abandoning it. Its historical importance and its commonality across varied traditions are too important to push it aside, not to mention its theological basis. Rather, we must seek a holistic and broad interpretation of the Great Commission. We must broaden it from the narrow definition of church planting among unreached peoples *and* avoid cynical formulations that paint it as simply the ideological heart of Western colonial oppression. The mainline churches find themselves caught between the extremes of a narrow interpretation of the Great Commission and the secular criticisms of the age. The following suggestions may help us move beyond this impasse and reaffirm the Great Commission for the twenty-first century.

1. Proclaim Christ Rather Than Western Economic Interests

First, we should break the connections between globalization in an economic sense and the theological vision of the kingdom of God. The associations among capitalism, modernization, and Great Commission Christianity can be traced back to the days of William Carey and early Methodism. In an age of globalization, it is legitimate to ask whether disproportionate attention to numerical growth owes more to Western economic and cultural expansionism, or to a gospel of prosperity, than to biblical Christianity. To the best of our abilities, our interpretation of the Great Commission must emphasize proclaiming Christ without proclaiming Western economic self-interests.

Let us reexamine the Great Commission in light of pre-expansionist models of Christian mission by using 2 Corinthians 4:5-6 as a model for twenty-first-century mission: "For we do not proclaim ourselves; we proclaim Jesus Christ as Lord and ourselves as your slaves for Jesus' sake. For it is the God who said, 'Let light shine out of darkness,' who has shone in our hearts to give the light of the knowledge of the glory of God in the face of Jesus Christ." One advantage of placing these words of the apostle Paul alongside the Great Commission is that they focus on the glory of God rather than on human volition, organization, and efficiency. Prior to the age of capitalist expansion, seeking to glorify God was a primary motive for Protestant mission. The God whom the Puritans sought to glorify was the Creator who inaugurated human existence by bringing light forth from darkness. Through the face of Jesus Christ, God the Creator has shone light not only in the cosmos, but also in the human heart. If our mission is to extol the glory of God, we can shift our vision away from the profit motive or the success syndrome that haunts so much of the American psyche, including missionary Christianity.

In an age in which the church has finally spread all over the world, it behooves Western Christians to focus more on what it means to be faithful to the God of Jesus Christ. Criticism of globalization has parallels with the struggle over colonialism that confronted missions after World War II. At that time, prophetic mission theologians like Hendrik Kraemer and Max Warren emphasized the separation of Christ from Western culture as a precondition for the health of world Christianity. Warren spoke about a mission of "Christian Presence" in which Western missionaries would cultivate a "theology of attention" to other peoples, cultures, and religions.[21] Missionaries of Christian presence create a climate of integrity in which the message is proclaimed through deeds and not just words. In the wake of 9/11, the leading evangelical Islamicist, Dudley Woodberry, suggested that American missionaries have to withdraw from Muslim countries in favor of nationals from other countries.[22] To avoid confusing the message with the messengers, it becomes necessary for the globalized church to decide which ethnic and national groups can most effectively witness to Jesus Christ in particular settings. If we can separate the Great Commission from capitalist expansion, then our mission is clarified as one that glorifies God rather than ourselves or our Western way of life.

"For we do not proclaim ourselves; we proclaim Jesus Christ as Lord and ourselves as your slaves for Jesus' sake." These stirring words of the apostle Paul should be reclaimed as basic to the missionary message of the twenty-first century. There are quite a number of famous missionaries who became bicultural through the actual experience of being enslaved and then became effective cross-cultural communicators; for example, Ulfilas, the translator of Scripture into Gothic; St. Patrick, the English former slave of the Irish; Samuel Adjayi Crowther, a recaptured Yoruba slave who became the first African Anglican bishop and great mission-ary; and Anthony Ulrich, a former slave from the West Indies who per-suaded Count Zinzendorf to send Moravian missionaries to his homeland. Paul was writing to the Christians in Corinth that he was willing to be their slave for the sake of the gospel. He was willing to serve them, to be humble and not put himself forward in his efforts to glorify God. Perhaps when we talk about Pauline models of mission, we should emphasize Paul's willingness to serve as a slave rather than the usual focus on "Pauline" financial self-support. As we seek to imitate Paul in his preaching of Jesus Christ, we must be willing to proclaim Christ only, devoid of our Western egos. To see God glorified in the face of Jesus Christ means we must unmask our economic privilege as Western Christians, so that we do not make the mistake of putting our own faces where Jesus Christ's ought to be.

2. Rediscover the Great Commission as a Spiritual Discipline

A second way to emphasize the Great Commission in the twenty-first century is to rediscover it as a spiritual discipline. Those of us in the Wesleyan tradition have always considered spiritual growth an ongoing and necessary process in the Christian life. But geographic expansion is not the only definition of what it means for believers to "go into all the world"; we must bear faithful witness at home and in distant places. I do not believe that witnessing across barriers of culture, race, and nation-ality is a task that can ever be completed because the health of the church and our personal spiritual growth depend on it. The exploding populations in the Two-thirds World mean that there will always be a "mission field" among the evolving cultures of the world's young people, and the health of the church depends on growing and deepening our relationship to God through profound obedience to the Word. Especially for Protestants, devotion to the Great Commission is a criti-cal marker of spiritual vitality, and points to the core of what it means to be a faithful follower of Jesus Christ. We must always be prepared to testify to the hope within us (1 Peter 3:15), in our local communities and throughout the world that God has made. In the spiritual sense, the Great Commission can never be completed this side of the new creation.

3. Emphasize the Didactic Function of the Great Commission

In the twenty-first century, we should shift our focus to the second half of the Great Commission, "teaching them to obey everything that I have commanded you." A shift to the didactic function of the Great Commission is not a repudiation of "going into all the world," but a corrective that resonates with previous interpretations of the Great Commission. When women first became Protestant missionaries in the early 1800s, they focused on the teaching aspect of the Great Commission. They saw themselves as teaching women around the world and helping them achieve human dignity in relation to abusive social systems.[23] Holistic mission has always put equal weight on the discipleship and evangelistic aspects of "going into all the world."[24] Bishop Kenneth Carder spoke of the Great Commission in his opening remarks to the Board of Discipleship in 2002, when serving as its president. He stated, "We must continue to move beyond exclusive personal experiences in terms of what it means to make disciples of Jesus Christ. . . . Making disciples of all nations has to do with transforming communities, as well as human hearts; the creation of communities of love, of grace, of justice and hospitality that look like Jesus Christ."[25]

The urgency of the didactic function of the Great Commission becomes apparent in light of the rapid expansion of the church in the late twentieth century. In new Christian areas, there is a desperate need for religious instruction and for ethical reflection on the relationship between the gospel message and sociopolitical struggles. People may have joined the church, but their understanding of the gospel is limited by their lack of formation in Christian beliefs and practices. The hunger for basic teaching on the meaning of the Bible and the meaning of the Christian faith is overwhelming. The very success of the Great Commission as a motivator to send Christians "into all the world" means that the command to teach "everything that I have commanded you" has become an urgent priority in areas where church growth has been rapid and recent. If we fail to incorporate the teaching of the meaning of the holistic gospel in our mission work, then we will be like the sowers who threw the seed into shallow ground. The plants grew quickly, but then withered because their roots were stunted.

4. Ground Ourselves in the New Testament Church

The Great Commission in the twenty-first century must be regrounded in the New Testament church. When Christ commanded his disciples to go into all the world, he was not speaking to people whose nation was the strongest country in the world or possessed of modern technology, unlimited transportation resources, or pension plans for missionaries. Rather, the Great Commission was a sign of hope among simple, persecuted believers whose leader had been crucified and then raised from the dead. Christian tradition claims that Thomas went to India, Philip to Africa, Peter to Rome, Mark to Egypt, and Paul to Spain. The disciples witnessed across national and ethnic boundaries not because they were powerful, but because they were faithful to the vision of the kingdom of God they had glimpsed in Jesus Christ.

The true context for the Great Commission is that of the persecuted minority church, not our dominant Western culture. Like in the New Testament church, Christians in an age of globalization are rediscovering a theology of the Cross. As Christianity grows in minority communities around the world, we see renewed persecution against believers. Christians who witness in the world today must be prepared to be arrested by Islamic authorities in Saudi Arabia, captured by revolutionaries in Colombia, harassed by the Chinese government, abused for supporting minority and human rights in places like Rwanda, Indonesia, and India—or ridiculed by secular intellectuals in the West.

For those of us who are Westerners, it is difficult to disassociate ourselves from the trappings of power even if each of us takes a personal vow of poverty. We face the difficult challenge of separating Christian mission from the anonymity of modernization, and the increasing contrasts between wealth and poverty in a global economic system. We are trapped in the culture, which the rest of the world ascribes to us. I am sure I am not the only person who has had the disheartening experience of going to a poor country in the Two-thirds World only to be objectified as a representative of Western wealth, and indeed, I am part of that system even as I struggle to live out my Christian commitments. Missionaries are trapped between the needy and unreached of the world and the material resources of the West. All over the world, there are missionaries in vulnerable situations, scapegoats of the resentment against globalization and Western dominance. For North Americans, our mission in the twenty-first century may mean glorifying God as slaves, just as Paul was willing to do in 2 Corinthians 4:5-6. The Great Commission was a victorious statement of Resurrection, but its backdrop was the experience of the Cross.

Conclusion: A Resurrection Vision

In the final analysis, to follow and live out the Great Commission in the twenty-first century means to continue anticipating God's kingdom of peace and justice for all. In other words, the Great Commission has an eschatological dimension; it commands us to work for the inbreaking kingdom of God, for the new creation, while we remain in the midst of the world still groaning toward completion. We live as signs of hope to all the world. The hope for all of God's people, united in justice and truth under Jesus Christ, is a Resurrection vision that sustains people around the world. This Christian message of hope is not finished, as God's reign presses toward fulfillment. Rather, it is the deeper meaning that lies at the heart of the Great Commission.

CHAPTER 3

The Global Mission of The United Methodist Church

Elaine A. Robinson

I n The United Methodist Church, the official or formal language of "mission" can be understood in two distinct, but related senses. First, the broader and primary sense of mission refers to the basic purpose or raison d'être of the UMC: "The mission of the Church is to make disciples of Jesus Christ."[1] In this broader perspective, we would understand the formation of disciples as the primary task of the church.[2] Second, mission is used in a related, but narrower sense of mission as "outreach."[3] In this narrower sense of mission as outreach, the primary administrative responsibility is assigned to the General Board of Global Ministries. Although the relationship between mission as the task of the church and as outreach will figure prominently in the subsequent discussion, our primary concern in this essay will be the overarching mission of making disciples of Jesus Christ.

Making Disciples of Jesus Christ

The mission or task of making disciples, as defined and articulated by the 2004 *Book of Discipline*, can be understood as a multifaceted process. To enable us to more precisely discern the scope and contours of this mission, we might suggest there are four overlapping dimensions of the process of making disciples: (1) theological, (2) structural, (3) contextual, and (4) dispositional (i.e., the ethos of discipleship). Together, these four dimensions of the discipleship process provide a fuller understanding of the mission of the UMC as currently formulated.

1. The Theology of Discipleship

The theology of discipleship arises out of what are considered to be our "distinctive Wesleyan emphases" and may be framed, initially, in terms of the outreach and ingathering work of grace. Albert Outler once expressed the relationship between grace and mission in this way: "the essence of mission is the GIFT OF GRACE, the outreach and ingathering of grace, the promotion and support of the RULE OF GRACE in the hearts and lives of human beings."[4] God's grace, especially prevenient grace, is available to all persons, though it can be resisted. Unless we respond to the gracious divine initiative and accept the gift of faith, we cannot enter into the discipleship process. As such, the witness of Christians, in word and deed, is central to the process of enabling others to be awakened to the condition of sin and the offer of grace. With the acceptance of grace and the gift of faith, disciples begin a lifelong process of responding to the promptings of grace, as it roots out sin and enables our growth in love manifest as the love of God and the love of neighbor, or inward and outward holiness. We thus affirm that "God's grace calls forth human response and discipline."[5] Good works, works of piety and mercy, flow from the love of God "shed abroad in our hearts by the Holy Spirit."[6]

The United Methodist Church's theological understanding of discipleship is thus premised upon the relationship between the inward and outward or personal and social holiness evoked by grace. As the *Book of Discipline* claims, "personal salvation always involves Christian mission and service to the world. By joining heart and hand, we assert that personal religion, evangelical witness, and Christian social action are reciprocal and mutually reinforcing."[7] This sense of mission and service to the world, social holiness, is grounded in and pursued by the worshipping community as it nurtures personal holiness: "The communal forms of faith in the Wesleyan tradition not only promote personal growth; they also equip and mobilize us for mission and service to the world."[8] Although the use of "mission" in this statement refers to the narrower sense of mission as outreach, it is presented as one aspect of the broader mission of making disciples. Theologically, the broader mission of making disciples is premised upon the twin pillars of personal and social holiness.[9]

Third, discipleship has a trinitarian basis, highlighted in the "rationale for our mission," which indicates that the mission of The United Methodist Church—and, arguably, the church universal—is "to make disciples of Jesus Christ by proclaiming the good news of God's grace and thus seeking the fulfillment of God's reign and realm in the world."[10] It then continues, advancing the claim that this mission is "our grace-filled response" to the good news "*embodied* in the life, death, and resurrection of Jesus Christ [and] *experienced* in the ongoing creation of a new people by the Holy Spirit."[11] In response to God's grace, the gospel takes on flesh as the Body of Christ, the church, and enables a vital experience of the living God present among us by means of the Holy Spirit. The process of making disciples functions to save persons and to transform social structures as a means of "changing the world."[12] This language of "changing the world" is intended to convey that our response to grace facilitates the inbreaking realm of God in tangible ways.

Fourth, discipleship is a universal calling and task that mirrors the understanding of personal and social holiness. As a calling, the church "affirms the worth of all humanity" and calls "all persons into discipleship under the Lordship of Jesus Christ. . . . We seek to reveal the love of God for men, women, and children of all ethnic, racial, cultural, and national backgrounds and to demonstrate the healing power of the gospel with those who suffer."[13] The universality of Christ's atonement and the universal offer of God's grace mean that all persons, regardless of any physical characteristics, whether individual or collective, are called to be disciples of Jesus Christ, and accordingly, no one is excluded from the church's mission, either as the subject or as the object of it. In other words, the mission is directed toward all persons, and in turn, all persons who are in Christ are to participate in the church's mission.

Those who accept the gift of faith and follow Christ in the world are to participate in God's inbreaking realm through the ministry of servanthood, the universal task of Christians. The *Book of Discipline* defines the ministry of servanthood in terms of the narrower sense of mission, but premised upon the broader conception: the "heart of Christian ministry is Christ's ministry of outreaching love. [It] is the expression of the mind and mission of Christ by a community of Christians that demonstrates a common life of gratitude and devotion, witness and service, celebration and discipleship."[14] This ministry or task as disciples takes shape in particular, concrete settings and forms such as diverse locations, interests, and denominational expressions, "yet [is] always catholic in spirit and outreach."[15] Every Christian is called to participate in the ministry of outreach toward others. Here it should be noted that baptism (and confirmation for those baptized as infants) renews the believer's life for the sake of mission and service to the church and the world. Baptism by water and the Spirit initiates every Christian into the ministry of servanthood.

Finally, an eschatological *telos* guides the understanding of the ministry of all Christians, as mission is figured in terms of "active expectancy."[16] The "ministry of all Christians consists of service for the mission of God in the world," and this mission is expressed most clearly in the Lord's Prayer, which calls us to "live in active expectancy: faithful in service of God and [our] neighbor; faithful in waiting for the fulfillment of God's universal love, justice, and peace on earth as in heaven."[17] While awaiting the promised fulfillment, the ministry of all Christians is "shaped by the teachings of Jesus." In other words, discipleship, as the calling of all Christians, involves ongoing formation in the doctrines and practices of the faith as we await the completion of the promised renewal of the whole of creation.

2. The Structure of Discipleship

The structure of discipleship, or what we might understand as the church's polity as it is structured to promote the mission of making disciples of Jesus Christ, is based upon two organizational features: connectionalism and the itinerant system. Indeed, the *Book of Discipline* understands the ministry of all Christians, the work of making and being disciples, as the "journey of a connectional people,"[18] and it affirms the way in which the itineracy[19] makes "visible" and promotes the "connectional nature of the United Methodist system."[20]

Richard Heitzenrater defines the principle of connectionalism, as it was originally conceived, as "the covenantal association of preachers committed to a united mission to spread scriptural holiness (and to abide by the doctrine/discipline of the organization designed to implement that mission) under the direction of John Wesley and the conference."[21] The connection, as implemented in today's United Methodist Church, is formed by two primary means. First, the shared (albeit continually evolving) discipline is intended to empower the mission of the church through a democratic form of polity. The democratic principles of American Methodism, which form the basis of today's global United Methodist

Church, take shape primarily through the system of conferences that serves as the decision-making body of the church.[22] Here, we should understand that the mission of making disciples is premised upon the combined wisdom of the delegates to the various conferences and, most important, the General Conference, which sets the disciplinary requirements for a given quadrennium. Of course, the executive and judicial branches of The United Methodist Church (i.e., the Council of Bishops and the Judicial Council) also play a role in church decision making, though formal authority for establishing disciplinary standards lies with the General Conference.

The connection functions in relationship to the itineracy, "by which ordained elders are appointed by the bishop to fields of labor."[23] The intention behind this system is for appointments "to be made with consideration of the gifts and evidence of God's grace of those appointed, to the needs, characteristics, and opportunities of congregations and institutions, and with faithfulness to the commitment to an open itineracy."[24] Although the itinerant system "as a missionary order of preachers [has] given way to a more professional model with itinerants less and less able simply to go where sent," it nonetheless functions to promote the church's mission by appointing clergy to congregations and other settings where they are best able to use their gifts and graces for the larger good.[25] As Heitzenrater summarizes, "Itinerancy is a method for deployment of preachers who are willing to be placed in stations where and when they are needed most . . . in order to further the Methodist mission to spread scriptural holiness."[26] In this structure of connectionalism and itineracy, the UMC has a "centralized and united framework for developing and effecting a common mission" that remains largely democratic in principle and practice.[27]

3. The Context of Discipleship

The mission of making disciples of Jesus Christ involves a third element: the context in which the process of discipleship takes place. In this case, mission unfolds in the tension and interplay of the local and global contexts. The local church is the primary context in which the broader mission of The United Methodist Church unfolds, as is emphasized in paragraph 120 on the mission of the churches: "Local churches provide the most significant arena through which disciple-making occurs."[28] Thomas Frank has noted a distinct shift as the local church has grown in importance in recent years. In fact, the "mission statement" of making disciples, which assigns primary responsibility to the specific contexts of local churches, was moved to its current location in the *Book of Discipline* by the 1996 General Conference.[29] Even so, the mission of the local church, as currently formulated, is by no means clear since the various sections of the *Book of Discipline* speak about the local church in different ways and demonstrate "the varied expectations United Methodists have for their local churches."[30] In other words, although the primary responsibility for the mission of The United Methodist Church lies with the local churches, how to define the parameters and requirements of their mission of making disciples remains ambiguous.

In spite of this ambiguity, two disciplinary sections, in particular, provide discernment regarding the mission as it is embodied in the local church. First, in the doctrinal standards, the church's mission is articulated as "a congregation of faithful men [*sic*] in which the pure Word of God is preached, and the Sacraments duly administered" (Art. XIII, *Articles of Religion*; cf. Art. V, *Confession of Faith*), and which "exists for the maintenance of worship, the edification of believers and the redemption of the world" (Art. V, *Confession of Faith*).[31] Second, the local church's role in the broader mission can be discerned in paragraph 122, "The Process for Carrying Out Our Mission," which indicates:

> We make disciples as we:
> —proclaim the gospel, seek, welcome and gather persons into the body of Christ;
> —lead persons to commit their lives to God through baptism by water and the Spirit and profession of faith in Jesus Christ;
> —nurture persons in Christian living through worship, the sacraments, spiritual disciplines, and other means of grace, such as Wesley's Christian conferencing;
> —send persons into the world to live lovingly and justly as servants of Christ by healing the sick, feeding the hungry, caring for the stranger, freeing the oppressed, and working to develop social structures that are consistent with the gospel; and
> —continue the mission of seeking, welcoming and gathering persons into the community of the body of Christ.[32]

In this paragraph, we find the most explicit expression of the contours of the local mission of making disciples; however, this primary mission extends beyond the context of the local churches in the form of global outreach and as a globally connected church.

Paragraph 123 articulates the "global nature" of the church's mission: "The Church seeks to fulfill its global mission through the Spirit-given servant ministries of all Christians, both lay and clergy. Faithfulness and effectiveness demand that all ministries in the Church be shaped by the mission of making disciples of Jesus Christ."[33] The subsequent paragraph seems to indicate that the "global nature" spoken of here is that of universality more than a geographical or a spatial perspective: "Our mission in the world" affirms that God's self-revelation in Christ "summons the church to ministry in the world through witness by word and deed in light of the church's mission," and this ministry includes practices aimed at the upbuilding of the Christian community, calls all persons to discipleship, and struggles for justice and reconciliation for all persons regardless of race, ethnicity, culture, or national background.[34]

In terms of the geographical or spatial sense of the global mission of making disciples, the focal point is the General Board of Global Ministries, which exists as "a missional instrument of The United Methodist Church, its annual conferences, missionary conferences, and local congregations in the context of a global setting."[35] Mission, in the narrower sense, is "a sign of God's presence in the world."[36] Thus, the responsibilities assigned to the GBGM include such things as encouraging and supporting the development of leaders for mission in the world; challenging all United Methodists to "proclaim the gospel to the ends of the earth, expressing the mission of the Church"; equipping missionaries for service; strengthening congregations to be "units of mission in their places and partners with others in the worldwide mission of the Christian church"; and assisting "local congregations and annual conferences in mission both in their own communities and across the globe by raising awareness of the claims of global mission and by providing channels for participation."[37] Clearly, in this disciplinary section on the GBGM, the language of mission is used primarily in the sense of outreach, though as part of the overarching mission of "making disciples of Jesus Christ." The GBGM functions to facilitate the global outreach, but the primary responsibility for the church's mission of disciple making remains under the auspices of the local churches around the world.

4. The Ethos of Discipleship

From a practical theological perspective, the formation of disciples in the UMC involves a threefold "ethos" of discipleship or "dispositional" character, consisting of (1) personal holiness, (2) social holiness, and (3) ecumenism. Personal holiness or personal piety involves the inner workings of grace in which the individual is "being perfected in love." This dimension of formation involves a commitment to the General Rules of doing no harm, doing all the good we can, and attending upon all the ordinances of God (i.e., the daily reliance upon the means of grace including prayer, scripture study, and worship).[38] But personal holiness is inseparable from social holiness in the Wesleyan tradition. As John Wesley stated in the introduction to the 1739 collection of *Hymns and Sacred Poems*, "The gospel of Christ knows of no religion but social; no holiness but social holiness." The *Book of Discipline* expresses it thus: "Scriptural holiness entails more than personal piety; love of God is always linked with love of neighbor, a passion for justice and renewal in the life of the world."[39] The ingathering, transforming grace of God overflows in the outreach of God's love to others through good works. Piety always propels us toward "social action and global interaction, always in the empowering context of the reign of God."[40] Here the Social Principles and the *Book of Resolutions* provide guidance for witness and work in the world, but they are not binding upon church members. Thus, the theological understanding of personal and social holiness is intended to take shape in and be expressed through the *habitus* of discipleship.

Finally, the ethos of discipleship in the UMC involves an ongoing ecumenical commitment in which "Christian unity is not an option; it is a gift to be received and expressed."[41] It is best represented in terms of the "Catholic Spirit" or "universal love," which John Wesley preached and taught. In this spirit of love, the church is called to engage in interfaith encounters and "to be both neighbors and witnesses to all peoples."[42] The church's ecumenical and interreligious dialogue is intended to "raise all such relationships to the highest possible level of human fellowship and understanding. . . . In respectful conversations and in practical cooperation, we confess our Christian faith and strive to display the manner in which Jesus Christ is the life and hope of the world."[43] In other words, disciples are expected to see and respond to the image of God in the other person, whatever his or her faith commitment may entail. It is important to note, however, that the language used here in relation to interreligious dialogue may be somewhat at odds with the mission statement as defined in paragraph 124, which claims that The United Methodist Church calls "all persons into discipleship under the Lordship of Jesus Christ."[44] Nevertheless, the Wesleyan tradition has always included a commitment to ecumenism—at least in spirit, as guided by John Wesley's teachings—and such an understanding is an important dimension of the ethos of discipleship as cultivated in the contemporary United Methodist Church.

These four overlapping dimensions of the church's mission of making disciples of Jesus Christ—the theological, structural, contextual, and dispositional characteristics—are offered as heuristic categories and intended to delineate the complicated and sometimes elegant process by which the church's mission is to be carried out in the world. At the same time, these four dimensions are intended to demonstrate some of the conceptual, theological, and disciplinary lacunae or, perhaps, inconsistencies that arise out of the democratic decision-making process of The United Methodist Church. In the final sections of this essay, we will look briefly at the Methodist understanding of "mission" in retrospect and prospect.

Methodist Mission in Retrospect

A brief historical background enables us to place the mission of making disciples into a clearer context. Of primary importance is the understanding of mission as represented in the Methodist movement of the eighteenth century. Although in that context, the precise language of "mission" was used only in the narrower sense as outreach, Wesley often spoke of the overarching mission of Methodism as that of "saving souls," "spreading scriptural holiness across the land," and nurturing "altogether Christians." The Methodist movement was intended, of course, as a revival movement within the Church of England that would serve also to reform the nation. As Ted Campbell has argued, "Wesley was a 'home' missionary: he understood his vocation as being that of an 'extraordinary minister' called out to proclaim the Christian message in the context of his neo-pagan culture."[45] Campbell goes on to indicate that "what we know of his views of 'foreign' missionary outreach suggests that he saw it as a natural extension of the apostolic and ordinary ministry by which the unchristian of his own nation were to be reached."[46] In other words,

Wesley's primary mission was to rekindle the nominal Christians of his day and thereby—to use our contemporary language—"make disciples of Jesus Christ," but he recognized that his work was part of a global mission. The societies provided systems of nurture and accountability through bands and classes. The societies engaged in outreach ministries to the poor, the infirm, children, and others in eighteenth-century England. Wesley also sent missionaries to North America as an extension of the Methodist societies. In a sense, the Methodist societies engaged in evangelism at home and abroad, outreach intended to offer the love of Christ and alleviate suffering, and careful formation of the societies' members in the teachings and practices of the faith.

Wesley's renewal of the Church of England, his mission of making disciples, is often articulated in his sermons, which served as doctrinal guidelines originally and became doctrinal standards in the establishment of The Methodist Episcopal Church in 1784. For example, in his 1741 sermon "The Almost Christian," he suggests that an "altogether Christian" is one who loves God, loves neighbor, has faith in Christ "working by love," and lives according to the General Rules. In a recent essay, prepared initially for the United Methodist Bishops' Taskforce on Theological Education, Randy Maddox argues that in Wesley's late sermon "Causes of the Inefficacy of Christianity," we can find guidance on the central mission of the church.[47] According to Maddox, Wesley contends that Christianity has done so little good in the world because it has produced so few altogether Christians. Three factors play a vital role in the formation of disciples: (1) doctrinal formation (i.e., a biblically based, theological understanding of what it is to be a Christian); (2) discipline as spiritual practice (i.e., embodying the General Rules, including regular participation in the means of grace); and (3) self-denial as dispositional formation (i.e., denying our free will whenever it opposes God's will). This understanding of Wesley's approach to the making of disciples of Jesus Christ includes the sense of mission as outreach, in that works of mercy or the love of neighbor is integral to all three factors.

In the transition of Methodism to the New World and throughout the better part of the history of American Methodism, the language of "mission" has referred to the narrower definition of mission as "outreach," located primarily in the Board of Missions (the predecessor to the GBGM) as it was responsible for "home" and "foreign" missions. Such missional outreach has always been an important dimension of the church's task. It is worth noting that women in the nineteenth century played a significant role in the development of structures of missional outreach as they undertook foreign and domestic missions apart from the official structures of The Methodist Church, Evangelical Association, and United Brethren Church. Because the ordained ministry was closed to women in The Methodist Church until 1956 and in The Evangelical United Brethren Church prior to the 1968 union,[48] "the exclusion of women from leadership roles for the denomination as a whole led to their creating spheres in which their gifts could be utilized."[49] In this case, the church's polity was circumvented in order to engage in extensive outreach.

In The United Methodist Church, beginning with the 1968 union, the language closest to that of the contemporary mission of making disciples is found buried within the section on the local church and the meaning of membership, where it reads:

> A member of The United Methodist Church is to be a servant of Christ on mission in the local and worldwide community. This servanthood is performed in his family life, daily work, recreation and social activities, responsible citizenship, the issues of his corporate life, and all his attitudes toward his fellowmen. Participation in disciplined groups is an expected part of his mission involvement. He is called upon to be a witness for Christ in the world, a light and leaven in society, and a reconciler in a culture of conflict. He is to identify himself with the agony and suffering of the world and to radiate and exemplify the Christ of hope. The standards of attitude and conduct set forth in the social principles . . . should be considered as an essential resource for guiding each member of the Church in being a servant of Christ on mission.[50]

The mission statement, as we know it today, began to take shape in the 1980s. The 1984 General Conference established the Commission on the Mission of The United Methodist Church, which was "specifically directed . . . to identify 'Christ's call for our third century' and to set forth a unifying vision of its mission."[51] The year 1988 thus marks a particularly important juncture, as the commission's statement, " 'Grace Upon Grace': God's Mission and Ours," was presented to the General Conference. The document was recommended as an addition to paragraph 69 of the *Book of Discipline*, following Our Theological Task and before the Social Principles (¶70). It delineated, at some length, the biblical and theological rationale for mission, a unifying vision grounded in God's grace and our response as witnesses to it, our missional heritage, a call for personal and social transformation, and the undeniably global dimension to the church's mission.[52] In the 1992 *Book of Discipline*, a much-condensed version of the "Grace Upon Grace" statement appeared as paragraph 69, section 5, "Mission Statement."

In 1990, as the process of clarifying the mission of The United Methodist Church continued beyond the work of the commission, the Council of Bishops issued a pastoral letter, "Vital Congregations— Faithful Disciples: Vision for the Church." This document was intended to initiate reflection on and dialogue about American Methodism's "self-understanding" or identity, and the bishops issued a summons to local congregations to join them in the search for a new vision.[53] At this time, the language of "discipleship" emerged and began to gain prominence in church discussions. A comment made in 1991 by Bishop Melvin Talbert, secretary of the Council of Bishops, is insightful in terms of the impetus behind this period of rethinking the church's mission. He pointed to a pervasive sense of "confusion as to what our mission should be."[54] It is important to recognize, however, that the process itself of ongoing reflection on the church's mission in light of the contemporary context is faithful to the Methodist tradition. In other words, a sense of "confusion" may demonstrate that we are not "static" in our theological reflection but always in the process of rethinking the expression of God's grace in and through the church for the sake of the world.

In 1996 the mission statement was revised considerably and placed at the beginning of the chapter "The Local Church." Here we find, for the first time, the statement that "the mission of the Church is to make disciples of Jesus Christ."[55] The 1996 *Book of Discipline* included a new emphasis on "disciple-making" that indicates, in intent if not in language, a desire to recover the broader meaning of mission in the Wesleyan heritage. It also marks the increasing responsibility placed upon the local church for carrying out this primary mission. A second change in 1996 relates to the responsibility of the local church toward its members. Previously, the *Book of Discipline* of The United Methodist Church indicated, "Each local church shall have a definite membership and evangelistic responsibility."[56] Beginning in 1996, we find this requirement: "Each local church shall have a definite evangelistic, nurture, and witness responsibility for its members and the surrounding area and a missional outreach responsibility to the local and global community."[57] In sum, Methodism has been marked by a concern for mission as outreach, as well as some confusion over the broader task and identity of the church. In the 1990s, efforts began to broaden and deepen the church's sense of mission, though, of course, further reflection and ongoing deliberation on the mission of making disciples of Jesus Christ are warranted, as this iterative process is intrinsic to the Wesleyan tradition.

The Mission of the UMC in the Twenty-first Century

As the above discussion is intended to highlight, the mission of Methodism in America has been ambiguous and ill-defined, at times, based at least, in part, on the American context that diverged considerably from that of Wesley's Britain. The task of the Methodist Church lacked clarity for much of its history, and only in the 1980s did the church begin to reflect upon its mission in the broader sense. Indeed, one could speculate that the drive to create a "mission statement" reflects the rise of the managerial mind-set and the writing of mission statements in society-at-large during that era. Nonetheless, defining and clarifying the mission and vision of The United Methodist Church has been a valuable process. As The United Methodist Church has moved toward the centrality of the mission of making disciples of Jesus Christ, organizational and programmatic changes have been implemented, such as the growing importance of the local church and the launching of the "Open Hearts, Open Minds, Open Doors" campaign. Moreover, the recognition of our global connection has become more pronounced. Nevertheless, the church's ecclesiology is in need of ongoing development and refinement.[58] Perhaps, in some ways, the words of Bishop Francis Asbury in 1813 are still reflected in today's United Methodist Church. He concluded that in his forty years of ministry, "We were a Church, and no Church"—a statement that has been interpreted to suggest that Methodists have always struggled to discern "whether they would be a great church or a holy people."[59] Today, ongoing deliberation is warranted in several important areas of our ecclesiological understanding if we seek to be both a great church and a holy people, despite Bishop Asbury's astute observation.

First, the process of growing in holiness, sanctification, lacks clarity and sufficient emphasis in the disciplinary mission of making disciples of Jesus Christ. Making disciples also requires being disciples, a fact that John Wesley understood well. While the global context of the twenty-first century differs markedly from Wesley's context and presents a different web of challenges and concerns, the sense of encouraging personal holiness and social holiness through ongoing formation and accountability in community remains fundamental to the church's overarching mission. Today, we recognize that mission and evangelism are integrally related to this sense of ongoing formation and growth in the love of God and neighbor. The mission of the church is a process, not a product; it is a journey much more than a destination.

Second, as previously noted, since 1968 and the formation of The United Methodist Church, the Wesleyan ecumenical spirit has become more prominent, in large measure due to the work and vision of Albert Outler. Yet as the church's ecumenical and interreligious work has grown, the mission of the UMC maintains an evangelistic thrust that calls for all persons to come under the "Lordship of Jesus Christ." While these aspects of the church's mission need not be inherently contradictory, further theological discernment and reflection would deepen the understanding of the disciple-making mission at all levels of the church as the UMC's global presence continues to expand, especially in the Two-thirds World. Here, the work of Russell Richey on the church's ecclesiological understanding is insightful, as he highlights the divisions that exist within The United Methodist Church over the question of our ecumenical and interreligious commitment.[60] One might suggest there are "subcultures" within the church, groups that favor either the ecumenical dimension or the evangelical dimension of the Methodist heritage, but often at the expense of the other. Are these two commitments opposed to each other, or can both be affirmed as expressions of God's grace in the world that is still groaning toward completion? How do we reconcile missional aspects that include both "conversion" and "conversation"?

Finally, in 1981, Albert Outler, speaking against the tendency to pit the work of evangelism against the work of "liberation" or social action, offered this prophetic message:

> The great cause in the United Methodist Church today is to recover and renew the original sense of mission—the heralding by word and lifestyle the kingdom of God on earth, the Rule of Grace and righteousness; the proclamation of God's unmerited gifts of pardon, reconciliation, assurance, and dedication; and the transformation of persons and societies by the means of God's gifts and fruits more than human achievements.[61]

Richey reiterates this concern more than twenty years later, claiming that "the more progressive wing of the church believes that the conservatives slight justice and social transformation. The conservative wing believes that the progressives slight justification and evangelism."[62] Outler sought to reduce this tension, concluding that the church's mission arises out of the scriptural understanding of saving faith working by love, which Wesley also spoke of as personal and social holiness. In other words, the church's mission requires both social and personal transformation; we are called to be active in both dimensions of the movement of God in Jesus Christ in the Holy Spirit in the world.

In many ways, The United Methodist Church has initiated a renewal of its mission in the world by means of the deliberative process that led to the current mission statement of making disciples of Jesus Christ. Even so, the mission of The United Methodist Church can yet become a more powerful, grace-filled agent of the inbreaking realm of God in the world. As briefly noted here, further reflection and dialogue on the applicability of the historical Wesleyan conception of mission, the tensions of the local mission in a global context, the ecumenical and interreligious responsibility in the face of a traditional commitment to evangelizing the nation and world, and the balance between outreach and ingathering in the context of ongoing formation are warranted. In reclaiming and reinterpreting the church's mission in the present time, The United Methodist Church has the potential, once again, to renew the church and to reform the nation in light of the inbreaking realm of God in the world and to continue the process begun by John Wesley almost three hundred years ago.[63]

CHAPTER 4

Jesus Christ: The Heart of the Great Commission

W. Stephen Gunter

The conclusion affirmed in the *Book of Discipline* is clear: "We endeavor through the power of the Holy Spirit to understand the love of God given in Jesus Christ. We seek to spread this love abroad. . . . A convincing witness to our Lord and Savior Jesus Christ can contribute to the renewal of our faith, bring persons to that faith, and strengthen the Church as an agent of healing and reconciliation."[1] If one were to do a word search through the *Discipline*, Jesus Christ and the sentiment expressed in the sentences above would be the thread that holds Parts II, III, and IV (Doctrinal Standards and Theological Task, Ministry, and Social Principles) together. Indeed, Section 1—Our Doctrinal Heritage opens with these words: "United Methodists profess the historic Christian faith in God, incarnate in Jesus Christ for our salvation and ever at work in human history in the Holy Spirit."[2]

When we speak of the essentials of vital religion, there should be little doubt or hesitation that Jesus Christ is at the heart and center. When we say, "Beyond the essentials of vital religion, United Methodists respect the diversity of opinions held by conscientious persons of faith,"[3] this diversity is not an exclusionary clause for church members to opt out of incarnational Christianity. Although we are plural and diverse in our opinions about how to live out the implications of the "historic Christian faith in God, incarnate in Jesus Christ for our salvation," we are not pluralists in the sense that Jesus Christ may or may not be "incarnate . . . for our salvation and ever at work in human history in the Holy Spirit." Even as we make this affirmation, we know that there are many church members and even clergy for whom pluralism and pluralist is the option preferred to plural and diverse; but this is not a position that is in harmony with the tradition, teachings, and practices of Methodism.

A good example is the local member who came to the pastor after morning worship at the church on the campus of Emory University and offered the criticism, "Pastor, since you came to be our preacher [two years ago], we have been hearing too much about Jesus." She did not clarify about whom or what she preferred to hear each Sunday, but she was clear that hearing so much about the saving work of God in Christ made her uncomfortable. If what she heard each Sunday were a simplistic "Jesus-ology," then we might have sympathy for such a critique. It has been my privilege recently to worship often at this church, and the pastor, an Emory University New Testament Ph.D., carefully exegetes the text each Sunday (from the original languages, often with connection to the Old Testament reading for that day) and then draws explicit practical applications with regard to how the scriptural teachings impinge on our daily lives—a wonderful homiletical practice that models the maxim: "No motif in the Wesleyan tradition has been more constant than the link between Christian doctrine and Christian living."[4] Thankfully, we can report that the pastor did not yield to this church member, and that Jesus Christ as the heart of the Christian message remains at the center of his preaching. One good anecdote does not a case make, but in this instance it does point to an intellectual impasse that, for many, calls into question the missionary and evangelistic work of the church. In the following pages, an apologetic will be developed for the viability of the Great Commission, centering on the person and work of Jesus Christ. This will take place within the contours of two sets of parameters: first, why Jesus of Nazareth is our doctrinal center; second, how Jesus the Christ is to be proclaimed "in all his offices."

Christians are aware of Jesus and recognize him as the Christ because of the tradition of his deeds and words preserved in the New Testament, and from this the church has discerned the central content of its proclamation. As such, Jesus is the precipitating cause of Christian faith and Christian doctrine; indeed, we may accurately say that the history of Jesus of Nazareth was and is the crucible of Christian doctrinal possibilities. The church may not safely ignore the person and work of Jesus because what happened in the past is recognized as being charged with significance for the transformation of the church's present, as well as the construction of the future. What the first-century Christians knew, and what we ignore at our spiritual peril, is this: what we experience and believe about Jesus Christ is the axis on which the present possibilities and future realities hinge.[5] Put another way, Jesus Christ is the heart and soul of the church's evangelistic message.

One does not have to read far in the New Testament before encountering the teaching that Jesus is the one who brought divine judgment and, as a consequent reality, the possibility of conversion and transformation. While many, especially in United Methodist connections, are prone to pronouncements like, "We are not doctrinal," or "We are not a confessional church," the lack of epistemological rigor in such assertions is quickly apparent when we look closely at scripture. Within the New Testament there is a surprisingly large body of evidence suggesting that the earliest Christians began to adopt fixed confessional formulae as a means of summing up and passing on the fundamental content of their understanding of the personal relevance of Jesus to their faith. The term "Christ" is deeply embedded in the earliest church's witness to Jesus of Nazareth, and it references a deep and complex Jewish religious expectation.[6] One need look no farther than 1 Corinthians 15:3-4 to find an example of an early Christian interpretation of the messianic expectation: "For I handed on to you as of first importance what I in turn had received: that Christ died for our sins in accordance with the scriptures . . . was buried . . . was raised on the third day in accordance with the scriptures."

What Paul is doing in his Corinthian letter is ascribing a specific theological significance to Jesus of Nazareth, in fact, a doctrinal interpretation of the Jewish messianic expectation. He is leading the early church in its first doctrinal steps; he is birthing the theological image that subsequently came to define the early church's theological imagination with the resurrection of Christ as its center. Subsequently, the church birthed other theological images around Jesus of Nazareth in its attempt to make sense of its experience of Jesus as Messiah. One cannot read the New Testament carefully and miss the obvious dimension of the early church's theological imagination around Jesus of Nazareth, and it is not inaccurate to recognize these as seminal doctrinal assertions. In other words, from its earliest origins, the church has been doctrinal; moreover, when the church ceases the rebirthing of theological images related to Jesus of Nazareth, it stands in mortal spiritual danger. It would imply that the church has ceased to have fresh encounters with the resurrected Lord, encounters that demand doctrinal and theological imagination to make communicable sense of them.

There are many ways in which Jesus may be religiously or theologically construed, but when the church chose the assertion "Jesus is the Christ" as foundational, it was closing out a host of other less doctrinal and theological assertions about Jesus of Nazareth. "Jesus is the Christ" is not an arbitrary assertion by some individual; rather, it is a nomenclature suggested by the total narrative of the life and work of Jesus. It has been discerned within the narrative, not imposed from without. The theological interpretative framework is of great consequence, but the narrative about Jesus is primary. In fact, both are part of the New Testament; and when a supposed theologian of the church makes an assertion like, "We are not doctrinal," then that theologian is severing ties with the earliest confessional communities whose emerging confessional formulae are embedded in the New Testament.

We witness a terse affirmation of such formulae in Romans 1:3-5, which proclaims, "the gospel concerning his Son, who was descended from David according to the flesh and was declared to be Son of God with power according to the spirit of holiness by resurrection from the dead, Jesus Christ our Lord, through whom we have received grace and apostleship." This and other similar assertions call the narrative about Jesus of Nazareth to be viewed in a particular theological light, and they close out other available assertions. The early church was no less aware than we should be about the threat of theological lenses being placed over the Jesus narratives that would encourage different doctrinal conclusions. Gnostic interpretations come quickly to mind.

It is not accidental that the early Christian communities worked to close out Gnostic interpretations, for the early theologians of the primitive church were deeply and increasingly committed to a particular theological interpretation regarding Jesus of Nazareth, namely, the emergent doctrine of the two natures: Jesus is God and Jesus is human. Jesus was human is easily enough worked into our frames of reference, for with a historic human figure we can find points of affinity; however, the early church discerned that Jesus of Nazareth was not merely another religious teacher. He was rabbi to them, but he was more. He was God among us.

When we as "United Methodists profess the historic Christian faith in

God, incarnate in Jesus Christ for our salvation and ever at work in human history in the Holy Spirit," this is an ecclesial anamnesis (remembering) that connects us with the New Testament and the early ecumenical councils of the primitive church. To the extent that some among us cannot say this with full conviction, we are exhibiting a tendency to cut ourselves off from this divine remembrance. What is being doctrinally observed in the Incarnation is the early believers' conviction that two things that had theretofore been separate, the human and the divine, have in Jesus of Nazareth been brought together. Within the narrative of the New Testament, this is of salvific significance in order to interpret adequately the early disciples' experience of Jesus—for example, by Jesus pronouncing forgiveness of sins: "When Jesus saw their faith, he said to the paralytic, 'Son, your sins are forgiven.' Now some of the scribes were sitting there, questioning in their hearts, 'Why does this fellow speak in this way? It is blasphemy! Who can forgive sins but God alone?'" (Mark 2:5-7). The point to be made here is not about a theological abstraction. Indeed, it was the early church finding a way to connect the experience and meaning that they discovered in their encounters with Jesus.

Unlike some Protestant movements and denominations, the theological heirs of John Wesley have typically avoided approaching doctrine rationalistically. When some among us say that we are not doctrinal, it is hopefully this propositionalist construal of doctrine that they have in view and not all doctrinal assertions per se. The fallacy of a comprehensive nondoctrinalist assertion is fallacious on at least two levels: it does not do justice to the New Testament, and historically, it has never accurately described us as Wesleyans. We may be neither rationalists nor propositionalists, but that does not mean that we are not doctrinal. There is at least one other way in which we may be doctrinal, namely, a construal in which there is a dynamic relationship between doctrine, the scriptural narrative, and our experience of both. This construal is especially the case with regard to the doctrine of the Incarnation. The rationalist approach would be to discern whether the doctrine of the Incarnation is a proper deduction from the premises of what scripture records about Jesus. The fundamental fault with this approach is that it misconstrues the nature of scriptural accounts, interpreting them as rational constructions from which premises might be deduced. Scriptural accounts about Jesus, however, are narrative. They are story, and story is better interpreted by inference than by deductive logic. We might ask the question this way: "Amid the particularities of the narratives about

Jesus, what are the possible frameworks of conceptualities to be inferred that would help us make the most sense of who Jesus was?" In other words, the Bible is not fundamentally a set of propositions or premises from which we deduce truth claims; rather, it is a narrated story (set of stories) that in its wholeness emerges as a pattern of thinking that invites us to transpose the story into an interpretative framework. The church has called this framework "doctrine."

We have learned from the early church that the mere recitation of scripture is not adequate to inform the life of the church. Doctrine was required in order for the church to engage other modes of discourse that grew out of its experience, such as liturgy, poetry, and song. It is a well-intentioned but misguided platitude when a person says, "We don't want doctrine in our church. We just want the Bible." That would do away with most every activity save the reading of scripture. Whether we are aware of it or not, doctrinal assertions and assumptions inform almost every pronouncement we make the moment we move from the actual reading of the text. The question is not whether we have doctrine, but what kind of doctrine do we have?

It is only against this background of the importance of doctrine, especially the church's historic assertions that Jesus was both human and divine, that our underscoring the importance of proclaiming Christ as Savior retains theological coherence. And when we turn to a very specific Wesleyan form of that proclamation—proclaiming Christ in all his "offices"—the foundation of historic doctrinal affirmations is indispensable.

Proclaiming Christ in All His Offices

In many Protestant churches, especially those of the more evangelistic inclination, we often encounter a very specific construal of incarnational theology. Typically, it is an atonement theology that points rather exclusively to the "saving work of Christ on the cross," and the Atonement is viewed as penal (suffering the punishment due the sinner) and substitutionary (suffering sacrificial death in our place, like the "unblemished lamb" in the Levitical sacrificial system). In John Wesley's theology and, hence, in subsequent Methodist doctrinal emphases, this reference to the past work of Christ on the cross is not absent, but it is not the primary focus of our soteriology. What Christ has done *for* us is foundational for what God through Christ will do *in* us: "By justification we are saved from the guilt of sin, and restored to the favour of God: by sanctification we are saved from the power and root of sin, and restored to the image of God."[7]

From the earliest days of Methodism, Wesley theologically shaped the movement to view Christ's atoning work less through a lens oriented to the past and more oriented to the present and looking toward the future; furthermore, he urged his preachers to proclaim not only "Christ dying for us" but also "Christ reigning in us."[8] Wesley's way of accomplishing this was to exhort the Methodist itinerants to preach Christ "in all his offices": Priest, Prophet, and King.[9] Randy Maddox has argued, and I think correctly, that this sequencing (Priest, Prophet, King versus Prophet, Priest, King) of the offices is most appropriate to the logic of Wesley's soteriology, the priestly role being foundational to the prophetic and kingly offices,[10] and all of these together being Wesley's shorthand for the whole of Christ's saving work. Already in 1744 we read in the "Minutes" of the preachers' Conference:

> Q. 15. Is there not a defect in us? Do we preach as we did at first? Have we not changed our doctrines?
> A. (1) At first we preached almost wholly to unbelievers. To those therefore we spake almost continually of remission of sins through the death of Christ, and the nature of faith in his blood. And so we do still, among those who need to be taught the first elements of the gospel of Christ.
> (2) But those in whom the foundation is already laid, we exhort to go on to perfection; which we did not see so clearly at first; although we occasionally spoke of it from the beginning.
> (3) Yet we now preach, and that continually, faith in Christ, as the Prophet, Priest, and King, at least as clearly, as strongly, and as fully, as we did six years ago.[11]

The significant and comprehensive import that Wesley attaches to the offices language is reflected by his including reference to it in the *Explanatory Notes* on Revelation 5:6, "And I beheld in the midst of the throne . . . a Lamb [Christ] standing as if he had been slain . . . ," about which Wesley comments, "He is now in a posture of readiness to execute all His offices of prophet, priest, and king."[12] Given its foundational significance to the Methodist movement, it is incumbent on us to sketch, at least the main points of emphasis of what it means to proclaim Christ as Priest, Prophet, and King.

Proclaiming Christ as Priest

Wesley takes the orthodox doctrine of sin with the utmost seriousness, and he often refers to this sinfulness as the Fall. Because of the Fall, all of humanity has lost the comprehensive freedom given by the Creator, and every human being without exception has become satisfied with a lesser virtue than God originally intended. The result is a condition of the deepest sin and corruption that is both personal and systemic. For this desperate "lostness" humanity requires a High Priest, and with regard to Christ's priestly office, Wesley concentrates on the personal dimension. This loss of moral and spiritual capacity is permanent and irreversible unless aided by divine grace. Lostness is the natural state of humanity apart from grace. Wesley is one with St. Augustine who, with reference to John 15:5 ("Without me you can do nothing"), writes, "the Lord did not say, 'Without me you can with difficulty do something,' . . . in that same gospel statement he did not say, 'Without me you can complete nothing,' but *'Without me you can do nothing.'* "[13] Wesley is clear with regard to the implications of human sin: there is complete human impotence apart from divine initiative for the human soul, feeling, will, or abilities to participate in salvation.[14] The priestly work of Christ is an absolute necessity.

Wesley's logic is this: there is no salvation apart from faith, yet this faith is the gift of God's grace. It is the faithful who are saved, and those who remain faithful will finally be saved. Faith and salvation are inseparable. Answering those who wished to interpret Christ's priestly work as a finished salvation that logically led to predestination, John Wesley published "Serious Thoughts upon the Perseverance of the Saints" in 1751.[15] In this piece he emphasizes two corollary aspects of Christ's priestly work for our salvation. First, unbelief leads to damnation. Second, only faith and belief lead to salvation. The complicated logic regarding cause and condition for salvation are wrestled with in Wesley's 1765 sermon "The Lord our Righteousness."[16] This sermon contains the essential components of Wesley's doctrine of Christ in relation to human salvation, and his apologetic is consistent. Wesley's emphasis on the priestly work of Christ centers not on a salvation already determined by a salvific work in the past tense, but on the present and future implications of that priestly work. If the righteousness of Christ is imputed to us *before* we believe, then election is unconditional; but if Christ's righteousness comes after believing, then faith is the condition and all believers are truly righteousness. Wesley asks, "When is it that the righteousness of Christ is *imputed* to us, and in what sense is it imputed?" [¶II.1]. As to the question, "When?" the response is patently clear: "When they believe. In that very hour the righteousness of Christ is theirs. It is imputed to every one that believes, as soon as he believes: faith and the righteousness of Christ are inseparable." If we pursue Wesley's words to their logical conclusion with regard to causality and ask, "Is this then human or divine?" the answer is also unambiguous: this is Christ's divine priestly work. Wesley maintained against all his detractors that he did not deny the imputed righteousness of Christ to the believer as a result of Christ's priestly work; rather, on the basis of this priestly office, he asserted that both the active and the passive righteousness of Christ are the "whole and sole meritorious cause of the justification of a sinner before God" [¶II.15].

Evangelism in the Wesleyan spirit requires that we, like Wesley, take the doctrine of sin, pervasively personal and systemic, with due seriousness. Likewise, it is incumbent on us to proclaim the priestly office of Christ as the one whom through his death and in resurrected life intercedes on our behalf. The priestly work of Christ is foundational to Wesleyan soteriology, and Wesley's sermonic corpus is replete with references to it, as well as to the prophetic and kingly offices as, for example, in the sermon "The Law Established through Faith, II":

> To preach Christ as a workman that needeth not to be ashamed [2 Tim. 2:15] is to preach him not only as our great 'High Priest, taken from among men, and ordained for men, in things pertaining to God' [Heb. 5:1]; as such, 'reconciling us to God by his blood' [Rom. 5:9, 10], and 'ever living to make intercession for us' [Heb. 7:25]; but likewise as the Prophet of the Lord, 'who of God is made unto us wisdom' [1 Cor. 1:30], who by his word and his Spirit 'is with us always' [Matt. 28:20], 'guiding us into all truth' [John 16:13]; yea, and as remaining a King for ever; as giving laws to all whom he has bought with his blood; as restoring those to the image of God whom he had first reinstated in his favour; as reigning in all believing hearts until he has 'subdued all things to himself' [Phil. 3:21]; until he hath utterly cast out all sin, and 'brought in everlasting righteousness' [Dan. 9:24].[17]

Regarding Hebrews 7:25, "Wherefore he is able to save them to the uttermost . . . ," Wesley comments: "From all the guilt, power, root, and consequence of sin."[18] The priestly office of Christ is foundational to the prophetic office.

Proclaiming Christ as Prophet

Although words like "prophet" and "prophetic" are used in everyday parlance to refer to future events, Wesley interprets Christ's prophetic office to be directly linked with God's salvific work to deliver the believer from the power of sin. If the judicial work of pardon is the first step on the way of salvation, then deliverance from the power of sin in the life of the believer is the consequent second step. Explaining the reference in Matthew 1:16, "Jesus, who is called the Christ," Wesley comments: "The name Jesus respects chiefly the promise of blessing made to Abraham; the name Christ, the promise of the Messiah's kingdom which was made to David . . . and Messiah in Hebrew signifies 'Anointed'; and imply [sic] the prophetic, priestly, and royal characters which were to meet in the Messiah." With specific respect to the office of prophet, Wesley asserts: "And with respect to ourselves, we find a total darkness, blindness, ignorance of God, and the things of God. Now here we want Christ in His prophetic office, to enlighten our minds, and teach us the whole will of God."[19]

There is clearly no artificial distinction implied between the priestly and the prophetic offices in the Wesleyan evangelistic message, for what Wesley is endeavoring to make clear is that pardon for sin and actual transformation of the pardoned believer are part and parcel of one salvific work: imputed righteousness *and* imparted righteousness. Indeed, in Wesley's mind Jesus' Sermon on the Mount is the vision for humanity God has in view: "The beauty of holiness, of that inward man of the heart which is renewed after the image of God. . . . This inward religion bears the shape of God so visibly impressed upon it that a soul must be wholly immersed in flesh and blood when he can doubt of its divine original."[20] Time and again in his expositions on the Sermon on the Mount, Wesley reflects his opinion that these teachings of Jesus are "the noblest compendium of religion which is to be found even in the oracles of God."[21]

Wesley would have no part in exegesis that interprets Jesus' words as intended for some time later in God's heaven. Not only Christ's priestly work of pardon, but also the divine work of renewal and transformation are part of what God's grace can do in the present. To proclaim fully the offices of Christ is to proclaim both justification and sanctification as integral to Christ's saving work in the world.

Proclaiming Christ as King

John Wesley's most extended explication of the kingly office is to be found in his sermon "The Law Established through Faith, II."[22] The kingly office represents the logical culmination of Wesley's evangelistic message, and it reflects an amalgamation of the priestly and prophetic offices in all their dimensions. The logic and flow in the sermon is this: Christ's Kingship involves (1) giving laws to all those he has bought with his blood, (2) restoring those to the (moral) image of God whom he had first reinstated in his favor, and (3) reigning in all believing hearts until he has "subdued all things to himself."[23]

We are not truly faithful to the Wesleyan tradition when we preach continually on grace without reference to the law. A radical doctrine of grace makes salvific sense only if there is a radical sense of need and falling short; but there must be something to fall short of: "We 'establish the law', first, by our doctrine: by endeavouring to preach it in its whole extent, to explain and enforce every part of it in the same manner as our great Teacher did while upon earth."[24] Wesley repeatedly names all three offices as interrelated, and he gives specific content to the kingly office in connection with lifting up the law and Christ as the fulfillment of that law, our "disciplinarian" (lit. schoolmaster) to lead us to Christ.[25] Preaching a legalistic gospel is not authentic to Wesley, but neither is it a Wesleyan soteriology when we preach grace without reference to law.

Wesley turns the logic of typical "grace-oriented preaching" on its head, for he pays much closer attention to Jesus' and the apostle Paul's teaching than we are prone to do. While we might be prone to ignore any emphasis on the law, Wesley wants to "establish the law." He wants the transforming power of the evangelistic message to "fulfill the law" in the heart of the believer:

> This is therefore the main point to be considered: How may we establish the law in our own hearts so that it may have its full influence on our lives? And this can only be done by faith. Faith alone it is which effectually answers this end, as we learn from daily experience . . . faith in general is the most direct and effectual means of promoting all righteousness and true holiness; of establishing the holy and spiritual law in the hearts of them that believe.[26]

The heart of what Wesley wants to proclaim about the office of Christ as King, as an amalgamation with the priestly and prophetic offices, is that we cannot fulfill the law if we do not know what the law has taught. God's intention for the law cannot be internalized without reference to the law. He concludes, "In how amiable a light do you now see the holy and perfect will of God! Now, therefore, labour that it may be fulfilled, both in you, by you, and upon you. Now watch and pray that you may sin no more, that you may see and shun the least transgression of the law. . . . So shall you continually go on from faith to faith. So shall you daily increase in holy love, till faith is swallowed up in sight, and the law of love established to all eternity."[27]

It is clear that a Wesleyan soteriology is less rooted in specific moments of spiritual crisis (as important as they are experientially to the person) and more inclined to an entire life of spiritual development. A Wesleyan construal of Jesus Christ as the heart and soul of the Great Commission is more incarnational than it is penal and substitutionary. A decisive moment of pardon for sin and guilt (the priestly office of Christ) is fundamental, but this is the beginning rather than the end of the *via salutis*. The prophetic and kingly offices of Christ are indispensably integral to the journey of the believer in order that an ever-increasing Christlikeness might be realized as the evangelistic goal. Wesley was not reticent to name the comprehensive goal: *holiness*. Richard Heitzenrater sums it up nicely for us with these words: "Wesley was convinced that his position on justification and sanctification was crucial to the goal of spreading scriptural holiness. His preaching and his organization had taken on quite a different shape from those of Whitefield over the years, in no small part because evangelism itself takes on a different form when holiness is the goal."[28] I am fond of telling my students, "The real evangelistic question is not, 'If you died tonight, do you know that you would go to heaven?' The really crucial question is this: 'If you live for twenty more years, will it make any difference in this world?'" In other words, will God be embodied in us? Is our understanding of Jesus' saving work rooted in an incarnational theology?

Jesus Christ as the incarnate God among us is the heart and soul of the church's evangelistic message, and proclaiming Christ in all his offices— Priest, Prophet, and King—is essential to the church's proclamation if we are to be true heirs of our Wesleyan evangelistic heritage, one in which comprehensive Christlikeness is the goal toward which all believers are moving along the *via salutis*.

PART II
Contextualizing the Great Commission

CHAPTER 5

Megatrends That Challenge an Evangelizing Church[1]

Achim Härtner

Evangelism After September 11, 2001

The church in the twenty-first century is challenged by far-ranging changes in Western societies. The single historic event of September 11, 2001, came to stand as a symbol dreadfully indicating the vulnerability and the unpredicted risks of Western civilization. No matter if people are Christian and "churched," if they belong to some other religion, or if they are indifferent to religious sensibilities, the shock wave of September 11 affected them all. In many parts of the Western world, we sense an amorphous uncertainty in spite of all that we hear from government officials about national strength, military power, and national security. Many individuals feel deeply a fear of worldwide terror and war, a lack of confidence toward the future. The terrorist attacks of September 11 and various actions since then have led to what I call an "emotional globalization." The omnipresent electronic media is a key reason for the emotional interconnectedness that exists today as never before. In the U.S., medical experts like psychologist Jean Twenge of Cleveland speak of rising numbers of clients with "general phobia syndrome";[2] in Germany, experts say that some 15 percent of the adult population suffer from fear-related symptoms at least periodically; and in

Greece, the population shows the highest numbers of fear-related symptoms in central Europe. The impact upon children and youths will have to be examined over time. In my view, the theme of existential fear will become increasingly important in individual counseling as well as in sociological, political, and theological discourse. I also believe that a latent spirit of fear and fright will affect an evangelizing church, which is called to witness in word and deed to the biblical truth of a loving and caring God, who loved the world so much that he gave his only Son to open up a livable, secure future for all humankind.

Ten Megatrends in Central Europe and North America

During the last two decades of the twentieth century, deep-rooted changes took place in the Western world and, indeed, worldwide. Some of these changes came to pass at a breathtaking speed: the process of disintegration of the former East and West power blocs, the ongoing globalization of economics based upon a model of maximizing profit, the uninterrupted progress of much of the world from industrial to information societies. With these global, national, and regional upheavals, the necessity for interpreting the present situation has not decreased but increased, for the individual as well as for our societies as a whole. The questions of how to interpret the present situation and what conclusions might be drawn from it for the future are questions that are important to many people. The question, however, about the role the church can play in contributing to a livable future is barely posed outside the church in many contexts. To live out the Christian mission in the world requires us to be aware of the global context. That is why evangelization and mission, in general, and local congregational development, in particular, cannot avoid working through these social realities. The successful evangelizing church must come to terms with today's changing global culture. In what follows I want to analyze the social factors that shape the minds of people in the Western world today by highlighting the commonalities that exist amid the great diversity among individuals and societies.[3]

In focusing on this theme, we stand in the tradition of, on the one hand, futurologists such as Hermann Kahn, David Riesman, Anthony J. Wiener, Vance Packard, and Horst W. Opaschowski, and on the other hand, trend researchers like John Naisbitt, Faith Popcorn, and Matthias Horx. Likewise, the term "megatrends" points toward general phenomena that shape a society for a longer period of time, generally, five to fifteen years. Changes in the general social climate cannot be seen simply as the sum of individual phenomena, but need to be viewed as vastly interconnected factors that provide the frame of reference for today's social trends.[4] There are four basic factors of societal change in the Western world:

1. The *globalization* of economics, science, cultural, political, and other social matters,
2. The *demographic* development that includes an increasing percentage of older people and migration and ethnic shifts due to economic and political factors,
3. The growing *economic* disparity between the "haves" and the "have nots,"
4. The development of *mass communication* has led to the omnipresence of electronic media, which delivers a flood of information that must be analyzed and interpreted.

With these factors in mind, we will turn to our analysis of ten megatrends or interrelated currents that shape today's societies in significant but ill-defined ways.

1. "More Is Better!"—The Differentiation and Pluralization of Life

Standing in front of the shelf at the supermarket, we may experience a strange feeling of helplessness. Which yogurt should we purchase? The one with fruit on the bottom, fruit mixed in, or a crunchy topping? In the cosmetics aisle, it seems there is not an inch of skin that lacks a customized cosmetic product. To choose or not to choose—that is the question in today's world of commerce and in almost every area of our lives. We are dependent on expert authorities to analyze the complex realities and choices confronting us. Indeed, the vast number of possibilities before us challenges not only individuals, but also persons responsible for decisions affecting the economy, politics, and culture. Historically, after World War II, a movement toward individualization has shaped the far-reaching change "from fate to choice," as described in the late 1970s by Peter L. Berger in his book *The Heretical Imperative: Contemporary Possibilities of Religious Affirmation*.[5] Francis Fukuyama went a step further when he wrote with a sense of urgency about the "end of history."[6] He claimed that almost all of the traditional systems of values and meaning-making have dissolved, leading him to question the possibility of a civilized future.

However optimistic or pessimistic our view of the situation may be, one thing is clear: the days of monolithic ideals are over. There is no one set of values or foundations that is shared by all or even the majority of a society. We live among ever-increasing variety in a "Multioptional Society," as Swiss sociologist Peter Gross proposed in 1994. The motto of pluralism is "more is better!" We must learn to cope with the plurality of alternatives, even as the multitude of options gains a meaning and momentum of its own. This differentiation and variation leads to segmentation within human communities. People who share less and less in common come together only occasionally; they become part-time citizens in part-time societies. In the postmodern age, people become wanderers among different worlds, and many people understand themselves as "island-hopping" from one life-island to another.[7] Life spheres like work, leisure, education, and family exist in a generally unconnected manner. On each of these life-islands a certain language and set of values are applicable, but may not be understood or deemed as valid in other social locations or contexts.

This sense of variety and multiple options is significant for the religious situation, in general, and the life of our churches. Christianity must deal with an external pluralism (other religions) and an internal pluralism (within the Christian faith). In the Western world, the market principles of supply and demand apply to religious life, and this leads to a situation of compromise more than it does to conflict. In a 1992 study on the religious situation in Germany, published by the weekly political magazine *Der Spiegel*, the country of the Reformation was depicted as a "heathen country with a Christian past and Christian leftovers."[8] This description is true for other European countries, and it may someday be true in North American countries, if it isn't already. In the situation of realized pluralism, the question of truth is posed with new urgency. As Christians, we are challenged to be held accountable for "the hope that is in [us]" (1 Pet. 3:15). By all means we should renounce quick-fix answers in order to avoid running into some kind of fundamentalism, on the one hand, or into an indifferent reduction of the Christian message to a least common denominator, on the other hand.

As such, there are two major challenges to a future-oriented, evangelizing church. The first is that people should take residence and make themselves at home in the Christian faith,[9] thus being nourished and cared for in the ongoing process of becoming better disciples of the living Christ. The second challenge is to provide people with the capacities to negotiate the situation of pluralism, namely, to help them develop a sense of tolerance rather than ignorance. It is encouraging that the motto of our days—"choose your life!"—corresponds with the fundamental doctrine and basic structure of The United Methodist Church as a "free church" (which in Europe has a different meaning than in North America) or one that permits us to "think and let think." We want people to make up their minds to become followers of Christ and to join a congregation of believers to grow spiritually and socially. Our task is to identify and communicate the values of our doctrines and biblical roots and the goals of our Christian understanding of life in order to make this a viable option.

2. "Me, Myself, and I!"—Individualization and Segmentation of Life

The February 2001 issue of *Der Spiegel* showed the face of tennis star Boris Becker beside the title "Me." Becker, like other international media stars, can be understood as a representative of the "ego society" of the turn of the millennium. From a historical perspective, there has never before been a time in which the Western man and woman thought and lived in such a self-centered way as today. Sociologists confirm that in Western civilization it seems the only authority left is the individual.[10] The increasing number of options to choose from inevitably brings with it a higher degree of possibilities for individual development, but it likewise fosters enormous pressure for deciding among alternatives. So many persons seek actively to escape from the "gray mass" and yearn for an individual and differentiated lifestyle. While variety and pluralism have grown, so, too, has the compulsion to mold one's individuality. The destandardization of life patterns that accompanied the thrust of individualization (leading to what has been called *patchwork identity* or *bricolage*) has now revealed its shadow side. Under the guise of individual freedom, new standards have been established based upon certain patterns of enjoyment or pleasure, leading to distinct milieus or subcultures with characteristic sets of rules and conventions. People are attempting to invent themselves anew daily; but it is clear that this is not viable. As human beings, we need stability and continuity to be able to live in a multioptional society.

The most significant change to be noticed in terms of the philosophy of life is that large numbers of people cease to follow their "native" religions and go through a selection process among different religious alternatives on the market. As proclaimed in Bob Dylan's song "Universal Soldier," people feel free to choose and change their religion or even to create their own by blending aspects of different world religions with neopagan fragments.[11] Sociological studies and various questionnaires include the category of "religious preference."[12] As the term indicates, religion is a choice that we can subjectively take or leave: tomorrow things can be entirely different as long as the religion fulfills our personal needs. Individualism and pluralism have led to an unprecedented level of secularization of religious life. However, as Edmund Burke had supposed in his day, the human creature "is constitutionally a religious animal," such that the quest for meaning in a chaotic world cannot be cut off entirely by secularization, even as it is disguised in the language of self-fulfillment and self-definition. When it comes to the question of truth, the consequences of that change are glaring. If "what concerns us ultimately,"[13] as Paul Tillich described the subject of theology, becomes a matter of individual construction from various traditions and sources, it will lose its ultimacy and its power. As Jesus said to his disciples, it is God who chooses us: "You did not choose me but I chose you. And I appointed you to go and bear fruit, fruit that will last, so that the Father will give you whatever you ask him in my name" (John 15:16).

3. "I Want It All, I Want It Now!"— The Quest for Holism

"I want it all, I want it now!" is one of the most popular songs of the British rock group Queen. The title can also be heard as the motto of society at the end of the twentieth and beginning of the twenty-first centuries. Published research indicates that adventure is a key concern for scores of people in Western societies and that the desire for instant gratification has become a shaping life-pattern for many.[14] Material possessions, however, can neither grant or guarantee true meaning nor create quality public spirit; the quest for instant fulfillment and accumulating material goods can hardly mask the inner void that remains unfulfilled. American writer and Nobel Prize winner Saul Bellow speaks of a kind of longing that is characterized by the inability to comprehend that something is missing. Bellow explains that we are surrounded with everything we need for a comfortable life, a life filled with movement and pleasure. Yet he adds, "And there is something in us all that says to us: What's next? And what now?"[15]

Undeniably, a longing for fulfillment of wishes and dreams is deeply planted in our human hearts and minds. In our day, the pursuit of holism, a well-rounded life, or as some would say, a life "in unity with the cosmos," typifies the understanding of our generation, including the understanding of religion. We may live in an age of "transcendent homelessness" (Lutz Friedrich),[16] in which people are stirred and moved by expectations of conducting their lives according to their own desires; nevertheless, people also hold deeply sensed expectations toward "God" or an unnamed transcendence as a meaning-making authority.

What makes life worth living in a time of high expectations? Austrian psychologist and founder of logotherapy Viktor E. Frankl, who survived a Nazi concentration camp, pointed out that a life filled with positive experiences and ample self-reflection is not the only life worth living.[17] Indeed, he reminds us that crisis and suffering and even stagnation can prove to be sources of growth and development. German philosopher Odo Marquard offers a similar appraisal, when he claims that what we need today is a diet in terms of meaning-making. Not everything, he argues, needs to make sense; not all the chapters in our autobiographies need to be pleasurable. We don't have to persistently check our "individual satisfaction" pulse and run from one highlight to another to be able to say at the end that it was a good life.[18]

I remember what theologian Fulbert Steffensky said at a church congress in Stuttgart, Germany. He argued against a totalizing compulsion, saying this:

There is a suffering that comes out of excessive expectations. The expectation that my marriage is perfect, that my partner fulfills me utterly, that I get wrapped up in my work totally, that the education of my children works out exactly as it should: Life just isn't that way. Most of our loves succeed halfway, most of our parenthood is at half measure; we are half-good as teachers, half-happy as human beings. And even this is quite a lot. Against the terror of holism, I want to praise a successful halfness. The sweetness and beauty in life does not lie in perfect success and wholeness. Life is of finite nature, not only in the sense that we have to die. Life is finite in itself, in the limited happiness, in the limited success, in the limited fulfillment. Great passion can hide in half a thankful heart.[19]

Indeed, the urge for holism in many lives has to do with the dwindling of trust in God. Those who believe in God do not have to play God with their lives, but when faith in the Creator and Sustainer of life shatters, the creature has to bear the full burden of responsibility for the entirety of life. When it comes to talking with people about expectations in life, we can share the prescription for some kind of diet in terms of meaning-making. Furthermore, we need to make sure that we ponder all possibilities to show to what extent the Christian message and faith are capable of providing direction for living in uncertain times and refreshment that quenches the spiritual thirst and deepest longing for warmth and security in a hostile world.

4. "Faster!"—Life's Accelerated Pace and the Shrinking of the Present

The individualization of life brings not only the sense of greater freedom and relief from conventions, but also increasing demands on our ability and willingness to change. Employment, life partnership, cultural interests, religious life, and other features of life are in flux and subject to constant change. The tendency in highly developed societies is toward the continuing acceleration of the pace of life, which leads to a consciousness that philosopher Hermann Lübbe calls the "shrinking of the present." Transportation and communication means get faster and faster, and our physical and mental limits become strained. Sociologist James Gleick, in his book *Faster: The Acceleration of Just About Everything*, projects the twenty-first century as an age of "speed."[20] Is he right?

A characteristic of what we can call an "acceleration society" is that the pace of change occurs gradually and tends to be underestimated. Sociologist Robert Levine has compared ways in which different societies deal with time.[21] He highlights the global diversity in a number of areas such as the precision of public clocks, the speed at which people walk, and the speed at which people work. The result can hardly be considered surprising: eight of nine countries with the quickest pace of life are in Western Europe; Japan is ranked fourth, immediately after Germany. The slowest societies are countries like Brazil, Indonesia, and Mexico, where people work and live in an attitude characterized by *mañana* (tomorrow). Furthermore, there is a remarkable difference between rural and urban areas. Levine found that, in general, the more productive, industrialized, and mechanized a national economy is, the faster the pace of life becomes. As Levine puts it, wasting the time of a businessman is as bad as robbing his wallet.[22]

How do the accelerating pace of life and the consciousness of a "shrinking present" affect people? On the one hand, many people are willing to adapt to the heightened pace. Their hunger for adventure and success is a strong motor that keeps them on track, and this is especially the case with younger people. They enjoy living in an active, exciting world. But the reality is that the increasing commercialization of today's Western societies requires an emphasis on achievement and higher output. This emphasis puts pressure on people with which they must cope every day. Some people are driven by the dread of social regulation and feel heavily constrained by their life circumstances. Others suffer from a social context that focuses on money and achievement as status symbols. In many cases, the price to be paid by those who will not or cannot adapt to the faster pace and demands is a reduced quality of life.

This megatrend has consequences for our church work as well. As church leaders, we love high levels of attendance and vigorous participation by our members, but we also sense the challenges of leading and preaching in a rapidly changing congregation. Have we learned how to cope with people dropping in and dropping out of our congregations? For example, when a person who has attended our church for a year or more moves to another city and discontinues his or her church activities, we can say, "We're losing another active member," or we can say, "We are sending out a disciple of Jesus into the world." In the twenty-first century, flexibility will be one of most important skills we can have. We will need to practice and teach the skill of flexibility in our local churches if we want our congregations to continue being homes for people who live in this fast-paced, success-oriented world.

The Bible testifies to a God who is dynamic. Yahweh tells Moses "ehyeh asher ehyeh," or "I AM WHO I AM" (Exod. 3:14). This statement is to be read not as a word of arbitrariness, but as one of constant love and care through shifting times and ages. At the end of the Gospel of Matthew, the risen Christ promises his enduring presence to the disciples after entrusting them with the Great Commission: "And remember, I am with you always, to the end of the age" (Matt. 28:20). Christ, who "is the same yesterday and today and forever" (Heb. 13:8), is not abandoning the world; therefore, we can count on God's presence through the Holy Spirit (Acts 1:8) when we seek to mold our congregations to be present-day places of rest and spiritual renewal. As Christians, we live according to a different understanding of time.

5. "You Are as Young as You Feel!"— The Blurring of the Generation Gap

I recently read an article in a local newspaper that argued that inline skating is just the right exercise for senior citizens. As a father of three children, I know how dangerous this joyous sport is, and I can only surmise that the author of the article is subsidized by an interested company. This random example may be typical of the trend of diminished or even vanished generational boundaries. Everything seems to be just right for everybody. Journalist Florian Illies, biographer of "Generation Golf" (the cohort born between 1965 and 1975), makes this point in assessing the marketing of the new Volkswagen automobile: "In the advertisement for the new Golf model, a smart looking and handsome thirty-something man sits next to his 75-year-old father. Both seem to enjoy life. . . . Then the younger one says or thinks: 'I wanted to do things completely different from my old man. And now—we are driving the same car.'"[23]

Sociological surveys of central Europe and North America confirm this image: younger and older people adapt to each other or, at least, involve themselves with each other. Young and old find a way to cooperate based upon a partnership involving mutual advantage or necessity. A prominent survey of German youths indicates that never before, in the history of such surveys, have children seemed to be as content with their parental generation as they are today.[24] Although such findings point to a spirit of mutual understanding and respect in numerous families, this result needs to be interpreted *cum grano salis* (with a grain of salt). Especially in those Western European countries where studies on youth violence are being done, it has been suggested that many teenagers today lack the opportunity to demarcate their territory from that of the adults. To live in opposition and distinction from the adult world has been considered an important element of successful adolescence by educators and youth psychologists. In putting their interests first, many parents neglect what is in the best interest of their children. Yet this is a new kind of neglect attending to affluence and material accumulation: these parents neglect their youngsters' needs not by refusing to furnish them with enough material goods or give them various rights, but by depriving them of personal attention and sufficient self-determination to develop a healthy personality. In many cases, education today is delegated—as we delegate services of all kinds to "authorities"—to kindergartens, grammar schools, nannies, and so forth. But boys and girls need parents, who show their love not only by turning themselves toward the kids with patience and trust, but also by providing education as *pedagogues* (Greek: to lead a child), that is, by demonstrating values such as how to live with limitations and how to go through conflicts with mutual respect.

Perhaps more significant than the changes in lifestyle, sociological studies indicate that countless young people have reduced expectations not only in relation to adults but also toward their own adulthood. There are as many children acting remarkably mature as there are adults acting like little children. "It's the end of the world and I feel fine," a line from a song by the group REM, represents the stance of many people across the generations when it comes to facing the world's problems. A tendency toward an "infantilization" of Western societies has been observed; a brief look at magazines or the average TV program can easily convince those who doubt that propensity. If children and youths see adults existing in an attitude of easy-living and striving for instant gratification to a significant extent, it is no surprise that, among young people, a spirit of doubt toward the problem-solving ability of adults is growing. Indeed, the adult world of doubtful politics and unbridled capitalist economies has proven in many cases to be incompetent or unwilling to overcome hunger and war. We appear to be unable to establish peace and justice—ideals and values that have been talked about for decades, in the church no less than in society. We can't blame young people who display an openly disinterested or even cynical mind-set and wonder, "What good is it to become an adult?"

Although in the year 2000 youth and societal surveys showed a more positive outlook on life and the world among younger folks,[25] after September 11, 2001, experts predicted an increasingly pessimistic attitude toward the future and the problem-solving competence of adults. We don't yet know how the awareness of the latent danger of terror, and news about political mismanagement, economic downturns, and the depletion of natural resources will affect the upcoming generations. Certainly, the credibility of adults is a key to providing youths with a perspective of the future that is worth living. The interaction and cooperation among the generations are crucial challenges for the church, which must not be underestimated in its importance. Programs that link the age and social cohorts, which in daily life are separated, help mutual understanding and exchange of thoughts. This can be realized by all-age worship services, by common educational, cultural, and leisure amenities, as well as by common projects of various kinds where the energy of the young is needed as much as the experience of the older generation. These forums would also enable young people to take responsibility in various ways. Beyond such programs, adult Christians are challenged to rethink how we are modeling expectations, ways of relating, and values for the young.

6. "How Nice!"—Aesthetics as a Leading Category for Decision Making

By the rise of the aesthetic dimension of life, we mean a fundamental alignment of human thinking and action according to its spirit of adventure or the general excitement generated by an object or event. "Nice" and "ugly" more and more replace "good" and "bad" as the values of our days. "To look good," "to feel attractive," and other ways of expressing positive appearances have become a leading category shaping daily life. Sociologist Gerhard Schulze, author of the influential work *Die Erlebnisgesellschaft* (The Adventure Society),[26] perceives this development as an increasing orientation toward "the project of a pleasant life." No matter if it is in the sphere of consumption or healthy interhuman relationships. In the Western world, assessments related to quality or durability have fallen behind external assessments or whatever may give the impression of being good. *Good is what makes you feel and look good.*

In order to have some relatively stable framework for living (which becomes increasingly indispensable in times when we sense constant change is the reality of our lives), people form diverse clusters, milieus, and subcultures that follow distinctive aesthetic schemas, and they tend to dislike those from whom they want to differentiate themselves. This development shows up in the church in a similar way and affects our evangelism and mission. It is often stated that we simply want to do just one thing: to powerfully communicate the gospel in its essence. At the same time, a growing number of churches accept the notion that whatever you do in communicating the gospel, there is always a cultural aspect to it.[27] As hard as it may sound, our congregations are not open to everybody in the true sense. What we do or leave undone has to do with culture; each of our programs *de facto* has its target audience or, for those who dislike this term, spectrum of people. If the cultural facet of mission is not attended to, however, people with enjoyment patterns other than our own may quench their religious thirst in some other church or denomination or outside the Christian church. The challenge for the evangelizing church is to make it clear—and credible by deed—to the people they want to reach: "We want you to become and continue being Christians, but you don't have to become exactly like us!" We should give careful attention to this point in our worship services, outreach ministries, children's care, and educational programs. We have to ask ourselves: What role do matters of taste play in our congregational life? And due to this, who is included, and who is excluded?

7. "What Do I Get Out of It?"— The Pragmatization of Religion

In the early 1910s, Max Weber, one of the founders of modern sociology (of religion), developed the concept of *Zweckrationalität* (rationale of purpose). He meant that the lives of people tend to be progressively determined by a logic that is function-oriented and focused on embracing life before death. The main reason for this development, Weber argued, is the increasing comprehensive commercialization of modern societies. An implemented rationale of purpose, for example, shows up in an occupation that becomes a mere job whose function is to provide for living on a desirable level. Interpersonal relationships, which are basically purpose-driven, are determined by individually validated price-performance ratios and lead to new definitions of love and fidelity. One significant indicator of the tendency toward a dominating rationale of purpose is the falling birth rate in the so-called highly developed countries. Having children for an increasing number of couples has become subject to stringent calculation and evaluation of individual options. It is hard to deny that a spirit of "gain or lose" has been pushed forward along with the global economy and is reaching deep into the hearts of our societies and their value systems, including religion.

In faith issues, the key question no longer is "How can I be righteous before God?" as it was for Paul, Luther, Wesley, and other forebearers of the Christian faith, or even more basically the question of truth itself, but instead, the "economic" question of "What do I get out of it when I believe in (your) God?" This trend also resonates within our churches and provokes constructive reaction from the leadership. In our congregations, too, a pragmatization of the faith and church relationships can be detected, and the primary interest has shifted toward personal gain in religious practice.[28] As church leaders, we have our problems with this development. God's supreme love is the same for all people of all times, and "God shows no partiality" (Deut. 16:19; Rom. 2:11). Trusting God, worshipping Christ as Savior, praising the presence of the Holy Spirit, and loving our neighbor stand alone without any special interest added on. The gospel isn't a message promising sustained personal health, unbroken happiness, and affluence to all. Protestant doctrine makes the point that it is exactly in *looking away* from our individual interests and personal gain that we can gain the freedom to believe, to trust, and to love. Salvation in Christ and a new life as a disciple are gifts of the gracious God that cannot be earned or worked out in the way the market teaches; and that is truly good news for those who suffer under the daily pressure of achievement. For others who are fully adapted to living according to a business-shaped schedule and value system, it is hard to accept a gift and trust in love that is freely offered. The gospel, nevertheless, teaches just that message: "We proclaim Christ crucified," as the apostle Paul writes to the Corinthians, "a stumbling block to Jews and foolishness to Gentiles" (1 Cor. 1:23).

On the other hand, we need to take into account what surveys have indicated,[29] much like the experiences in many local churches have demonstrated, that people *do* have—against myths that may say the opposite—substantial expectations about the Christian church and its message. As countless stories in the Old and the New Testaments testify, it is not only justifiable but legitimate for people to come with expectations toward God and his "ground personnel"—the church. As Methodists, we know that seeking "holiness and happiness" is a virtue of our tradition. We need to say a decisive "No!" to any attempt to turn the Christian message into a "gospel of prosperity," just as surely as we welcome those who knock at the doors of our churches or homes expecting significant change for their inner and outer lives. The gospel isn't a lifeless memorandum to be passed on, but a dynamic, life-changing message. As Paul said in Romans 1:16: "It is the power of God for salvation to everyone who has faith." Do we still have the *basic trust* that the living God not only can but will change lives for the better?

8. "My Little Kingdom!"— The Privatization of Life

From a historical perspective, the process of modernity in the Western world can be described as a step-by-step development away from common to individual interests. Property, occupation, sexual preference, social bonds, and religion have become almost completely private matters; any interference in those areas from outside will be questioned, if not repudiated. In tribal societies, the common worldview and religion were identical; in premodern times, religion shaped the general image of the world. Since the Enlightenment, instituted religion and the common philosophy of life have been moving apart, such that in our postmodern era we face a plurality of equally ranked world concepts and individual, privatized forms of religion.[30] Modern democracies are eager to guarantee a maximum of personal freedom and individual self-determination; freedom of religion is a precious element therein. To talk about a personal decision for a particular faith does require a certain amount of religious freedom, and in our postmodern societies, it generally takes the shape of personalized and privatized faith options.[31] As twenty-first-century people, we are the makers not only of our own luck, but also of our own salvation, and what is true for us is not necessarily true for others. Since personal faith belongs to the private or even intimate sphere—the legacy of the modern and liberal mind-set—influencing others will likely be seen as an intervention into private affairs. Those who live a "missionary" lifestyle, who speak about their faith publicly and claim truth for what they believe, are suspected of religious fundamentalism. Authentic evangelism, for that reason, needs to state clearly what is decisive and distinctive about the Christian faith without touching the individual's realm of freedom.[32] George Morris and Eddie Fox have discussed this issue and suggested speaking of "non-manipulative dialogue" in order to develop means for appropriate *faith sharing*.[33]

Sociologist Richard Sennett has comprehensively described "the decrease and end of public life." He has spoken of a "tyranny of intimacy," pointing to the radical shift away from public and common interest toward the private life in Western societies.[34] Certainly, distrust and disinterest toward political affairs or social tasks compromise the notion of democracy and jeopardize a future with communal sensibility. Moreover, from a psychological point of view, the private sphere has come to be a place of compensation. Those elements of the personality that cannot be lived out in one's work will be compensated in the private sphere, which can and often finds expression in the field of religious practice. Lacking influence, status, power, emotions, and so forth provides the subject matter for conscientious parish and evangelistic counseling, as well as for competent congregational leadership.

The fact that the megatrend of privatization exhibits these two sides can be found in the word itself. The Latin verb *privo* unites two opposite meanings: to liberate and to deprive. The liberation that came with a privatized society is the valuing of the individual by which all of us benefit. We should not too quickly wish ourselves back in the Middle Ages. The deprivation that came along with privatization of life is the loss of the "big picture," the slackening of the social fabric that holds us together as human beings, as nations, regions, congregations, or families. From a theological perspective, the love of God is poured out for the individual but, by all means, aims to the public. Because *ekklesia* stands for a public concept, proper evangelism can't teach or foster an individualistic perception of salvation,[35] but will lead persons into responsible discipleship. Consonant with John Wesley's claim that there is no holiness apart from a social holiness, to live faithfully in the realm of God's kingdom can never be reduced to a wholly private matter.[36] The tradition of a Social Creed was begun by The Methodist Episcopal Church North, followed by The Evangelical United Brethren Church in 1946 with its Social Principles; both traditions are still breathing within United Methodism and need to be kept going further by women and men with warm hearts and cool heads. The biblically and historically handed down connection between *proclamation* and *incarnation* of the gospel must not be discarded, but displayed powerfully and publicly without shame.[37] Indeed, a church's withdrawal from the public and social spheres of life is not without consequences; it will most likely lead into a severe crisis of credibility for those who are entrusted to bear witness to God's care for the world.

9. "God Yes—Church No!"— The Decreasing Influence of Public Institutions

In the days of the early Christian church, Cyprian, bishop of Carthage (ca. 190–258), made the statement: "You cannot have God as your father unless you have the church as your mother." By this he meant that being a Christian necessarily means accepting the given rule for everyday life.

For Augustine (354–430), even the authority of scripture is dependent on the church: "I would not believe in the gospel if it weren't for the authority of the catholic church which made me to do so."[38] By insisting on the most common conviction of the early church, *extra ecclesiam nulla salus* (there is no salvation outside the church), institutionalized Christianity has succeeded for centuries in determining "what has to be believed by everybody, every time, everywhere" (Vincent of Lerinium, ca. 450 CE).

Logically, the greater the degree to which individualization and privatization exist in a society, the more the influence of public institutions will decrease. This development is true not only for most public authorities like elected officials, political parties, and such, but also for the field of religious life. In central Europe, the vast majority of institutional functions (of whatever religious cult and practice) have suffered from a serious loss of influence and power; and in North America, the situation is not all that different. Standing under the "heretical imperative" (Peter L. Berger),[39] people have extended their search for spiritual fulfillment and orientation in a chaotic world, their quest for excitement far beyond the church walls to overcome daily routine and their longing for interhuman solidarity. The effect is that churches and denominations are facing massive losses in membership; the trend is toward further "de-churching" and "de-confessionalization" of the religious market. Especially in central and northern Europe, congregations and denominations have to come to terms with cutbacks in parishioners' donations, with federal withdrawals of tax allowances, and other benevolent communal privileges; in numerous cases, churches are forced to reduce their public services and ministries. At the same time, pastors and other church officials can no longer benefit from the supposed status that attends their office, but are challenged to practice a lifestyle that demonstrates distinct and faithful Christian witness.

While we should not underestimate the painful consequences that this megatrend will bring for many, there also exists an immense opportunity for evangelism. If church leaders, trusting in God's enduring love, model what they believe and teach their parishioners to do the same, the outcome will be telling. Wouldn't people in our world today be willing to seriously consider the Christian faith as the basis for their lives? Many encouraging stories of faith-sharing congregations suggest the answer is yes.[40] In times of privatized religion, it no longer is a paradigm of "doing church for others," but one of "being church with others" that can make the Christian community attractive, relevant, and persuasive once again. The church must be a *community of seekers and believers*. In turn, the church, as institution, can reclaim cultural significance, integrity, and a healthy amount of authority and public influence. What the General Conference of The United Methodist Church agreed to in 1996 points the way:

> The local church shall be organized so that it can pursue its primary task and mission in the context of its own community—reaching out and receiving with joy all who will respond; encouraging people in their relationship with God and inviting them to commitment to God's love in Jesus Christ; providing opportunities for them to seek strengthening and growth in spiritual formation; and supporting them to live lovingly and justly in the power of the Holy Spirit as faithful disciples.[41]

Finally, by practicing evangelization and social action in the sphere of the kingdom of God and not just within the limitations of a single denomination, and by seeking further cooperation with other Christians and church bodies, Methodism can be released from an unhealthy fear for its continued existence, which so often in church history has paralyzed courageous steps forward.[42] The time for ecumenical cooperation has come, and we must seek to move from striving for "unity with others" as well as "unity within ourselves." The "dismembering" of the historical Body of Christ has created a major credibility gap in terms of its mission down through the centuries; the biblical perception in John 17:21 "that the world may believe" testifies to a missionary perspective for Christians working together.[43] The ultimate goal of evangelization is not to build a strong denomination of whatever kind, not even to develop strong local churches, but to help people to live their lives according to God's will and to develop a living and dynamic faith that grows to maturity.

10. "We'll See about That!"—
Changes in Bonding and Commitment

In many areas of public life, we notice significant changes in the way people bond with each other or make commitments in the personal or public sphere. Concerning jobs, life partnerships, religious habits, and other aspects of life, a diminishing longevity can be discerned; commitments often are made hesitantly or partially. In many churches throughout Europe and North America, a tendency toward an attitude of "wait and see" can be observed when it comes to becoming a full member of a congregation or denomination or accepting the responsibility for occasional tasks. A survey published in 1994 by the German government's minister for family and generational affairs compared figures concerning active membership in various societal groups. The results were thought-provoking: "If you compare the percentage of young people who are active in church-related groups (8%) with the percentage of those who are active in political parties (1%), labor unions (3%) or civic action groups, it is proven that the church is an organization, which, at present, can fall back on the largest reservoir of active youth."[44] The church's position as the frontrunner offers little comfort. Figures like these vary from country to country and from region to region; in our case, we must read them as indicators of a *social listlessness*, a trend that has reached far into our fun-oriented societies across the generational boundaries.[45] Despite our individualistic societies, as public catastrophes such as the terror attacks in the U.S. in 2001 or the devastating flooding over large parts of central and Eastern Europe in summer 2002 have proven, there remains an interest in joining forces to help others; but this desire tends to be situational or project-oriented, and does not lead, for the most part, to a regular, ongoing engagement in a social group or organization.

Experts have been questioning the reasons for this unwillingness to participate in communal and social groups, especially among young and middle-aged persons in Western societies. It is not just the overwhelming market of consumer and leisure amenities available, but as psychologists have suggested, there is a growing incapacity to develop and sustain relationships in the personal and the social spheres. What journalist Florian Illies claims about his own "Generation Golf" has a self-critical undertone: "Because we, high-handed people, aren't afraid of anything as much as the feeling of disappointment, we always have a ripcord in our heads. We enter into a relationship only so far as we sense that we can get out of it."[46]

As a denomination that historically has been and presently is dependent on spiritually devoted lay participation, both theologically and practically, we have the challenge to find healthy and persuasive ways to talk about the call to dependable service that comes with the gift of discipleship in Christ. Calls for solidarity and appeals for charity will not necessarily reach deaf ears. It still is a minority of social scientists, such as Amitai Etzioni, who suggest that the tide is turning in regard to communal activities in individualized societies. In his book *The New Golden Rule*, Etzioni sums up indicators for a future society in which responsibility for one another will be normative to some extent.[47] He envisions a kind of communitarian *me-and-you-paradigm*, arguing that in the U.S. one out of two people already engages in an average of 4.2 hours of volunteer work per week, without neglecting individual interests and needs. In Germany, too, there are signs of an emerging "ego-fatigue." A representative survey across generations indicates that 40 percent of the interviewees answer the question, "What is important for your meaning in life?" with the notion of "working for a better society." This figure represents an increase of 9 percent in comparison to the year 2000.[48] Examples like these may encourage church leaders to take the chance to talk with people about social involvement and responsible commitment. In talking to new church members, I have found that positive expectations have been communicated to them, in many cases, and this attitude was one crucial point for newcomers to stay and become involved. I believe that entrusting others with meaningful work on behalf of the kingdom of God, like Jesus entrusted his disciples, will always be a significant factor in winning people to join a caring community of seekers and believers.

Megatrends: Threats or Opportunities for the Church?

1. Finding a Critical "Yes" to Societal Change

In talking with fellow Christians about megatrends, I repeatedly hear lament or resignation. In addition to those people who are working for a progressive church and critiquing its lethargy, there are a number of church folks who long for the "good old days" of traditional evangelism and church growth to be restored. This is understandable since many of those people had their formative spiritual experiences in years past and have been serving faithfully since then. But at the same time, they realize we need to go forth from that point. How do we go about it? Two points demand our consideration.

First, we must recognize that not everything about the late- or postmodern period is bad or to be rejected. We enjoy tremendous individual liberty and mobility, personal self-determination, and independence in various spheres of life, which benefit most of us. The variety of options and the (relative) freedom to choose from among them have proven to be more suitable for individuals than an enforced uniformity of any kind. I believe that is also true for personal faith development. We should not underestimate the efforts of those who have been working for political and individual rights, including freedom of religion in our societies and nations.

Second, the flip side is also true: not everything about the late- or postmodern period is good or to be accepted. The loss of the "big picture" is the price we have to pay for a galloping plurality, which fosters abandoning traditions, as well as an increasing pace of life. If a rationale of purpose is lived out as egoism, it will lead to ever more privatization. Privatization includes within itself, as previously noted, an aspect of deprivation. In a number of publications, the present situation has been compared or even identified with the early Christian missionary situation of the ancient world. There is some truth to this comparison, but it needs to be added, that for large parts of central Europe and parts of North America, we have to speak of a post-Christian era.[49] It is not just secularism and new religiosity that mark our Western religious situation; there is also a widespread *civil religion,* as Robert N. Bellah has noted,[50] that still has Christian characteristics, seemingly vaccinated and immune to the gospel message itself.

If we accept that people in our societies *are* striving for meaning in life and spiritual fulfillment, who would not be encouraged by the story of the apostle Paul in Athens, confessing the crucified and risen Christ in the face of similar obstacles to faith? Facing the altar "To an unknown god," he publicly stated, "What therefore you worship as unknown, this I proclaim to you" (Acts 17:23). Critical to the future of evangelism and church development is the incarnation of the gospel: To what extent will we manage to be contemporary Christians who take societal changes as a challenge to make proclamation relevant in our own day? From its beginnings the Christian community has been built *within* the world, yet without being *of* the world (John 15:19). The saying, "Who gets married to the spirit of the times most likely will be a widow," in our case challenges a church that says "Yes" to the present situation as the basis for faith and congregational development. We must identify those points of societal development where it is necessary, in the tradition of biblical prophecy, to say "No." When people are denied fundamental human rights, when commercialization and an unhealthy spirit of success gain ascendancy over humanity, then the church must speak in a prophetic voice, modeling a *contrast society,* to use Gerhard Lohfink's phrase,[51] that goes beyond simply "being against" something to display positive images of "succeeding" in life without harming others.

2. Learning to See People Through God's Eyes

If we speak a critical "Yes" to the society in which we live, we are talking primarily not about structures, but about people. People want to be treated as people, with all their obvious needs and hidden desires, which is exactly what many stories in the Old and New Testaments testify that God has been seeking to fulfill. People are central to evangelistic endeavors of all kinds: those whom God has created so different from and yet but a "little lower than God" (Ps. 8:5), those who will miss their final destination in life if they do not cultivate a relationship with their Creator.[52] It is those people who join in singing the chorus, "I just want to live while I'm alive," as rock star Jon Bon Jovi has put it,[53] for whom God's passionate offer of life, now and in the future, is intended.[54] If we, as a church, want to treat people as people, then we must learn to see them through God's eyes. God's passion to save and renew people as shown in Jesus Christ must come again or cease to be ours.[55] Since God is "the first evangelist," we are called to follow Christ and be evangelists, following his example. An evangelizing church, for that reason, will be careful to respect the needs, capacities, and limits of those to whom it is reaching out, including respecting their cultural proprieties.[56] At the same time, a promising evangelizing church must provide the same attention and live according to the same values when dealing with its own employed and volunteer workers. In fact, this may be an even greater challenge. The way we "are" and "do" church must be identical, in its spirit of love and truth and forgiveness, within our walls as beyond them.

3. Keeping the Faith: The Good News Remains

The megatrends we have explored are bundled together like a kaleidoscope as they reflect today's reality in its colorful fragments. When the church accepts the challenge to enter into conversation with thoughtful persons of any age or ethnic group, discussing the questions and realities of their lives in light of the gospel message, churches that care about people are most likely to gain or reclaim relevancy and develop a positive energy that people will find attractive. It is the gospel, the good news of God's love in Jesus Christ, that was, is, and will be providing life-unfolding truth for us and the generations to come. It is the gospel that directs and inspires our mission and evangelism in all ages and through all of life's trends and challenges.

Suggestions for Further Study

Bellah, Robert N. *Habits of the Heart: Individualism and Commitment in America.* Updated ed. Berkeley: Univ. of California Press, 1996.

Berger, Peter L. *A Far Glory: The Quest of Faith in an Age of Credulity.* New York: Free Press, 1992.

Cobb, John B., Jr. *Grace & Responsibility: A Wesleyan Theology for Today.* Nashville: Abingdon Press, 1995.

Etzioni, Amitai. *The New Golden Rule: Community and Morality in a Democratic Society.* New York: Basic Books/HarperCollins, 1996.

Frankl, Viktor E. *Man's Search for Meaning.* 78th ed. New York: Simon & Schuster, 1988.

Gunter, W. Stephen. *Resurrection Knowledge: Recovering the Gospel for a Postmodern World.* Nashville: Abingdon Press, 1999.

Härtner, Achim, and Eschmann Holger. *Learning to Preach: Fundamentals—Practical Guide—Consolidation.* Cliff College Academic Series. Calver, UK: Cliff College Publishing, 2004.

Hunter, George G. *Radical Outreach: The Recovery of Apostolic Ministry and Evangelism.* Nashville: Abingdon Press, 2003.

Naisbitt, John, and Patricia Aburdene. *Megatrends 2000: The New Directions for the 1990s.* New York: Harper & Row, 1990.

Opaschowski, Horst W. *Wir werden es erleben: Zehn Zukunftstrends für unser Leben von morgen.* Darmstadt: Primus, 2002.

Runyon, Theodore W. *The New Creation: John Wesley's Theology Today.* Nashville: Abingdon Press, 1998.

Schulze, Gerhard. *Die Erlebnisgesellschaft: Kultursoziologie der Gegenwart.* 8th ed. Frankfurt: Campus, 2000.

Sweet, Leonard. *Aqua Church: Essential Leadership Arts for Piloting Your Church in Today's Fluid Culture.* Loveland, Colo.: Group Publishing, 1999.

Welsch, Wolfgang. *Unsere postmoderne Moderne.* 5th ed. Berlin: Akademie-Verlag, 1997.

C H A P T E R   6

Building the Church in Africa: Church Planting as an Inclusive Praxis

John Wesley Zwomunondiita Kurewa

I n preparation for the Eighth Assembly of the World Council of Churches in 1998 in Harare, Zimbabwe, the executive secretary for Faith and Order in the World Council of Churches' Programme on Unity and Renewal, Thomas Best, made the following statement: "In the southern hemisphere, churches are growing and acting increasingly as if their historic divisions have been healed."[1] At the close of the last millennium, Andrew Walls, former missionary in Sierra Leone and now professor emeritus at the University of Edinburgh, wrote, "Today, at the brink of a new millennium, Christianity's identity as a Western religion is being challenged and changed as never before. Due to the growth of Christians in the developing world, the church's demographic center of gravity has shifted from the north and west to the south and east: Latin America, Africa and Asia. . . . This shift happened quickly, and the church in the West has hardly begun to grasp this reality."[2] David Barrett's comparative study of churches and religions in the modern world shows that in 1900, Africa had a population of 107,854,260 persons, of which only 9,938,448 (or 9.2 percent) were Christians. He goes on to forecast that, by the year 2000, the population of Africa will have grown to some 813,390,700, and the Christian community will have risen to an astonishing 48.4 percent of the population.[3] These statements represent three of the many claims now being forwarded, regarding the phenomenal growth of the church in Africa today. As an African living within this phenomenal growth of the Christian community, I want to reflect upon a biblical and theological basis for the praxis of church planting in Africa today.

Paul the apostle provides us with a starting point for our reflection when he writes to the church in Corinth, using the metaphor of planting and watering the seed—a metaphor that speaks effectively and persuasively within African thought. Of course, Paul wants the church in Corinth to understand that there should be unity and not divisions among the servants of the God in whom the Corinthian Christians had come to believe (1 Cor. 3:1-9). He writes, "I planted, Apollos watered, but God gave the growth" (v. 6). Paul and Apollos are not only servants; they are also "God's servants, working together" (v. 9) or allies in his service. Thus, the Corinthian Christians are "the field which God, through his servants, is cultivating; the building which God, through his servants, is erecting."[4] As C. K. Barrett has suggested, "This must mean that Paul was the first evangelist to work in Corinth (note his principle, stated in Rom. 15:20. Ambitious to preach the gospel not where Christ had been named, lest I should build upon someone else's foundation); Apollos arrived later, continued the work of evangelism, and helped in the task of building up the church."[5] Paul is thus understood as the one who plants, and Apollos is the one who waters those seeds as he continues the work of building the church. But independent of God, neither the work of Paul nor that of Apollos has any significance, as the "only significance of the planter and waterer is that God accepts their labour and works through them (v. 9)."[6] Paul also wants the church in Corinth to know that everyone who plants, and everyone who waters—every single person—does it in accordance with his or her commission from God.[7]

Indeed, Paul must have recalled and reflected on those onerous days of church planting, when he stayed in Corinth "a year and six months, teaching the word of God among them" (Acts 18:11). He would not, of course, forget the night when the Lord gave him the assurance of his presence in a vision: "Do not be afraid, but speak and do not be silent; for I am with you, and no one will lay a hand on you to harm you, for there are many in this city who are my people" (Acts 18:9-10). Despite the difficulty of Paul's labor, he understood the importance of church planting; indeed, church planting is integral to the ministry of evangelism. As Paul's letters demonstrate, it is the gospel of God's grace that remains central in the task of church planting. The centrality of God's grace remains true for us today, and for this reason, we must turn to the biblical and theological presuppositions that undergird the work of church planting. With the rapid pace of growth on the African continent, these biblical and theological presuppositions guide our ministry. Paul reminds us that the church in its many expressions belongs to God. A servant of God may be planting a new church in a new area, or one may be watering the seeds where another servant did the planting. In either case, whatever the role one plays in church planting, that church belongs to God. Paul is very particular about this point whenever he talks about the church. He addresses the Christians in Corinth as "the church of God that is in Corinth" (1 Cor. 1:2; 2 Cor. 1:1). As J. Robert Nelson has pointed out, in one instance, Galatians 6:16, Paul speaks of the Christian church as "the Israel of God."[8] What Paul suggests is that the church consists of a people who, through Christ, have been reconciled to God (2 Cor. 5:19), or a people who have responded to God's call to salvation (Rom. 11:29; 1 Cor. 1:26; Eph. 1:18; 4:1).[9] Clearly, at the heart of the church is the relationship between the people's response to God's offer of reconciliation and salvation. It is not a matter of what any person or group of people has done, but what God in Jesus Christ has done for us.

Indeed, for Paul the Atonement plays a central role. The church belongs to God because God purchased it "with the blood of his own Son" (Acts 20:28). Although Paul writes to the church in Rome, he claims that "God proves his love for us in that while we still were sinners Christ died for us" (Rom. 5:8). That is the price God in Christ paid for the salvation of all humankind, and today Africa is rejoicing in that gift. Today, the continent of Africa celebrates the growth of Christianity numerically, as stated at the outset of this essay. Equally, if not more important, we receive the news of churches that have split apart due to leadership conflicts, corruption, and so forth, as unbecoming and unchristian practices because the church belongs to God and what God in Christ has done for us. This is the reason for the call to a biblical and theological basis for evangelism and church planting in Africa today. We must remember who we are or, better, whose we are. It is essential that we emphasize, first and foremost, that the church belongs to God. The churches arising today in Africa, just like every other church in the world, belong to God.

Second, the church of God is built on the Word of God, which is Jesus

Christ. The church cannot be planted without sharing or proclaiming Jesus Christ to those who have not heard of his name. Someone needs to share or proclaim the good news to such persons if they are to hear and believe (Rom. 10:14). Jesus Christ, the Son and the Word of God, constitutes the gospel, the good news, the message that the world needs. Not only is Jesus Christ the Word of God; he is, at the same time, the unique foundation on which the church of God is built. Paul writes, "No one can lay any foundation other than the one that has been laid; that foundation is Jesus Christ" (1 Cor. 3:11). Gustaf Aulen explains this understanding of Jesus Christ as the sole foundation of the church in terms of relationship: "The decisive point in the question of the relationship between Jesus and the church is in the final analysis the fact that the foundation of the church is the finished work of Christ and that the church appears as a living reality in and through the exaltation."[10]

Thus, we can summarize by noting that (1) Jesus Christ is the foundation on which church planting takes place through proclaiming Jesus Christ as the Word of God; and (2) the subsequent, emerging church is a result of the proclamation of Christ and not merely a social organization. The church is a living reality—the spiritual body of the risen Christ. The pastor of a church or its members may possess special talents or gifts; indeed, Paul would tell us that God gives gifts and graces for the sake of the mutual upbuilding of the church. These talents may be realized and expressed in a number of ways and different forms, including rhetorical flair, charming personality, beautiful voices, organizational ability, stewardship of resources, and a number of others. These talents or gifts are important, for they are needed "to equip the saints for the work of ministry, for building up the body of Christ" (Eph. 4:12). Nevertheless, Christ, and Christ alone, is the unique foundation upon which the church of God must be erected by human hands as the Body of Christ. Indeed, this is the message of the familiar hymn that proclaims,

> My hope is built on nothing less than Jesus' blood and righteousness.
> I dare not trust the sweetest frame, but wholly lean on Jesus' name.
> On Christ the solid rock I stand, all other ground is sinking sand.[11]

From the atoning work of Jesus Christ, to the proclamation of his name, to the foundation upon which we build, the church cannot exist without God in Jesus Christ.

The third theological and biblical basis for church planting is that the church of God is empowered by the Holy Spirit. At Pentecost the Holy

Spirit came upon the disciples of Jesus, acting as the midwife through whom the church was brought into existence. At the same time, the Holy Spirit was the empowering agent of the newly born church, as Jesus had promised his disciples: "You will receive power when the Holy Spirit has come upon you" (Acts 1:8). It is, of course, a power to act as God's agents, as the Body of Christ, on behalf of the kingdom of God. Thus, on the day of Pentecost, not only were all the disciples "filled with the Holy Spirit" (Acts 2:4) for the power to witness to Jesus Christ, but they became fully equipped for the hostile world into which Christ was sending them. They were encouraged to put on "the whole armor of God," wearing "the belt of truth," "the breastplate of righteousness," "the gospel of peace," "the shield of faith," "the helmet of salvation, and the sword of the Spirit, which is the word of God" (Eph. 6:13-17). Jesus knew that his church would experience turbulent situations throughout generations; thus, this armor is undergirded by the assurance of the omnipresence of the risen Lord himself, when he said, "I am with you always, to the end of the age" (Matt. 28:20).

When one considers the suffering that many African nations face today and the turbulent moments the church has gone through historically, with many of its leaders and members facing martyrdom at times, it is remarkable that the church continues to grow. One begins to trust in the promise of Jesus when he said, "I will not leave you orphaned; I am coming to you" (John 14:18). In the face of the tide of refugees sweeping across the continent, what message can the African church share? In the face of the devastating pandemic of HIV/AIDS, what other promise could bring as much comfort as Jesus' words in John 14:27: "Peace I leave with you; my peace I give to you. I do not give to you as the world gives. Do not let your hearts be troubled, and do not let them be afraid"? Even as Africans face these and other difficult situations, those who are believers begin to affirm once again that the Spirit of God is hovering over the difficult, chaotic, disjointed situation, with the voice still breaking through, saying, "Let there be light" (Gen. 1:3). The church of God is not simply a human or a social organization; it is not bound together only by a written code or constitution. Rather, it a spiritual reality of God dwelling among the people all the time, and bound together in love by the Holy Spirit. It is a spiritual reality of those who are forgiven in Christ and empowered by the Holy Spirit. It is for this reason that Aulen says the Christian church is the church of Easter and Pentecost.[12] This is the truth that every evangelist—be it the individual or a church—should understand. The power to propagate the cause of the gospel in and through the church is the work of God, Jesus Christ, and the Holy Spirit.

A fourth basis for the inclusive praxis of evangelism is that the church of God in every community evolves a new self-consciousness and assumes a new identity. The Christians in Palestine "appropriated for themselves the title of 'the community of God', the true Church."[13] They understood themselves as "God's chosen" (Col. 3:12; 1 Pet. 1:2), "God's elect" (Titus 1:1), and "the saints" (Col. 1:4), or as Paul says, "the Israel of God" (Gal. 6:16). They were also known as the people "who belonged to the Way" (Acts 9:2; 19:9, 23; 22:4; 24:14, 22). "The Way" was a term that was used "by the early Christians to denote their own movement, considered as the way of life or the way of salvation."[14] One could compare the previous texts with Acts 16:17 and 18:25 where the understanding of "the Way" is incomplete or misconstrued.

The people who belonged to the Way had a new consciousness or a new understanding of themselves, which led them to act in a spirit of community before God. Thus, "they broke bread at home and ate their food with glad and generous hearts, praising God and having the goodwill of all the people" (Acts 2:46-47). The extent of this communal spirit is uncertain: "Whether they met as a whole congregation or in separate groups (Acts 12:12), we do not know."[15] We can only guess that, as the number of the people who belonged to the Way increased on a daily basis (Acts 2:47; 4:4), they must have met in their homes in various groups of different sizes. What we do know is that they realized they were a *koinonia* (fellowship) of believers in Christ, and as such, they belonged together. We are told that "it was in Antioch that the disciples were first called 'Christians,'" instead of speaking of "the Way" (Acts 11:26). The self-understanding of the people of the Way, Christians, is located in their relationship to Christ and to one another in the Body of Christ.

One of the recent developments in African churches is the search for self-understanding in light of the gospel and our cultural context. In some churches, the cultural past or context is not often appreciated. In this case, it continues to be condemned as a heathenish cultural past, which should not have a place in the life of the church. Others are proud of the fact that God has raised up the church in the context of Africa with its own history and culture. Nevertheless, the struggle continues, and it is very important in church planting that at some point in the process, people understand who they are in the sight of God, who brought them salvation through Jesus Christ. For example, in Zimbabwe

Christians have come to understand themselves as *Makristu*, meaning Christians; *Vatendi vaKristu*, or believers of Christ; *Chechi yaKristu*, the church of Christ; *Vanamati*, the people who pray; and many other similar identifiers. These names or titles may sound like a direct translation of the missionary and/or biblical terms. That is true, because the mission stations were the "cradle" or "birthplace" of Christianity in Africa. The first Christian converts in Africa were brought to the mission stations where they were stripped naked of their culture and then clothed with the Christianity of Western forms of civilization. That was the place where they also learned to articulate their new faith.

Placed in one's environment, however, one may articulate one's self-identify in Christ in a very natural manner. My mother often told us of a story of an elderly woman who had just been baptized in our village church, Sherukuru United Methodist Church, in the 1930s. As she came from church that afternoon, she passed through the gardens where the other women of the village were working. The newly baptized woman began to greet the other women, shouting, "*Ndati mwana mutsva! Ndati mwana mutsva*," which means, "I am a new child! I am a new child!" In this case, the metaphorical figure, "child," symbolized the purity, innocence, and utter dependence on someone. That was the self-understanding of the newly baptized woman; she had the sense of having a new identity in God. Indeed, "if anyone is in Christ, there is a new creation" (2 Cor. 5:17). Church planting, which takes the ministry of evangelism seriously, will always bring people to the realization of a new identity or self-understanding in their relationship to God, and this understanding may be found within their cultural context where God is at work.

Fifth, the church of God is called into existence for God's task of evangelization. It has been said before, "God is a missionary God."[16] The Father, who sent his Son into the world (John 20:21), did not leave his Son in this hostile world alone. He was and is with him (John 8:29). The time came for the Son to send his disciples into the world to continue with God's mission (John 20:21). As if he had known that some of the disciples would rather have been out of this world, Jesus prayed to his Father for them: "I am not asking you to take them out of the world, but I ask you to protect them from the evil one" (John 17:15). God's mission is in the world—the world that he loved to the extent of giving his one and only Son for it. God has never called a people without also giving them a mission. It follows that no church that God calls into existence has no mission, especially in the community in which it is located.

Indeed, the church exists for God's mission. Often, God's mission seems hidden to church people. There are people who have conceived of God's mission for the church as that of getting people ready to go to heaven. This is typical during evangelistic revival meetings. No one would question that proposition, as Jesus himself assured his disciples: "And if I go and prepare a place for you, I will come again and will take you to myself, so that where I am, there you may be also" (John 14:3).

At the same time, we cannot prepare for being with Christ in eternity through a preoccupation with the thought of going to heaven. The church must be preoccupied with God's mission in the world, which is what God calls his people to do. Jesus emphasized this point when he taught his disciples to pray, "Your kingdom come. Your will be done, on earth as it is in heaven" (Matt. 6:10). He also prayed for his disciples who were going to be engaged with God's mission in the world when, in John 17:15, he asks that the disciples not be taken out of the world but, rather, protected. The world is where the church finds and carries out God's mission; and it begins with our own communities, in our own neighborhoods, within our own cultural contexts. But it is not simply a comfortable life that comforts people and encourages them to accept life as it is and has always been. Rather, as David Bosch says, "Mission is the conscience of the Church, for it always questions, uncovers, digs down, prods, and irritates. It is always contrary to the human deliberations and convictions and preferences, whether they are to the 'right' or to the 'left.' "[17] God's mission stirs up the people of God to seek a new way, to don new clothes. Often, it is after a local church has discovered or realized the fullness of its new identity in Christ that it begins to discern the mission placed before it. When that occurs—and that special day comes to each one of us and to each community of faith—we will then be surprised to hear Christ say, "Just as you did it to one of the least of these who are members of my family, you did it to me" (Matt. 25:40).

The sixth theological and biblical basis for the inclusive praxis of church planting is that the church of God in every place needs leadership. With the origin of the church, Jesus chose the twelve from among his many disciples, "whom he also named apostles" (Luke 6:13). The disciples worked with Jesus for three years, learning their new vocation from the Master himself, who had called them with the words, "Follow me and I will make you fish for people" (Mark 1:17). For the rest of his followers, present and future, Jesus assured the disciples of another Counselor, who would be not only with them, but also in them and the church forever

(John 14:17). That promise was fulfilled on the day of Pentecost, in Jerusalem, when the disciples of Jesus were all "filled with the Holy Spirit" (Acts 2:4). The Holy Spirit raises up, empowers, and guides the leadership of the church of Jesus from within the church. The Spirit's role has remained in keeping with what Jesus told his disciples in the beginning. The Holy Spirit is the Spirit of truth (John 14:17); teaches the church all things (John 14:26); guides the church into all truth (John 16:13); testifies about Jesus' teachings (John 15:26); and does many other things, including raising up the leadership of the church. Although there are times when the human element seems strong in the selection of church leadership, the joy of this process is that—in spite of the mistakes human beings often make—God can use any person as an instrument of the building of the Kingdom. The assurance of this reality comes through the message to Timothy, who also indicates that we must respond to God and seek to live holy lives under the guidance of the Spirit: "In a large house there are utensils not only of gold and silver but also of wood and clay, some for special use, some for ordinary. All who cleanse themselves of the things I have mentioned will be special utensils, dedicated and useful to the owner of the house, ready for every good work" (2 Tim. 2:20-21). Indeed, God will use every Christian for the work of the Kingdom if we are willing to follow God's way.

Lately, we have witnessed how the church has cleansed itself from the historical barriers of ethnic racism, the cultural barriers that exclude women from the ordained ministry of the churches, and many other barriers imposed by human systems of injustice. These are truths and guidance that come to us—though not so easily—through the indwelling power of the Holy Spirit who raises up courageous leadership in the church of Christ and can and does use all persons for the sake of the gospel. Even so, two factors temper and color the leadership of the church. The gospel itself has a way of providing leadership for the church and community. Often the positions of leadership in churches are held by the believers who are baptized and are already full members of the church—that method is generally the safest way for any church as an institution to proceed. However, when it comes to planting churches in new areas, where full members of the church may not yet exist, the church still has to have leadership, and it is always important to choose leaders from among the local church and the local culture. A few years ago, I served in a charge where, at one of the preaching houses, a woman from whom a demon had been exorcised, and who was a probationary member, became the lay leader. That small preaching house changed into what any pastor would have wanted to see happen; under her leadership, it overflowed with great zeal to serve the community. She was sensitive to other women who had suffered from the same powers of evil that had tormented her for years in that community. At the same time, she testified to the power of Christ and to the change that Christ brought to her own life and family. She became a strong Christian leader to her church and the community. Yes, church planting produces leaders, and those leaders must come from the local church. Paul writes about such leaders of the early church like Tychicus (Eph. 6:21) and Onesiphorus (2 Tim. 1:16) of Ephesus, Epaphroditus in Philippi (Phil. 2:25), Epaphras (Col. 1:7; 4:12) and Onesimus (Col. 4:9) of Colossae, and many others.

Another factor that tempers and colors the leadership of the church in every locality is culture. Culture is always a human way of organizing life; and hence, it involves communication. God calls the church into being and leaves it to the people to name the church and to articulate what they discern as God's mission in their community. Thus, the tasks of naming, reflecting upon the identity of the church, and articulating its mission are colored by the cultural brush. As God created and calls us in this rich variety, so the expressions of the church will flow out of these many cultural colors. We remember that Paul says, "We are God's servants" (1 Cor. 3:9); we are coworkers with God. In the Genesis story, we also observe that God created everything and then made the first human a cocreator by asking him to participate in the process by naming all that God created: "The man gave names to all cattle, and to the birds of the air, and to every animal of the field" (Gen. 2:20). God and people continue to work together in creating and naming our magnificent world. Indeed, from one land to another the names of these creatures differ because of culture.

This observation leads us to another factor about culture: there is no one "superculture" or overarching culture that structures the church in every place. In evangelism and church planting, it is possible to have people respond to the gospel message—a universal message of salvation and God's love for humanity. However, if the structure of the church put in place is not culturally tempered and colored, all that might have been gained through evangelism could be lost, as the church does not feel like "home," but someone else's "home" to which they have been invited. Church structures must respond to culture for purposes of authenticity, communication, and identity. That was the reason the elders of the early church in Palestine were called *presbyters*, while in the Hellenistic world, they were known as *episkopoi*. The two titles were synonymous, meaning elders. It is culture, including the differences that exist in our languages as bearers of culture, that assures us of the incarnational nature of the gospel.

The seventh and final basis for church planting as an inclusive praxis is that, as soon as the church of God is planted, it needs to attend to the stewardship of its resources. A steward is a person who manages or cares for the property in business as, for example, found in 1 Kings 16:9[18] or a person who "manages someone's affairs for him (Luke 12:42)."[19] As a servant of Christ, Paul talks in a metaphorical sense in referring to himself as a steward (*oikonomos*), who is entrusted with the mysteries of God (1 Cor. 4:1). The concept of stewardship is commonly applied to money, but actually involves much more. The "Christian concept of stewardship before God involves time, talents, possessions, and self (Luke 12:42; Eph. 3:2)."[20] Therefore, a church that is newly planted must not be deprived of the opportunity to practice and teach Christian stewardship in all its expressions. Exercising the power of Christian stewardship is part of the human response of the people of God to the challenge of the gospel and its mission. As David Shenk and Ervin Stutzman have noted, "Giving is an important way of expressing appreciation for the grace of God as revealed in our Lord Jesus Christ."[21] New believers should not be denied the opportunity to share their various resources either as an act of appreciation or as a way of commitment to God's mission.

In 1973, for the first time in its history, the (then named) Rhodesia Annual Conference of The United Methodist Church planned and promoted a program of Christian stewardship by recognizing a special Harvest Sunday on the conference calendar. It happened that at the Annual Conference of 1974, Nyakatsapa Circuit under Pastor Willas Makunike "was lifted as a teaching example."[22] That circuit had put together about fifteen bags of maize as a thanksgiving to God, a thing that had never happened in the history of the conference. In 1975, the Rhodesia Annual Conference as a whole raised $6,000 on the Harvest Sunday, again, a thing that had never happened in its history. Through the constant teaching of Christian stewardship in the two Zimbabwe Annual Conferences (East and West), today each conference is talking of raising millions of dollars on Harvest Sunday. In spite of the economic hardships Zimbabwe is going through today, in the year 2001, "over $22 million was raised by the Zimbabwe East Annual Conference alone."[23]

There is no doubt that everything has a beginning. At the same time, for a church that started in 1897, we did not have to wait until 1973 to assume the responsibility of promoting Christian stewardship; we could have begun this teaching much earlier. The teaching and practice of Christian stewardship has manifested itself not only in financial giving; many Christians in the two conferences have thanked God by sharing with others in a variety of ways, including the sharing of talents, time, and possessions. The point is that, as soon as a church is planted and made aware of its mission through its leadership, it should be ready to respond with whatever resources it has for the sake of God's mission. If we think only in terms of money, many contributions will be lost. Yet we must also recognize that church planting and growing require financial support. This is what Paul is instilling in the church of God in Corinth when he writes, "Now concerning the collection for the saints: you should follow the directions I gave to the churches of Galatia. On the first day of every week, each of you is to put aside and save whatever extra you earn, so that collections need not be taken when I come" (1 Cor. 16:1-2). Good stewardship should be practiced whether the leadership is present and watching or not.

In summary, we have said that church planting as an inclusive praxis is integral to the ministry of evangelism. Wherever we are involved in church planting, there are biblical and theological presuppositions we need to observe. As the church in Africa continues to expand across the continent, there is still much work to be done planting the seeds and watering them. But the leadership and God's people in every place must be God's servants and coworkers in this important task of church planting. As Paul said to the church at Corinth, "you are God's field, God's building" (1 Cor. 3:9). As God's field, we must grow together toward the rich harvest that has been promised to us in Christ.

C H A P T E R   7

Evangelization and Church Growth: A Lesson from the Barrio

Harold J. Recinos

M any historians consider the twentieth century one of the bloodiest and cruelest known in history.[1] The threat of nuclear arms, global and regional wars, the use of torture and death squads to repress and exploit people, and the rise of racial, ethnic, and religious genocide have all raised powerful questions about God and human rights. Evangelism strategies that hoped to encourage persons to take seriously the mandate to bear witness to the gospel have been forced to think about the daily life circumstances of people in the context of sin and suffering in the world. The early years of the twenty-first century challenge us to continue to rethink how the good news of the reign of God will be "proclaimed throughout the world, as a testimony to all the nations" (Matt. 24:14).

That sin and suffering figured as subjects of evangelization in the recent history of the church is not surprising. Christian preachers have reacted to the natural and historical roots of impiety concerned to understand, rise above, or coexist with it. They have talked about sinfulness from such central notions as the self; racial, gender, and class conflicts; or the problem of meaning in human experience. They have explained the origin of suffering, justified its existence, or made it a spiritual virtue. Evangelists have argued for overcoming human sinfulness through the moral renewal of life in the gospel and a clear commitment to God. Many found Isaiah's remarks ripe for our time: "Wash yourselves; make yourselves clean; remove the evil of your doings from before my eyes; cease to do evil, learn to do good; seek justice, rescue the oppressed, defend the orphan, plead for the widow" (Isa. 1:16-17).

In the following pages we will explore the themes of sin and suffering in the world from the perspective of barrio evangelization. Barrio evangelization conveys that the good news of Jesus of Nazareth cannot be separated from the world God aims to deliver into new arrangements of power and social relationships. Barrio evangelization seeks to embody the plan of salvation through a commitment to respond to the world of the poor and the concern to struggle against oppression and suffering among the beaten-down sons and daughters of God. Evangelization has recently emerged with fresh urgency among mainline Protestant churches facing declining membership, shrinking budgets, and growing levels of marginality with respect to the wider culture. Barrio evangelization offers a critique of mainline Protestant evangelization strategies and a vision for announcing the good news. In the following essay, we will examine these two dimensions of barrio evangelization.

The Church Growth Required by God

Mainline Protestant denominations' interest in evangelism reflects a new focused attention on congregational revitalization and evangelizing efforts that promote church growth. Sadly, this emphasis may often reflect a motivation on the part of many church leaders that has little to do with sharing Jesus' message about a God who seeks to be involved in human affairs by unfolding relationships of compassion, justice, solidarity, and peace. Church growth strategies dominate what many denominational leaders mean by evangelism; thus, the concern to convey God's invitation to practice justice and live in solidarity with oppressed-suffering humanity is downplayed. Evangelists excitedly promote the idea that the vitality of the church depends on preaching a "user-friendly gospel," learning new management skills, and nurturing congregational contexts for private spiritual renewal.

Church growth evangelists correctly ask: How can we stir mainline Christians to effectively address dwindling membership roles and the aging membership in churches? Still, the theological assumption held by this brand of evangelism in the mainline Protestant context is that the business of God is church growth. Church growth evangelists use the latest social scientific approach to community studies to strategize how to especially reach out to the nonchurched public. Their growth-oriented approach to faith witness sidelines the view that God's focus for humanity is not numerically growing churches or cultivating congregations whose faith witness is loath to confess the system-shattering claims of the gospel. Church growth evangelism rarely talks of crossing cultural, ethnic, and racial boundaries, while it prefers to preach a saccharine gospel and individual salvation.

Apparently, evangelists focused on church growth tend to pursue their endeavor emphasizing the verbal proclamation of the gospel, which is believed to be the best way to express the Great Commission, "Go therefore and make disciples of all nations" (Matt. 28:19-20). They are upset that a growing numbers of persons have abandoned personal faith in Jesus Christ, which is implied in the directives of the Great Commission. In an age when people are more doubtful of the inherited religious traditions' offer of salvation, church growth evangelists can be credited with situating faith-talk in the context of the church's missionary call. Certainly, these evangelists challenge people disenchanted with organized religion and turning inward for divine insight to see the church anew as a vehicle for the sacred. But, ultimately, the Great Commission needs to be linked to the Great Commandment, "Love one another as I have loved you" (John 15:12).

Church growth evangelists focused on techniques that grow and multiply congregations forget the importance of raising to the level of theological and ethical concern the situation of crucified humanity. They cheapen the gospel by narrowing it down to winning people for the pew, instead of calling persons to a discipleship that responds to oppressed-suffering and sinfulness in the world. Crucified people now require the Christian way of life be defined in ways far more engaged in social and political witness than the congregation growth approach allows. In the face of the abysmal suffering of the crucified people of history, the fullness of Jesus' good news about the coming of God's rule on earth requires the church to point to larger social and political realities. That Jesus embodied the revelation of God in person and history suggests this way of Christian discipleship.

In the barrio, Latinos and Latinas who are economically exploited, politically excluded, and racially humiliated are critical of church growth evangelists who remove the gospel from their world of painful lament. These crucified people at the edges of U.S. society find no value in a growth evangelism that proclaims "a conscience-soothing Jesus, with a scandal-less cross, an otherworldly kingdom, a private, inwardly limited spirit, a pocket God, a spiritualized Bible, and an escapist church."[2] Multiplying congregations that have little concern for announcing the reign of God in a world of suffering and death or that are single-mindedly centered on "fattening the pews" produces Christians who lack the resources to truly preach and hear God's Word. One Salvadoran remarked about the true task of the church, "The best way to deceive ourselves as Christians is to separate faith from life. Salvadoran martyrs helped me to see this because they removed the dust from God's Word and placed it on our streets, in our weakness, limitations, miseries, and gifts. For me the church needs to proclaim the kingdom of God as something real in this world. It is a place of justice, liberty, peace, solidarity, and love, and we must struggle to construct it with God."[3]

Contemporary national church conferences often reflect that church growth thinking has captured the imagination of mainline Protestant denominational leaders. For instance, in the aftermath of the Rodney King riots, The United Methodist Church unfolded an urban strategy and sponsored national conferences framed by church growth views that generally featured what Harvey Cox called "designer churches," those with fast-growing congregations, funds, and other visible signs of "success."[4] Interestingly, the urban reality these conferences were intending to address is filled with people in churches far more like those of the early Christian community, which lacked impressive congregations, were constituted by marginal people not bound to earthly patterns of success, and who confessed Jesus as Lord and proclaimed Christ's good news of a new life on earth ruled by God.[5]

I remember standing outside one urban church whose leadership drew mission energy from church growth thinking. I met a Latino beggar dying of AIDS, sitting on the church steps, waiting for people to come out of worship. He grew up listening to sermons about a compassionate Christ and the justice of God. This young man talked of spirituality without big churches, doctrines, creeds, or educated pastors. He found daily hope and human dignity in finding Christ present in his crucified existence. On the church steps, he faced poverty and a premature death, fully aware that his Jesus sat with him outside the church. He bore witness to the risen Christ in the profound way that comes only with the experience of

Jesus as a living reality, whether or not we acknowledge him (Luke 24:13-35).

The church growth messages heard in crowded pews on Sunday morning are contradicted by the gospel vision of the world's power arrangements radically transformed to favor oppressed-suffering humanity. Evangelism understood as reconciling union through Christ must be accompanied by activity that reflects the justice of the reign of God Jesus preached all the way to the cross. Cheap evangelism issues forth from bearing witness to the good news of God by simply declaring Jesus is a personal Savior and believing there is no further expectation in Christian life or greater ethical preoccupation than church growth. As Mortimer Arias observed, "The church . . . cannot name Jesus Christ if it does not name also the idols and demons that must be cast out from the inner life of [persons] and from the structures of society (Luke 3:1-20; 6:20-23; Matt. 23)."[6]

Evangelism that stresses subjective matters and institutional growth alone is hardly a reflection of the good news of God's reign. Jesus first announced the good news of God by preaching liberation to the oppressed and poor, and by vitalizing faith for service in society from a point of departure in the world of rejected, despised, and unheard persons.[7] From the perspective of the barrio, proclaiming the gospel requires staying close to human suffering, where the God of grace revealed by Christ is revealed with a vision toward a new future world. Persons evangelized into growing churches are also called to mission where Christ waits for them amid the sick, the hungry, the naked, the destitute, the beaten-down and the despised of the world (Matt. 25:31-46). Let us now turn to an examination of barrio evangelization.

Barrio Evangelization

Mainline Protestant churches in our highly urbanized society cannot avoid the growing presence of Latinos and Latinas. Today, the Latino/a Christian community says that confronting the reality of a troubled world longing for the renewal of life means remembering the barrio where God is hidden in the drama of the weak and crucified. Although the Latino perspective on evangelism has been largely disregarded by mainline Christian institutions, Latinos and Latinas proclaim that Jesus reveals God among them and calls for the revival of mainline religion from the margins of society. Church growth evangelists can stand to hear from Latinos/as that in North American society, where a crucified people live, mainline Christians are invited to complete "what is lacking in Christ's afflictions" (Col. 1:24) in the setting of the barrio.

Listening to Latinos/as speak about matters of faith and action from the perspective of the barrio will result in an evangelized mainline Protestant church converted to the world of those not counted among the notable. This conversion to the margins of life is one way to remember that God-in-the-risen-Christ began the church, not focused on ecclesial enhancement, but with mostly despised, lowly, powerless rejects of society (1 Cor. 1:26-29). Certainly, the overwhelming gift to the mainline Christian community that a conversion to the margins facilitates is that in a world threatened and dehumanized by militarism, poverty, political oppression, terrorism, economic exploitation, racism, sexism, and egotism, faith is more than feeling good in big and successful congregations. Faith presupposes a deep commitment to live the good news of Christ in the bad news situations of a world beaten up by poverty, oppression, and death.

Barrio Christians know the good news of God is a gift extended to human beings that directs our attention to life's deepest purpose. This good news is given to hearers in the barrio who live in a poverty that produces tormented existence and an inevitable unease about economic and political structures. Thus, from a barrio perspective, evangelization means the good news proclaimed by Jesus questions the basic alienation of human beings from God and the structures of sin that negate the kingdom of God is at hand. For this reason, Latinos/as understand that evangelizing does not simply mean bringing people to church to hear the gospel, but it demands bearing witness to the mystery of Jesus of Nazareth and God's reign as life's defining reality as well as the basis for transforming societal institutions that are deaf to the clamor of the poor.

The people of the barrio are critical of church growth evangelists who encourage inner-city mission based on the verbal proclamation of the good news of Christ, which always falls short of effective saving action. From the barrio, downtrodden men, women, and children confess that the church must evangelize others not only by declaring the saving knowledge of the risen Christ, but also by offering Christian witness that expresses fidelity to a crucified God, Jesus' option for the poor, and genuine solidarity with degraded people. Barrio people tell church growth evangelists who knock on their apartment doors that God evangelizes the baptized every day with the reality of the Cross—a sign that is a persistent criticism of all death-dealing ways of life. In the daily passion of the barrio, Christians are invited much like the disciples on the road of Emmaus to discover the power of the Resurrection in the midst of suffering.

Barrio evangelization means enabling others to become increasingly aware that Jesus proclaimed the love of God and showed it at work in cures, miracles, and especially prophetic action in the Temple where religion was associated with oppression and exclusion; at table fellowship sharing meals with people discriminated against and rejected by the privileged; and in breaking the cultural rules that erected barriers between classes of people.[8] Certainly, in the barrio where people live on the edge of death and their humanity is not of compelling interest to mainline Protestant churches, evangelization means deepening and intensifying the commitment to the reign of God by way of a preferential option of love for the excluded. Conversion to God-in-Christ without commitment to the poor in whom God is incarnate hardly develops Christian existence according to the faith of Jesus.

Barrio evangelization places the church in tension with the values of the wider dominant culture. The good news issuing forth from the mouths of degraded men and women in the barrio confronts the mainline church's distorted theological view of God ruling in almighty power and ignorant of the plight of the poor; indeed, the good news can never be unconcerned with young children struck down by poverty; youth disoriented by feelings of facing a hopeless future; racial and ethnic people degraded by social values, institutions, and economic structures; exploited workers unable to organize their labor rights; the unemployed and underemployed pushed into homelessness and despair; the elderly poor who are disregarded in a society focused on youthfulness; and prostitutes forced by poverty and drugs into humiliating sex work, yet yearning for the gospel that assures their dignity in the sight of God.

The good news of Christ that comes to us unexpectedly and freely given was preached in history to address life-denying conditions of life. Barrio Christians confirm this by pointing to the answer given by Jesus to John the Baptist's disciples: "The blind receive their sight, the lame walk, the lepers are cleansed, the deaf hear, the dead are raised, and the poor have good news brought to them" (Matt. 11:5; Luke 7:22). Thus, barrio evangelization requires that faith and the practice of the gospel establish congregations that confront dominant social, political, and economic orders. The Bible hardly encourages us to go out and build designer churches; instead, God rejects such profit churches in favor of calling persons to a discipleship concerned with doing justice to trampled human beings (Mic. 6:6-8). Barrio evangelism celebrates God present in the poor who yearn for a world without exploitation and injustice.

In the barrio, the good news of Jesus confronts the everyday reality of Latino/a families who are threatened by poverty, language isolation, limited access to good jobs and wages, barriers to education, racial discrimination, and problems obtaining adequate social and legal services. Latino/a children are especially affected by these challenges and often become vulnerable to at-risk behavior, being drawn into the urban world of drugs, gangs, and chronic community violence. In the harsh and hopeful reality of the barrio, the poor carpenter from the city of Nazareth in Galilee exhorts his followers to look for God's reign and justice in the world (Matt. 6:33). In short, evangelization in the barrio reflects less the concerns of dominant culture and mainline Christianity than faithfulness to the liberating news of Jesus of Nazareth.[9]

From the viewpoint of the barrio, the work of evangelism means recognizing that in Jesus God takes the form of a poor, unemployed, and marginal worker, who lacks formal educational titles; indeed, Jesus revealed in no uncertain terms that God opts for the poor and the oppressed whose lives are always threatened by structures of death. He manifests a God who deeply understands the situation of the poor and loves them with infinite mercy and the promise of abundant life. In this light, barrio evangelism holds that the church is called to bear witness to God in the service of love to the poor who are isolated from mainstream society and who constitute the great majority of human beings on earth. The will of God is found in the setting of the poor, and those who are most deprived of life seek through Christ to "build houses and inhabit them . . . plant vineyards and eat their fruit" (Isa. 65:21).

In the twenty-first century, the mainline Christian community needs to hear the good news again from a barrio Jesus who calls us to walk with forgotten people in justice and love. As I argued in a previous work,[10] a hard-hitting barrio Jesus is identified with the poor, denounces the accumulation of wealth, praises individuals who give up their love of money, rejects oppressive behavior, condemns the separating practices of mainline religion, requires service to others, and opposes social injustice. This hard-hitting Jesus tells marginal people that their poverty implicates the rich (Luke 6:24; 12:13-21), religious authorities (Mark 11:15-19; Luke

11:39-44, 46-52), and powerful officials (Mark 10:42). Thus, the good news Jesus asks us to preach may include the possibility of social conflict (Mark 13:9; Luke 21:12-13; 22:36).

Barrio evangelism claims a hard-hitting Jesus historically revealed God as a friend of outcasts and helpless people. He shed light on oppressive systems of economic exploitation in light of the hope of the poor to make the gospel flesh in concrete life situations (Matt. 6:24; Luke 6:24). When evangelists place the concerns of the barrio above those of fattening the church with new members, then the full gospel of the hard-hitting Jesus who proclaimed the truth of outcasts to those in power will illuminate our hearts. As the mainline Protestant church is evangelized anew by the barrio, it will critically reflect on the meaning of Jesus who acted in history and continues to act, seeking to transform the racial, political, social, spiritual, and cultural structures that negate life and human dignity (Luke 13:26).

For barrio evangelists, the hope inspired by their hard-hitting Jesus gives rise to a freedom that seeks to enact a new vision of human purpose and equality in society (Gal. 5:1). Barrio evangelists know there is no greater joy than freely confessing Christ in the service of outsiders, beyond the religious, ideological, political, and cultural compound, in places lacking money, security, and comfort, in the service of a mission that claims worldly knowledge of God in the suffering and dying of rejects and unwelcome strangers. Marginalized Latinos/as know that once mainline Protestants follow the hard-hitting Jesus in the struggle of the barrio poor, they will learn to tell the story of how Jesus offers universal salvation from a point of departure in the world of lowly people. They also know that mainline Christians discover how not to be faithful clients of the power establishment by following Jesus in the barrio.

Barrio evangelism offers to free the mainline Protestant church from the dead weight of the past, beginning with these questions: How has the church interpreted its mission within the totality of human existence? Whose interests has it served? Have the poor had good news preached to them? Do persons disabled by socially structured oppression walk? Do the blind to human suffering regain sight? Do the deaf to the cries of humiliated people hear? Surely, those wonderful designer churches that provide a safe place for self-indulgent Christians are living a false piety when they believe it is unimportant to look toward the interests of lowly others and largely overlook in their liturgies, prayers, worship life, and Christian practice that though Jesus "was in the form of God, [he] did not regard equality with God as something to be exploited, but emptied himself, taking the form of a slave" (Phil. 2:3-7).

The crucified God is absent from churches interested only in their growth instead of making the world better and more human. Barrio evangelists believe that if mainline Protestant churches are to have any credible future, their dominant culture value system will need to be penetrated by the hard-hitting Jesus present in the barrio in each face of a people who know what it means to exist between suffering and death. The recovery of the logic of evangelism at the core of the mainline Protestant church's mission can no longer remain captive to the proclamation of a shallow, self-centered, and undemanding gospel. Indeed, the prevailing culture Christianity found within mainline Protestant congregations that mostly communicates Christian faith in an alienating fashion must be identified as negating the life and ministry of Jesus.[11] Indeed, barrio Christians suggest that mainline Christianity is perhaps most in need of God's gospel illumination!

Today, church growth evangelists and mainline Protestant churches need to remember that the Latino/a poor of the barrio keep alive the ethical demands of the gospel and the question of God in a sinful world; indeed, the witness of barrio Christians confronts the false gods that operate in so many mainline Protestant churches that assure the idolization of wealth and structural violence toward the poor. Latinos/as do not hesitate to speak out at designer church conferences, where the logic of a prosperity gospel overrides compassion for the poor, the words of Isaiah: "You make many prayers, I will not listen; your hands are full of blood" (1:15). In short, barrio Christians believe an evangelized people should deal with everyday problems by confronting dominant political and economic orders. If the barrio remains ignored and trivialized by mainline Protestant churches, the good news of Jesus Christ will then remain distorted.

Conclusion

Surely, the cruelty and violence of the twentieth century leave any would-be evangelist crying out with Jeremiah, "We look for peace, but find no good; for a time of healing, but there is terror instead" (14:19). This essay began discussing how church growth evangelism dominates the discourse of mainline Protestant churches with a message concerning the importance of numerical growth and the creation of economically successful churches. Church growth evangelists are less likely to preach about practicing good news toward others and living in awareness of relationship to the God of the poor than declaring a "user-friendly gospel" and promoting the development of so-called designer churches. I argued that evangelists hoping to take the good news of Jesus Christ seriously for the mission of the church will need to preach and practice faith in the context of the poor and oppressed.

Unlike church growth evangelism, barrio evangelization insists that naming Jesus Christ includes denouncing the structures of sin in society; indeed, barrio evangelists insist that the mission of the church is far more than simply "saving souls," building bigger congregations, taming the gospel, or focusing on becoming better individuals. Evangelization implies following Christ in service to the sick, hungry, naked, destitute, beaten-down, and crucified people of this world. Barrio evangelization focuses on at least five aspects of Jesus' call to follow him: (1) embracing discipleship that encompasses Jesus' option for the poor and crucified people, (2) developing Christian life according to the faith of Jesus, (3) living a Christian life in service to those who lack money, security, and comfort, (4) discovering God present in people degraded by power elites, and (5) continuing Jesus' ministry of radically transforming the structures of life in accordance with God's reign.

Suggested Reading

Banuelas, Arturo, ed. *Mestizo Christianity: Theology from the Latino Perspective*. Maryknoll, N.Y.: Orbis Books, 1995.

Costas, Orlando. *Christ Outside the Gate*. Maryknoll, N.Y.: Orbis Books, 1982.

———. *Liberating News: A Theology of Contextual Evangelization*. Grand Rapids: Eerdmans, 1989.

De La Torre, Miguel, and Edwin David Aponte. *Introducing Latino/a Theologies*. Maryknoll, N.Y.: Orbis Books, 2001.

Diaz-Stevens, Ana Maria, and Anthony M. Stevens Arroyo. *Recognizing the Latino Resurgence in U.S. Religion: The Emmaus Paradigm*. Boulder, Colo.: Westview Press, 1998.

Maldonado, David, ed. *Protestantes/Protestants: Hispanic Christianity within Mainline Traditions*. Nashville: Abingdon Press, 1999.

Rodriquez, Jeanette. *Our Lady of Guadalupe: Faith and Empowerment Among Mexican American Women*. Austin: University of Texas, 1994.

Segovia, Fernando F., and Ada Maria Isasi-Diaz, eds. *Hispanic/Latino Theology: Challenge and Promise*. Minneapolis: Fortress Press, 1996.

CHAPTER 8

Saving Women: Re-visioning Contemporary Concepts of Evangelism

Laceye Warner

Introduction

In a context of increasing secularization and religious pluralism, the study of evangelism is a vital resource for the church.[1] However, most studies related to the theology and practice of evangelism have yet to give substantial attention to a group that forms more than half of the church's constituency.[2] Although, historically, women have comprised the majority of church members and active participants in evangelistic ministries, their contributions are only beginning to be studied. One significant reason women are absent from categories of discourse related to evangelism stems from an understanding of evangelism as verbal proclamation, most often in the form of preaching—a practice to which women have had only limited access.[3]

An examination of selected women invites the re-visioning of concepts of evangelism, as it relates to preaching, that emerged in the eighteenth and nineteenth centuries and remain influential today. This essay focuses primarily upon women connected to Wesleyan traditions in eighteenth-century Britain and nineteenth- and early twentieth-century America. Drawing on the nature of evangelistic ministries of women during this formative period, this essay challenges an understanding of evangelism as merely verbal proclamation. In the ministries of these women, a profound synthesis of verbal proclamation and evangelistic practices embodied the gospel message.

My argument proceeds as follows. First, I will demonstrate the narrow use of the language of evangelism—predominantly confined to preaching—in the historiography of women's ministries and in contemporary sources, which leads interpreters to miss the integrated nature of women's evangelism. Verbal proclamation of the gospel message is an essential, scripturally grounded component of evangelistic practice. However, a brief survey of contemporary sources reveals an emphasis on verbal proclamation to the exclusion of compassion for physical or material well-being. This contrasts with New Testament foundations, as well as canonical themes, that tie spiritual formation to the care of whole persons. Second, the essay explores the particularity of women's historical practices of evangelism that, although linked when possible with preaching, have been associated more often with ministries of compassion, with the aim of initiating disciples of Jesus Christ into the reign of God. The complexity of women's evangelistic practices closely resembles those ministries embodied and commissioned by Jesus Christ in the Gospels. I am not arguing for an understanding of evangelism that neglects verbal proclamation. Rather, women's practices of evangelism include ministries of compassion that, when introduced to the discourse of evangelistic theology and practice, broaden contemporary conceptualizations of evangelistic ministry. In this study, women's evangelistic witness emerges as an integrally connected web of practices that provides a multifaceted paradigm beyond the simplified concept of evangelism as solely verbal proclamation.

Women, Proclamation, and Evangelism

Practices of evangelistic ministry in the eighteenth and early nineteenth centuries tended to focus on personal holiness as a means to social holiness. During the First Great Awakening in Britain and America, women began to serve as domestic visitors and Christian educators. Women offered Christian witness in the homes of the spiritually and physically impoverished through ministries such as prayer, encouragement, health and employment consultation, and the provision of clothing, food, and medication. Connected with communities of faith, they offered Christian instruction to seekers of all ages. As women's local associations organized into vast networks during the nineteenth century, their evangelistic ministries also developed into complex programs at home and abroad, training and supporting male and female missionaries as physicians, nurses, and educators in hospitals, schools, and urban mission facilities.

The focus on the primacy of personal holiness within North American Protestantism was followed by a separation of social reform from evangelistic ministries as the Social Gospel and fundamentalist movements grew more estranged from one another. This increasing separation culminated in the fundamentalist-modernist controversy of the early twentieth century. As Jean Miller Schmidt has argued, women's ministries during this period exemplified greater wholeness in evangelistic social reform in contrast to the general trend of fragmentation.[4] Donald Dayton's research also points toward the balance of evangelical piety and social reform within Wesleyan holiness traditions, particularly among the ministries of women.[5] Shaped by a strong evangelical faith, women's evangelistic ministries in the late nineteenth and early twentieth centuries took seriously the implications of systemic evil in their efforts to improve the plight of the disenfranchised—the imprisoned, the mentally ill, the immigrant poor, and the enslaved and, later, segregated African Americans.

William Abraham argues that the contemporary Protestant church in North America has inherited the sixteenth-century reformers' emphasis on proclamation. This emphasis has further encouraged the church to limit its concept of evangelism to verbal proclamation of the gospel as a practice distinct from social reform and works of justice.[6] As the exegetical and theological reflections of recent scholars have shown, evangelism relies significantly upon verbal proclamation, but it is also closely related to other ministries that sustain the process of the initiation of persons into the reign of God.[7] Thus, an understanding of evangelism focused solely on preaching can be richly expanded in light of recent scholarship and models based upon women's evangelistic ministry from the eighteenth- and nineteenth-century Wesleyan tradition.[8]

Most women who were appointed to or bravely assumed the role of preacher in the eighteenth and nineteenth centuries engaged in a complex web of evangelistic practices that complemented their verbal proclamation of the gospel. The number of women who confronted the challenges of eighteenth- and nineteenth-century church and society to fulfill their vocation to preach was relatively small. Women preachers were more prevalent in splinter groups because of the relatively permissive ethos with regard to female preaching often associated with congregational autonomy or intense pneumatology. As smaller movements, such as Methodism in Britain and America, grew in numbers and resources during the First Great Awakening, they moved away from the less respectable practice of female preaching.[9] Indeed, strong resistance to women's preaching, based on biblical as well as constitutional arguments, began to mount. In Britain, support for female preaching, among other innovations encouraged by John Wesley, quickly waned following Wesley's death in 1791.[10] For example, the 1803 Wesleyan Conference disallowed female preaching (after the relative openness of Wesley's leadership of the movement) as a result of opposition within the denomination and a growing sufficiency in the number of male preachers. Not until more than a century later, in 1910, were women allowed to preach to other women. Then in 1911, women were allowed to preach to a consenting gathering of men and women.[11]

In America, some Wesleyan traditions afforded women ordination and the right to preach during the nineteenth century. The Methodist Episcopal Church granted local preacher's licenses in some districts beginning in 1869; seventy or more women received them during the 1870s. However, the licenses were rescinded by the 1880 General Conference in the midst of petitions for women's ordination, which were flatly denied. Women were not granted preaching licenses in The Methodist Episcopal Church until 1920.[12] In an ecclesial context in which evangelism was synonymous with verbal proclamation, this almost fully excluded women from engaging in traditionally recognized evangelistic ministries.

Scholars writing about the historical contributions of women to religion, following the example of eighteenth- and nineteenth-century practitioners such as John Wesley and Charles Finney, have tended to use language related to the term "evangelism" to describe the ministries of verbal proclamation assumed by these female preachers. According to James Logan, "Wesley never employed the term 'evangelism' itself. This noun was simply not in currency in his day, though he did speak of his itinerant preachers as 'evangelists,' denoting their sole responsibility to preach."[13] Charles Finney used the language of evangelism similarly, adding a subtle nuance by claiming that reform lectures were a corollary to evangelism.[14] Thus, the language assumed by Bettye Collier-Thomas in her text on preaching women in the African American tradition, and

Nancy Hardesty in her study of the reform work of evangelical women, uses the terms "evangelism" or "evangelists" synonymously with "preaching" or "lay preachers," usually as distinct from those holding ordination.[15] Alternative terms such as "mission," "outreach," and "reform" then represent practices other than preaching. Catherine Brekus demonstrates that connotations of female evangelism, understood merely as preaching, too narrowly construe the contributions of women and hinder the implications of women's examples for contemporary evangelistic theology and practice. She writes, "A Mother in Israel or Sister in Christ was not a crusading evangelist who traveled from town to town preaching the gospel, but a Sunday school teacher, a temperance reformer, or an antislavery activist who deferred to the authority of her local pastor."[16] Jean Miller Schmidt, in her description of Phoebe Palmer's encouragement of urban mission work at the Five Points Mission in New York City, acknowledges the significance, for Christian witness, of activities other than preaching. According to Schmidt, Palmer "was convinced that something more than evangelism was required."[17]

A small but significant number of women within the First Great Awakening's early Methodist movement were afforded the privilege of preaching by John Wesley. Women and men who pursued the office of preacher were not simply admitted to the role. Wesley undertook a process of strict discernment to determine the presence of an extraordinary call and the demonstration of fruits. As a result of the movement's considerable pneumatology and less developed ecclesiology, women were given some opportunity to preach. As Paul Chilcote argues, the roles of women in early British Methodism expanded in a logical and natural progression, leading to a small number of Methodist women preachers in the 1760s.[18]

When we look at the work of women preachers, a richer picture emerges. Sarah Crosby (1729–1804), the first woman informally authorized by Wesley to preach within the Methodist movement, and Mary Bosanquet (1739–1815), the writer of what is probably the earliest defense of women's preaching within Methodism, not only served as preachers within the movement but also established an orphanage and provided care for the impoverished. In 1763 Bosanquet and Sarah Ryan, later joined by Crosby, organized a home at Leytonstone, near London in Essex, similar to the home in Christopher Alley where these women began their work among London's poor in the late 1750s. Over the course of five years, thirty-five children and thirty-four adults at

Leytonstone received shelter and care for their physical needs as well as formation as disciples in the Christian faith.[19] The ministry of this community of women was significantly expanded with the move in 1768 to Cross Hall, near Leeds in Yorkshire, a vital area of the Methodist movement. At Cross Hall, the home established by Bosanquet, Ryan, and Crosby continued, with the addition of Ann Tripp, its ministries of compassion for both bodies and souls, while developing into a center for corporate prayer and worship. It is difficult to determine their understanding of the relationship between word and deed, specifically whether they perceived them as united. Despite this ambiguity, their intentional community of faith created a fertile ground for the cultivation of women preachers and provided a context for the formation and initiation of disciples into the reign of God.[20]

As mentioned earlier, opportunities for women preachers in British Methodism declined sharply after John Wesley's death in 1791, as the movement transitioned toward denominational institutionalization. As a result, many preaching women within British Methodism left that connection for less institutional traditions such as the Quakers, Primitive Methodists, and Bible Christians. However, most of the women who remained within the Methodist connection continued their ministries of evangelism, persisting in practices considered appropriate for women of the time.

Preaching women within nineteenth-century American Wesleyan traditions, particularly the holiness movement, are well known for their participation in international evangelistic campaigns. With the powerful ministries of proclamation also existed ministries of compassion. The impetus for this multivalent ministry was the recognition of the transformative power of ministries of compassion and social justice related to conversion. Phoebe Palmer (1807–74), through her preaching and visitation, interacted with the poor living in the slum area of Five Points in New York City. With her encouragement, the Ladies' Home Missionary Society of The Methodist Episcopal Church began a mission there in 1854 that eventually included a place of employment for five hundred people, a day school, and various social programs.[21] Church members had been visiting the poor and sick and holding Bible classes, Sunday schools, and prayer meetings in the area since 1843.[22] As a result of Palmer's encounters with the poor through door-to-door visitation, Five Points House of Industry was established to minister to the poor. The mission grew out of the empowerment Palmer received from her experience of holiness or entire sanctification.[23] The mission work at Five Points eventually concentrated on children—saving them from street gangs, educating them, and providing day care and adoption services.[24] In addition to establishing a school, the Five Points Mission contained a chapel and twenty apartments to accommodate impoverished families.[25] Use of the language of evangelism as verbal proclamation, mentioned earlier, is consistent with contemporary conceptualizations of evangelism. However, such missions, in their multifaceted work, ministered to physical needs as an integral part of proclaiming the gospel. A more complex understanding of evangelism emerges as recipients of compassion began to participate and assume membership in local communities of faith, thus demonstrating the integration of compassion and verbal proclamation in evangelism. Palmer, with Bosanquet and her intentional community, persevered in cultivating opportunities to preach while at the same time participating in numerous evangelistic ministries, including ministries of compassion that cared for the bodies and souls of persons.

Saving Women: Moving Beyond Preaching in Evangelistic Practice

Women's practices of evangelism in eighteenth- and nineteenth-century Wesleyan traditions built upon ministries of verbal proclamation with ministries of compassion and social reform through their roles as missionaries, deaconesses, and leaders in temperance, abolition, and other reform movements. Ecclesial hierarchies did not consistently allow women to preach in the larger, more institutionalized, and "respectable" denominations of the day. These other, complementary ministries were pursued in part because they were considered appropriately feminine for middle-class (most often), European-American churchwomen. Women's ministries of compassion and reform have significant contributions to make to the discourse and practice of evangelism. The following sections explore the evangelistic ministries of women within Wesleyan traditions, demonstrating the array of activities pursued with the purpose of making disciples of Jesus Christ.

Women in Early Methodism

The majority of participants within early British and American Methodism were women.[26] Women assumed a large portion of leadership roles within the movement, most often as visitors of the sick or as band or class leaders.[27] Methodism, particularly in eighteenth-century Britain, provided a unique opportunity for leadership by those of low socio-economic status, namely, the uneducated, the impoverished, and women.[28] Although John Wesley never affirmed a general policy in support of women preachers, he did, as mentioned earlier, encourage gifted women of spiritual maturity to assume leadership within the movement, leadership that often included preaching. Women's roles in the Methodist movement, while varied, had an evangelistic character that involved a web of practices related to verbal proclamation and ministries of compassion.

Numerous women engaged in evangelistic work within the British Methodist movement.[29] One, in particular, bears mentioning to demonstrate the interrelatedness of activities that contributed to evangelism. Dorothy Ripley (1769–1831) was born in Whitby, England. Her father was a Methodist preacher well known for his hospitality to strangers and his compassion for the poor and outcast. After his death, Ripley described her father's ministry that strongly influenced her own: "Believing it his duty, he fed the hungry, clothed the naked, and so increased his treasure above winning souls to God by the merchandise of his wisdom."[30] Like her father, Ripley embodied a ministry of evangelism that did not sunder care for souls and bodies. In 1801, Ripley received a special call to minister among the slaves in the New World, where Charleston, South Carolina, was her base.[31] Ripley understood the gospel to include the ceasing of oppression particularly in relation to the Africans in the American colonies. Ripley wrote, "And it sufficeth me to believe that he [God] will soon cause the oppressors to cease their oppression and reward with peace such who travail in spirit for the spread of the gospel of our Lord Jesus Christ."[32]

Ripley's vocation to minister to the disenfranchised addressed a union of spiritual and material brokenness. For example, on July 2, 1802, Ripley included in a written account a description of "five or six little wretched children, naked, from the age of two years up to nine."[33] According to Ripley's account, many questioned her response of shock and affection to the children's plight. "Why do I? Because a gracious God leads me to feel for them—weep for them—and pray in faith also for them that they may be blessed with the same blessings which are poured down upon my head and others, who groan in spirit with me for their redemption from sin and thralldom of the oppressors."[34] Ripley ministered to slaves and slave owners and heard the promise of many youths to free their parents' slaves upon inheritance so "that they might free themselves from the curse of their fathers."[35] Although Ripley did not consistently undertake the ministry of preaching, her verbal proclamation of the gospel and its relationship to practices of compassion provide an example of how women's evangelistic ministries in early Methodism cared for the spiritual and the physical well-being of persons.

Missionaries and Evangelistic Practices

Women participated in evangelistic ministries as wives of foreign missionaries from the early nineteenth century. Eventually, the role of single women as foreign missionaries was recognized and supported, first in The Methodist Episcopal Church with the founding of the Women's Foreign Missionary Society in 1869. The WFMS, the second such society to organize in North America (following Congregationalist women),[36] described its missiology as "Woman's Work for Woman." The aim of the work was evangelism: the invitation of indigenous women to Christianity in the context of communities of faith. Because of the limitations on ministry roles available to women, their evangelistic impulse was most often embodied in a variety of practices considered appropriate for women of the time, such as teaching and nursing. An important aspect of the "Woman's Work for Woman" missiology was the argument that preaching (a primarily male practice) should not be valued over teaching (a primarily female one), as had been proposed by the male leadership of the modern missionary movement.[37] Implicit in this argument was an awareness of the complex web of practices necessary for effective evangelism. The missiological vision of the WFMS valued women's contributions to evangelistic ministries that complemented the practice of preaching.

"Woman's Work for Woman" comprised three areas of ministry —education, medical care, and evangelization (preaching)—each directed toward the empowerment of women in foreign mission contexts.[38] The women considered their work essential to the overall missionary movement; indeed, they considered all three areas of ministry to be evangelistic.[39] However, public support for women evangelists lagged behind that for women teachers and doctors, since the title "evangelist," because of its limited definition related to preaching, required explicit approval for women.[40] Still, women's preaching was more accepted in foreign mission contexts than in domestic ones. Brekus describes the greater acceptance of women as preachers in foreign contexts this way: "As missionaries, both women [Sarah Thornton, a Freewill Baptist, and Eliza Barnes, a Methodist] continued to preach informally, but instead of facing questions about their morality or femininity, they earned wide praise for their self-sacrificing devotion to the 'heathen.' "[41] Because of the urgent needs confronting mission efforts in foreign contexts, the assumption of preaching roles by women was typically less contested in these settings than at home.

In addition to verbal proclamation, which remained central to the evangelistic impulse of the WFMS, missionaries such as Isabella Thoburn (1840–1901) and Clara Swain (1834–1910), the first single women supported by the WFMS beginning in 1869, made significant contributions to the education and medical care of indigenous women. Thoburn worked diligently in India during the late nineteenth and early twentieth centuries to establish boarding schools for girls and higher education for young women. For Thoburn and the WFMS, the preparation of indigenous women for leadership in evangelism was a missiological goal in itself.[42] Female missionaries aspired to equip these women with knowledge as well as practical skills. Clara Swain, the first female medical doctor to serve as a foreign missionary, not only practiced medicine among Indian women of all classes but also trained women in medicine and established a hospital. Swain's evangelistic ministry reached beyond medical mission work to include teaching Sunday school, training women to teach the Bible, preach, provide medical care, and witness to upper caste Zenana women who needed medical assistance.[43] For Thoburn, Swain, and the WFMS, a multitude of ministries—from teaching to practicing medicine to preaching—were evangelistic. "Woman's Work for Woman," although subject to currents of cultural imperialism not discussed in detail here, represented a missiology that valued the interwovenness of evangelistic practices available to women in foreign mission contexts. These practices worked together, offering ministries of wholeness to bodies, minds, and souls, as individuals were initiated into the reign of God and local communities of faith.

Deaconesses and Evangelistic Practices

The role of deaconess emerged within the Protestant church in the first half of the nineteenth century, beginning in Germany in 1836 when

Theodore Fleidner, a Lutheran pastor, with his wife, Frederika, established a home for released female prisoners at Kaiserswerth. The role of deaconess at Kaiserswerth expanded into teaching and nursing, each including strong evangelistic components. The role of deaconess soon spread across the European continent and to North America, beginning again with the Lutheran Church. In Great Britain, deaconesses and sisterhoods initially emerged in the Church of England, followed by Nonconformist traditions. In North America before the end of the nineteenth century, women were encouraged to serve as deaconesses by the Episcopal Church, followed by the Methodists and Baptists.

Deaconess homes and training schools often provided for women's ministry in three areas, similar to those addressed by female foreign missionaries: education, medical care, and evangelism (practiced most often through visitation rather than preaching). However, deaconess ministries generally embodied a significant interplay of each of these areas in response to particular needs. In addition to leading class meetings for adults and teaching Sunday school for children, deaconesses trained youth in industrial schools, preparing them for employment in various trades. Their ministries in both education and medical care represented holistic practices of evangelism that combined verbal proclamation with ministries of compassion.

Deaconesses were usually organized into the two relatively distinct roles of nurse and visitor. In the Methodist Episcopal tradition, deaconess nurses and visitors shared an evangelistic impetus while their training diverged to allow specialization in the distinct areas. Deaconess nurses began their ministry in the homes of those unable to afford medical care. With the development of financial resources and the training of women as nurses, an impressive number of deaconess hospitals were established in the late nineteenth century. The Methodist Episcopal deaconess movement founded each of the sixteen Methodist hospitals established between 1887 and 1900, a number that is striking in comparison with the two Methodist hospitals founded between 1880 and 1890.[44] The ministries of deaconess nurses, although most obviously focused on physical need, did not ignore the spiritual need for Christian formation through prayer, Bible reading, spiritual counsel, and teaching. According to Florence Parker, a Methodist Episcopal deaconess nurse, the motto of the deaconess nurse was "Help for Perishing Bodies—and Souls," an important complement to the work of the deaconess visitor, whose motto was "Help for Perishing Souls—and Bodies."[45] Deaconess visitors often organized into deaconess homes or affiliated with local churches. Under the supervision of clergymen, they engaged in domestic visitation, usually to the impoverished, often to immigrant women and children concentrated in urban areas. The visits established a means to provide other ministries of compassion such as nursing, always with an evangelistic purpose that included the verbal proclamation of the gospel.

Deaconesses in the late nineteenth century worked under the auspices of clergymen, usually in individual local church appointments. They served in clearly supervised roles with little autonomy, roles that remained consistent with the dominant ideologies of femininity of the time. Confined by ideologies of domesticity and femininity often espoused by denominational leaders, deaconesses, particularly in The Methodist Episcopal Church, seldom had opportunity to preach. Such opportunity was slightly more common in other denominational traditions, typically, the less structured and less affluent traditions that had critical shortages of male preachers. These opportunities often arose in more remote settings. The language and tasks related to deaconess movements tended to follow the Victorian ideals related to the roles of mother and sister. Implicit in these ideals were the responsibilities of mothers for the formation of children as moral and religious citizens. As celibate women, deaconesses assumed the roles of mothers and sisters to the lost and broken. Although deaconesses were limited by these essentialist interpretations of gender-appropriate roles, the maternal and sisterly character of their roles did afford opportunities for spiritual nurture and evangelism beyond the domestic setting.

Frances Willard and the Woman's Christian Temperance Union

Protestant women engaged in numerous efforts for reform in the late nineteenth and early twentieth centuries, from temperance and women's ecclesial rights to racial justice. Many of these efforts, together with the many women who championed them, demonstrate the complexity of ministry practices that often emerge from an evangelistic impetus. The work of Frances Willard (1839–98) within the Woman's Christian Temperance Union (WCTU) serves as a prime example of the evangelistic impetus of late nineteenth-century reform, especially her leadership within the temperance movement and her contributions to the movement for ecclesial rights for women.

Frances Elisabeth Caroline Willard attended Northwestern Female College and joined First Methodist Episcopal Church in Evanston, Illinois, as a full member in 1861; she was described as "an active worker, seeking to lead others to Christ."[46] The ministry of Phoebe Palmer and her spouse facilitated an experience of holiness or entire sanctification received by Willard in 1866.[47] Willard claimed to have lost the purity associated with her experience of holiness.[48] Willard served as an educator and administrator within educational institutions[49] before joining the temperance crusade that commenced in earnest in Ohio during the winter of 1873–74.

Under Willard's leadership the WCTU, already the largest women's organization in the United States and, presumably, one of the largest in the world, increased the effectiveness of the women called to work for moral reform. Willard's personal vocation and the significance she attributed to reform influenced her leadership within the temperance movement, first as secretary (1874–79) and then as president (1879–98). Willard struggled with a call to ministry, which she discerned to include a call to preach and receive ordination. Such roles were not readily accessible to women in The Methodist Episcopal Church at the time. Willard expressed her vision for the church in a letter written to Mrs. D. L. Moody in 1877, in which she supported women as evangelists and alluded to the role of preaching by women evangelists, but also indicated the expansion of this role was "such that most people have not dreamed." She writes, "I firmly believe God has a work for them [women] to do as evangelists, as bearers of Christ's message to the ungospeled, to the prayer meeting, to the church generally and the world at large, such that most people have not dreamed. It is therefore my dearest wish to help break down the barriers of prejudice that keep them silent."[50] In her first presidential address to the WCTU, Willard described women as two-thirds of Christ's church, whose voices are "a reinforcement quite indispensable to the evangelizing agencies of the more helpful future."[51] Willard referred to Charles Finney's statement that "the Church that silences the women is shorn of half its power."[52] The goal of Willard's evangelistic vision was "the Christianizing of society,"[53] revealing relatively early glimpses of the American Social Gospel as well as a multivalenced conceptualization of evangelistic ministry.

As early as 1874, the WCTU sponsored gospel temperance meetings where local unions offered the gospel cure for intemperance in religious services that were modeled on revival meetings and culminated in a conversion to the cause. This conversion was demonstrated by signing the pledge.[54] By 1877, these gospel temperance meetings mingled salvation from intemperance, "tens of thousands have been saved and redeemed from the appetite of rum," with salvation in Jesus Christ. The WTCU notes, for example, that "Connected with Friendly Inns in Cleveland are chapels, in which evangelistic services are held."[55] In 1877, 50,000 attended these evangelistic services, in which 200 professed conversion to Christianity; "multitudes who came only for the bread and meat stayed to pray and were saved."[56] While working for temperance reform, these women cared for the spiritual and temporal needs of persons.

As the ministries of the WCTU expanded under Willard's leadership, so did the women's participation in a variety of compassionate ministries that emerged as inseparable from the saving of souls. As mentioned earlier, the goal of Frances Willard's evangelistic vision was "the Christianizing of society." The complexity of the WCTU's evangelistic reform can be seen in the ministries sponsored by its Chicago chapter: two day nurseries, two Sunday schools, an industrial school, a mission that sheltered four thousand destitute or homeless women each year, a lodging for men, and a low-cost restaurant. Similar ministries were represented in the forty departments of the national organization.[57] Willard's presidency ended with her death in 1898, but her legacy was substantial. In the first decade alone of her leadership, the WCTU quadrupled its membership, as well as carving out space for women to practice holistic ministries of evangelism.

Conclusions

This essay began with the premise that women's contributions have yet to be included in the categories of discourse related to the study of evangelism. This circumstance arises at least in part because conceptions of evangelism have been too narrowly associated with verbal proclamation of the gospel. By integrating the contributions of selected women from the eighteenth and nineteenth centuries, a more complex and nuanced concept of evangelism emerges, one that resonates with contemporary themes in the academic study of evangelism. Based on their evangelistic practices, these women proclaimed the message of salvation through the fullness of ministries that reached beyond the role of preacher. Such a conception of evangelism recognizes the intricate web of ministries and roles that contribute to the care of whole persons and their initiation into the reign of God. Such a conception also demonstrates the significance of women's evangelistic practices to the church's mission in and to the world.

The Means of Grace and the Promise of New Life in the Evangelism of John Wesley

Henry H. Knight III

Apreacher warns of God's judgment and calls for a decision on the part of the hearers to accept God's forgiveness. A stranger approaches and, through a presentation of spiritual laws or a series of questions about our eternal destiny, invites us to accept Christ as our Savior. In both cases there is the urgent call for a decision now, at this moment, because whether one spends an eternity in heaven or hell could depend upon it. These are among the images that come to mind when North Americans hear the word "evangelism." But such images are stereotypes. Some who practice evangelism do come close to the stereotype; others are more careful, caring, and theologically nuanced than the images suggest. But whether done poorly or well, these forms of evangelism all understand salvation as a matter of eternal destiny—of going to heaven rather than hell. They believe that destiny is settled by an immediate decision to accept Christ and the forgiveness of one's sins. There is an urgency to share this message lest someone miss that opportunity and be lost eternally.

John Wesley and the movement he led were certainly concerned with the eternal destiny of persons. There was an urgency to proclaim the good news of salvation through Jesus Christ. Yet Wesley never equated being saved with a decision we make; salvation was foremost a work of

God. Salvation involved much more than whether one went to heaven or hell; fundamentally, it was the reception of and growth in a new life of love. These two emphases—the content of salvation and the nature of divine activity—may be where Wesley is most different from many recent understandings of evangelism, and they are certainly his greatest contributions to our own evangelistic theory and practice.

Salvation as New Life

Wesley's understanding of human salvation was at the heart of a larger eschatological vision for all of creation. Ultimately, God will put an end "to sin and misery, and infirmity, and death" and reestablish "holiness and happiness" throughout the world.[1] Within this larger vision, Wesley believed it was God's intention to restore human beings to the divine image in which they were created and to do so in this life. Indeed, Wesley believed this eschatological transformation had already begun: through restoring the *imago Dei* in humans, God was already "renewing the face of the earth."[2]

Wesley understood the *imago Dei* to have three components. The first of these, the *natural image*, consisted of understanding, will (with various affections), and liberty (agency). The *political image* involved the responsibility to govern the creation. Most important was the *moral image*, in which humanity reflected the righteousness and holiness of God. Just as God is love, love for God and love for neighbor are the governing affections of humanity created in God's image. The effect of the fall into sin was the corruption of the moral image and the consequent distortion of the natural and political images. With the loss of love for God, the relationship with God was broken. With the loss of love for one's neighbor, immense suffering was unleashed by humanity upon the world. Because the affections had become unholy, the tendency to sin became rooted in the heart, so determining motivations and clouding vision that humanity could not escape the condition into which it had fallen. Only God could deliver humanity from this corruption by sin. That is precisely what God has done through the death and resurrection of Jesus Christ and is doing through the ongoing work of the Holy Spirit. The goal is the restoration of humanity "not only to the favour, but likewise to the image of God; implying not barely deliverance from sin but the being filled with the fullness of God."[3] This, then, is salvation; "nothing short of this is Christian religion."[4]

Now if this is the goal, then evangelism cannot be construed in any way that would imply a salvation short of this goal. The end of evangelism is not justification but sanctification; growth in love is not subsequent to salvation—it is salvation. Evangelism in the Wesleyan tradition therefore must initiate persons into and sustain them in the process of sanctification that culminates in the heart perfected in love.

Grace as Transforming and Enabling

In his examination of how God works, Wesley simultaneously avoids two extremes. While insisting we have moral agency, or liberty, he denies we have absolute free will. Rather, in our fallen condition, our motivations for action, criteria for choices, and perspective on the world are governed by sin. The corruption of the will by sin is total; it is a disease that affects the entirety of human existence. This understanding Wesley holds in opposition to the views of some in his day that humanity is free by nature. If humanity did have natural free will, then the work of God would be, at most, persuasive. Through proclamation or other evangelistic means, the Holy Spirit would seek to elicit a decision, and because humanity could make that decision, the resulting conversion would not be so much an inward transformation of the heart as the resolution to turn to God and live a moral life. For Wesley, however, the corruption of sin was such that, apart from a gracious act of God, we could not make such a decision, much less live a moral life. Salvation is, indeed, by grace alone.

It is this consideration that has led many in the Augustinian and Calvinist traditions to insist grace must be irresistible. The logic is, if we cannot exercise our will to accept (much less procure) salvation due to its bondage to sin, then salvation can come only through a prior act of God transforming our will. This transformation must necessarily come at God's initiative. Once the will is transformed, it has a new set of motivations, orienting the person toward God. Moreover, the fact that not everyone responds implies that God selects (predestines) those who will receive salvation. In this case, evangelism would consist of proclamation with the assumption that those who respond and persevere in the faith are the ones chosen by God.

Wesley rejects this position—that all is of God's choosing—almost as strongly as the first position of absolute free will. Irresistible grace would not restore the *imago Dei*, but change it, denying the liberty that is essential for humanity to have moral agency. Without the capacity for moral agency, humanity could not be restored to the image of God, for the moral image, centered as it is in love, necessarily requires agency or the ability to respond. Love is not truly love unless it is freely given. Put differently, if God loves in freedom, then humanity cannot partake of that image unless it, too, can love in freedom. We must be free or, better, freed to love God and our neighbor.

While insisting salvation is by grace alone, Wesley understood grace differently from the Calvinists. For Wesley, grace enables human response and invites it,[5] restoring a measure of freedom to the human will. Reminding his readers of their own experience of grace, Wesley notes that God "did not take away your understanding; but enlightened and strengthened it," and likewise, God did not "destroy any of your affections; rather they were more vigorous than before."[6] Above all, God did not "take away your liberty, your power of choosing good or evil"; God "did not *force* you; but being *assisted* by his grace you, like Mary, *chose* the better part."[7]

Because grace is enabling but not coercive, Wesley can envision grace as universal without implying universal salvation. Because God does not want "any to perish, but all to come to repentance" (2 Pet. 3:9), God's grace reaches out to every person, enabling each to respond. Through this prevenient grace, says Wesley, "everyone has some measure of that light"; it not only gives us a conscience but is the source of the unease we feel when we act "contrary to the light of . . . conscience."[8] Evangelism does not "bring" Christ to persons, but announces the good news of salvation in Christ to those whom God is already at work among. Thus, in contrast to those who advocate natural free will, Wesley insists persons are bound by sin and need to be set free by the transforming power of God's grace. In contrast to those who see transforming grace as selective and irresistible, Wesley argues it is enabling and universal. When this view of grace is linked to salvation understood as a new life governed by love (and the restoration of the *imago Dei*), it has profound implications for how we do evangelism.

Evangelism as Proclamation

We have not, as yet, defined evangelism. While it is generally acknowledged that Wesley did evangelism, it was not a term he used—in fact, the term "evangelism" comes into common usage only in the nineteenth century.[9] Two definitions of evangelism are helpful in understanding Wesley's practice. At this point we can introduce the first, which understands evangelism to be either the proclamation of the gospel or personal witness to persons who are not Christians. Most contemporary definitions of evangelism, while differing in details, would be compatible with this understanding. Of course, a definition like this depends in practice on what is meant by "being a Christian." For Wesley, a Christian is minimally a person who has been regenerated or born again. Such a person has been so transformed by grace that love for God and neighbor, as well as other holy affections, has taken root in the heart and begun to grow. That is, a Christian is someone in whom the restoration of the *imago Dei* has actually begun.

If this is the case, then there are persons who have been baptized or who are on church rolls but are not Christians and, therefore, should be considered appropriate recipients of an evangelistic message. This claim—that a person can be baptized, yet not be a Christian—is disturbing to many because it seems to diminish the importance of baptism. Yet it points to the very heart of God's promise of salvation according to Wesley, which is not merely a change in status before God but an actual transformation of the heart and life by God that leads to a continual response by the person. For Wesley, baptism is denied by failing to actually live as one who has been baptized.[10]

We can now see how God utilizes evangelism to effect salvation. In some, who may not even believe there is a God, prevenient grace is at work, manifested as an uneasy conscience or a sense that life is somehow not what it is meant to be. With others, the nominal Christians, there is an extremely diminished understanding of salvation that does not include the new birth, or perhaps what was once a living reality in their lives has now become a distant memory. To all of these, evangelism proclaims the salvation that God has promised through Jesus Christ. It gives an account of the fallen human condition, what God has done in Christ to remedy the situation, and a description of the new life God offers. It emphasizes that this offer is by grace alone and is received by faith. Evangelism, then, is preeminently invitational, urging persons (enabled by grace) to turn to God and to receive forgiveness and new life.

Evangelism as Initiation

In later centuries, with the advent of the altar call, persons responding to an evangelistic invitation were expected to leave the meeting as

Christians.[11] In nineteenth-century revivalism, those responding would perhaps undergo a struggle, as they went through the throes of repentance, culminating in an experience of the joy of salvation. With later revivalism, the focus was less on experiencing salvation and more on making a decision. These later revivalistic practices are all in sharp contrast to Wesley's practice. Those awakened to their condition and, therefore, seeking salvation were invited to enroll in a small group that met weekly and to practice a set of spiritual disciplines.[12] The goal was not to elicit a decision, but to enable participation in the means of grace.

Wesley defines "means of grace" as "outward signs, words, or actions ordained of God, and appointed . . . to be the *ordinary* channels" through which God conveys "preventing, justifying, or sanctifying grace."[13] Among the means of grace are works of piety, such as prayer (both public and personal), receiving the Lord's Supper, searching the Scriptures (through hearing, reading, meditating), fasting, and Christian conference. These are means through which we may be in relationship with God. Other means of grace are works of mercy, wherein we care for the souls and the bodies of our neighbors through meeting the needs of those who are poor, sick, hungry, or otherwise in need, sharing the good news of Jesus Christ, and nurturing faith. As we engage in these means of grace, the Holy Spirit works in our lives, enabling us to grow in grace. Thus, the awakened sinner, seeking to know that his or her sins have been forgiven and to receive a new birth, does so by using the means of grace. The newborn Christian, seeking now to grow in sanctification and be perfected in love, does so by continuing to use the means of grace.

It might be wondered, if persons cannot be moral on their own, why would they faithfully do acts of piety and mercy? Even with a small measure of freedom restored through prevenient grace, this performance would seem to be spotty at best. Wesley sees the problem of remaining faithful to these means of grace as even more difficult. In addition to the dominance of sin prior to the new birth and the persistence of sin afterward, he describes us as "encompassed on all sides with persons and things that tend to draw us from our centre,"[14] which is God. This dissipation, as he terms it, involves much more than the many temptations to sin; it includes all the busyness of life, all the activities, deadlines, demands, and pursuits that can so occupy our time as to move God to the margins of life. A dissipated person is "habitually inattentive to the presence and will"[15] of God; dissipation is "the art of forgetting God."[16] The result of unchecked dissipation is that the awakened sinner is drawn from the path to justification, the nominal Christian is reimmersed in his or her illusory Christianity, and the growing Christian falls away. Persons may profess Christian beliefs and attend church, but their hearts and lives are no longer oriented toward God and their neighbor.

It is the difficulty of consistently participating in means of grace coupled with the serious threat of dissipation that makes the small groups and spiritual discipline essential. In Wesley's day, a Methodist was someone who was committed to the discipline—the Rules of the United Societies—and to attend the weekly class meeting. The discipline was structured around three rules: (1) do no harm (that is, refrain from known sinful actions); (2) do good to the bodies and souls of persons (works of mercy); and (3) attend upon the ordinances of God (works of piety).[17] At the weekly meeting, the Methodists were held accountable for how well they had kept the discipline, as well as received advice and encouragement to enable them to do so more faithfully.

The Methodist classes were fundamentally designed to counter dissipation and encourage Christian formation. They provided the structure, support, ethos, and accountability that enabled Methodists to participate in the means of grace. By such continued participation, awakened sinners came to know forgiveness and receive new life, and then began to grow in love as God restored them to the divine image. The goal of evangelism was for awakened persons to commit to this discipline and begin attending the weekly meetings, that is, to initiate persons into a life of Christian discipleship. It is no wonder, then, that Wesley records that "I was more convinced than ever, that preaching like an Apostle, without joining together those that are awakened, and training them up in the ways of God, is only begetting children for the murderer."[18]

An increasing number of contemporary writings on evangelism express dissatisfaction with traditional definitions that center on proclamation and seek, in some way, to relate evangelism to some form of Christian initiation. William Abraham defines evangelism "as primary initiation into the Kingdom of God" and provides a set of six distinct activities necessary to that initiation.[19] Scott Jones builds on Abraham, adding a seventh activity, and makes the focus of initiation communal discipleship.[20] George G. Hunter III, a leading church growth theorist, calls for the recovery of the Celtic style of evangelism that emphasizes conversion through communal participation.[21] Robert Webber and Daniel Benedict seek to recover the ancient catechumenal process for a postmodern culture; Webber understands this as "liturgical evangelism."[22] Richard Peace notes the processive nature of the conversion of the twelve apostles in comparison to the instantaneous nature of Paul's conversion and proposes forms of evangelism through small groups and worship that facilitate the former.[23] These proposals are by no means identical, but they all share with Wesley a commitment to evangelism as entailing a process of initiation as well as proclamation and witness.

There has also been an increasing emphasis on cell groups as integral to evangelism and church growth, frequently with Wesley cited as the historic progenitor. Certainly, cell groups have been a major feature of church growth around the world, sometimes leading to congregations numbering in the tens of thousands. But while there may be much to celebrate about cell group ministry, Wesley's own practice was not as concerned with cell groups themselves as with helping persons adhere to spiritual discipline. The key question Wesley raises for all contemporary practice is whether evangelism leads to participation in the means of grace and to salvation as the restoration of the image of God.

The Means of Grace and Salvation

To underscore the necessity of evangelism's initiating persons into faithful participation in the means of grace, we must examine the believer's growth in the Christian life. We can begin by recalling the role of affections in Wesley's theological anthropology.[24] Abiding affections or holy tempers are dispositions that together constitute the will. Affections make us the persons we are. The affections determine our spiritual and moral character. The Christian life is marked by such holy tempers as love for God and neighbor, faith, hope, humility, joy, peace, and other fruit of the Spirit. In fact, Wesley claims that "true religion, in the very essence of it, is nothing short of *holy tempers*."[25]

Now it is clear that these affections are not abstract qualities. We do not simply "love," but we love God and neighbor; we do not simply "hope," but we hope in God (or hope for God's kingdom). In other words, affections are directed toward particular objects. Unholy affections, such as pride or the love of status or wealth, are directed toward objects other than God; holy tempers are directed toward God. The life that one lives is decisively shaped by the affections that one has. A life centered on love of wealth is quite different from one governed by love of God. The heart, consisting as it does of various affections, determines the shape of the life. A holy life is a product of a holy heart. Yet, to an extent, the reverse is also true: works of mercy and works of piety, when done by those who are seeking God and open to receive grace, are means of grace through which affections are evoked and nurtured.

What is true for the growing Christian is also true for those awakened by evangelistic proclamation or witness. These persons recognize their lives are ruled by unholy affections, and they desire for God to give them holy affections instead. Yet their very seeking, prior to receiving the new birth, has evoked fear of God, together with what Wesley calls the "faith of a servant"[26] and a beginning hope in the gospel promise of forgiveness and new life. They bring this faith of a servant to the means of grace and begin to grow as they expectantly await justification and new birth.

This system of means of grace, spiritual discipline, and weekly meetings makes three important contributions to receiving and growing in the Christian life. The first we have already noted: the discipline linked to accountability in the class meeting enables one to counter dissipation and remain faithful to practicing the means of grace. The second has to do with the object of the affections. It is one thing to love God or hope in God, but it is another to say just who this God is. The means of grace provide an ethos in which we experience the identity of God. I use the word "experience" deliberately, as participation in the means of grace involves the whole person. God is not whoever we think God is, but God is who is actually revealed in the history of Israel and preeminently in Jesus Christ. To prayerfully search the Scriptures, to come to the Eucharist with expectant faith, to pray, or to sing, enables us to experience this distinct and particular God. Thus, participation in the means of grace enables us to grow in the knowledge and love of God, for as we come to know God more fully as the object of our affections, our affections (and our lives) are shaped accordingly.

The third contribution has to do with how we actually live. It is one thing to have hearts increasingly governed by love for God and our neighbor, but another to determine exactly what it means to serve God or love our neighbor in the concrete circumstances of life. Wesley believed that even attaining Christian perfection would not remove our ignorance or other limitations of finite existence. Culture has its shaping influence on our lives, giving us ways of looking at the world that are at variance with the reign of God. The means of grace are continual reminders of what God's reign requires and what God's love entails; through them, the Holy Spirit shapes us in the reality of the new life that

God gives instead of the fallen existence that is passing away. The class meetings provide regular opportunities to discuss what it means to live out this new life in relation to our neighbor. Over time we can increasingly come to see the world as God sees it.

The Witness of Christian Communities

What might be the impact of communities of Christians who actively seek to love God and their neighbor, either to receive new life or to grow in it? We have seen how Wesleyan evangelism necessarily leads to initiation into a formational discipline involving participation in means of grace. Now we can add that this way of life has implications for the practice of evangelism in two ways. First, Christians find they have good news to share. Their lives have been decisively and joyously transformed, and there is every reason to tell others not only what they have received, but that God's promise of new life is for all. Moreover, because they have begun to love their neighbor, they have every motivation to let others know what God offers them in Christ.

The second implication is what persons will find as they encounter such a community. Certainly, they will not find the kingdom of God in its fullness. Nor will they find a people free of suffering or removed from all the difficulties of life. What they will find are persons who believe in the promises of God and who seek to be open to receive the life God gives. They will find people who love and want to grow in love and who seriously desire to learn how to love their neighbor and one another in the world today. Above all, they will find persons growing in their devotion to God, as manifested in their worship and their service to others.

If, as Lesslie Newbigin has said, the "congregation is the hermeneutic of the gospel,"[27] then through meeting such a community, persons will come to know the reality of God's love. It will be a concrete interpretation of what the good news of Jesus Christ can mean in this world and for human lives. Such a community gives the gospel credibility, for it is a sign, as Wesley said, that God is indeed renewing the face of the earth.

PART III

Practicing the Great Commission

CHAPTER 10

Evangelism and the Practice of Hospitality[1]

Joon-Sik Park

I n this essay, I view evangelism in relation to the biblical practice of hospitality. Hospitality is neither equal to evangelism nor simply a means to evangelism; it is a primary context for evangelism, within which an authentic evangelism takes place. Evangelism in the context of hospitality is particularly crucial in the post-Christendom society in which North American and Western European churches find themselves today. In this post-Christian era, the church is no longer in a central position of power and influence, but is rapidly becoming marginal. In his article "Can the West Be Converted?" Lesslie Newbigin writes that our society is a pagan society. Yet "it is far tougher and more resistant to the Gospel than the pre-Christian paganisms," since it is "a paganism born out of the rejection of Christianity."[2] As Douglas Hall aptly describes, "It is a society that has some awareness of the enormous gap between Christian theories and Christian practice and that mistrusts easy declarations of salvation."[3]

Verbal proclamation of the gospel is an essential dimension of evangelism; evangelism is definitely a word event. It is not, however, solely verbal, as demonstrated in Jesus' incarnation, the paradigmatic event of evangelism, in which the Word became flesh. As Niles claims, "The Christian Gospel is the Word become flesh. This is more than and other than the Word become speech."[4] As people hunger for evidence of the life of the gospel, the practice of biblical hospitality compellingly embodies the gospel and makes its witness "credible and inviting."[5] An evangelist is not simply a detached and mechanical communicator. In evangelism, one's whole being is to be involved and shared. In the context of hospitality, the gospel becomes vital and visible.

Hospitality as the Context for Evangelism

When we practice hospitality, we intend to enter into fellowship with those whom we welcome. Evangelism practiced in the context of hospitality is not simply the sharing of our knowledge of the gospel, but of our lives redeemed, transformed, and sustained by the grace of God. When the good news is shared, the lives of the witness and the one invited to Christian faith are also to be shared. In this way, hospitality is more than simply a context for evangelism; it is integral to the gospel. In fact, the whole life of Jesus was that of hospitality, as Pohl suggests: "Jesus gave his life so that persons could be welcomed into the Kingdom."[6] Koenig puts it this way: "When Paul urges the Romans to 'welcome one another . . . [just] as Christ has welcomed you' (15:7), he is revealing something close to the heart of his gospel."[7]

The driving force for evangelism is felicitously described in 1 John 1:1-4, particularly in verse 3: "We declare to you what we have seen and heard so that you also may have fellowship with us; and truly our fellowship is with the Father and with his Son Jesus Christ."[8] Thus, our motivation for evangelism is based, first, upon our own experience of God's invitation to eternal life in Christ, out of our gratitude for God's welcoming of us in Christ to fellowship. Second, our motivation is based upon our desire to invite others into the same welcome of God, into this fellowship, which is not only with God but also with one another. The practice of evangelism in hospitality "both reflects and participates in God's invitation of welcome to all."[9] With this in mind, one of the most important questions in evangelism is whether we are willing to share our lives with others and to share in the lives of others.

In Christian hospitality, the ultimate host is Christ. We, as Christians, invite unbelievers not to the table of our own resources, but to the table of Christ. And to that table "we come as equals."[10] Niles emphasizes that a Christian is merely a guest at Christ's table. "In the Christian's role as evangelist, he or she calls others to come to that table."[11] Again and again, we are pointed to the way mission is described in Luke and Acts as—what Koenig names—"spiritual-material welcoming." Luke carefully seeks to prove "the essential unity between ministries of the word and ministries of the table."[12] A vivid example is found in Luke 15 where Jesus presents three parables that "are a classic description of what evangelism is."[13] These are the parables of the lost sheep, the lost coin, and the lost son. Jesus aptly tells these parables of the lost precisely when he is accused of receiving and associating with tax collectors and sinners and having meals with them: "This fellow welcomes sinners and eats with them" (Luke 15:2). Here is a significant connection between evangelism and the hospitality of shared meals. Evangelism is to be practiced in the context of the welcome table, which is a sign of acceptance, inclusion, and equality.

Seeking to understand evangelism in relation to biblical hospitality, I deem three elements crucial for evangelism to be authentically practiced: evangelism in hospitality as a boundary-crossing practice; the church as the witnessing and hospitable community; and evangelism in hospitality sustained by spirituality.

Evangelism in Hospitality as a Boundary-Crossing Practice

For evangelism done in the context of hospitality, an intentional and genuine effort to cross significant racial, ethnic, and socioeconomic boundaries is an essential and integral part. As Koenig states, "The kingdom breaks in on meals and other occasions of welcoming; or it somehow advances through alliances with strangers."[14] Hospitality to the stranger, particularly to the marginalized, is then both intrinsic to the gospel and crucial to its proclamation.

For the early church, hospitality to needy strangers "became one of the distinguishing marks of the authenticity of the Christian gospel," and "a fundamental expression of the gospel."[15] The very credibility of our witness to the gospel is at risk when our ministry of evangelism fails to cross boundaries, when it is limited to those who are culturally or racially similar to us. The true nature of the gospel is contradicted when our witness becomes selective and does not reach past racial, ethnic, and other boundaries established by society. But evangelism in the context of hospitality recognizes the equal worth of every person and does not accommodate the gospel to discriminations based upon cultural and socioeconomic differences. Thus, the evangelistic practice of hospitality defies prevailing practices of society and can offer a prophetic witness to the prevailing culture.

At the synagogue in Nazareth, Jesus read from Isaiah 61: "The Spirit of the Lord is upon me, because he has anointed me to bring good news to the poor. He has sent me to proclaim release to the captives and recovery of sight to the blind, to let the oppressed go free, to proclaim the year of the Lord's favor" (Luke 4:18-19). Most New Testament scholars agree that, in the brief phrase "to bring good news to the poor," we find Jesus' statement of his primary mission. The question then is, "Who are the poor?"

The term "the poor" should not be deprived of metaphorical meaning, and thus it should not be limited to the spiritually poor or to the economically poor. However, as Tannehill points out, it first of all refers to those economically oppressed and poor.[16] Green extends the meaning of "the poor" to embrace not simply the economically oppressed but also "the excluded, and disadvantaged," all who are on the margins of society and devalued by society.[17] One contribution of liberation theology is the rediscovery of the poor as a hermeneutical focus, which leads to a new understanding of the Christian gospel and to a legitimate attention to the priority of the poor in mission and evangelism. The emphasis of liberation theology upon "the preferential option for the poor" implies not that God is interested only in the salvation of the poor, but that "the poor are the first, though not the only ones, on which God's attention focuses and that, therefore, the church has no choice but to demonstrate solidarity with the poor."[18] It cannot be denied that Jesus particularly demonstrated his solidarity with the poor and made them the principal recipients of the good news. The rediscovery of the poor in theology has had significant implications for mission and evangelism. Considering solidarity with the poor "a central and crucial priority in Christian mission," Bosch argues that "once we recognize the identification of Jesus with the poor, we cannot any longer consider our own relation to the poor as a social ethics question; it is a gospel question."[19]

Korean Protestantism has experienced remarkable church growth for the last thirty years. Recently, however, it has been losing the credibility of the gospel it preaches because it has not been on the side of the poor and marginalized and it has been rather silent in the face of injustices. It has become too rich to hear the cry of the needy and powerless. In the

Korean church, there likely is a strong connection between its experiences of becoming culturally captive and becoming gradually stagnant. If the gospel is to be announced credibly, believers should follow the evangelistic practice of Jesus, paying careful attention to the kind of people with whom he associated throughout his ministry. Then, as Costas stresses, evangelism is "to be undertaken from below . . . from the depth of human suffering, where we find both sinners and victims of sin."[20]

In the book of Acts, the Holy Spirit keeps urging the church to move beyond its boundaries. In fact, in Acts almost every evangelistic endeavor involves the crossing of boundaries. One of the most significant events in Acts is the conversion of Cornelius. It was the first full-blown encounter between a Christian Jew and a Gentile, with significant implications for the future mission and evangelism of the early church. Here the issue is not the legitimacy of a Gentile mission, but how that mission should be carried out in the face of Gentile uncleanness, which prevents Jews' free association with Gentiles.[21] Throughout the whole incident, hospitality becomes and remains a pervasive and thorny issue. Thus, in the subsequent episode, when Peter goes up to Jerusalem, the Jewish Christians criticize him for having gone to uncircumcised people and having eaten with them (Acts 11:2-3). Here "the inclusion of Gentiles and table-fellowship with Gentiles are inseparably related."[22]

It is clear that the Cornelius story is about the social barrier to the Gentile mission. For the Jerusalem church to overcome such a barrier, Peter first has to experience a conversion, learning firsthand that "God shows no partiality" (Acts 10:34). Peter's conversion then leads to the conversion of the church from ethnocentrism to multiculturalism. According to Gaventa, "Indeed, in Luke's account, Peter and company undergo a change that is more wrenching by far than the change experienced by Cornelius."[23]

Unfortunately, the church in the twenty-first century is still faced with the same kind of challenge—to overcome its ethnocentrism and homogeneity and to reach people of different races, cultures, and economic classes. No Christian could possibly deny that God's love is for all, and that God shows no partiality. Yet many Christians and churches still need to have a conversion experience, as Peter and the early church did, so that they can fellowship willingly and joyfully with persons of different cultures and practice mutual hospitality. For the witness of the gospel, we need intentionally to cross many boundaries established by society and to create relationships with those who are different from us.

Any church, which is neither multicultural nor seeks to become so, should carefully examine itself and ask why it has become stuck in a monocultural mode. There is always a danger that the church will pursue "culturally exclusive forms of Christian witness and church formation" that could result in "the pollution of Christian witness with racism, classism, and ethnocentrism."[24] However, evangelism in the context of hospitality invites believers to go beyond their comfort zone to meet and form a community with people who are different from them, challenging the prevailing patterns of homogeneous human relationships in society.

The Church as the Witnessing and Hospitable Community

Second, for evangelism to be carried out in the context of hospitality, what is critically needed is a Christian community that is evangelistic and, at the same time, demonstrates a life of hospitality within itself. Evangelism should be understood not simply as a program of the church, but as integral to its identity and calling. Faithful and effective witnessing to the gospel is based upon the congregation's sense of identity. Only when members of a Christian community understand evangelism or mission in relation to its basic identity, can the biblical sense of evangelism be recovered. In other words, what is required is a radical transformation in its ecclesiology.

Bosch in *Transforming Mission* states, "There is church because there is mission, not vice versa."[25] The church is a missionary community by its very nature and vocation. Hence, mission and evangelism are intrinsic to the very life and calling of the church. The church is called to participate in mission and evangelism not for institutional survival, but for the kind of community it has been created to be. What has to be recovered is "the biblical sense of mission as belonging to the whole disciple community."[26] The evangelistic work should not be considered an individualistic labor only of some who are gifted. It is a ministry committed to the whole people of God; the church as the body has been called to be and live as an evangelizing community.

When the church understands itself as a witnessing community, evangelism cannot be disconnected from the corporate life of the church. This is so because the concrete life of a believing community is an essential expression of the credibility of the gospel to which it bears witness.

The life of the church should not invalidate its witness. Evangelism is practicable and feasible only when there is a community whose life reflects authentic differences from the rest of the world. Thus, John H. Yoder says, "There can be no evangelistic call addressed to a person inviting him or her to enter a new kind of fellowship and learning if there is not such a body of persons."[27] In fact, the very being of the church is a witness. The church as a witnessing community is to live its life as a community of hospitality, a community for which "hospitality is an organizing practice."[28] The authenticity of evangelism is heavily dependent upon the way the believing community lives and practices hospitality.

The community of hospitality, above all, should be inclusive. The question is whether our community of faith has a place for strangers within itself, and whether it is willing to be a home for all. Churches willingly provide various social programs and yet remain unwilling to extend community to people of differences.[29]

There are, however, some churches in the United States that seek to build relationships across racial, cultural, and socioeconomic differences, with their biblical visions of a community. In *We Are the Church Together*, Foster and Brelsford carefully examine the life and ministry of three multicultural congregations in the Atlanta area. Among the distinctive characteristics of these multicultural congregations, two are particularly important. First, there is an emerging ecclesiology different from the one prevailing among homogeneous congregations. The three congregations have endeavored to embrace racial and cultural diversity as integral to their identity as a community of faith, and to draw upon it as a resource for their life and mission. In other words, the "differences have come to be viewed not so much as problems to be overcome but as gifts to be accepted, explored, and affirmed."[30] Second, they bear a sign of the cross. In living against the persistent and dominant practice of cultural and racial homogeneity, both in congregational life and in society, they cannot avoid facing difficulties. They constantly live in ambiguity and uncertainty. The sense of loss is inevitable, since not every one understands their vision and some longtime members have left in search of a more comfortable and familiar congregational setting.

What these churches possess is "a particular sort of faith, . . . a faith without the certainty of uniformity and sameness. It is a faith that does not rely on what is, but lives instead with multiple possibilities and imagines what might be. This is not an easy faith."[31] These three congregations demonstrate a life of vibrancy in the midst of fragility. One of the pastors often refers to a particular vision from Revelation 7:9-10: "There was a great multitude that no one could count, from every nation, from all tribes and peoples and languages, standing before the throne and before the Lamb, robed in white, with palm branches in their hands. They cried out in a loud voice, saying, 'Salvation belongs to our God who is seated on the throne, and to the Lamb!' "

The vision is a constant reminder to the congregation that the church is to bear faithfully the multicultural nature of the kingdom of God.

The call to mission and evangelism is given to the individual Christian and to the whole community of faith; as such, we should respond to the call as individuals and as a community. For the church to be a faithful witnessing community, it has to be a community of hospitality. As Kirk aptly puts it, evangelism "must proceed from a community that believes in evangelism and it must result in people becoming part of a community that knows how to welcome 'strangers' and make them part of its family."[32]

Evangelism in Hospitality Sustained by Spirituality

The practice of evangelism when carried out in the context of hospitality is, in itself, a spiritual experience and, at the same time, needs to be sustained by spiritual disciplines.[33] Evangelism is not about methods or techniques. It is not simply a task of memorizing and reciting salvation prescriptions. The Christian witness is to be born out of the depths of our being; it is to be an encounter at the deepest level. It thus involves our spirituality more than any other ministries of the church. As Escamilla maintains, "The answer to the crisis in evangelism does not lie in innovative programs, or in just trying harder. The nature of crisis is much deeper—it is spiritual!"[34]

In Acts, the Holy Spirit initiates and guides every evangelistic and mission activity. In fact, the main evangelizing actor is the Holy Spirit, "the great mover and driving power" of the evangelistic witness of the church;[35] we participate in evangelism as co-agents with the Spirit. But what has not been given due attention is the fact that spirituality is missional by its very nature: "Spirit and speaking therefore belong together."[36] The Holy Spirit is not simply concerned about our inner spiritual life, but encourages and enables us to speak in witnessing. Guder rightly states, "Witness is an essential form of spirituality: in and through witness to the gospel, the Holy Spirit is experienced as the enabler and encourager."[37]

It is unfortunate that the practice of evangelism has not been considered as one of the essential spiritual disciplines in the Christian church. I believe that evangelism deepens our spirituality and is sustained by it. Particularly when the ministry of evangelism is done in the context of hospitality, it touches us at our deepest being: it compels us to examine our spirituality, our relationship with God. Our spiritual growth is thus directly linked to our participation in the ministry of evangelistic hospitality. Without faithful involvement in evangelism, "we deny ourselves a unique and compelling form of spiritual growth, a unique and compelling sort of communication with God."[38] In other words, evangelism is an intrinsic part of our spiritual journey.

If evangelism is an essential form of spirituality, it needs to be nurtured and cultivated. John Wesley's understanding of God's prevenient grace, as preceding any conscious human responses to God, encourages us to anticipate the active presence and operation of God in every person. God seeks all and takes the initial step in the human experience of divine grace. If God is already present and active in the life of a person whom we invite to the Christian faith, we definitely need spiritual sensitivity to discern such divine presence and activity and to respond accordingly. As witnesses, we are to have a deepened awareness of and sensitivity to the Spirit's presence and work in our spiritual journeys, so we can help others relate to the Spirit's presence and work in their lives. We first need the discipline and practice of speaking *with* God before we speak *of* God. For us to help others begin their relationship with God, we have to be in communion with God. The journey inward through disciplines of prayer, word, and silence nurtures our ability to invite others to the same journey. We need to cultivate and nurture a spirituality that freely and joyfully witnesses.

Welcoming strangers and sustaining our commitment to engage in fellowship with them at the deepest level are long, hard work. Doing evangelism in the context of hospitality is quite demanding and exacting. Such witness requires sustaining strength and perseverance, which can flow only from our daily communion with Christ. Pohl writes, "The demands of hospitality can only be met by persons sustained by a strong life of prayer and times of solitude."[39] Without constant access to spiritual nourishment, human resources will quickly drain. What we need is a spirituality that can sustain our willingness and commitment to carry out the ministry of evangelism in the context of hospitality.

The church should help its members cultivate spiritual resources that enable them to endure and to find sustenance in their work of witnessing. We can draw on powerful resources when "we learn to read scriptures missionally," that is, "to read scriptures from the basic assumption that they are intended to equip the community for mission."[40] The church should be a place where such a missional reading of the Bible takes place, helping the members discover and live the call to be a witness. Our commitment to integral evangelism is to be nourished and deepened by our constant encounter with God. Every day we have to renew our commitment to follow Christ and to be his witnesses in the world. The spirituality of our churches and individual Christians should be missional; at the same time, our spirituality should nurture and sustain the ministry of evangelistic hospitality.

Conclusion

The multicultural congregation I pastored in Cincinnati has been involved in urban ministry in a racially diverse community since the spring of 1998 through a coffee house and basketball ministries. Since the summer of 1999, it has extended the ministry to Over-the-Rhine, the most drug-ridden and crime-ridden area in Cincinnati (where the riot erupted in April 2001, following the police shooting of an unarmed African American teen).[41] Every Saturday afternoon, we met and talked with people on the streets of Over-the-Rhine, seeking to communicate the gospel to them. I never drove to Over-the-Rhine without anxiety or apprehension of meeting and talking with strangers. Often, I went out of obedience rather than out of willingness; yet I always returned full of joy and thankfulness, realizing that I was where Jesus had already been at work.

Walking around the sections of Over-the-Rhine, with trash-riddled lots and boarded-up buildings, we often felt overwhelmed by the depth of brokenness and hopelessness among the people, and by the vicious cycle of poverty and despair. In the face of extreme human suffering, the practices of evangelism and social concern, though distinctive, were so closely interrelated that they could hardly be separated. Talking with strangers on the street corners, and trying to build friendships with them, we discovered that a great number of them had already heard the gospel and many once belonged to the church. The good news was not new to them; rather, it had to be proven good and true. Without genuinely caring about them and seeking to serve them as whole persons, that is, without practicing biblical hospitality, we could not communicate God's redeeming love in Christ with credibility. We needed to share our lives with them and to share in their lives. It was extremely challenging, but there was no other way. We came to realize the essential need of hospitality in the ministry of evangelism.

Practicing hospitality is quite difficult and arduous. It involves one's whole being, not just a part, and demands all we have, not just a portion. It requires "the kind of courage that lives close to our limits, continually pressing against the possible, yet always aware of the incompleteness and the inadequacy of our own responses," and thus deepening "our dependence on, and our awareness of, God's interventions and provision."[42] Since evangelism in hospitality is so demanding, we can carry it out only with the guidance and in the power of the Holy Spirit. We also need a witnessing and hospitable community in which every Christian can be equipped, nurtured, and supported for the self-conscious and intentional witnessing.

Being a witness is at the core of our identity and calling as Christians and as the community of faith; it is not optional. We have to understand it "as defining the entire Christian life, both individually and corporately."[43] In D. T. Niles's words, evangelism is "being a Christian" and "a way of the church's life."[44] Indeed, our motivation for evangelism should be based upon our own experience of God's love for us, and on our realization of the truth that every person is the object of God's love. Without an undeniable personal encounter with Christ and an experience of his grace, one cannot become a witness. Furthermore, without love and the willingness to practice hospitality, our witnessing becomes empty words and vain rituals. It is because evangelism is "a labor of love"[45] and a form of participation in the cross of Jesus that biblical hospitality can thus be seen as an authentic context for evangelism. In a similar context some two thousand years ago, Paul wrote to the Thessalonians: "So deeply do we care for you that we are determined to share with you not only the gospel of God but also our own selves, because you have become very dear to us" (1 Thess. 2:8).

CHAPTER 11

Evangelistic Hospitality in Preaching: Welcoming Everyone to the Story

Rob Weber

The question at hand is how to use media and experiential communication in the local congregation in order to evangelize new generations. In this question there are several elements to be considered. One is the work of evangelization. A second is the focus on new generations (even if not exclusively). A third is the necessity of using media and experiential communication to carry out the task. Implied is the assumption that preaching, as evangelistic communication through words alone, will not suffice, however central and essential it may be. In a new image-rich multimedia world, the art of preaching must be transformed in order to yield the desired results. Later in this essay, I shall provide some examples of how I have experienced and used imagery and experiential communication in effective ways. However, first I must comment on each of the aforementioned three elements. What concept of evangelism is to be employed here? Why are generational differences important? Why is it necessary to use media and experience in combination with verbal proclamation?

What is most important in reaching newer generations, as well as continuing to reach older generations, is the understanding of evangelism as *evangelistic hospitality*. Evangelistic hospitality is a concept of evangelism that involves preparing others to receive grace and creating space in

God's story for those who come. This concept of evangelism will shape our congregational assumptions and structures as well as our methods of communication. Hospitality is an integral component in an effective congregational evangelism program, because no matter how good the marketing piece that brought a person to church—no matter how excellent the music, the facilities, or the sermon—if the congregation is not experienced as a place of welcome and care, a visitor will be unlikely to consider further participation in the community of faith. No matter how impressive the wrapping, the message will appear worthless without the presence of a hospitable community. If people are cold to visitors, or visitors don't understand the practices or the cultural language that is being spoken, then it is highly unlikely that the congregation will be able to reach them for Christ.

Hospitality, however, has much broader meaning than simply making people feel physically welcome. Hospitality, or in particular, evangelistic hospitality, is a larger concept that has to do with creating a space in a congregation's common life that allows the guest or the stranger to feel welcome, to observe, to inquire, and to experience the reality of what we proclaim. Evangelistic hospitality, at one level, is a matter of inviting persons into the congregation and making them feel at home. At a deeper level it means inviting them into the story that is the reason for the congregation's existence. They enter as strangers and guests, but the purpose of the hospitality is not only to treat them nicely so they will want to come back, but also to enable them to participate and take ownership. This is the process of community building.

For the purposes of this essay, we will focus much of our attention on this type of community building through preaching. Preaching has been and will continue to be a fundamental instrument for inviting people into the Christian story. However, preaching must be accommodated to certain realities of the church's social setting. One is that persons in the society are at different degrees of closeness to or remoteness from the Christian experience and its founding and formative story. There are those who are embedded in it quite deeply, those who once knew it to some extent but have become estranged, and those who hardly know it at all but may become interested. Preaching must encourage hospitality for all three, but in different ways. Cutting across these degrees of relationship are generational differences. Developing evangelistic hospitality in preaching means to communicate in such a way as to provide multiple windows through which people from different perspectives can observe the story, as well as multiple doorways through which they can enter and experience the story.

Ezekiel and Congregational Analysis

Ezekiel was living in a situation very similar to ours. He was trained to be a preacher, a minister, a priest in a *temple-centric* community. He was trained to do the ritual, the rites, the feast days, and the high holy days, to change the paraments at the right time, and to be sure the correct responsive reading corresponded to the hymns being sung (I'm mixing time periods and liturgical practices, of course, but you know what I mean). He was trained to do ministry in one particular way. The problem was that things changed. Assyria and Egypt went to war, and the Israelites were cast out of their land. They were sent out into the Babylonian Diaspora, scattered all over the place. The people of God who had been centered in the Temple were scattered, and what made the situation more complex was that while they were scattered, they *were not* enslaved. They were scattered, but they were not downtrodden. They were disconnected from their source of the story, but not rendered uncomfortable. It was in this setting of transition that Ezekiel was forced to discern how to live out his calling.

In the Diaspora there were three primary types of people. There were the ones who had temple-memory as central to their identity. There were other people who vaguely remembered the Temple as the center of the community, but were getting used to living in Diaspora, getting used to living not only in a different place, but also in a different mind-set, a different set of cultural perspectives. Finally, there were some people who had no memory of the temple-centric society. These people lived in Babylon and were comfortable there. They might have been related to people who had experienced the centrality of the Temple, but they had found a new home in Babylon. Ezekiel had all three kinds of people: (1) the temple-centric people, (2) the people who remembered the Temple, but were getting comfortable in Babylon, and (3) the people who were born in Babylon and had no memory of the Temple.

When I look at my congregation, as well as the larger community, I can see those same three types of people. It is not that the church has been picked up and moved somewhere, not that we were deported from our land, but instead that the culture has so changed around us that we, in effect, while remaining stationary, have entered a time of diaspora—a spiritual diaspora. There are people inside the church who have temple-memory. There are people inside the church who are getting much more used to the cultural Babylon surrounding us. Finally, there are those inside and outside the church who have no understanding of what temple community, or Christian community, is all about. The challenge for the preacher as pastor, leader, and evangelist is to discover how to communicate to those different types of people all at once. That was what Ezekiel had to do. He was trained to do one thing, but found that he had to act in a totally different way.

The first church I served after seminary was in a rural community, and the church was modeled on a type of temple-centric understanding. The community got its first traffic light about a year and a half after I left. The people who were in that church were, for the most part, longtime residents of that community. They shared history, background, and experiences. They had the same general perspective and worldview. They knew what church was supposed to be about. They knew what they were supposed to do in church. They knew the basic Bible stories. They knew their responsibilities, and every once in a while someone new would venture in or we would reach out into the community to serve or invite in new people, but the majority of the new people were also *like* the people already in the church.

My next congregation was a very different situation—a diaspora church that included all three audiences. I was given the opportunity to serve as founding pastor for a congregation that was to be situated geographically between areas of affluence and poverty, between commercial and residential developments, in a community that used to be stable (perhaps even static) but, due to changing economic forces and the distribution of employment and educational opportunities, had developed a high level of social mobility. The congregation that was born in this new setting drew people from many different backgrounds and many different social, cultural, educational, and economic situations.

One of the greatest elements of diversity among participants in the life of the congregation is the placement of religious memory in individual worldview. There are some who have long and deep memories of the Christian faith. There are people with a little church background (what some call the "church inoculated"), who went as children to Sunday school and got a little taste of the Bible stories. There are those who rejected church because they had been burned by abusive ministers or toxic members of previous congregations. There are those who felt too intellectual for church because they understood the message of the church to be: "If you are going to be a Christian, you can't use your mind; you can't ask questions." The new congregation is made up of many different kinds of people—people from different generational groups, different backgrounds, people who are coming from all kinds of different addictions and broken places in life. When I look at that congregation, I can see many of the different places from which all these people are coming. I can see the diverse backgrounds. I can see the different worldviews out of which they think, ask questions, and interpret reality.

Learning from Ezekiel's Communication Style

Ours is a context that finds a great deal of similarity with the situation of the prophet Ezekiel: building and maintaining faithful community, communicating with the disenfranchised, and trying to create a new shared language, memory, and direction. From experience, I know that it is an easier task to communicate with a group of people who have a shared understanding of reality. However, times have changed, the makeup of the communities in which Christians are called to share the good news has changed, and so has the task of preaching. The task of evangelistic preaching in the contemporary world is a complex, multidimensional event that takes place in a synergy between church and marketplace. The task of the preacher encompasses simultaneously the elements of pastoral care, leadership, apologetics, and evangelism. In this media-savvy, image-rich world, preaching as the communication of words only will not suffice, despite its ongoing importance. Preaching as evangelistic hospitality must employ multiple images and means of communication and must invite the hearers to become doers through dramatic and effective participation in the proclamation of the Word.

Ezekiel could have chosen to continue to operate as he had been trained. He might have decided that in order to build community in the Diaspora, he was required to maintain the familiar. He might have reasoned, "If we focus on the traditional practices I was taught, people will be stirred to participate." With that approach, most likely he would have drawn the people who were temple-centric. Another possibility would have been to develop a "Babylonian Diaspora seeker service" and gone after one segment of the people in a different way. He would have had to figure out how he was going to choose his target, and develop his communication technique to address that particular segment of the population. Ezekiel, however, was not given those choices by God. God did not say, "I want you to reach one particular segment of this group." God said, in essence, "These are all my people, they are to be called back to me, and here's how you're going to do it."

Picture Ezekiel in the Diaspora setting with those three different types of people. They are far away from the Temple. Their king is living with the Babylonian king in the palace, and people have jobs, so it seems that it is a nice place to be. Then God comes to Ezekiel and says,

> You, O mortal, take a brick and set it before you. On it portray a city, Jerusalem; and put siegeworks against it, and build a siege-wall against it, and cast up a ramp against it; set camps also against it, and plant battering rams against it all around. Then take an iron plate and place it as an iron wall between you and the city; set your face toward it, and let it be in a state of siege, and press the siege against it. This is a sign for the house of Israel. (Ezek. 4:1-3)

It's an interesting set of instructions. Ezekiel, trained to be a priest, is cast out of the Promised Land into an entirely different situation. What is Ezekiel to do in this situation? How is he to communicate in the midst of this diversity? He is asked to take a brick, a soft piece of clay shingle (the soft clay tablets on which Babylonians used to write cuneiform), and draw Jerusalem on it. The Hebrew people did not draw physical pictures. They were word people. They told stories. Then, the artist was to place the tablet on the ground in front of everyone, begin to build warrior models, tiny battering rams, and other siege paraphernalia, and finally arrange them all around the picture on the brick that he had drawn. Next, in front of everybody, he had to lie down on the ground and hold an iron pot in front of his face, turn his face toward the pot, and attack the city with his other hand.

Imagine the reaction of the people on the busy street who were witnesses to this strange display. "What happened to Ezekiel?" "What is he doing? Come here. Look at this!" They all gathered around—the old ones, the young ones, the ones who had no temple memory at all— everybody came to look at this priest gone crazy, having a little war with clay figures and a pot in his face. They gathered and asked, "What are you doing?" Ezekiel responded with something like, "Well, now that I've got your attention, you see, this image represents the setting in which we find ourselves. The pot represents our disobedience in front of the face of God. Even though God would desire to save us from this destruction, our disobedience creates a barrier. This is our common history and our common experience. We have to remember that we have a different future from where we are right now."

Ezekiel had a diverse and scattered "target audience." His "congregation" was made up of the same three audiences. In this context of Diaspora and at the intersection of multiple cultural and spiritual perspectives, Ezekiel as preacher used a new method of communication. Through the multilayered, multileveled communication system that drew upon a variety of different experiences from people in the group, Ezekiel was able to grasp the attention of a vastly diverse group of people and communicate with them the reality of their situation. As they experienced the reality of that shared situation, they began to realize a common memory, a common history, and a common present. They would develop a common foundation from which they could move toward a new vision for tomorrow. Ezekiel's task as communicator in a shattered time was to use whatever means necessary to remind the people who they were, to help them remember the image of God that was in them, and then to develop a shared experience so the people could move into a common future. Ezekiel used media from the surrounding culture, common imagery, the spectacle of a one-man show, and the connecting power of the overarching story of God. His methods, media, and message provided space and places of entry for all of the different audiences, and through imagination, we can envision in the midst of all this the creation of space for diverse hearers—evangelistic hospitality.

In many ways, we face that same situation in our churches. All around us there are people who have some memory of what it means to be Christian, there are others who have participated in that memory all their lives, as well as some who have no memory of what it means to be Christian, and finally, there are some who have extremely negative opinions of that meaning. As was the case with Ezekiel, many of our ministers have been trained for preaching and ministry in one particular setting and have been called to share the gospel in another setting with another kind of group. The good news is that God accomplished God's purposes through Ezekiel with a brick and some army toys, calling the people to repentance and calling the dry bones back to life. If God could do that with a priest, taken out of his element, using strange and different forms of media for communication, then too in our situation can the fragmented places of our society and our lives be drawn back together in the wholeness of Christ. The questions we must ask as we prepare to preach are, "How can I paint a picture? How can I invite people into a shared story? What images or experiences can I use to meet diverse people where they are? How can I draw them to a shared place so that they can enter into the life that God has for them?"

Ways of understanding change in relation to our methods of communication, and our methods of communication have to change along with our ways of knowing. Hanging on the wall in the office of one of my seminary professors was a drawing of a preacher in a pulpit surrounded by the word "words" written in many different ways. The "words" filled all of the space around him as he preached. The understanding of preaching in this picture was one of "wordsmith"—one who shaped words in such a way as to communicate the gospel to the gathered congregation. The art of preaching has much to do with the formation and distribution of words; however, in this era of rich, layered images in electronic media and other forms of communication, the question must be posed: "Is the model in the picture adequate for those in our emerging generations?" Preaching is an art form that has undergone a great deal of transformation in style and delivery across the history of the church, but today's challenge is even greater as the preacher struggles to bring the gospel to light through forms of expression that will cut through overcrowded streams of information and activity and reach the hearts and minds of those who have yet to know Christ.

Communicating to Multitasking Generations

Keeping in mind the idea of evangelistic hospitality in preaching and our call to speak across generational lines, we do well to understand some of the principles of communication that are effective with the generations born into the age of digital communication and imagery. I have firsthand knowledge of the development because my son is a member of this group of young persons, the millennial generation, who were born between 1982 and 1999.[1]

Psalm 145:4 tells us, "One generation shall laud your [God's] works to another, and shall declare your mighty acts." I had one of those transgenerational experiences at a retreat center in the piney woods of central Louisiana. Because my wife and I were involved in the retreat, we brought along our son's video game system, a small TV with VCR, and a table for art supplies. We were going to be teaching and leading all day for two days, and we wanted him to have plenty to do. At the conference center in the corner of the room, we set up his little makeshift technology, arts, and entertainment studio. He also brought his scooter and his inline skates for exercise and adventures outdoors. Yet his behavior demonstrated what is perhaps a characteristic developing in the brain of later generations—he *multitasks*. By that I mean that he can listen to information and learn while he is engaged in another activity—drawing, writing, engaging a character on a video screen, and so on.

If you were to observe him in the corner of that room, he might have appeared to be oblivious to his surroundings and completely absorbed in his immediate activity. But, in fact, the operating system of his brain had multiple windows open at the same time. Even though he was focused on one activity by himself, he was able to comment on everything that was said during the group presentation. Moreover, he was not always absorbed in the technology or entertainment before him; he was also highly relational. After a while, he started trying to initiate conversations. Most people were polite and would stop for a moment, listen to him or tell him a joke, and walk on. One woman, however, stopped, skipped part of the conference, and spent about a half hour with him. She used her watch to time him zooming down to the end of the parking lot and back. She talked to him about different ideas and adventures. When the session was over, he came back in and told me all about it.

At the next break, I put him up on my shoulders, and we walked around the meeting room looking at and discussing pictures of the different disciples. We were remembering some of the stories in the Bible. Then we got to the picture of Jesus sending the people out two by two, and I explained that Jesus was sending them out to share the good news. I thought, *Maybe this is one of those teachable moments, and I can explain to him what ordination is, why all those ministers are here, and why I do what I do.* I explained that the bishop had put his hands on me and sent me out to tell the good news, and the church has done that for a long time ever since Jesus did it. He didn't seem too impressed, so we moved on.

Later that afternoon, we were developing worship services in groups around the room. Each group had been given the same scripture text and a different setting, with instructions to design a worship experience using image and language that would reach the imagined audience. They were practicing "evangelistic hospitality" in communication. One group wanted to use a skit as an element in the service, and they asked Jonathan to participate. When it was time for that group to present, he was attentive and happy to be part of the action. Then, in the evening, we went to the chapel for worship. The woman who had stopped to visit with Jonathan was preaching. In preparation for her message, she had gathered a big box of different items with which to illustrate her sermon. When she talked about an idol, she pulled out something that was an idol from another culture. When she talked about each piece of scripture, she pulled out objects that added an extra dimension to her communication. Toward the end of the message, she picked up a big mallet and told of the Crucifixion. Then she talked about the sacrifice Christ made on our behalf. She simply carried the mallet. She didn't get overly graphic or dramatic with it; she simply carried the big mallet and set it down beside large spikes at the foot of the cross. I looked at my son sitting next to me. He was weeping. "Why did they have to kill him?" he asked. At prayer time we went to the altar rail, kneeling, holding hands, and praying. When we came back to our seats, he sat on my lap as the rest of the congregation continued to come forward to pray. He turned to me and said, "Dad, will you lay your hands on me so I can go out and tell the good news?"

The Principles of Sharing Evangelistic Hospitality

What happened to cause that experience? I believe some principles are important to remember and employ as we strive to preach and communicate in order to reach younger generations. First of all, *he was with people*. Second, *he learned the story* as we remembered the stories of the disciples while looking at the pictures. Then, *he became part of telling the story* as he was in that drama. Because he became part of telling the story, it became more real to him; it was not just something that he had heard or that his father talked about. In other words, as he became part of telling that story, it communicated with him at a different level. Finally, *he experienced evangelistic hospitality in communication* (through one of the people with whom he had spent time earlier in the day).

Here is a boy who is totally image-oriented. His mind, like those of many others in this new digital generation, is image-oriented and used to multiple streams or layers of information. When the preacher that evening lifted up those objects as she spoke, they became part of the communication, a multilayered communication. He found his way into the story she was telling because she communicated in a way that related to his way of hearing. She used a hospitable form of communication that invited him into the story and the experience. In that combination of experiences, he was able to enter—as were we all—a shared sacred space. We walked into that larger story; we lived in it together; and this brought him to the point where he wanted to become one who could share it with others.

If we examine the principles at work in this experience, six categories emerge. Understanding these categories and principles can help us move toward evangelistic hospitality in our preaching and communicate across generations. In brief, the categories involve interaction, familiarity, ownership, invitation, story dwelling, and storytelling.

1. Being with People: Interaction

Whereas the boomer generation was to be reached by presentation-oriented "seeker services," members of the postmodern and millennial generations desire and respond to relationships in a powerful way that boomers do not. Some theorists predicted that the generations reared on technology and Web surfing would be technologically savvy, but relationally distant. To the contrary, my experience indicates that the opposite may be the case. The high-tech culture has not drawn them into isolation and separated them from the need for relationships; instead, it has increased connectivity and the desire for interaction. Churches that will effectively evangelize emerging generations should enhance opportunities for relationships to develop. Having integrity and being real will be important for any leader or communicator who would hope to invite, welcome, and involve emerging generations.

2. Learning the Story: Familiarity

Stories have a universal character to them, and the biblical stories are entry points into the larger story of God in which Christians live. In our culture, we face a serious deficiency of familiarity with the biblical stories. These stories were originally told and retold among those who shared oral traditions. On the contemporary scene Disney and Pixar Studios understand the power of story for capturing the imagination of younger generations, and these movie studios have mastered the art of telling and retelling stories. Children and youths can name the characters of the latest Disney movies, as well as provide a narrative summary of the story line and a definition and analysis of the Pixar characters. Many, I have heard, can also interpret moral and spiritual lessons from these stories on the movie screen. This is not anything negative about Disney or Pixar; on the contrary, it is a call to understand the power of telling and retelling our stories in a way that allows us to learn and to remember what we have learned.

3. Becoming Part of the Story: Ownership

Knowledge is only one dimension of understanding. People can know the details of a particular system of thought or belief, yet remain distant and detached. This sense of intellectual distance leads to compartmentalization, and compartmentalization rarely leads to transformation. The dynamics of knowing change when the knower becomes responsible for sharing in the story. It is no longer something from which a person can remain easily detached, but instead, the person develops a sense of belonging or participatory ownership. Involving people not only in hearing the story, but also in opportunities to engage in and live out the Christian story deepens the ownership and encourages connecting with the rest of the Body. In other words, people begin to take responsibility for belonging to the story.

4. Experiencing Hospitable Communication: Invitation

Invitations are not always verbal. Think of the phrase, "That looks inviting." It implies the reality of a visual "hook" that attracts the attention of the viewer. Preaching that utilizes a layering of objects, images, and experiences offers to the increasingly image-oriented mind, several possible points of entry into the meaning and message. For the image-oriented mind, words alone do not prepare a space of welcome. Images and objects are not to be included in communication for their own sake, but used judiciously, they can provide additional access points for the central message of the gospel. Invitation is an ongoing process of drawing the person more deeply into the message and reality that is offered.

5. Entering Shared Sacred Space: Story Dwelling

Entering shared sacred space occurs when people move beyond the basic observation of a situation or the simple mental perception of a message. It goes beyond that first sense of belonging to the story. It occurs when the recipient becomes an experiential participant in the reality of the story at a deeper level, sharing that reality with others in the gathered community and beyond the walls of the church. At one level, the sacraments are designed as multidimensional, experiential doorways through which participants can enter into a shared sacred space. The same multidimensional passage is offered through the appropriate layering of word, image, and experience. This entering of the story provides a deeper level of ownership than the previous stages in that it is centered in experience. The person now understands the reality of the message on the basis of personal experience rather than from simply an intellectual or interpretive perspective. The person is now a dweller within the Christian story with the whole of his or her life and being.

6. Desiring to Share the Story: Storyteller

This final principle of evangelistic hospitality in communication is really the principle of replication and contagion. As individuals find a welcoming place in the congregation and in the communication of the story of God, and as they begin to experience that story, not as something outside oneself, but as something in which they live and move and have their being, they become natural agents of invitation through their testimony to what they have come to understand and experience.

Reflecting on the previous story about the conference, I have come to realize that no amount of linear communication alone, no amount of text on a page, would have communicated so deeply with my child. The same is true for the majority of the millennial generation, a generation of image-oriented multitaskers, many of whom have not heard the story of Christ. In that experience, the words and music that have been such an important part of telling the story were not jettisoned. The story was not changed to make it more palatable for a new generation. The other participants in the worship experience were also engaged in a variety of ways, many of them familiar, and yet in this process of experience and interaction, we were reminded of the overarching story and that we are story dwellers, dwellers in the story of God. More than that, we were reminded that we are not simply passive recipients of the story but must be active, contagious storytellers.

Creating Contagious Communities of Transformation

When we consider the guest and the stranger, it may be necessary to make the existing methods of communication more accessible to those who would come. The art of communication and leadership for reaching new generations has to do with more than evangelistic proclamation alone; it requires the building of contagious communities of transformation. In this section we will look at two examples that demonstrate some of the practices of interactive, experiential, multimedia communication that build such a community. Some examples have a direct connection to the preaching event; others seem more remote but, if observed closely, will prove to be true to the principle of evangelistic hospitality in communication, as well as instrumental in inviting people into the story and helping them to become contagious storytellers.

1. Asking Questions That Reframe the Story

An important place to begin to develop the contagious community of transformation is the children. In developing experiences for the children in our church (some born into the church culture, others newcomers to the story), we have tried to help them see the larger story of scripture and how their lives find a home there. This means not only helping them see that it is their story, but also helping them to become communicators of that story. We have tried to work on asking questions in such a way as to reframe the story and develop new eyes or new ways of seeing in the children. One attempt at this experiential reframing is the development of the Children's Worship Team.

At the first meeting, each child was to come with a parent or guardian, not for safety, but for interaction. We introduced ourselves and then distributed packets we had assembled in advance. Each child got a disposable camera and a list of tips on how to take pictures—simple things such as, "What you see in the viewfinder is what you will see on the film. This is how to frame a picture." There was another list in the packet as well. It was a series of questions: Where do you see God? Where do you see God's people loving? Where do you see God's people serving? Where do you see the beauty of God's creation? Where do you see God's people giving? They were then charged with the task of going out and answering the questions by taking pictures. They wouldn't be allowed to explain the pictures; instead, they were to become photojournalists reporting on epiphanies. We prayed and dispersed the gaggle of fledgling "God reporters" equipped with new eyes, opened to the presence of God. They were alert and looking for the realities of God's kingdom unfolding in relationship and in the creation around them.

We developed a children's technology center in the church composed of several computers loaded with PowerPoint, KidPix, and a variety of other software programs. Key to the success of the center was the hiring of a part-time children's technology staff person, who helps the children tell the stories using the tools of the digital age. She also helps incorporate a technological dimension into the existing Sunday school curriculum. For the second meeting we gathered the "God reporters" in this center.

Each child was given the CD containing the images he or she had captured and shown how to access them on the computer. Soon the children began pouring out stories about what they had seen and experienced. Their "God reports" were on target. Their God-quest eyes had been activated. They were seeing themselves in the context of the story of God. The director then helped the children understand the basics of PowerPoint—a software program for displaying words and images on a screen. They discussed which pictures to include and selected several of them for use in a presentation about how they see God. In a worship service, the congregation was shown each question the children were asked, followed by the corresponding pictures they had taken. During the presentation, the children were singing. Beyond the immediate experience, on a larger level, people were being trained and encouraged to look with those God-quest eyes when they left that place. They were asking themselves, "Where do I see God's people loving, serving, giving? Where do I see God's touch in creation?" It was an image-based communication. Media can become an extension of our ability to communicate, but using electronic media just for the sake of using electronic media can be counterproductive. We must know why we are using media in order to use it most effectively. There are many elements of media that can make for a rich experience of communicating the gospel.

2. A New Take on an Old Meal

The sacrament of Holy Communion is a powerful and spiritually nourishing experience for Christians, yet it can be confusing and even uncomfortable for those who are not familiar with the life of the church.

The people come from a variety of backgrounds with different experiences of the sacrament, but many do not understand its place in the theology, tradition, or story of the church. In order to develop a shared understanding of this experience and to help orient individuals and community toward God and the reconciling work of God in the world, we began to develop a multilayered experience seasoned with story, image, and evangelistic hospitality.

One Friday evening, we assembled the Children's Worship Team and brought in a church member who enjoys cooking. We asked him to bring a simple bread recipe so that he could lead the children in the process of making bread. It was wonderful to watch them together in the kitchen making bread. The children were covered in flour as they kneaded the dough. While they were mixing and kneading and baking, I was taking video and digital pictures of them. When the bread went into the oven, we gathered around a table, and as the smell of bread filled the area, I told them stories about bread in the Bible: Passover, manna from heaven, the Last Supper. We talked about the meaning of the bread and the cup.

When the bread was ready, I took the children into the worship area to talk with them about Communion: what it means to participate in Communion, what it means to serve Communion, how it is a sacrament, and how it connects to the story of the scripture. Then I asked them if they wanted to help me serve Communion that weekend; they were excited. Some of the other adults who were helping with the children brought some of that fragrant, still warm, fresh bread into the sanctuary, and we served each other. That weekend, as I told the congregation during the sermon what we had done with the Children's Worship Team, we showed some of the video clips[2] and images of the kids mixing, kneading, and baking—with flour all over them. Then the children came up and took the bread they had made, held the cups filled with grape juice, and assisted in serving.

In the sermon, the retelling of the scripture stories, and the images of the children who were doing the baking, the congregation heard the words *this is the Body of Christ broken for you, the Blood of Christ shed for you*. Then they saw these words in the faces of the children, and they tasted in the bread that the children had made and broken. The multilayered images and experiences came together to communicate the truth of the larger story—the story of who we are and whose we are and how that relationship is expressed over time. That congregation will never experience Communion the same way again because they have a shared memory, a shared experience, and a shared story. The layering of information, story, experience, relationship, and participation in the construction of the preaching and worship event created a setting in which we entered into *shared sacred space* and grew to become tellers of the story.[3]

Conclusion

Ezekiel used clay, iron pots, and miniature homemade war paraphernalia to call forth truth in ways deeper than words alone can convey. We, as preachers or as church leaders, have opportunities to share the faith story in deeper, more hospitable, and multilayered ways, much as Jesus did. When he told a parable or a story, he didn't say, "After I read to you from this scroll, I'm going to tell you exactly what this passage means." Instead, Jesus would look at a situation and the people involved, and then offer a story that could give them a window into a larger reality. As people grasped that reality, they were invited to live in it. The stories became pathways—not instructions or "how to" manuals—but pathways to Kingdom living.

We, like the prophet Ezekiel, find ourselves in the middle of a fragmented society with a scattered people. Our task is to draw together the faithful in sacred memory, as well as to introduce those who do not know Christ to the ever-new story of God's creative, redemptive, and sustaining work. In our changing world, like Ezekiel, we are required to tell the story in new ways that provide access at many different levels. To this end, preaching becomes an activity that seeks to practice evangelistic hospitality in communication by using media, experience, relationship, and process. This is not something that can be done in a vacuum or prepared hastily on a Saturday evening. It is a process that requires the involvement of creative and faithful people from a variety of areas of the church body.

Preaching in worship is a primary instrument of evangelistic hospitality. Its aim is to ground the Christian community in the story and to orient the gathered people toward God, calling (inviting) people to be reconciled to God and neighbor and to become agents of God's reconciling work in the world. Keeping in mind the people who already live in and express the story, this preaching will also reach across generations to invite and welcome strangers and receive guests. As evangelistic hospitality, it emphasizes drawing everyone into the story through hearing, seeing, and participating. It enables them to feel at home in witness, service, and community. In order to fulfill that task, the church must assure that the particular practices and the language of the worshipping community and the preacher are comprehensible to those whom they are trying to reach. Otherwise hospitality will be neglected, and evangelism will fail. When we remember to be hospitable, to use those varied means of communication, we facilitate a shared sacred memory for those who are welcomed into the community of the faithful for the first or five-hundred-and-first time. That is evangelistic hospitality, and it is real preaching for all generations.[4]

CHAPTER 12

New Church Development

Bryan Stone

Throughout Christian history and around the world, the birth of new churches has served as one of the most vital and effective forms of evangelism. This is not simply because starting new churches is a useful evangelistic "technique," a clever way to reach individual souls for Christ, but because the salvation that we have been given in Christ and to which Christian evangelism invites persons is, by its very nature, ecclesial. To accept the invitation is to be incorporated into a visible, Spirit-created, forgiven people called the church—the Body of Christ. Another way of saying this is that, in some sense, the church does not really need to create evangelistic strategies; the church is the evangelistic strategy. Certainly, the Christian gospel must be heralded in the world by individuals and received by individuals. But the gospel that Christians herald is forgiveness and formation made possible by transformation into a new world, a new creation, and a new society. Christian evangelism, then, is not primarily individual and then derivatively social. Rather, the church *is* the visible and public witness to the world of God that is now made possible by the Holy Spirit.

All of this means that starting new churches ought to be among the most ordinary of Christian practices, flowing naturally from what it means to be Christian, and at the same time, a practice that is extraordinary and miraculous—indeed, a suprahuman practice insofar as the church is "built" by Christ himself (Matt. 16:18) and given as a gift by the Spirit (1 Cor. 12:12). It is unsurprising, then, that when we begin to talk about the birth of churches, our words often fail us. No wonder we so frequently rely on images and metaphors to guide us. Note, for example, the abundance, if not excess, of metaphoric language in the apostle Paul's descriptions of his efforts at starting new churches:

> I planted, Apollos watered, but God gave the growth. . . . For we are God's servants, working together; you are God's field, God's building. According to the grace of God given to me, like a skilled master builder I laid a foundation, and someone else is building on it. Each builder must choose with care how to build on it. For no one can lay any foundation other than the one that has been laid; that foundation is Jesus Christ. (1 Cor. 3:6-11)

Commentators have frequently noticed Paul's mixing of metaphors in this passage. In fact, to the metaphors of planting and building, we could easily add other biblical metaphors, such as birthing or parenting.[1] Paul even describes himself as "in the pain of childbirth" while Christ is being formed in the church at Galatia (Gal. 4:19).

Metaphors frequently help us envision the nature and mission of the church (for example, "body," "temple," "ark," "city," "nation," "family," a "people"), and metaphors also shape how we construe the relationship of the church to the gospel. Paul's planting metaphor points to the quality of the "seed," the need for adequate soil preparation, and the importance of watering, fertilization, and tending. His building metaphor depicts Christ as the church's "foundation" and Christians as "fellow workers" with God.

But metaphors also help shape, both positively and negatively, how we construe the relationship of Christians to the churches they start. The metaphor of planting or "seeding," for example, can connote a rather remote and extrinsic relationship that might result in an interventionist rather than incarnational evangelization—one in which the gospel is either thrown at the world or forcefully inserted. Moreover, the objectification of other persons or of whole cultures of people as a "harvest" waiting to be reaped, whatever its usefulness in mobilizing evangelistic zeal, may inevitably work against an evangelism that aspires to treat others and their cultures with gospel dignity and respect. The metaphor of birthing, on the other hand, may point to a more organic and symbiotic relationship between those who start churches and the churches that are started.[2] Still, it is not unlikely that one could imagine situations where both metaphors would be helpful. Parenting metaphors are also important in discussions about new church development, and while they might promote paternalistic or maternalistic distortions, they are just as likely to foster the sense of connectedness among Christians that is central to the biblical vision of how the people of God continue through history.

Some discussions of new church development have employed military metaphors, complete with concerns about establishing a "bridgehead," developing "campaigns" for the purpose of "expansion," and acquiring skill in employing the tactics of "power encounters" in the service of "spiritual warfare."[3] Whether such metaphors can be faithful to the message of shalom rather than perpetuating Constantinian assumptions about power and influence is doubtful. Moreover, such metaphors lose the intrinsic relationship of the church to Christian salvation, reducing the church, as I have already noted, to a technique or instrument. So, for example, church growth advocate Peter Wagner has said that "the single most effective evangelistic methodology under heaven is planting new churches."[4] On one level, Wagner's words are true, but when new church development is understood from within an individualistic soteriology in which the church has merely instrumental value as a means to "winning" souls, something important about the gospel has been lost. Stuart Murray, author of *Church Planting*, notes that whereas the church growth movement has been largely fixated on the *number* of churches planted for the purpose of "saturation," "the kinds of churches we plant are more important than the numbers."[5] So, for example, in a culture where churches have become used to accommodating themselves to the preferences, tastes, and felt needs of consumers in order to grow, planting more of these marketing-oriented churches may not be the answer.[6] As Murray argues, "Church planting is *not* just about establishing more churches. It is not even primarily about establishing more churches. . . . Church planting is an opportunity for theological reflection and renewal, for asking radical questions about the nature of the church and its task in contemporary society, and for developing new kinds of churches."[7]

How Do New Churches Get Started?

There is no single best way to start new churches, no guaranteed method that a new church will survive or thrive. Despite the many books and conferences that promote their own "ten steps" to starting new churches, we are dealing here with one of the central mysteries of the faith, that is, the church as the Body of Christ. It is, therefore, an enterprise before which we must stand with humility and awe. The Holy Spirit—not denominational boards and agencies—constitutes the church as Christ's Body. That fact, however, is not to diminish the importance of human beings in the process of church planting, but to insist upon it and to accentuate the significance of church planters who are open to and gifted by the Holy Spirit. What we have learned over time is that the Christians who start new churches are more crucial than the methods they use.

What kinds of Christians start new churches? Without question, they are Christians who have a strong sense of mission, the capacity to envision the ecclesial embodiment of that mission, and the ability to communicate that vision to others in compelling ways. The purpose of starting churches is to serve God's mission in the world. Church planters must be grasped by God's mission and able to imagine their work as serving that mission. This means that new church development can never be an end in itself. Yet if we understand God's mission in the world as the election, calling, and formation of a people who will worship and obey God and, through that worship and obedience, bear witness to God's ways in the world, then there is also a sense in which the birth of churches *is* God's mission in the world. The church is, as John Howard Yoder says, "the new world on the way,"[8] and church planters bear the noble calling of midwife.

The characteristics of an effective church planter are almost impossible to summarize, since a range of abilities, temperaments, and gifts is needed and valuable and no one person can possess them all. As Aubrey Malphurs says, church planting requires those who are visionaries, who can implement a vision for the first time, who can develop a vision further, who can organize and maximize the implementation and development, and who can bring rescue, renewal, and hope when struggles are inevitably faced.[9] This, from the outset, may warrant our thinking seriously about team approaches to new church development. It may also prompt us in thinking about leadership to ask about the particular stage of the new church start since every ministry, as Malphurs notes, has a life cycle.

Charles Ridley's list of thirteen qualities of effective church planters is frequently cited in this regard.[10] Ridley's list was the result of his research among church planters in North America, and it is a list worth consulting and one that continues to be used by a number of assessment instruments and denominational boards today. In addition to what has already been said about the leadership traits of new church planters, the following qualities (some of which are included in Ridley's list) should be highlighted:

1. Strong spiritual formation and an ongoing commitment to spiritual accountability, disciplines, and practices (such as prayer, Sabbath keeping, reading, study, theological reflection). Because church planting is demanding and exhausting, it requires not only passion and commitment, but also balance and nourishment.

2. Imagination and creativity. Starting new churches requires the ability to think outside the box and something of an entrepreneurial spirit or the willingness to risk something new.

3. An ability to call forth the gifts of others and to create in others a sense of ownership of ministry.

4. A keen ability to exegete and analyze a community along with the surrounding culture and, likewise, an ability to contextualize the gospel and the practices of the church within that community in appropriate ways.

5. Flexibility, adaptability, energy, and resilience. Enough cannot be said about the importance of a new church developer's capacity to solve problems and make decisions on the go. Obstacles arise, but a church planter must be steady and know where to locate personal resources that prevent being swallowed whole by frustration.

6. Intrinsic motivation. This quality, mentioned by Ridley and others who have studied church planting, is vital. Most of the responsibilities involved in new church development require a person who can manage time well, does not need to be told what to do, and finds joy in following tasks through to completion, even when no one is around to notice, to care, or to offer reward or accountability.

7. Finally, while they are not character traits, some mention should be made of the need for church planters to be trained and supported. One of the best ways to sustain excellence in new church development is to provide, from the beginning, basic skills in leadership and character formation, administration, contextualization, and interpersonal communication, and of course, an astute ability to think theologically about the nature of the church and its mission in the world.

Organizational Models

Some persons in Christian history have held that "since the true church is invisible, therefore the church we organize cannot be the true church anyway. Thus nothing stands in the way of our organizing it as we please, or more precisely, as good public order demands."[11] But if God's mission is the creation of a visible people who bear witness to God's world in their public, social, material, and economic practices, then questions of organization and structure are as important as questions of mission, vision, and leadership. In fact, they are not two different sets of questions at all. The church, *in se,* is a visible social option in history, a recognizable pattern in the world that can be accepted or rejected. In any discussion of the nature and mission of the church, then, form and content are ultimately inseparable.

Still, there is much about new church organization and structure that admits to variation and is open to experimentation. Churches, like humans, come in all sizes and shapes, each with distinctive contextual features and styles. And while churches are to be organized in such a way as to serve the purposes of God's mission, rather than fashioned in such a way as to accommodate consumer tastes and preferences or to suit denominational structures, cultural patterns and expectations along with denominational polities will always shape the way new churches are started. One of the most important considerations for questions of organization and structure is how we understand the relationship of the proposed new congregation to its community and, in fact, what understanding of community is presupposed. Consideration of several models of new church development—and of their approach to the relationship between congregation and community—can provide helpful insights.

One of the most basic organizational models is the *neighborhood parish,* a church that identifies itself with a specific locality and intends to serve it, frequently even naming itself after the neighborhood. This model is sometimes criticized as being inappropriate for postmodern Western cultures where networks of relationship, interests, and affinities generated by shifting patterns of mobility and communication have shaped our connections with others more so than geographic considerations. Murray notes that since the parish model was developed under the conditions of Christendom, it tends to be more suited for churches operating within a pastoral paradigm when what we need today are churches operating within a missional paradigm.[12] Yet the parish model may still serve missional purposes in neighborhoods where a high degree of geographic community is present—a situation that proves to be the case, for example, in many low-income neighborhoods. A church that hopes to bear embodied witness to God's reign and to be Christ's presence in a neighborhood with severe economic problems would do well to understand itself as a "neighborhood" church from the outset, a church that lives as if its own well-being and the well-being of its immediate neighbors go hand in hand (Jer. 29:7).

A second model for starting a new church is that of the *regional church*, a church that serves a large geographical area, perhaps an entire metropolitan area, a metroplex, or a network of villages, towns, and cities that are within driving distance. Like those living in a neighborhood, the identity of those living within a region will be shaped geographically, but obviously within a much larger territory. The church planter will need to do ample homework on this question, since sometimes people will identify themselves "regionally" in ways different from those who may live just a few miles away from them, depending on factors such as topography, political districts, or location relative to major highways. A city in Connecticut with rail access to New York City, for example, may consider itself part of metropolitan New York in a way unlike that of a nearby city without a rail connection. Commuter patterns have long played a critical role in shaping regional identities. While regional churches will share the same sorts of questions with other churches about worship style, ministry priorities, building location, and visibility, those questions may take different forms.

A third model is that of the *network church*, a church that emphasizes relationships and commonalities rather than geography, even if geographic considerations still play some role. These churches often draw people from miles around because of their appeal to a shared ethnicity, age, denominational affiliation, or even sexual orientation. Or they may draw people from within a single neighborhood, though not for geographic reasons, but because they study at the same school or live in the same retirement home.

While the appeal to relational networks or affinities may be effective at achieving a new church start and at producing growth (and so, on one level, may "work"), there are significant theological questions to be asked about any model that puts a premium on homogeneity rather than heterogeneity, especially when one considers the heterogeneous vision of the church recorded in Revelation 7:9: "After this I looked, and there was a great multitude that no one could count, from every nation, from all tribes and peoples and languages, standing before the throne and before the Lamb, robed in white, with palm branches in their hands." A defining feature of the church, proclaimed in baptism, is the reconciliation of diverse peoples into a new social creation, the Body of Christ. In fact, if Paul is right, a central feature of the witness of the church to an unbelieving world is its visible inclusiveness in Christ where distinctions like social status, gender, or ethnicity, while nonetheless present, have ceased to be determinative (Gal. 3:28).

One must also ask whether this model will tend to lead to a cultural or nominal Christianity where one *belongs* simply because of one's ethnicity or age rather than discipleship. Of course, this question must be asked of the parish or regional models as well, for cultural Christianity has proven to be just as easily incubated, if not more so, within models where belonging is premised on geographic rather than other relational affinities. Here I find Stuart Murray's discussion of the homogenous unit principle (HUP) promoted by church growth advocates to be especially useful for any new church planter. This principle is expressed in Donald McGavran's claim that people like to become Christians without crossing racial, linguistic, or class barriers,[13] and that, therefore, our attempts to reach people for Christ should not require that they cross such barriers, at least at first.

Murray claims that this principle is frequently misunderstood by critics and by supporters and that this misunderstanding derives from "confusion between the use of the HUP as *one component* in a mission strategy and the planting of homogenous churches."[14] In fact, any church that ministers in such a way as to target a specific population, whether that is offering support groups for those with addictions, a Bible study for single mothers, or a high school youth group, is employing the homogeneous unit principle. Thus employed, this principle need not lead to homogeneous churches. And yet, as Murray warns, "network churches do tend to be homogeneous, and so their development is viewed with suspicion."[15] Of course, it is also the case that other churches likewise tend to be homogeneous, and in fact, the creation of new network churches around ethnic or cultural affinities can enable the church to break through to unreached peoples (e.g., ethnic groups or age groups) that existing homogenous churches seem either unprepared or unwilling to reach. The network church, then, provides at least one answer to the question of how we can break free from the homogeneity of existing churches, even if it does so by using homogeneity as a strategy. One of the strongest arguments against the network church, however, is that "the development of more and more churches that simply mirror the divisions in society is not only questionable as a sustainable mission strategy, but is objectionable as a perversion of the gospel."[16]

Cell churches are a fourth model of new church development. These groups of anywhere from eight to thirty members (depending on which model is being discussed) meet weekly for worship, instruction, discipleship, ministry, and pastoral care, and may be united to one another through a common denominational or organizational structure or for regular, though not necessarily weekly, gatherings centered on celebration and common projects. Though cell churches have a limited but growing exposure in North America,[17] they are also exemplified in the grassroots associations that have come to be known as "base communities" in Latin America.

Cell churches insist strongly on their difference from cell groups created by more traditional churches for ministry, discipleship, spiritual formation, or outreach. A traditional church might organize itself into several cell groups. Cell churches, on the other hand, consider their individual cells *to be* churches. They emphasize relationality, community, sharing, and lay leadership rather than hierarchy, programs, and buildings. James O'Halloran refers to these "small Christian communities" as comprised of members who "share the same faith in Jesus the Savior" and who "relate deeply to one another and fit into a community vision of the Church."[18] He stresses that the catholicity, or universality, of a church is derived not from its size or geographic spread but, as it grows and matures, from its possession of "the characteristics of the universal Church, namely, faith, love, worship, mission, prophecy (concern for justice), service, animation/coordination and communion with pastors." Thus, "even a local small Christian community is universal in nature."[19]

Cell churches, then, even though they are small, are no *less* church nor are they merely a *fragment* of the church. On the contrary, their grassroots and more fully inculturated practices of sharing, formation, service, and community building embody features of Christian *ecclesia* that frequently go missing in large churches. In fact, one could even say that the family unit itself is a cell church and, thus, what John Paul II has repeatedly referred to as the "domestic church."[20] Cell churches, accordingly, are neither additional ministries nor evangelistic programs of a church nor are they seeking to grow into "real" churches. They *are* real churches in their own right. Cell churches may also be distinguished from house churches that, when they grow, become larger house churches. Rather, "when cells grow, they multiply into more groups."[21] Cell churches challenge those philosophies of church growth that tend to think in terms of size and expansion rather than reproduction and multiplication. Their supporters would argue that, even though it is the nature of the church to "grow," that does not mean it is the nature of the church to "grow large." Perhaps that is why cell churches are frequently called "metachurches" rather than "megachurches."

The question of church size and church growth requires closer consideration at this point, for it turns out to be an extraordinarily important issue for new church developers. Not only are there concerns about the size to which a congregation should aspire to grow and which would mark a probable level of self-sustainability, but also, as the case of cell churches suggests, it is worth asking whether the church can be the church if it does not foster worship and formation on a personal level. Perhaps there is something intrinsic about the very nature of the church that leads it to reproduce itself so that, as Roger Ellis and Roger Mitchell claim, "if a church exists which never thinks about reproducing itself . . . never expects or anticipates that this is the natural business of growing up, then it is actually sterile."[22] In that case, the church's reproduction is not a marvel, but intrinsic to what it means to be the church. And yet, enamored with size, churches that have exceeded the limits of their own space rarely think of planting or of multiplying. Among the most seductive assumptions facing new church planters is still the simple but ubiquitous identification of evangelistic effectiveness with the quantitative growth of the church. In mainline and evangelical churches the persistence of this identification is staggering. Larger churches are still presumed to have more successfully reached the world with the Christian message and more faithfully embodied the gospel of Jesus, while smaller churches, consequently, are presumed not to have done so well.

Walt Kallestad, pastor of one of the fastest-growing Lutheran congregations in the United States, argues explicitly for this identification:

> The basic conviction of most evangelical Christians is that the New Testament presumes the growth of the church. In the Gospels and in Acts, we see that Jesus and the early church want the church to grow, to reach the entire world with the news that Christ is risen and that Jesus is Lord. The claim that three thousand persons were baptized at Pentecost speaks more forcefully about the power of the Spirit to transform lives than if only three had been baptized.[23]

The logic here is beguiling, but ultimately perverse. Though Kallestad's argument contains an element of truth and is undoubtedly offered out of the best intentions, it relies on a very worldly way of construing what counts as power—"more is better" and "bigger is better"—and thus runs counter to the values Jesus associated with the reign of God. In fact, if we follow the strict logic of the argument, we must inevitably conclude that the Holy Spirit was not as powerful at Pentecost as it could have been (so, for example, if six thousand persons had been baptized, that would have been a more "forceful" example of the Holy Spirit's power; if only ten thousand persons had been baptized, then we would know that we *really* serve a powerful Spirit). Once we adopt this logic, we will even need to conclude that Jesus' evangelism was not as powerful as that of the apostles at Pentecost. After all, Jesus was able to gather around him only a dozen or so committed followers, maybe even up seventy. In fact, when we measure him by worldly standards of success, we must finally conclude that Jesus was an abysmal failure.

Jesus' life and teaching stand in contradiction to this quantitative standard for measuring power, success, and effectiveness in starting new churches. And though we believe that the Holy Spirit was powerfully at work at Pentecost, it is not the size, but the character of the early Christian community that speaks "forcefully about the power of the Spirit." What is truly remarkable in the Pentecost story is the way lines of race, gender, and ethnicity were crossed so that "every nation under heaven" was able to hear the gospel in its own language (Acts 2:5-11) and the Spirit was poured out on men and women alike (2:18). What is remarkable is that those who believed "had all things in common" and began selling their "possessions and goods" and distributing "the proceeds to all, as any had need" (2:44-45). What is remarkable is that not one of them considered his or her belongings to be private property, but "everything they owned was held in common" and "there was not a needy person among them" (4:32-34). Whether there are twelve people or twelve hundred people, it is the embodied witness to the subversive values of God's reign that makes the church the church, and it is this witness to which new churches should aspire and by which they should measure their success.

A fifth model of new church development is that of *seeker-sensitive* or seeker-targeted congregations, of which the most frequently mentioned example is Willow Creek Community Church located in the suburbs of Chicago, Illinois. This is not the place to launch a full investigation or close analysis of this important ecclesial movement.[24] What should be mentioned here, however, is the relevance of such churches as a model for starting new churches and especially their mission to be "a church for the unchurched." Seeker-sensitive congregations are passionately concerned about understanding and building relationships with people outside the church. They make it a point to know, understand, and reach them in creative and contextually appropriate ways. Seeker-targeted churches emphasize quality programming, effective preaching, user-friendly worship, and a welcoming atmosphere for guests. They avoid a "churchy" ethos whether in appearance, jargon, or music. In essence, they try to be sensitive to what will likely engage their target audience and just as sensitive to what will likely be a turnoff—so much so, that they frequently receive criticism for being overly oriented toward a marketing paradigm with the net result that people are treated as consumers and the gospel as a commodity.

The challenge to such churches is to find ways to escape from a consumer mentality once they have so thoroughly bought into it. As Philip Kenneson and James Street, authors of *Selling Out the Church*, suggest, "if you treat people like customers, they will act like customers. Or the flip side: When people come [to church] expecting to be treated like customers, you will likely benefit if you so treat them."[25] In a marketing orientation, the "strangeness" of the church is perceived as the problem; therefore, new church development strategies revolve around how to get rid of this strangeness. But one may certainly ask whether Christianity is not inherently an invitation to be "strange." Seeker churches challenge us to make sure we locate the scandal of the gospel in the gospel itself, not in a stained-glass culture that has grown up around it.

A sixth model of new church development could be called the *community center* or social ministry model. This model is especially effective in the urban context where there is likely to be a high concentration of social and economic need and where the very nature of the gospel demands a holistic approach to new church development that incorporates a range of ministries including economic development, low-income housing, job training, education, and community-based health care. While community center churches frequently carry out many of these ministries directly from within the congregational structure itself and may even employ a small group structure for spiritual formation and social ministry, many such churches have taken the additional step (often from the very outset) of creating alongside the congregation a separate nonprofit corporation to administer and manage these forms of social outreach with the more public sets of controls and accountability that come with that designation. A nonprofit corporation or, as it is sometimes called, a public charity can also be a helpful vehicle for securing outside funding for its projects from foundations, corporations, nonprofit organizations such as the United Way, and the various levels of municipal, county, state, and federal governments.

The perennial question in this model is how the new church can keep all these ministries from consuming the church itself, its worship, community life, spiritual practices and disciplines, and evangelism. At its best, and with a holistic vision, all of this can be kept together and viewed integrally as "church." But it is also possible, especially where a separate nonprofit corporation has been created, to lose sight of this unity, and for the congregation to awaken one day only to find itself dwarfed by and alienated from the social ministries that once embodied their witness to the surrounding community.

Procedural Models

The foregoing list of organizational models is in no way intended to be exhaustive of the possibilities for what a new church might look like (other models such as house churches or multicongregational churches would also warrant an examination). But perhaps these few examples may have sparked the reader's imagination about what is possible. Just as important as organizational models, however, are models that focus more on procedure, method, and leadership. How does one actually go about starting a new church, what is the driving motivation, and who does the starting?

One of the standard and historically proven approaches to new church development relies on a single pastor or a planting team that is sent to a targeted location, usually based on demographic study indicating either the likely success of or the need for a church there, and typically equipped with an initial budget (or a one- to three-year commitment) raised by the sending denomination, congregation, or evangelistic organization or agency. Though a good argument can be made for providing ample financial resources so that, in the initial stage of development, leaders can devote themselves wholly to the new start, church planters are often bivocational, not only to conserve finances, but also to avoid the insulation of the church's leadership from the world outside the church and the failure to develop a culture of shared ministry by an over-reliance on ordained professionals. There is, of course, a long history of bivocational new church development that goes back to Paul and his fellow tentmakers, Priscilla and Aquila (Acts 18:1-6). Likewise, it is important to remember that not all new churches need to be started by clergy. Some of the most effective church planters are lay pastors or lay "coordinators" or "animators."

Much has been written about the advantages of starting a church with a team. This team could be a married couple or a group of individuals or families with complementary abilities and gifts. David Shenk and Ervin Stutzman, in *Creating Communities of the Kingdom*, list several compelling arguments in favor of a team approach to church planting, including:

1. To begin with a team is already to begin with a church, however small;
2. To begin with a team is to have the opportunity to embody cross-cultural diversity and reconciliation from the outset;
3. To begin with a team is to provide the possibility of modeling shared power from the outset;
4. To begin with a team is to bring together a community of co-laborers for mutual assistance and support (no less than 38 persons are mentioned by Paul in his letters as co-workers in new church development);
5. To begin with a team is, through synergy, to create a whole that is greater than the sum of the parts;
6. To begin with a team is to provide mutual support, encouragement, and accountability, all of which are essential in any congregational development project.[26]

At the end of the day, of course, the more important question is not whether church planting leadership is present in the form of an individual or a team, but what type of leadership is present. Lone planters with vision, creativity, evangelistic gifts, contextualization skills, and the ability to lead by consensus and to evoke the gifts of others will likely prove far more effective than a team of bickering individuals who are visibly poor models of Christian sharing, love, simplicity, and forgiveness.

Parenting Approach

An exciting approach to new church development follows on the decision by a "mother" congregation to birth a "daughter" congregation. The excitement of this approach lies in the way it gives Christians a palpable way to extend and multiply their ministries to others through the creation of something new, somewhat like the excitement of giving birth to a child. It may afford new leadership opportunities and provide a way of developing unused and undiscovered gifts and talents. Indeed, it can even prove to be a vehicle for stimulating renewal in the planting congregation itself. At the same time, there are also possibilities for harm to the parent church through a "loss of vision, inertia, feelings of bereavement, disappointment with the new church, strained relationships, and financial pressures."[27]

Typically, a new church is parented by beginning with a group of members from within the parenting church (usually, anywhere from five to thirty) who are selected and commissioned to serve as the "core group" for the new congregation, whether as a long-term commitment or "on loan" for a more finite term of perhaps one or two years. Most church planters will testify to the importance of establishing a core group of committed, mission-minded, discipled Christians early on, whether the project takes a parenting approach or not. The core group functions as an essential leadership team and provides a spiritual base to the new church project through worship, service, disciplines of accountability, and practices of spiritual formation. Some church planting approaches even advocate the formation of a large core group (fifty to one hundred) through discipleship programs before officially launching the church. The formation of an initial core group may prove to be one of the wisest uses of time for a church planter in the long run.

One clear advantage of beginning a new church by parenting, of course, is that the project begins with a core group, thereby reducing the risk of failure. Not only will the planting congregation have provided financial resources, but also that most precious of resources, leadership. It is often the case that the new church will be planted in an area where some church members already live, so there is a natural geographic connection that makes it easier to begin initial gatherings for worship, study, or prayer. A danger inherent in parenting models (over and above the feelings of loss, dilution of vision and energy, and financial pressures previously mentioned) is the temptation to model the daughter church after the mother church, thereby hampering the creativity that every new generation of churches brings with it, stifling the process whereby the new church forms its own vision, and forfeiting the important tasks of contextualization—for example, by mimicking size dynamics in the new church that are appropriate only to a larger church.

Similar to the parenting approach is "satellite church planting" or "second campus planting" in which the groups sent out from the church do not function as fully autonomous churches. The location of the satellite congregation may be in a home, a rented space, or an apartment building's community room, and the worship may be led by laity or by rotating members of the church staff. Satellite churches may eventually be organized apart from the parent church, but that is not necessarily their purpose.

The "Lazarus" Approach

When a congregation is dead or dying, but still has a few committed believers or resources in the form of property or endowments, one approach is to close down the church—in effect, to let it die—with the purpose of starting a new church at a later date with new leadership, a new core group, and the resources of the old church through conversion of the endowment and sale of the building. Some keys to the success of a Lazarus church are a full change of leadership, a new name, and a complete break with the past, including the location and building. A trickier consideration here can be what to do with any remaining members from the old church, since what is needed is a new vision for a new church with new leadership. There is nothing wrong with a few of the existing members getting on board with this and becoming part of something new, but a Lazarus church cannot be resurrected if it is not allowed to die fully; that is, if some of the prior members want to carry forward pieces of the past or their old leadership roles and worship styles into the new venture. Obviously, the sort of transition required by a Lazarus project is radical and should be taken only with the most careful forethought and precaution and only with the wisest and most sensitive leadership. Churches (including the names of those churches and everything about their buildings) almost always embody multiple generations of a people's hopes and dreams. To allow the old to die in order to make way for something new is a delicate undertaking, to say the least.

What About Buildings?

Nowhere in the New Testament is the word "church" ever used of a building. Jesus relativizes considerations of form and structure in worship—or, better, he "reorients" those considerations—when he says to the Samaritan woman that the worship of God is not tied to this or that sacred place, but must be performed "in spirit and truth" (John 4:24). And yet the worship, life, and ministry of the church take place within an unavoidable physicality, sociality, and temporality that bear witness to gospel priorities and allegiances. However much worship is to be carried out "in spirit and truth," thereby rejecting every "morphological fundamentalism,"[28] it is nonetheless a physical act that occurs in space and time, with the use of artifacts, as our bodies, minds, habits, and awareness of time are scripted into the pattern of Christ. Moreover, inherent in the very meaning of "church" is the idea of a people who have gathered to worship God together, and gathering implies a place of meeting. Although the church is not a building, but a people, an event, a body, this people is nonetheless "gathered" in space and time as a people who "meet" God while "meeting" together. Then, too, any church that is serious about ministry to the world must take seriously how it will do this physically, geographically, contextually, that is to say, incarnationally.

All this does not mean that church planting is about the building of new church buildings; far from it. Some of the most creative and sustainable approaches to new church development do not require new buildings at all, but meet in houses or rented halls, share space with other churches, or gather in the open air as in the case of Common Cathedral, a church for the homeless that meets every Sunday afternoon in Boston's historic Commons. Whatever physical or temporal restrictions we must take seriously in starting new churches, the most severe limits (though usually self-imposed) are those of our imagination. As a rule, then, mission should determine the use of buildings rather than the reverse in new church development. Buildings should be used or built with a vision of how they embody and make possible the mission of the church and with a critical awareness of how they inevitably "build" us, often in ways that dilute our mission, turn us inward, distort our focus, drain our finances, consume our energy, make us prideful, and tempt us toward idolatry. As one who has planted a church with a wide array of social ministries in a low-income neighborhood, I can testify to the extreme importance of buildings as a way the church is able to "be the church" in its community. But it is worth asking whether our witness can be stymied by reinforcing outside perceptions that Christians spend too much money on themselves and on their buildings.

The church is an event, a gathering of people, but it is a material and visible event in space and time. Better, perhaps, than thinking about what sorts of facilities are necessary to begin a church, we would do well to think of how the event called church would transform any space and time into ecclesial space and time. This requires a work of the imagination, first and foremost. It does not mean, however, that every place and time can be transformed into Christian space and time without either a radical, and impractical, alteration of the space and time or a radical, and theologically unacceptable, alteration of the Christian story. Extravagant buildings, for example, can communicate the very opposite of the Christian story, not to mention the financial burden they impose, even for those who are quite willing to shoulder that burden. But just because persons are willing or able to pay for extravagant new church buildings does not mean they should be built. Again, form should follow mission.

Do We Really Need More Churches?

Whether we really need more churches in a land where it sometimes seems there are churches on every street corner is a final question worth asking. Indeed, a major argument against the starting of new churches is that our primary strategy, energy, and effort should go toward the renewal of existing churches. Given the tremendous amount of energy, time, and finances required in starting new churches, why should we focus on starting something new if we already have property, history, and leadership in place?

Any attempt to answer this question must first insist that we do, indeed, need to give passionate attention to efforts at revitalization of existing churches, not only so that we avoid the needless re-creation and duplication of administrative, financial, and leadership structures that the planting of new churches would require, but also for the sake of the health of those very congregations. And yet, as a number of church planting experts have argued, the administrative, financial, and leadership structures in some congregations are precisely the problems rather than resources potentially overlooked or needlessly duplicated. White elephant church buildings with no parking and a dilapidated infrastructure, especially in aging urban areas, can be more of a deficit than a benefit in reaching a community, as can a church's long history of intransigent leadership and fortress relations with its neighbors. Though a new church may have to reinvent some wheels, they may very well be wheels that need reinventing. Perhaps most important, starting new congregations is a way to reach entirely new groups of people that present congregations, however healthy, are not presently reaching and are unlikely to reach. In other words, the argument for starting new churches is not premised on the inadequacies of present churches. For that reason, a new church development strategy should always be paired with a church revitalization strategy. In fact, to both of these we might add the importance of a church "closing" strategy. The death of an existing congregation may be painful, but there is no reason to expect congregations to live forever, and in fact, there may very well be life cycles to congregations that require their termination at some point. Those churches that are not able to die well or to be reborn or resurrected will inevitably fail to be the church.

As I hope this essay has shown, new church development raises numerous ecclesiological and missiological questions. Any effort at starting new churches implies an answer to the question, What is the nature of the church, and what is its mission in the world? Or what is its role in God's mission? The theological premise that has guided this discussion is that it is through the calling and formation of a people that God accomplishes God's mission in the world. The church, therefore, is not a missional afterthought or an evangelistic gimmick or technique; it is what God desires. Today, there is a growing and appropriate interest in churches coming to understand themselves as intrinsically missional, and this is the type of church that needs to be planted in order for the church to bear faithful witness to the reign of God in the world.

For Further Reading

Conn, Harvie M., ed. *Planting and Growing Urban Churches: From Dream to Reality*. Grand Rapids: Baker Book House, 1997.

Malphurs, Aubrey. *Planting Growing Churches for the 21st Century*. Second ed. Grand Rapids: Baker Book House, 1998.

Murray, Stuart. *Church Planting: Laying Foundations*. Carlisle, UK: Paternoster Press, 1998.

O'Halloran, James. *Signs of Hope: Developing Small Christian Communities*. Maryknoll, N.Y.: Orbis, 1991.

Shenk, David W., and Ervin R. Stutzman. *Creating Communities of the Kingdom: New Testament Models of Church Planting*. Scottdale, Pa.: Herald Press, 1988.

CHAPTER 13

Faithful Discipleship: A Conjoined Catechesis of Truth and Love

Dean G. Blevins

Introduction

Attempts to articulate the relationship between the ecclesial disciplines of mission and discipleship, evangelism and education, often appear strained. Descriptions of the relationship resemble a Texas two-step, struggling to find the lead partner. In some settings, evangelism is portrayed as the key concern, with education in the supporting role. At other times, education is seen as the primary need with missional concerns ignored. Nevertheless, for Methodists, education remains a primary concern in the midst of evangelistic endeavors worldwide.[1]

Without a doubt, Methodism has enjoyed a long relationship with education, whether in congregational contexts, in formal settings such as higher education, or through denominational commitments.[2] Why does the Wesleyan tradition value Christian education so highly? One obvious source lies in the educational passion of the Wesleys, particularly John's efforts. However, these concerns are most succinctly, and poetically, stated by brother Charles in his often-lauded lyric, "Unite the pair so long disjoin'd, / Knowledge and vital Piety."[3] This phrase is located within a stanza that elaborates fully the necessity of faithful discipleship:

Unite the pair so long disjoin'd,
Knowledge and vital Piety:
Learning and Holiness combined,
And Truth and Love, let all men see,
In those who up to Thee we give,
Thine, wholey thine, to die and live.[4]

Knowledge, Learning, and Truth conjoined with Piety, Holiness, and Love are portrayed, through the baptismal/Eucharistic imagery of dying and living, as existing in total dedication to God. Charles Wesley hereby captures the passion of the Wesleys' concerns for educational preparation as part of the total transformation of a person. The lyrics suggest a form of ongoing, dynamic catechesis—a "way" of discipleship reminiscent of early Christian formation that ultimately situates all educational efforts as forms of faithful discipleship resulting in Christlikeness. Methodism today should embrace the same form of discipleship if we are to remain faithful to our heritage and, more important, acknowledge the transformational vision that leads this tradition into a global future.

To understand the nature of this form of faithful discipleship, one might begin by seeing the comprehensive range of John's educational ministry through the rubrics set forth by Charles. Identifying John Wesley's educational methods, goal, and content assists our understanding of his contribution to today's mission/discipleship discourse.[5] John has been characterized as "a theologian, a theorist, and a pragmatist,"[6] and theorists interpreting Wesley's educational writings and practices reflect the same diversity.[7] Nevertheless, Wesley's endeavors reveal a form of Christian education best understood as mediating grace for the sake of holiness of heart and life. The result is a form of faithful catechesis designed to engender sacramental expressions of Christlikeness in the lives of believers.

Knowledge and Vital Piety: Wesley's Pedagogical Assumptions

John Wesley's educational ministry was comprehensive, if not uniform. Wesley addressed the educational needs of children and adults, seeking social empowerment and personal transformation in the lives of the Methodists. His multiple efforts appear more like a patchwork quilt than a seamless educational strategy, though collectively they have been portrayed as his ecology of total transformation.[8] Certainly, his sources and strategies appear eclectic, at times, and even questionable to con-temporary readers, as in the rearing of children. In light of this disso-nance, what knowledge or what set of philosophical assumptions guided Wesley?

Several philosophers may have influenced Wesley's view of education, including William Law, John Locke, John Milton, and John Amos Comenius.[9] Locke's influence is most often noted, particularly his empiricism.[10] Both Locke and Wesley emphasized childhood education as a form of formation "by precept and practice."[11] However, to what degree each philosopher determined Wesley's understanding appears sub-ject to conjecture and dispute.[12] Historian John English, for instance, believes John Norris, a Cambridge Neoplatonist, contributed to Wesley's understanding of spiritual senses and knowledge more than did Locke.[13] Reliance upon educational philosophies alone appears insufficient, par-ticularly since Wesley's concept of "knowledge" lies beyond strictly cog-nitive categories and included the education of the affections.[14] Ultimately, Wesley drew from theological and sacramental sources in defining his educational theory.

A better source for Wesley's educational efforts might be found in the conjoined emphasis of "vital piety," particularly piety formed through the means of grace. Wesley's definition of the means of grace, developed in Henry Knight's essay above, identifies a number of "outward signs, words, or actions," that God ordains as "*ordinary* channels" conveying "prevent-ing, justifying, or sanctifying grace."[15] Among the various practices, none more defines the means of grace than the Eucharist, which Wesley includes as a crucially important means anchored in God's initiating grace coupled to the responsive faith of the participant. Wesley did not believe that the Eucharist, or any means of grace, could confer grace "*ex opere operato*, 'by the work itself.'"[16] Wesley believed that participation required "a mind well-instructed, a sound belief and a heart well-inclined" for the sacrament to be efficacious.[17] Knowledge was to be con-joined with practice for the sake of efficacy. Whether drawing upon the traditional means of grace, such as prayer or scripture reading or other "prudential" (i.e., "wise") practices, each faithful action can convey grace.

Based on this definition, Wesley could easily use multiple educational approaches to engender grace within the lives of Methodists. Educational practices could be means of grace with the intended purpose of commu-nicating saving knowledge.[18] Christian education involves "mediating grace," a sacramental approach whereby knowledge obtained through learning shapes and mediates God's grace, whether in convicting one of one's sinfulness, awakening one to the possibilities of grace, or expanding the spiritual senses to the fullness of God's salvation.[19]

Education and Holiness: Strategies and Purpose

For all the possibilities of mediating grace, Wesley did intend a particular outcome. To reach his goal, Wesley was willing to educate children and adults through a number of educational strategies. The overall purpose for these various activities included the total transformation of Methodists into holiness of heart and life.

The Education of Children

Wesley was deeply interested in the spiritual welfare of children. His advice on child rearing and his work with schooling children were influenced by his childhood.[20] John's writings and practices concerning both child rearing and formal childhood education, however, can prove disconcerting to many contemporary educators.

1. *Wesley on Child Rearing.* Wesley's child-rearing practices indicate he was a disciplinarian who believed in bending or breaking the wills of children to make them pliable to their parents and educators and, therefore, to God. In his sermon "On the Education of Children," Wesley writes, "A wise parent . . . should begin to break their will the first moment it appears. In the whole art of Christian education there is nothing more important than this. The will of the parent is to a little child in the place of the will of God."[21] Wesley includes this observation in a list of practices that parents are to engage, in order to correct the natural "diseases" apparent in children: atheism, self-will, pride, love of the world, anger, dishonesty, and being unjust and unmerciful.[22]

Wesley built upon William Law's *Serious Call to a Devout Life*, attempting to restore the rational nature of persons through their training and helping students "begin their lives in the spirit of Christianity, in such abstinence, humility, sobriety, and devotion as Christianity requires."[23] Wesley believed forming Christian character in children entails both a radical submission of the child's will and a rational instruction in the Christian virtues. Yet Wesley's understanding of child rearing actually began earlier, with his mother, Susanna, a strict disciplinarian in her own home.[24] John explicitly acknowledged his mother's influence, reprinting her letter in his journal and using a select portion in his sermon "On Obedience to Parents."[25] Life in the Wesley household, however, was not totally oppressive. Susanna's writings reveal that each child was given special attention daily and that there was a real concern for the child's religious state.[26] Samuel Wesley influenced his sons through his devotion to scholarship and through his Anglican sensibilities.[27] John's childhood offered a strong blend of Puritan devotion and Anglican sacramentality and churchmanship, all of which influenced Wesley's educational practice.[28]

An anthropological understanding that children were, "by nature," willful and inclined toward self-sovereignty undergirded Wesley's child-rearing position. This view was informed theologically by a rather strong view of sin in the early life of children. However, the need to break the will of the child need not be the same as destroying the initiative and personality of the child; Susanna's own children offer an example, where submission did not destroy capabilities.[29] Wesley offered a more charitable view of child rearing in his sermon "On Family Religion."[30] Wesley admonished parents that children are "immortal spirits whom God hath for a time entrusted to your care, that you may train them up in all holiness, and fit them for the enjoyment of God in eternity."[31] Parents are to restrain children, yet use correction (physical punishment) only as a last resort. Children are also to receive instruction the first hour of the day, frequently and plainly.[32] Wesley acknowledged that his message is challenging:

> It is undoubtedly true that if you are steadily determined to walk in this path; to endeavour by every possible means that you and your house may thus serve the Lord; that every member of your family may worship him, not only in form, but in spirit, and in truth; you will have need to use all the grace, all the courage, all the wisdom which God has given you.[33]

For all of the perceived harshness of Wesley's intent, these words communicate an educational passion and an assurance of God's abiding grace, courage, and wisdom in the process.

2. *Formal Childhood Education.* Wesley also had distinctive views on formal education in childhood. His formal education, in his childhood and in his college years, reveals its importance yet also leaves some questions concerning consistency. Susanna required six hours of formal

education even for young children.[34] Wesley later attended the well-known grammar school Charterhouse, which probably influenced his view of education, but little is known of his formal schooling during this time and few conclusions can be drawn from this period.[35]

Wesley initially entered into the education of children in Georgia, where he catechized children under his parish care.[36] Even in this early period, Wesley provided education and support for the poor children of the colonies.[37] He gave his full support to Kingswood School (initiated originally by George Whitefield) as a response to the needs of poor colliers' children in a hamlet located just outside the seaport of Bristol.[38] The school went through a number of transitions, beginning in 1738, culminating with Wesley's leading the way for construction of the permanent boarding site, "New House," in 1748.[39] The residents at Kingswood ranged from poor collier children to Methodist children from various locations, Methodist ministers' children, and any others who would accept Wesley's standards.[40]

Rules for the school were strict, including early rising (4:00 a.m.), regular public worship, education, prayer, and a fixed regimen of work, as well as planned meals and regular codes of conduct (including no play).[41] The school actually had a stormy existence, both in funding and in leadership.[42] After colleges at Oxford University rejected several Kingswood graduates, the school established an additional four-year academic regimen for an advanced degree.[43] Wesley also initiated a Charity School in 1739 at the Foundry in London where the class schedule was equally arduous.[44] The school at the Foundry included not only the daily instruction of poor children but also a weekly meeting between teachers and parents to connect the activities of home and school.[45] In addition John wrote and edited a large amount of literature to support his educational efforts with families and in formal settings. Wesley wrote at least ten tracts including *Lessons for Children, Instructions for Children,* and *Tokens for Children.*[46] In his preface to *Instructions,* Wesley reveals his desire that education penetrate to the level of the child's understanding:

> Above all let them not read or say one line without understanding or minding what they say. Try them over and over again; stop short, almost in every sentence; ask them, "What was it you said last? Read it again: what do you mean by that?" So that, if it be possible, they may pass by nothing, till it has taken some hold upon them. By this means they will learn to *think* as they learn to *read;* they will grow wiser and better every day.[47]

Wesley desired that children truly comprehend material and respond with appropriate behavior to strict guidelines. Wesley also wrote or edited the curriculum at Kingswood School along with a collection of abridged books known as *A Christian Library*, recommended to Methodist ministers for reading.[48]

Wesley's interest in the education of children went beyond formal settings.[49] As early as June 28, 1746, he began to publish a number of childhood conversion stories from children as young as two and a half years of age.[50] Wesley was an advocate of the emerging Sunday school movement, supporting the efforts through visitations and writings.[51] Wesley also required all Methodist ministers to be involved in encouraging family devotion and in the training and care of children.[52] This interest may have related directly to Wesley's early experiences in Georgia and his interest in the religious experiences of children.[53]

Wesley and Adult Discipleship

Wesley's educational ministry was directed toward adults as well as children. His approach included individual attention through spiritual direction and more corporate practices via group gatherings and codes of conduct. Wesley encouraged discipleship (and consequently adult literacy) through a large number of publications. A connection can be seen between his personal pursuits, including his formal education, and his selection of discipleship methods. Wesley's interest in adult discipleship began with his entry into adulthood during his college years. Although Wesley was celebrated as an Oxford don, the quality of his advanced education is often shrouded with a poor performance early in his career.[54] Oxford was in the middle of a hundred-year educational slump, which influenced the quality of student and the quality of teaching.[55] Oxford, nevertheless, was also a place where Wesley experimented with "practical divinity" and developed an appreciation for a wide range of devotional reading, spiritual direction, and group guidance from his days as a teaching Fellow at Lincoln College to his ministry in other settings.[56]

1. *Personal Spiritual Direction.* Wesley's interest in individual spiritual guidance probably found expression through two primary activities: pastoral visitations and letter writing. A number of devotional resources influenced Wesley during his early years at Oxford.[57] He seems to have read and discussed various texts with others, including young ladies like Sally Kirkham.[58] John's efforts continued via letter writing in 1730 with

Mary Pendarves and Ann Granville. This method, called "a correspondence course in the methods of Christian Living," included a daily schedule and reading texts for academic growth and devotion.[59] As his journals reflect, Wesley also conducted pastoral visits to discuss people's religious condition. Letter writing was reserved primarily for devout women who were new converts, probably for the sake of propriety, and Wesley continued this form of direction, as well as pastoral visitation, throughout his life.[60]

2. *The Methodist Societies.* Wesley's efforts in organizing and directing the various groups within Methodism are well known. The emphases of Wesley's groups were spiritual renewal, mutual accountability, mutual responsibility, and Christian practice in the world.[61] He was personally involved with such groups during his early adulthood and later synthesized small group strategies from Anglican religious societies and Moravian communities to create the Methodist class meetings and band gatherings.

Wesley became involved with the famed Oxford Holy Club in 1729, which was actually comprised of several groups.[62] In some ways, the club was an extension of Anglican religious societies formed fifty years earlier.[63] Wesley's reading of Monsieur de Renty's small groups and his initial contact with Moravian missionaries also influenced his missionary formation of societies in Savannah, Georgia, from 1736 to 1737.[64] The first formal "Methodist" society began in 1739 in Bristol when John built the first preaching house or "New Room" to accommodate two smaller societies already deeply influenced by George Whitefield and Wesley, organized around rules established earlier for the Fetter Lane community.[65] However, this was not the first (or last) Methodist community.[66] Wesley also started the Foundry Society in December of 1739 and, during the next three years, was able to articulate the basic structure of the various bands and societies, which ensured the success of the societies.[67] Early class meetings, begun in 1742 as a strategy to relieve debt, blossomed into spiritual gatherings as persons participated in prayer, hymn singing, and mutual accountability.[68] Ultimately, these groups became so successful that Wesley incorporated them at the Foundry; they also expanded to be a major influence in the entire Methodist movement throughout the eighteenth century.[69]

The Christian Conference provided different levels of fellowship and accountability based upon the particular needs of the individual.[70] The groups were designed to transform people at various stages of the

Christian life. Strong leadership was advocated for the larger groups (such as the society and class meetings) to maintain control and to protect members from callous judgment and interrogation.[71] Leaders were developed from the laity, both men and women. In 1742, the Foundry Society reported that women led forty-seven of their sixty-six classes.[72] Wesley made sure that leaders were supervised and trained; they could also be transferred as needed in case of problems or larger needs in the society.[73] Wesley wanted competent leadership in order to ensure that the needs of each group were met. The societies became locations for empowering men and women, providing new opportunities to demonstrate leadership beyond their usual status in life.[74] After Wesley's death, the group structure within Methodist societies began to decline. A number of religious and cultural factors contributed to the decline including the broad popularity of Sunday school, a theological emphasis on immediate religious experience, and a reliance on untrained laity.[75]

Wesley may have provided another form of "education" (or socialization) through the various Methodist practices. Methodism challenged the local popular pastimes of the lower class (drinking, hurling, wrestling, bullbaiting, and cockfighting as well as certain feasts, festivals, and fairs).[76] Wesley noted how new faith often ended the practices in local communities like Cornwall, which could be destructive to local inhabitants or others. Wesley writes, "They who had been eminent for hurling, fighting, drinking, and all manner of wickedness, continued eminent for sobriety, piety, and all manner of goodness."[77] The strong moralistic code of Methodism, better known as Methodist discipline, left little room for such distractions.[78] David Hempton notes, "Serious Methodists could be recognized by their dress, hairstyles and physical detachment from the world of revelry, sports and dancing."[79] While general characteristics are often fraught with limitation and were open to caricature by Wesley's contemporaries, it would be fair to claim that Wesley intended Methodists to adopt rather strict lifestyles, often opposing the "popular cultural" characteristics of many in the English social system.[80] In total Wesley hoped to create an alternative way of life replete with positive practices (society gatherings) and restrictions that modeled a thoroughly Christian perspective in English culture.[81]

3. *Wesley's Publications.* Wesley's writings and editorial abridgments provided spiritual resources, practical guidelines for living, and opportunities for literacy practice for the Methodist people. His insistence on competent leadership included his desire for a literate constituency.

Wesley published a number of written materials, including his sermons, his journals, and many tracts.[82] Wesley often edited his journals so that they could be economically purchased and easily read by the lower classes within Methodism.[83] Indeed, Methodist societies can be seen as centers of education, empowering individuals by creating a community where mutual discussion could occur over texts like those in *A Christian Library*.[84]

Wesley also sought to provide reading materials to the poor. In 1782, he issued a broadsheet, *A Plan of the Society Instituted in 1782, to Distribute Religious Tracts among the Poor*.[85] The tract acknowledges that poor people might not take time to read the Bible, but might read a small tract designed to engage their attention.[86] This same rationale engendered a number of Wesley's publications. Ultimately, Wesley's publishing concerns resulted in the creation of a central distributing office known as the Book Room. The range of publications distributed by the Book Room varied in topic and in cost, and the writings included everything from daily etiquette to medicine to religious instruction.[87] In all, Wesley provided a large source of reading materials for adult Methodists.

Holiness of Heart and Life

With such a large array of activities it is important to keep in mind the goal of Wesley's educational activities. Wesley's conjoined use of holiness, particularly "holiness of heart and life," might best characterize the "tenor" of his theology of the Christian life and the essence of Methodism.[88] It is a phrase that he used repeatedly in sermons and other writings.[89] One taxonomy from Wesley's writings describes what is significant for his theology: (1) sin and repentance (i.e., self knowledge), (2) justification and pardon (i.e., assurance) and (3) holiness of heart and life—the final term Wesley considered a comprehensive term for salvation.[90] Holiness of heart and life characterizes an inner disposition of the heart (reminiscent of conversion) and an outward conduct of life (including moral and ethical behavior).[91]

The term "holiness of heart and life" provides a goal for Wesley's educational purposes. This transformative goal relates to his theological convictions for Methodism concerning personal salvation and the transformation of the world.[92] Wesley's efforts to transform Methodism (and, indirectly, the world through Methodism) provide an expanded view of the mission of the church. Discipleship then conjoins with mission in a view of transformation that is broader than many contemporary expressions, indicating that personal transformation is linked to communal and even cosmic renewal from God's perspective.[93] Wesley's view for the long haul more adequately captures the need for the total transformation of the person and the community. This view actually hearkens to an older view of discipleship reminiscent of the early church.

Truth and Love: The Christological Purpose of Wesley's Activities

Wesley's educational practices integrated devotion and discipline, practicality and holiness. The entire educational project was sacramental and soteriological, focused on the transformation of the total person in holiness of heart and life. If knowledge and vital piety reveal a sacramental method, and education and holiness reveal a purpose or goal, what constitutes the "content" that informs Wesley's educational desire? Perhaps the conjoined phrase, "truth and love," expresses this content, best represented in the exemplar of Jesus Christ.

Wesley, commenting on "truth" in 2 John 1:2-4, notes, "For the truth's sake, which abideth in us—As a living principle of faith and holiness."[94] Wesley often associates "truth" with the total soteriological activity of God, and with our ongoing walk by the power of God's Spirit. He continues, "This is the very foretaste of heaven itself, where it is perfected."[95] Wesley considers faith and truth as synonymous (2 John 1:3), yet truth for Wesley also includes the objective reality of Jesus Christ and Christ's gospel (Eph. 4:20-21).[96] Echoes can be heard of the Pauline vision of the total church, "speaking the truth in love" and growing into the very likeness of Christ (Eph. 4: 12b-16). As Wesley says, "To that maturity of age and spiritual stature wherein we shall be filled with Christ, so that he will be all in all."[97] Truth (in Christ) and perfect love become conjoined phrases for Wesley's vision of structured discipleship leading to a transformed life.

Wesley's comprehensive yet focused educational ministries, for all of their diversity, resemble early Christian practices to ground new converts in the "way" of Jesus Christ. Such a comprehensive focus on Christlikeness is reminiscent of early manuals of discipleship, like the *Didache*, which called for the transformation of the whole person.[98] In many ways, Wesley did not diverge that dramatically from his early efforts as a catechist in Georgia and a mentor in Oxford. Instead, Wesley expanded his vision to embrace any practices that would mediate grace and guide Methodists in the "truth" of Jesus Christ in order to manifest perfect love in their lives. Wesley often referred to the "mind of Christ" as part of the process of sanctification. His trinitarian perspective associated following Christ with our renewal in the image of God, concomitant terms for the process of sanctification.[99] On the Methodist emphasis of Christian perfection Wesley writes:

> Look at it again; survey it on every side, and that with the closest attention. In one view, it is purity of intention, dedicating all the life to God. It is the giving God all our heart; it is one desire and design ruling all our tempers. It is the devoting, not a part, but all our soul, body, and substance to God. In another view, it is all the mind which was in Christ, enabling us to walk as Christ walked. It is the circumcision of the heart from all filthiness, all inward as well as outward pollution. It is a renewal of the heart in the whole image of God, the full likeness of Him that created it. In yet another, it is the loving God with all our heart, and our neighbour as ourselves. Now, take it in which of these views you please, (for there is no material difference,) and this is the whole and sole perfection, as a train of writings prove to a demonstration, which I have believed and taught for these forty years, from the year 1725 to the year 1765.[100]

The range of biblical metaphors reveals the depth of the associations between Christian perfection and a particular way of living as Christ had lived. Wesley always understood sanctification within a triune vision of grace, "the grace of our Lord Jesus Christ which is the love of God manifest in the *koinonia* of the Holy Spirit."[101] Yet, as Richard Heitzenrater notes, "'Having the mind of Christ and walking as He walked' (see Phil. 2:5; 1 John 2:6) was one of Wesley's continuing descriptive explanations of Christian perfection."[102]

Holiness of heart and life is anchored in the objective reality of Christ's sacrificial act and actualized by the same "spirit of Christ." Wesley writes, "They to whom the righteousness of Christ is imputed are made righteous by the spirit of Christ, are renewed in the image of God 'after the likeness wherein they were created, in righteousness and true holiness.' "[103] Although not a common term for Wesley, "Christlikeness" can define the source and the practice of discipleship, as well as its goal of perfect love. Truth and love conjoin under this framework to remind Wesleyans that holiness does have a structure and "love" does have content, both found in Christ.

Conclusion

Faithful discipleship for Methodism demands a way of life that is totally transformative. This form of "walk" or way, associated with Jesus Christ, describes the comprehensive efforts of Wesley in his educational endeavors. The "truth" in Jesus Christ is deeply linked to the "love" manifested for God and neighbor (2 John 1:3). This comprehensive "way" included a number of educational strategies at every age level, all for the sake of holiness of heart and life. Each educational practice carries the potential of mediating grace sacramentally, but only as each practice is framed in the "knowing" participation of the person.

For Wesley, like the early church, this is catechesis in its fullest understanding.[104] John Westerhoff notes that this form of catechesis combines the efforts of *kerygma* and *didache*, proclamation and illumination.[105] Westerhoff continues: "Catechesis involves all those actions within a community of faith that enhance and enliven faith, that make divine revelation known, and that aid persons and the community in realizing their vocation."[106] This vision seems to correspond to Wesley's emphases mentioned above, as well as to Methodism's pervasive interest in education in the midst of ongoing mission.

Following Charles's stanza, the conjoined desire of discipleship concludes with the sacramental "means" for holiness and a cruciform "way" of life lived in Jesus Christ. "Dying and rising" imagery is often associated with Christ's oblation in the sacrament of the Eucharist, as well as our participation in the Body of Christ in baptism (and resulting transformation as new creations in Christ). Such imagery frames what Wesley understands as "faithful" discipleship. John Wesley appears to summarize this desire of "dying and living" in one of his written prayers for the family:

"My Lord and my God," I know that unless I am planted together with thee in the likeness of thy death, I cannot in the likeness of thy resurrection. O strengthen me, that by "denying myself and taking up my cross daily," I may crucify the old man, and utterly destroy the whole body of sin. Give me grace to "mortify all my members which are upon earth," all my works and affections which are according to corrupt nature. Let me be dead unto sin, unto every transgression of thy law, which is holy, merciful, and perfect. Let me be dead unto the world, and all that is in the world, "the desire of the flesh, the desire of the eye, and the pride of life." Let me be dead unto pleasure, so far as it tendeth not to thee and to those pleasures which are at thy right hand for evermore. Let me be dead unto my own will, and alive only unto thine. I am not my own; thou hast "bought me with a price," with the price of thine own blood. And thou didst therefore die for all, "that we should not henceforth live unto ourselves, but unto Him that died for us." Arm thou me with this mind; circumcise my heart, and make me a new creature. Let me no longer live to the desires of men, but to the will of God. Let thy Holy Spirit enable me to say with thy blessed Apostle, "I am crucified with Christ: Nevertheless I live; yet not I, but Christ liveth in me."[107]

For Wesley, any prayer for "vital piety, holiness and love," shaped by a way of life enriched and informed by "knowledge, education, and truth" includes the desire of dying and rising. For Methodists, education has often involved an element of sacrifice as well. Sacrifice when providing education as a part of mission, sacrifice in confronting obstacles to our learning and teaching, sacrifice in accepting that full salvation is found in the long haul of transformed living as persons and as communities. For the future of Methodism, this sacrificial perspective may well overcome the battle over who gets to lead in our Texas two-step. The Lord of the dance will hold together our mutual desire for education and mission. The result will be faithful discipleship, a conjoined catechesis shaped in truth and love; one that embodies the full reality Wesley intended, a transformed creation.

Suggestions for Further Study

Hels, Sharon J., ed. *Methodism and Education: From Roots to Fulfillment.* Nashville: General Board of Higher Education and Ministry, The United Methodist Church, 2000.

Henderson, D. Michael. *John Wesley's Class Meeting: A Model for Making Disciples.* Nappanee, Ind.: Evangel Publishing, 1997.

Matthaei, Sondra Higgins. *Making Disciples: Faith Formation in the Wesleyan Tradition.* Nashville: Abingdon Press, 2000.

Price, Elizabeth Box, and Charles R. Foster, eds. *By What Authority: A Conversation on Teaching Among United Methodists.* Nashville: Abingdon Press, 1991.

Watson, David Lowes. *Covenant Discipleship: Christian Formation through Mutual Accountability.* Nashville: Discipleship Resources, 1991.

Chapter 14

Sanctified Singing: The Role of Hymnody in Shaping Wesleyan Evangelism, 1735–1915

Candy Gunther Brown

Scholars of Methodism have long recognized the importance of the doctrine of entire sanctification to Wesleyan traditions. Yet the role of hymnody in shaping Methodist worship and spirituality has received relatively scant attention, despite the close connection between sanctification and hymnody. In this essay, I argue that the hymnody tradition initiated by John and Charles Wesley has historically played a critical role in integrating the pursuit of sanctification and Methodist worship practices. Through analyzing Methodist hymnal production and organization, the practices of hymn singing, reading, memorization, and composition, and individual hymn texts, I demonstrate how eighteenth- and nineteenth-century Methodists used hymns to embody the Wesleyan doctrine of entire sanctification.[1]

Hymns can be defined as poems sung or read in worship of God that are, in most instances, remarkably nonspecific as to time, place, or circumstance of composition. Unlike temporal narratives such as those found in novels, memoirs, or periodicals in which a sequence of events produces a different situation at the end than at the beginning, hymns articulate atemporal narrative structures that merge separate events into an overall explanatory pattern. Early Methodists used hymns to rehearse a universalizing framework that sanctified everyday life experiences as significant within a larger story of God's redemptive purposes for the world. In the language of the literary scholar Brian Stock, hymns offered "procedural knowledge," a script that taught singers how to connect theology with their own attitudes and behavior. Writing, reading, and singing hymns extended the reach of Christian community to embrace every event when people used hymns, on Sundays and weekdays, at church and at home, in all moments and places of experience. By repeatedly performing hymn narratives, Methodists reenacted the story of divine redemption and intensified that story's authority to infuse the world with sacred influences.[2]

During the religious revivals of the mid-eighteenth century, John and Charles Wesley wrote thousands of hymns for use in Methodist meetings. The Wesleys strove to promote not only religious conversion, but also growth in grace throughout the Christian life cycle. According to John Wesley, God's perfect love could so fill Christians that they ceased to commit intentionally sinful acts. Christians might receive entire sanctification in an instant by mere faith, but gradual growth continued before and after; individuals could also lose the blessing through willful neglect. Wesley urged Christians to pursue sanctification earnestly by employing means of grace such as worship. Following the Wesleys' example, eighteenth- and nineteenth-century Methodists used hymns during Sunday church services, at class and band meetings, in private devotions and family worship, and at camp meetings, love feasts, revivals, and gospel-song services; children memorized hymns before they could read, and the aged recited hymns on their deathbeds.[3]

John Wesley initiated the Methodist practice of publishing hymnals for the purpose of directing congregational worship toward systematic growth in holiness. Wesley published his first hymn book, a nondenominational *Collection of Psalms and Hymns*, in 1736–37, while traveling in Georgia. Of the seventy hymns included in the volume, the Calvinist Isaac Watts wrote more than a third, and John or Charles Wesley wrote or translated the remainder. Wesley organized his *Collection* into three sections: hymns for Sundays, Wednesdays or Fridays, and Saturdays. The Sunday hymns focused on praise; the Wednesday or Friday hymns on humiliation, repentance, and prayer; and the Saturday hymns on adoration of God as Creator of the universe. Each day's hymns commemorated a different stage in the Christian journey toward holiness: encompassing creation, sin, redemption, and worship.[4]

As Methodism developed into fuller institutional dimension, hymnal publication continued to play an important role in regulating congregational worship. The Wesleys' *Pocket Hymn-Book*, published in 1781, circulated widely in England and America. In 1808, the pioneering Bishop Francis Asbury oversaw the publication of the first American Methodist collection: *A Selection of Hymns from Various Authors: Designed as a Supplement to the Methodist Pocket Hymn-Book*. When lay Methodists began to issue their own, unofficial Methodist collections, such as *The Wesleyan Harp* (1834), the General Conference in 1836 prohibited the use of such books during Sunday worship services. The preface to the 1836 Hymn-Book urged, moreover: "We must, therefore, earnestly entreat you, if you have any respect for the authority of the Conference, or of us, or any regard for the prosperity of the Church of which you are members and friends, to purchase no Hymnbooks but what are published by our own Agents, and signed with the names of your Bishops." The African Methodist Episcopal hymnal of 1837, cued by the General Conference's precaution, included an almost identical plea. Church leaders early recognized the importance of hymnody to unifying Methodist worship practices.[5]

Nineteenth-century Methodist editors, following Wesley's lead, organized their hymnals in such a way as to promote growth in holiness, by systematically addressing every doctrine of the church and each stage of Christian pilgrimage. *The Hymnal of the Methodist Episcopal Church* for 1878 began with hymns marking the daily and weekly cycles of "Morning" and "Evening" devotions and "Sabbath" worship. The book proceeded through the doctrines of "God," "Christ," the "Holy Spirit," the "Scriptures," the "Sinner," the "Christian," the "Church," and "Time" and "Eternity." Organizational headings taught singers to interpret even unpleasant or banal life experiences such as "Trial" and "Suffering" as contributing to the spiritual phases of "Justification," "Regeneration," "Adoption," "Consecration," "Entire Sanctification," and "Christian Growth." The preface to *The Methodist Hymn Book* for 1883 explicitly framed the volume as a means to help Christian pilgrims find their "way to heaven by these songs." The language of pilgrimage conveyed an expectation that Methodists would find the hymns useful throughout the salvation process: in entering the path to salvation at the moment of conversion, and then as an aid to traveling through "every stage of progress in the divine life."[6]

Although concern for entire sanctification arguably diminished within Methodism by the end of the nineteenth century, pushing many church adherents to new holiness denominations, hymnody functioned to conserve church doctrines and practices over time. Because denominational hymnals cost anywhere from forty cents to six dollars per copy, the General Conference felt reluctant to revise its official hymnbook more frequently than once in sixteen years. Even when committees met to revise this collection, they resisted making substantial changes in the contents. The 1878 committee affirmed that "every excellent hymn must be retained, and that no good hymn should be ejected except to make room for a better." As multiple generations selected from a relatively stable core of hymn texts, they reaffirmed traditional Wesleyan theology.[7]

Nineteenth-century congregations combined eighteenth-century hymn classics with new compositions, adapted to changing worship tastes and social contexts. The editors of unofficial hymn collections, such as *The Golden Harp* (1857), applied the timeless narrative of Christian pilgrimage to the world of nineteenth-century America by coupling almost fifty eighteenth-century British hymns with more than twice as many new camp-meeting songs and choruses.[8] "The Gospel Steamer" affirmed "Yes, We'll land on Canaan's Shore; / Oh, He'll land us on the shore; / Yes, We'll land on Canaan sure, / And be safe forever more." The repetitive diction, rhyme, narrative structure, and heavenward focus of such hymns reflected the timeless theme of Christian pilgrimage adapted to vernacular camp-meeting traditions.[9]

The desire of congregations to express their worship through song exceeded the bounds of published hymn collections. The Methodist minister S. W. Christophers, writing in 1874, regretted the "oral rhyme" tradition that had "always been afloat among Methodists."[10] Alongside the singing of Wesley's hymns, "now and then some zealous, though uncultured, brother or sister has been known to start up under rhyming inspiration and set all like-minded fellow worshippers a singing at the poet's dictation. Many a ditty never submitted to an 'editor' has become more popular in its oral form than it would have been as shut up in print."[11] Christophers had little regard for the poetic quality of improvised ditties popular among Methodist congregations, yet he acknowledged the power of the oral song tradition to stimulate fervent worship.

Coupled with official and unofficial congregational worship practices, private devotional use of hymns furthered the sanctification process. Used at the beginning of devotions, hymns "banish[ed] intruding worldly thoughts, and lift[ed] the soul out of its dull round of earthly care," composing the mind for "communion with God."[12] Hymns sharply distinguished between the profane and the sacred worlds, transporting the reader from one to the other, regardless of physical location. At the same time, hymns integrated every "earthly care" into a sacred framework: "ten minutes spent each day in reading the hymnbook . . . [purportedly] spread a blessed influence over all the hours and engagements of the day."[13] Hymns played an important role in the spiritual practices of individuals as well as congregations.

Because of the premium they placed on hymns as a vehicle of spiritual growth, Methodists encouraged their children to memorize hymns from before the age of reading. Methodists believed that hymns memorized in childhood could "inform the memory and impress the heart," exerting a "permanent influence" that even shaped the "language and aspirations of declining age."[14] As one example of this emphasis, the Methodist *Youth's Magazine* (1839) presented a brief biographical sketch of the hymnist "Good Bishop Ken," informing readers that the bishop began his morning by singing with "holy feelings": "Awaken my soul with the sun, thy daily course of duty run," which prepared him to live "through the day" in the same holy manner as he began it. The article advised: "it would be well for us to learn by heart" Bishop Thomas Ken's hymn, using it as a catalyst to sanctify the remainder of the day.[15] Whether sung during congregational worship on Sundays, camp meetings, or private devotions or memorized in childhood, those hymns included in published collections and those more informally circulated played a pivotal role in orienting Methodists to view their lives in terms of heavenward pilgrimage.

Throughout the body of hymns popular among eighteenth- and nineteenth-century Methodists, verbal metaphors define the Christian life as pursuing a journey, fighting a battle, and running a race. Hymn narratives culminate with Christians' arrival in heaven, a land of rest, home, and eternal day, where one united church will forever worship God. One of the most popular hymns in the eighteenth and nineteenth centuries was British Methodist John Cennick's "Children of the heav'nly King," a text written in 1742 that ranked as the thirteenth most frequently reprinted hymn in both Methodist and non-Methodist Protestant hymnals published from 1830 to 1890.[16] The hymn encourages its singers to envision themselves as heaven-bound pilgrims: "We are traveling home to God, / In the way our fathers trod: / They are happy now, and we / Soon their happiness shall see. / Lift your eyes, ye sons of light, / Zion's city is in sight; / There our endless home shall be, / There our Lord we soon shall see."[17] The singing congregation encouraged one another to keep traveling home to God by recalling the journey that previous generations had undertaken and by anticipating arrival in heaven.

Although some hymns, like Cennick's, frame life in terms of a literal journey, others focus on the spiritual journey of Christians struggling against sin and longing for sanctification. "Love divine, all loves excelling," written by Charles Wesley in 1747, ranked sixteenth in number of occurrences in nineteenth-century hymnals.[18] Wesley's hymn traces the pilgrim community's journey through each stage, from the beginning of faith to its end in perfect heavenly worship. The first stanza addresses Jesus as the source of love and asks for his presence in the heart of every Christian:

> 1. Love divine, all loves excelling,
> Joy of heaven, to earth come down;
> Fix in us thy humble dwelling,
> All thy faithful mercies crown:
> Jesus, thou art all compassion,
> Pure, unbounded love thou art;
> Visit us with thy salvation,
> Enter every trembling heart.

The second stanza appeals to the Holy Spirit to take away the bent to sin, freeing hearts from the power of sin.

> 2. Breathe, O breathe thy loving Spirit
> Into every troubled breast!
> Let us all in thee inherit,
> Let us find that second rest:
> Take away our bent to sinning;
> Alpha and Omega be;
> End of faith, as its beginning,
> Set our hearts at liberty.

The third stanza envisions the possibility of pure worship on earth as in heaven, in enjoyment of perfect love.

> 3. Come, almighty to deliver,
> Let us all thy grace receive;
> Suddenly return, and never,
> Never more thy temples leave:
> Thee we would be always blessing,

> Serve thee as thy hosts above,
> Pray, and praise thee without ceasing,
> Glory in thy perfect love.

The final stanza anticipates continual growth in purity; Christians change from glory into glory as the Father perfects the new creation. Wesley thus writes,

> 4. Finish then thy new creation,
> Pure and spotless let us be;
> Let us see thy great salvation,
> Perfectly restored in thee:
> Changed from glory into glory,
> Till in heaven we take our place,
> Till we cast our crowns before thee,
> Lost in wonder, love, and praise.

Biblical references, interwoven throughout the text, offer Christians assurance at each stage of their journey as they experience trembling hearts, feel bound by their bent to sinning, bless God, and finally lose themselves in wonder, love, and praise. "Love Divine" weaves the word of the Bible into a narrative of Christian progress through this world toward heaven.[19]

Alongside texts like "Love Divine," Methodists even used hymns originating outside Wesleyan traditions and stemming from significantly different theologies to promote growth in holiness. The Calvinist Augustus Toplady wrote the hymn "Rock of Ages" as part of an article in *The Gospel Magazine* (1776) to refute the Wesleyan doctrine of entire sanctification. Toplady averred that Christians "never, in the present life, *rise* to the mark of legal sanctity," and that to the contrary, "our *Sins* multiply with every second." "Rock of Ages" appeared in the 1830 *Supplement* to the Methodist hymnal, and was reprinted in the 1878 edition of the Methodist hymnal, in a *significantly modified* form that approximated a version written by the Anglican Thomas Cotterill in 1815.[20]

Augustus Toplady (1776):	Methodist *Hymnal* (1878):
1. Rock of Ages, cleft for me,	1. Rock of Ages, cleft for me,
Let me hide myself in Thee!	Let me hide myself in thee;
Let the Water and the Blood,	Let the water and the blood,
From thy riven Side which flow'd,	From thy wounded side which flowed,
Be of Sin the double Cure;	Be of sin the double cure,
Cleanse me from its Guilt and Pow'r.	Save from wrath and make me pure.

2. Not the labors of my hands
Can fulfill thy Law's demands:
Could my zeal no respite know,
Could my tears for ever flow,
All for Sin could not atone:
Thou must save, and thou alone!

2. Could my tears forever flow,
Could my zeal no languor know,
These for sin could not atone;
Thou must save, and thou alone.

3. Nothing in my hand I bring;
Simply to thy Cross I cling;
Naked, come to Thee for Dress,
Helpless, look to Thee for grace,
Foul, I to the fountain fly:
Wash me, Saviour, or I die!

In my hand no price I bring;
Simply to thy cross I cling.

4. While I draw this fleeting breath—
When my eye-strings break in death,
When I soar to worlds unknown,
See Thee on Thy judgment throne:
Rock of Ages, cleft for me,
Let me hide myself in Thee.

3. While I draw this fleeting breath,
When my eyes shall close in death,
When I rise to worlds unknown,
And behold thee on thy throne,
Rock of ages, cleft for me,
Let me hide myself in thee.

The Methodist version transformed the hymn's theology from a statement denying the possibility of entire sanctification to a prayer for its attainment. Three exclamatory statements expressed Toplady's urgent sense of unrighteousness: "Let me hide myself in Thee!" (1:2), "Thou must save, and thou alone!" (2:6), "Wash me, Saviour, or I die!" (3:6). The intensity of the hymn's pleas for Christ's grace diminished in the Methodist version, which omitted all exclamation marks. More directly, the last line of the first stanza, "Cleanse me from its Guilt and Pow'r," became "Save from wrath and make me pure." Both lines refer to the "double cure" (1:5) of justification and sanctification, but the second version implies that purity from sin is possible in this life. The second and third stanzas merged in the Methodist version. The revision left out the couplet: "Not the labors of my hands / Can fulfill thy Law's demands," lines that assert human inability to live a righteous life. The hymn similarly modified absolute statements of human helplessness and divine sovereignty: "*All* for Sin could not atone," "*Nothing* in my hand I bring," and in the final stanza "See Thee on Thy *judgment* throne," attenuating the claims to read: "*These* for sin could not atone," "In my hand *no price* I bring," and "And behold thee on thy throne." The revision omitted another four lines that emphasize the extent of human sin and helplessness: "Naked, come to Thee for Dress, / Helpless, look to Thee for grace, / Foul, I to the fountain fly: / Wash me, Saviour, or I die!" Finally, the Methodist editors organized Toplady's text within a Wesleyan doctrinal framework. The editors chose not to place the hymn in the section "The Christian—Sanctification and Growth," even though Toplady intended the hymn to address the subjects of sanctification and growth in grace. Instead, the hymn appeared in the section "The Sinner— Repentance," thereby implying that the sin-consciousness that still pervades the hymn pertains to the beginning stages of the Christian life rather than to the mature Christian's experience.[21]

The hymn-writing practices exemplified by texts such as Cennick's, Wesley's, and Toplady's continued into the nineteenth century. The most prolific hymnist of all time was the nineteenth-century Methodist Fanny Crosby, the author of more than eight thousand hymns, many of which found a home in gospel-song services, as well as in more traditional congregational worship. Despite the speed at which she wrote, Crosby attested that some of her hymns had been "dictated by the blessed Holy Spirit," and that others resulted from "deep meditation" and prayer.[22] Hymns such as "The Pilgrim's Journey" expressed a longing for holiness closely akin to that voiced by the Wesleys more than a hundred years earlier: "Slow to anger, full of kindness, / Rich in mercy, Lord, Thou art, / Wash me in Thy healing fountain, / Take away my sinful heart. / I would go the pilgrim's journey, / Onward to the promised land; / I would reach the golden city, / There to join the angel band."[23] Crosby, like the Wesleys, envisioned her hymns leading congregations in heaven-bound worship.

Although Methodist theology and practice by no means stood still between Wesley's day and Crosby's, hymns written, published, memorized, and sung played a pivotal role throughout early Methodist history in orienting a pilgrim community to strain toward its entire sanctification. The evangelistic implications of this are clear: conversion is merely a good beginning, and the gospel goal is a life of growth in grace, going on to perfection.

Suggestions for Further Study

Bradley, Ian. *Abide with Me: The World of Victorian Hymns*. London: SCM, 1997.

Bruce, Dickson D., Jr. *And They All Sang Hallelujah: Plain-Folk Camp-Meeting Religion, 1800–1845*. Knoxville: Univ. of Tennessee Press, 1973.

Epstein, Dena J. *Sinful Tunes and Spirituals: Black Folk Music to the Civil War*. Urbana: Univ. of Illinois Press, 1977.

Hobbs, June Hadden. *"I Sing for I Cannot Be Silent": The Feminization of American Hymnody, 1870–1920*. Pittsburgh: Univ. of Pittsburgh Press, 1997.

Lorenz, Ellen Jane. *Glory, Hallelujah!: The Story of the Campmeeting Spiritual*. Nashville: Abingdon Press, 1980.

Rogal, Samuel J. *Sisters of Sacred Song: A Select Listing of Women Hymnodists in Great Britain and America*. New York: Garland, 1981.

Sallee, James. *A History of Evangelistic Hymnody*. Grand Rapids: Baker, 1978.

Sizer, Sandra S. *The Gospel Hymns and Social Religion: The Rhetoric of Nineteenth-Century Revivalism*. Philadelphia: Temple Univ. Press, 1978.

CHAPTER 15

DISCIPLE
Bible Study and
Changed Lives[1]

Stephen W. Rankin

Introduction

Since DISCIPLE Bible study's beginning in 1987, more than a million people have come together under its auspices to read, reflect, pray, and serve. It has subsequently expanded to thirty-four denominations and has been translated into seven languages.[2] If one types " DISCIPLE" into an Internet browser, one gets thousands of hits, providing a sense of the magnitude of local churches that include it among their programs. According to one report, more than thirteen thousand congregations use DISCIPLE.[3] Although people who have gone through the study readily acknowledge that it is but one of numerous grass roots efforts for spiritual renewal, they point to its remarkable growth as good reason to see it as a significant movement.

In one of the early brainstorming sessions leading to the creation of DISCIPLE, Albert Outler observed that the small group format they envisioned for the study was very much like the Wesleyan groups of old.[4] The question of whether and how DISCIPLE reflects Wesleyan practices and doctrinal themes sets the agenda for this essay. I will argue—following Outler's suggestion—that DISCIPLE embodies a Wesleyan praxis in quite important ways, even though Wesley's doctrines and disciplines remain unnamed, except in the covenant service that concludes DISCIPLE:

BECOMING DISCIPLES THROUGH BIBLE STUDY. The ministry of evangelism is central to a Wesleyan approach to the Christian faith. Given DISCIPLE's deployment throughout the church, it is worth considering its potential service to the Great Commission. Although the originators of DISCIPLE did not include evangelism as one of the goals for the study, in fact, it has produced fruit in this way. How a ministry that does not intend to be evangelistic turns out to be exactly that is another question worth considering.

The Spark That Ignited: The Impetus for and Development of DISCIPLE Bible Study[5]

DISCIPLE Bible study began in 1987 with the publication of DISCIPLE: BECOMING DISCIPLES THROUGH BIBLE STUDY. The designers originally intended only one stand-alone, thirty-four-week study of the entire Bible (in fact, about 70 percent of the Bible; it does not include all of the books of Kings and it skips the books of Chronicles). DISCIPLE became so popular, however, that the publishers began to plan for follow-up studies. Over the next approximately ten years, the now well-known DISCIPLE series came into existence. DISCIPLE: BECOMING DISCIPLES THROUGH BIBLE STUDY still surveys the whole Bible, DISCIPLE: INTO THE WORD INTO THE WORLD studies Genesis-Exodus and Luke-Acts, DISCIPLE: REMEMBER WHO YOU ARE covers the prophets of the Hebrew Bible and the letters of Paul, and DISCIPLE: UNDER THE TREE OF LIFE examines the Gospel of John, the Johannine letters, and the book of Revelation. If a person undertakes all four DISCIPLE studies, she or he will have effectively worked through the whole Bible twice.

According to Bishop Richard Wilke, who played a large role in the creation of DISCIPLE, the main aim from the beginning focused on transformation—to make disciples of Jesus Christ.[6] To a large extent, it grew out of the need for biblically formed and informed lay leaders in the church. The developers of the study admittedly did not foresee that it would become an evangelistic tool and a seedbed from which would grow a new crop of people responding to the call to various forms of vocational ministry.

The seeds for DISCIPLE were first planted in the 1970s. When Wilke was appointed pastor of First United Methodist Church in Wichita, Kansas, in 1974, he stepped into a common situation—a large traditional downtown church struggling to remain viable in the face of suburban sprawl. Few people lived close to the church. Many members lived forty-five minutes to an hour away. Wilke thus faced two challenges: the church had become evangelistically stagnant, and it suffered from a dearth of spiritually mature lay leaders. He entered this situation with the one overriding concern of making disciples. Wilke did what many pastors in large churches do; he tried big programs. By his assessment, however, these efforts brought no conversions and, certainly, no new disciples. The church first tried a Leighton Ford crusade. Then they participated in the "I Found It" campaign developed by Campus Crusade for Christ. Volunteers made five thousand phone calls, but the church did not receive even one new member as a direct result of the campaign. They started a television ministry, airing their worship service every Sunday morning. Although people expressed appreciation, the church saw no conversions or gains in membership.

In view of these frustrating results, Wilke began to reconsider the value of Sunday school for making disciples. One enduring quality of Sunday school is the small group feeling, even in larger churches where classes can include fifty or a hundred people or more. They offer intimate Christian community, a factor of enduring significance in Christian discipleship. But again Wilke encountered serious problems in his congregation. He discovered one class led by a person who taught the doctrine of reincarnation along with the Christian faith. Another group was led by a very determined young-earth creationist whom they actually paid to teach the class. The church suffered from the double-edged problem of low adult participation in Sunday school and, for those who did participate, little input that would help them develop into mature followers of Jesus Christ.

Frustrated but undaunted, Wilke pledged to overhaul and grow the Sunday school ministry because he knew the value of small group interaction. He immediately encountered strong resistance from the people he tried to recruit as leaders. They did not know the Bible and in no way felt qualified to teach it. Wilke began searching for the right tool to address their concerns and found the Bethel Bible Study series, which began with teacher training and then proceeded to the congregation at large. The church decided to try it, and for two years a group of people studied the Bible in the training phase. Although the congregational phase did not come to pass, Bethel did provide good training for teachers, and Wilke was able to realize his dream for starting and grounding biblically literate Sunday school classes. By the time he left the church in 1984, First United Methodist Church boasted one of the largest Sunday schools in United Methodism. Through trial and error, Wilke learned early how small group Bible study proved to be a crucial factor in growing disciples.[7]

One quickly begins to see similarities between the needs of people at First United Methodist Church and the spiritual needs addressed by various Wesleyan groups of the eighteenth and nineteenth centuries. People gathered into small groups with a common commitment, that is, to know God and to fulfill God's purpose. Openness to share one's heart with others, a willingness to be taught, faithfulness to a disciplined process, and a hunger for doctrine (understood in the sense of teaching that leads to holy living and not mere cognitive, dogmatic formulations) are common to the early Wesleyan communities and to what was forming in Wilke's mind.

Before we turn to the specifics of DISCIPLE, one strand of narrative remains to be told. In what amounted to an eleventh-hour decision (the vote literally took place late in the afternoon on the last day of the session), delegates at the 1984 General Conference voted to set a goal for increasing church membership to twenty million by the year 1992.[8] At that time, the number stood at just above nine million, so it meant more than doubling the membership in eight years. In hindsight the goal seems quixotic, but at least the church was thinking about its call to make disciples. Bishop Jack Tuell, speaking to General Conference in the Episcopal Address four years later (halfway through the time in which the twenty million member goal was to have been reached), said, "The action of the 1984 General Conference setting a goal of doubling our membership by 1992 has been soundly criticized with some justification. But that action did get the attention of the Church, and the Church is committed more than it has been in many years to becoming a growing church."[9] In 1984, the church had set a lofty and laudable goal for evangelism and discipleship, but it seemed that grassroots United Methodists had few resources to pursue it.

In July 1984 the South Central Jurisdiction elected Richard Wilke to the episcopacy. He was appointed to the Arkansas area, and because of his success with Sunday school in Kansas and his interest in discipleship, the Council of Bishops asked him to head up an effort to develop a strategy for church renewal. This work resulted in the book *And Are We Yet Alive?*[10] Published in 1986, it described a church in serious straits and summarized Wilke's call for change. It brought the church's evangelistic struggles—the 1984 General Conference notwithstanding—into sharp relief.[11]

Some serious denominational soul-searching ensued. A spate of books appeared in rapid succession, each offering its own analysis and prescription. In 1987 alone, for example, Abingdon Press published at least four books on the subject of renewal in United Methodism. Certain themes appeared in all of them: the church's need for a new vision of mission, the importance of lay leadership, the crucial role of pastors for making disciples of church members, the need for clarity in doctrine without lapsing into a doctrinaire or party spirit, the call for recovery of our Wesleyan ethos and fervor, and finally, the joyful and winsome commitment to evangelism.[12]

During the same period of time, United Methodist Publishing House executives began noticing a trend in requests for a deeper kind of Bible study. None of their current resources seemed to satisfy this hunger. Bishop Wilke was invited to Nashville for a consultation on this matter. In preparation for the meeting, he and his spouse, Julia, made a list of twenty principles that they believed should govern any new Bible study that the publishing house might produce. Several of those guiding values bear directly upon the focus of this essay: (1) the study should be explicitly Bible-based and should keep recourse to biblical commentaries to a strict minimum (the desire was for people actually to read the Bible, to engage its contents); (2) it should cover the whole Bible (rather than the typical studies that take small portions); (3) it should be—to use language from educational theory—learner-based instead of teacher-based, meaning that rather than having the teacher prepare the lesson, all the participants should study and share their discoveries with the whole group (i.e., the "teacher" should be a group facilitator while the content of the study should come from participants); (4) group size should be limited to approximately twelve; (5) video presentations by respected Bible scholars would help the group to focus and would provide important background information; and (6) the aim of the study should be transformation, not merely information.

Publishing house executives, led by Nellie Moser, liked the idea, so they called for a meeting that took place at Flower Mound, Texas, in 1986. Staff from the publishing house as well as scholars and teachers gathered to lay out the guidelines for the production of the new study. They agreed to make it rigorous, Bible-based, and highly creative with a variety of ways to encourage interaction. Participants would experience a range of approaches to help them engage the Scriptures in a lively way.[13] Bishop Wilke was appointed to write the manual, which he did in collaboration with Julia. Such a sense of urgency surrounded the project that The United Methodist Publishing House had the finished product ready for distribution a little more than a year later. The first DISCIPLE groups thus began meeting in 1987.[14]

What Is the "Study Structure" of DISCIPLE?[15]

Having summarized the story of the development of DISCIPLE, we can now turn to its main components. Each participant purchases a study manual to be used weekly, and in the description that is to follow, I will make note of each of its parts. The design team sought to strike the optimum balance between the need for substantial explanation of critical issues (so that students can develop some facility in interpreting diverse types of biblical literature and to gain some understanding of the Bible's more perplexing qualities) and the prospect that participants might have virtually no experience in Bible study. From an editorial point of view, this set of dynamics provided a steep challenge—to make a rigorous study based on the best of biblical scholarship while avoiding unnecessary detail and technical terms. It was this latter group that Bishop Wilke and the editors kept in mind as the manual was being written. Much care has been given to making serious critical issues accessible to people with little or no prior knowledge.

The study is arranged to encourage individual Bible reading and prayer, the rule of thumb being that a participant should spend at least thirty minutes daily, six days a week. Students gather weekly with a trained group facilitator for a two-and-a-half-hour period to watch a video presentation on the biblical book studied that week and to share what they have discovered in their personal reflection and prayer. A noted Bible scholar serves as the video presenter (most of the presenters are seminary professors, denominational executives, or pastors) and provides historical context, structure, and major themes for the book of the Bible studied that week.

Each week's study has a theme word and guiding scripture verse. For example, Week 1 begins with the word "authority." The theme verse comes from 2 Timothy 3:16, focusing on the nature of scriptural authority—as the verse says—"so that the person who serves God may be fully qualified and equipped to do every kind of good deed."[16] The first week is given to getting familiar with the overall structure of the Bible (the two divisions into Old and New Testaments, for example) and introducing participants to the various types of biblical literature. In addition, the manual includes a few pages of commentary to give readers guidance on how to distinguish and approach various types of literature.

In addition to a theme word and verse, each weekly chapter features "Our Human Condition," which is a statement summarizing the practical life problem (or set of problems) the scriptures address. This statement focuses the student's attention not merely on the content of the assigned readings, but on the life issues the assigned texts address. "Our Human Condition" thus encourages the reader to begin making connections between her or his life and the scriptures. The logic of this step is inductive, inviting the reader, first, to make observations about her or his situation or attitudes, then to move into the scriptures for interpretation and guidance. For example, Session 2 is called "The Creating God" (the theme word for the week is "wonder"). "Our Human Condition" states, "I wonder who made me and my world. If there is a Creator, what is this Creator like? Why was I made? . . . In a universe so big, surely I am only a speck of dust."[17] Here we find the effort to put into words the questions and struggles people commonly face.

One cannot overemphasize the study's aim to stay practical. The theme word and the statement of the human condition move participants beyond merely thinking about the content. Although DISCIPLE students gain a great deal of confidence in knowing and making sense of the Bible, cognitive grasp stands secondary and in service to discipleship. Each week contains some point that draws attention to attitude and practice. For example, in what many students find to be one of the most difficult parts of the Bible—the book of Leviticus with all its perplexing details regarding sacrifices and judgments about cleanliness—they are challenged to think about how lightly we modern Western Christians take corporate worship and, furthermore, to renew their commitment to worship.[18] In this way, the study seeks to help people avoid getting bogged down in detail and to keep clear the lifestyle and spiritual purposes of the study.

As a person reads each day, he or she is invited to take notes on the reading, and the manual provides space for them. Taking notes is an important part of the experience because time is allowed each week when the group meets for participants to share their discoveries and to ask their questions. Next in the manual comes a short commentary on the week's readings, never more than a few pages. Interspersed in the commentary are questions to guide reflection and space to write responses. At the end of each week's comments is a section titled "Marks of Discipleship," with a summary statement that focuses attention on what disciples do, that is, how disciples respond to the principles gleaned from the material studied that week. For example, in the session dealing with the Psalms, the manual summarizes, "Disciples trust God with all their thoughts and feelings."[19] Here one finds a set of questions for personal reflection and response. Sometimes this section challenges the participant to straightforward soul-searching. In the Matthew study, for example, after a participant has read the Sermon on the Mount, "Marks of Discipleship" asks, "Describe where you are in your discipleship. Have you responded to Christ's call, 'Follow me?' Is anything or anyone holding you back?"[20] This question is characteristic of the entire study. Most questions are gently, but persistently personal, even intimate. They invite the readers to examine their hearts.

Sometimes this section invites participants to share something that might be painful to reveal, but opens the opportunity for healing. After the group has studied the problems of the church in Corinth, for example, one question in "Marks of Discipleship" asks about participants' harmful practices with regard to food, exercise and health, sexuality, and alcohol or other drugs, then ends with the question, "Can you report this to the group? What would you have to do, with the Holy Spirit's help, to be freed from harm in these areas?"[21] This type of question is common in the study, and it demonstrates the risk and the power of the DISCIPLE experience. If a person is willing to share information about something this personal and if the group has formed authentic Christian community, then the sharing becomes a holy moment. Members of the group know to keep these matters in confidence, which helps to set people free to speak candidly. To be sure, it takes a while for members to grow into this level of intimacy, and some groups never manage it. It frightens people to speak in such a self-revealing way. It is risky, but if one courageous person takes the lead, others usually follow. The sharing associated with "Marks of Discipleship" often becomes the time of the meeting when transformation takes place.

Sometimes participants are challenged to do something during the week beyond just the study and prayer. The section on the book of

Hebrews, for instance, invites the participant—in view of the great cloud of witnesses mentioned in chapter 11—to write a thank-you note to another Christian who has provided a godly example and encouragement.[22] Occasionally, participants are asked to engage in some form of ministry, such as serving in a soup kitchen. Notably, the study pays special attention to spiritual gifts, which challenges people to go beyond such acts of kindness to considering, more generally, one's purpose.[23] The manual for this week (Week 33) contains no "Marks of Discipleship" because in effect the entire chapter is given to the "marks." When the group gathers for its weekly meeting, the manual provides space for each participant to write down the names of all the group members. Time is taken in the discussion for people to share their perceptions of their own gifts as well as those of others in the group. The manual provides space for participants to write down these thoughts, including a section for what "the group perceives my gift(s) to be. . . ."[24] Participants often report this experience as alternatively thrilling, affirming, humbling, and challenging.

I have paid extra attention to the "Marks of Discipleship" section of the DISCIPLE manual because it goes to the heart of this essay—practices leading to a transformed Christian life. I will have more to say in the concluding section, but it is worth noting at this point that the shaping effect of DISCIPLE takes place at two mutually reinforcing levels. Individually, people spend a significant amount of time in study, prayer, and reflection. DISCIPLE requires setting priorities and maintaining concentrated effort. It is intentionally rigorous; it requires participants to make a nine-month commitment to keep absences to a maximum of four meetings for the entire study. Beyond the bare time commitment, however, it calls for one to offer one's heart, so to speak, to be shaped by the experience.

In one's individual prayer and study time, one interacts with and lays one's heart open to God. At the corporate level, one does the same with a group of brothers and sisters in Christ. A dialectic process in discipleship formation is at work here between the individual and the group. Thinking something to oneself and writing in one's personal journal are beneficial, but when someone shares the same thoughts with peers, they become solidified and clear or modified and redirected through the interaction.

Up to this point I have mentioned only the design of DISCIPLE and its intended effects. Admittedly, I have been describing the study as it is *meant* to happen. The stories of participants indicate that spiritual formation is happening for a large number of people. Still, things do not always go so well, and "Marks of Discipleship" is the place where the breakdown often occurs, precisely because the questions and exercises aim at the heart. Sometimes it seems too difficult to participants to think about these questions; indeed, this section of the manual seems to be the one most often left blank. Sometimes, participants are too hesitant to share what they have discovered about themselves, or the issue is simply too painful. A discerning and sensitive facilitator will pay attention to this possibility and, with care, will try to draw out the hesitant persons in the group, to encourage them to share even the painful parts of their lives or, at least, to be intentional about offering it to God for healing.

As mentioned earlier, participants spend six days a week, roughly thirty minutes per day, in private Bible reading and prayer to prepare them for the weekly group session. It is designed for a two-and-a-half-hour period and is divided into several types of experiences. The session begins by drawing attention to the theme of the week. Often groups will read aloud the scripture verse and the statement in "Our Human Condition." Someone will offer a prayer, or the group will read the prayer (from the book of Psalms) printed in the study manual. Sometimes the group sings a hymn or praise song. Next, participants watch the video, which typically takes ten to twenty minutes. A brief time of questions and comments follows. The facilitator works to help the group avoid getting bogged down in trying to interpret some difficult or controversial passage, because this is often one of the temptations for new participants. Students who find the critical issues of special interest often want to launch into their questions, but the purpose of the opening video and discussion is to highlight the week's theme and get the group moving toward thinking about the "Marks of Discipleship." Because spiritual growth is the aim, debate over varying interpretations is discouraged. After the opening exercise, the group spends close to an hour discussing the week's reading and sharing participants' discoveries. The leader's manual offers the group facilitator a variety of means for drawing out the participants' learning. For example, the facilitator may ask participants to pair up, take one assigned day's readings, and discuss how they would summarize the content. Each pair then shares its insights with the group. Another exercise takes a list of key words from the biblical texts and invites participants to discuss what they mean. Simple maps and timetables are included in the manual to help the group put information into context.

After a brief break, the group reconvenes to engage in an experience called "Encounter the Word." Again, this exercise takes a variety of forms.[25] One of the most common exercises used in this section is known as "Theological Bible Study." Students read a passage together, then discuss three questions: (1) What does this passage say about God? (2) What does it say about human beings? and (3) What does it say about the relationship between God and human beings? Typically, the facilitator makes notes of participants' observations on a marker board. Students are challenged to "encounter" the text in a variety of stimulating ways. The aim of this section is to help students see something fresh, possibly to overcome some unhelpful preconception or otherwise to gain new insight. The session ends with participants' sharing their reflections from "Marks of Discipleship." By design, this is the high point of the meeting, as participants "get personal." Approximately twenty minutes is taken for this portion of the group session. "Marks of Discipleship" is not therapy, but a time of reflection and application.

One can see from the design that the two-and-a-half-hour session is highly interactive. "Lecturing" is limited to the video presentation. If the facilitator has supplementary information to share, it should never be more than a very few additional minutes. The purpose of DISCIPLE is discovery and application; it aims at interaction, not heavy content input. At this point it is worth returning to the values guiding the design: (1) the focus stays clearly on the Bible and not commentaries or critical concerns; (2) it covers the whole Bible so that students get the "big picture" of the biblical narrative; (3) it is learner-centered; (4) it keeps the group small so that Christian community has a chance to develop; (5) it uses "bite-sized" video presentations to manage the necessary content input; and (6) transformation or developing disciples of Jesus Christ is the purpose. With these values and the description of components of DISCIPLE in mind, we are now prepared to offer an analysis.

The Effectiveness of DISCIPLE

How well does DISCIPLE accomplish these aims? In other words, how fruitful is DISCIPLE in contributing to the Great Commission? It is impossible to quantify the impact of DISCIPLE, but a steady stream of anecdotal evidence suggests noteworthy influence.[26] As mentioned earlier, the program's developers did not envision it as an evangelistic tool, but it has turned out to be so for a substantial number of people.[27] This is significant for at least four reasons. First, although participation in DISCIPLE requires a large amount of time and energy, it nonetheless manages to make the Bible accessible even to people who have no prior experience with it. Here we encounter a fact that runs counter to conventional wisdom. Overattention to the whims of popular culture pushes church leaders toward a kind of "lowest shelf" mentality that seeks to put the gospel within reach of people allegedly too intimidated by religious vocabulary and practice to undertake serious engagement. DISCIPLE does exactly the opposite. It places challenging questions and substantial content in front of people and invites them to wrestle with them. Not only do they become familiar with the biblical story; they also deal with the basic critical issues of authorship, historical setting, and literary type and structure.[28] They have to work hard, but they consider it worthwhile because they have the sense that they are actually gaining access, as it were, to the "throne of grace."[29]

This sense of gaining access to God moves us in the direction of thinking about DISCIPLE's affinity to a particularly Wesleyan praxis. Given the testimonies one hears from participants, we can see why DISCIPLE is Wesleyan in its aims and practices. As Henry Knight and other scholars have made clear, "searching the scriptures" is one of several "instituted and particular means of grace."[30] "Grace," for Wesley, always refers to the activity of God's love in Jesus Christ poured out in the Holy Spirit and into the heart of a person, urging the person along the way of salvation toward full Christian maturity. In like manner, DISCIPLE shares this purpose. By keeping content input secondary to personal interaction and by asking questions and building community in which personal "heart" matters can be addressed, DISCIPLE conforms readily to the Wesleyan means of grace as it comes through searching the Scriptures and through Christian conferencing. In other words, people search the Scriptures in order to know God, not just to know the Bible, and in community, we see and hear grace illuminated. One is encouraged to place oneself at God's disposal. It is a process of both challenging and lending support.

The "challenge factor" of DISCIPLE leads to a second important principle: for activities that matter deeply, people will invest and extend themselves far beyond what we commonly expect. To draw an analogy from church administration, often in recruiting people to jobs we make the tasks sound too simple and undemanding. Generally, people do not want to do menial and meaningless things. The same holds for Bible study that really matters. To be sure, it can be "pitched" too high. The DISCIPLE experience, however, suggests that people see great value in spending time with other people grappling with their relationship to God and their purpose in serving God. Polls regularly demonstrate high interest in spirituality in our culture. People hunger to know God and to know that their lives matter. A Bible study that effectively gives them the opportunity to engage these big questions ought not to soft-pedal the challenges. People respond quite readily to DISCIPLE because they sense the significance of the work in which they are engaged.

A third important factor in the evangelistic impact of DISCIPLE is that it satisfies the hunger for sound doctrine. Again the study runs counter to conventional wisdom. One occasionally hears the old saw, "Doctrine divides." The statement implies that we should avoid it because it reminds people of differences and drains the love from Christian community. Or, worse, people talk of doctrine as if it were nothing more than abstract formulations hopelessly tied to a foregone era. These weaknesses are perceived to make doctrine impossible to understand (unless one studies theology as one's profession), but ultimately, it does not matter because doctrine has been deemed as having nothing to do with the "real world."[31]

On the contrary, DISCIPLE's popularity reflects a church hungry for biblical and theological instruction; not any kind, to be sure, but the sort of teaching that represents, in the best sense of the term, the wisdom of the ages. At this point, the qualities of high challenge, substantial content, and sound doctrine coincide. Naturally, the section of DISCIPLE: BECOMING DISCIPLES THROUGH BIBLE STUDY dealing with Wisdom literature provides the example. Chapter 14 deals with the book of Proverbs. The video presentation and the manual's commentary introduce participants to critical questions and then turn quickly to the biblical readings. In addition to the Proverbs, sections from Ezra and Nehemiah help students connect the Proverbs to real-life situations in the history of the exiled people beginning to return to their land and to reconstruct their nation. Participants readily see connections to their personal stories and to contemporary history and culture, and the Proverbs become a rich resource for them as well. This scenario represents the true function of doctrine and shows how DISCIPLE meets that need.

Finally, DISCIPLE's evangelistic effectiveness has to do with the natural enthusiasm of people for sharing their discovery of exciting and important knowledge. It stands to reason that a person who values her or his study and believes it to be personally important will naturally want to share with significant people what she or he is learning. This enthusiasm is infectious, and it provides the motivation for participants to suggest to their friends, family members, colleagues, and neighbors that they get involved in DISCIPLE. Occasionally, participants invite non-Christian[32] friends to join, who take up the offer and find themselves meeting and making commitments to Christ as Lord and Savior. In a way, this process represents evangelism in its most natural and fruitful form. It happens in the context of community, that of the one-to-one friendship and then that of the small group community of DISCIPLE students. In this case, people "belong," in a sense, before they believe. The transparency of disciples as they share their testimonies *and* their struggles helps the non-Christian see that being a Christian is both desirable and attainable. The small group community provides a safe place for a seeker to ask questions, express doubts, and find answers.[33]

Turning from evangelistic effects of DISCIPLE, we find one other serendipitous result. A number of people are entering seminary and vocational ministry via this study. For example, one United Methodist seminary admission officer found nine people currently enrolled as students who claim DISCIPLE as a significant factor in their hearing and responding to a call to ministry.[34] One should take care not to generalize too much from a few experiences, but two common features are worth noting. First, these students were provoked and inspired by their exposure to the Bible and to related critical questions. They discovered a zeal for God's Word that became, to some degree, their dominant interest and sent them digging for more. Students commonly refer to the "Bible coming alive" for them in DISCIPLE.

A critical factor for people hearing the call to ministry lies in the community and in the significant relationships formed in DISCIPLE. For leadership in the church, in general, and ordained leadership, in particular, the combination of personal study and reflection with group discernment is critical. A person has the chance to share what she or he may be sensing, to have it confirmed or modified by the group. Conversely, the group may recognize something in a person of which she or he has not been aware. Since this interaction comes very near the end of the nine months of study, prayer, and service together, the conversation surrounding the question of call should be both open and penetrating if the group has become a community. To put it another way, people are ready to take seriously what the community shares because they have spent a lot of intense time with other disciples, searching the Scriptures and sharing their hearts. Considering this quality of the DISCIPLE experience, it is not surprising that some people hear God's call to vocational ministry.

For some seminarians, DISCIPLE was the catalyst for them to *hear again* the call to ministry. Typically, they had experienced a call to ministry in their youth or young adult years through a summer church camp, a youth retreat, a campus ministry experience, or the like. For whatever reason,[35] they did not follow up on the call, and DISCIPLE became for them something of a "second (or third) chance." Again, no hard data are available, but one can safely say that a significant number of people entering ministry have done so from the DISCIPLE experience.[36]

In considering the community aspect of DISCIPLE, we find both similarity and difference with earlier Wesleyan groups, though the similarities outweigh the differences. In my opinion, DISCIPLE most represents the Wesleyan class meeting in terms of size, the spiritual and demographic characteristics of people in a group, and the role of the group facilitator. Both male and female form DISCIPLE groups, as they did in class meetings. The only requirement for joining a class was the desire "to flee the wrath to come" and to be willing to submit to its disciplines. The requirement for joining a DISCIPLE group is similar: a hunger for God and a willingness to submit to private and corporate disciplines. The class leader was one of the group, leading by example in being transparent with one's own victories and defeats and in helping the group stay focused on matters of the heart. Likewise, a DISCIPLE group facilitator is not the "expert" in the Bible, but a fellow disciple whose main purpose is to help the group stay focused on practical matters in order to grow into mature disciples. Although no class tickets are used for DISCIPLE, there is a similar accountability. Keep in mind the rule of thumb of a maximum of four absences over the course of the study. If a person must miss more than four sessions, he or she is encouraged not to start until able to devote the full time to DISCIPLE or, in some cases, to drop out of the group and pick it up again later. As with the class meetings, individual attendance is crucial to community formation. The group feels the gap when a person misses a meeting. Of course, class meetings did not incorporate a systematic Bible study into its group practices as does DISCIPLE, though here we must take into account the differences between the eighteenth century and today in terms of literacy and publishing.

Conclusion

To conclude this analysis, a few general reflections on the practices associated with DISCIPLE Bible study are in order. These observations derive from my thinking about DISCIPLE, specifically, but could well serve as guiding principles for any ministry related to evangelism and discipleship. First, and possibly most crucial, is the primacy of relationship over program. Big programs produce no long-term fruit if they lack opportunity for significant relationship, for getting people involved in community. Discipleship, on the other hand, is always grounded in relationship and intentional Christian fellowship. Programs that ask for a decision to follow Christ in a way that is disjoined from the relationships formed in Christian community get the cart before the horse.

Pastors play a crucial role in the lives of lay leaders, a point that too often gets lost in the busyness of pastoral care and administration. Transformative discipleship requires mentoring relationships between pastors and lay leaders. To be sure, mentoring can go both ways between laity and clergy, but on matters of discipleship, lay people look to their clergy for guidance, wisdom, and support. When Richard Wilke went to work starting the new Sunday school classes, he encountered a leadership vacuum and discovered that leaders needed to grow as disciples. It can come from peers, as they study and work together, but it depends to a large degree on the leadership and initiative of the pastor. Furthermore, a mentoring relationship between pastor and lay people must have discipleship (i.e., spiritual growth) as the main purpose. This means that time spent together is carefully planned, without becoming artificial, and everyone involved is willing to be held accountable to that plan.

Whether led by a pastor or a lay leader, DISCIPLE, by design, intends for the group facilitator personally to invite participants to join the study. It assumes that the leader has some acquaintance with potential participants. Thus, even before the study begins, new relationships begin forming or, if formed, take on new dimensions, precisely because they focus on growing together in Christ. If a pastor is leading the group, for example, it is quite possible that she or he has known invitees a while, but the invitation to join a thirty-four-week intensive study asks for a new level of intimacy, with the leader, with group members, and with God. The importance of this point cannot be overstated. Discipleship is an essentially relational phenomenon.

Second, reading the Bible in large sections has value for spiritual formation. It encourages people to read narratively and contextually, rather than in the smaller pericopes and verse units that tempt people to abstract ideas from the Bible and to proof-text. Reading the Bible narratively introduces people to big ideas and big pictures of God; to the overarching soteriological theme of God's determination to save and to restore humanity. John Wesley spoke often of the "marrow" of scripture as central to growing in grace.

Third, concomitant to reading large portions of the Scriptures is the time factor and the Christian formation that take place when people devote time to the task. Many DISCIPLE participants testify to having taken much more time than the thirty minutes required per day. Once they got into the Scriptures and began to realize that they could develop their own understanding, their hunger for the Scriptures increased. Furthermore, participants spend nine months with the same group of people doing the same thing: reading, praying, worshipping, sharing their thoughts and feelings, and attempting to practice in daily life what they are learning together.

Fourth, DISCIPLE participants are challenged to place the church in the wider perspective of the purposes of God's people in the world. In short, they develop a missional understanding of the church. For example, Session 31 includes 1 Peter, in which we find this vision of the church: "But you are a chosen race, a royal priesthood, a holy nation, God's own people, in order that you may proclaim the mighty acts of him who called you out of darkness into his marvelous light" (2:9). In the study manual for the same week, participants also read selected passages from Leviticus and Isaiah that highlight the covenant relationship between God and the people and the call upon them to be a servant people. Participants are thus challenged by the Bible readings and the commentary in the study manual to see themselves in the light of this covenant.[37]

Fifth, DISCIPLE encourages people to begin to think theologically. The "theological method" in the "Encounter the World" section does so effectively. Admittedly, they will likely not use the technical language associated with the academic study of religion (although at times they can pick up some of the terms), but they do start to think of daily experiences as opportunities to serve God and to develop a truly theological world view. This statement sounds like a truism until we compare it to the functional atheism that characterizes a good part of conventional church membership. A Bible study that provokes people to think theologically has a transforming impact.

Sixth, DISCIPLE's disarming effect of putting people on a level playing field with regard to knowledge of the Bible makes it useful and accessible to a wide range of people. By the study's design, "eager beavers" are encouraged to avoid wandering off into tangential matters. The focus stays on matters of the heart. Even though it is a high-demand study, if group facilitators follow the design, people are reassured from the beginning that one needs *no* knowledge of the Bible to be "qualified" to participate. Furthermore, the teacher is not the "expert" whose job it is to dispense information and insight. Rather, the study is designed to have members of the group share their insights. The teacher's main task is to guide conversation and to lead through the group exercises. The "expert" has already addressed critical issues and major themes through the video presentation. This quality puts the "expert" at some distance and allows the teacher to be a peer on the road to discovery. Participants understand that they are coming together as peers to search the Scriptures and to seek God. Because of the discussion and open dialogue in which people deal with real existential matters, DISCIPLE represents, in a contemporary form, the practical soteriology we associate with John Wesley.

Certainly, many other observations could be made about how DISCIPLE exemplifies a Wesleyan praxis. A study of how the religious affections might be shaped by the DISCIPLE experience would no doubt provide useful insights to church leaders. It also would be interesting to explore whether and how one might plot the Wesleyan *via salutis* through DISCIPLE to see what ideas we might glean for future work. Whether these studies take place soon or in the distant future, what we already know for certain is that DISCIPLE has made a profound impact on United Methodist and other local congregations where it has been faithfully used. If local churches using DISCIPLE continue to multiply, trends suggest that the denomination as a whole might indeed reverse its numerical decline. Numerical growth is not intrinsically a virtue for the church, but seeing the lives of people transformed through consistent DISCIPLE Bible study and accountable small group fellowship is a true mark of what is means to be the church.

CHAPTER 16

Forming Christian Witnesses Through the *Witness* Adventure[1]

Ron Crandall

And you will be my witnesses. —Acts 1:8

B
eing God's witnesses is as old and timeless as creation, as enduring as the last words of Jesus, and as recent as this morning's breakfast conversation. Those of us who have tasted divine grace and follow Jesus Christ cannot help becoming part of the great gospel cacophony: "So that at the name of Jesus every knee should bend, in heaven and on earth and under the earth, and every tongue should confess that Jesus Christ is Lord, to the glory of God the Father" (Phil. 2:10-11). Since even the "stones would shout out" if God's children did not (Luke 19:40), surely we as post-Pentecost disciples of Jesus must help one another find the best ways possible to cooperate with the Spirit and bear our witness.

The Biblical Call to Bear Witness

All creation is designed to bear witness to God's glory and power and majesty—even when this witness in its profound silence goes unnoticed. The psalmist declares:

The heavens are telling the glory of God; and the firmament proclaims his handiwork.
Day to day pours forth speech, and night to night declares knowledge.
There is no speech, nor are there words; their voice is not heard;
yet their voice goes out through all the earth, and their words to the end of the world. (Ps. 19:1-4)

Paul reminds us of the same reality and also notes that we often ignore this cosmic witness and live contrary to our own design and destiny. He writes:

For what can be known about God is plain to them, because God has shown it to them. Ever since the creation of the world his eternal power and divine nature, invisible though they are, have been understood and seen through the things he has made. So they are without excuse; for though they knew God, they did not honor him as God or give thanks to him, but they became futile in their thinking, and their senseless minds were darkened. Claiming to be wise, they became fools. (Rom. 1:19-22)

Even more than the creation itself, God's children are designed to be living witnesses. We are made in the likeness of God, flawed though we are by sin, so that we, too, might declare in words and works the glory of God and the wonder of God's redeeming love. Isaiah sets the stage for a great international trial in which God calls on all the peoples of the earth to come and hear testimony until they must declare, "It is true." And on whom does God call for his defense? Those he has chosen, chastened, and redeemed. They are his witnesses, as he proclaims:

But now thus says the LORD, he who created you, O Jacob,
he who formed you, O Israel:
Do not fear, for I have redeemed you;
I have called you by name, you are mine. . . .
Let them bring their witnesses to justify them,
and let them hear and say, "It is true."
You are my witnesses, says the LORD,
and my servant whom I have chosen,
so that you may know and believe me
and understand that I am he.
Before me no god was formed,
nor shall there be any after me.
I, I am the LORD,
and besides me there is no savior.
I declared and saved and proclaimed,

when there was no strange god among you;
and you are my witnesses, says the LORD. (Isa. 43:1, 9-12)

This image is carried over into the next chapter of Isaiah's prophetic announcement. God will raise up others, by the Spirit, to join in the chorus of testimony announcing, "I am the Lord's." And a recurring reminder is given to all of God's witnesses with the words, "Do not be afraid." Isaiah continues,

I will pour my spirit upon your descendants,
  and my blessing on your offspring.
They shall spring up like a green tamarisk,
  like willows by flowing streams.
This one will say, "I am the LORD's,"
  another will be called by the name of Jacob,
yet another will write on the hand, "The LORD's." . . .
Do not fear, or be afraid;
  have I not told you from of old and declared it?
You are my witnesses! (Isa. 44:3-5, 8)

This anticipation of the Spirit's outpouring to create a multitude of descendants who will announce, "I am the Lord's," is a constant theme. It is the theme of the new covenant as described by Jeremiah and Ezekiel and picked up by Paul and the writer of Hebrews.[2] It is also the image Joel uses (2:28-29), which is adopted by Peter as the primary interpretation for the day of Pentecost. The Spirit has been poured out, inhabitants of many nations have heard the word of God in their own languages, and Peter tells of Jesus whom God has raised up and made both Lord and Christ. Then, without fear, Peter says, "And of that all of us are witnesses" (Acts 2:32). What else could he say? Jesus had told him and the others to wait in Jerusalem until they received the Spirit and the power to become his witnesses (Acts 1:8). The disciples Jesus fashioned and then filled with the Spirit were created to reveal one transparent identity and accomplish one primary task: "You will be my witnesses."

Evangelism and Christian Witness

Being Christian witnesses and engaging in Christian evangelism are related but not identical activities. Evangelism is primarily the communication of the gospel itself as a message of hope and salvation and includes inviting persons to repent, place their faith in Jesus Christ, and follow him along the road of discipleship. Some of Christ's disciples are specially called and gifted for this work as evangelists (Eph. 4:11). We could quite successfully argue that evangelism is larger than just the work of evangelists and "preaching the gospel"; but it nevertheless is about offering the gospel in tangible ways and not just *witnessing* to our faith in it. Evangelism, offering the gospel, can be exercised for the larger public through preaching, teaching, outreach to the needy, writing, and even music, drama, and art. It can take place between just two persons as interpersonal evangelism; but whatever the mode of delivery, evangelism is primarily about communicating the content of the gospel message in word and deed. Not all of us are either gifted or called to be evangelists; however, all of us *are* called to be witnesses.

There is no way around it. To be a witness is to influence others, even if one is not directly an evangelizer. The goal of our witness as Christ's disciples is ultimately to enable others to acknowledge Christ as Savior and Lord, accept God's gift of the Holy Spirit and salvation as it is realized through the ongoing process of discipleship, enter the kingdom of God, and become part of the Body of Christ, the church. But the witness we offer can either help or hinder that possibility for others. I include hinder because part of what Christians say and do can become a "negative" witness, a witness against Christ.

For example, on one occasion I was in the back of a very full airplane. A man "snuggled" in next to me after lifting the armrest between us. As we got acquainted, he informed me that he was flying home to Texas from his brother's funeral in West Virginia. We talked about the years of suffering his brother had endured from Agent Orange poisoning. He showed me the obituary from the local newspaper; and noticing the home church of his brother, I asked him if he had grown up in this church. "Oh, yes," he declared, "saved and baptized at twelve, and traveled with a gospel quartet all around several states." In the course of our conversation, my seatmate told me he had been married seven times and had fourteen children in seven states; the youngest was now three and living with him and his newest wife. He asked me if I thought he should get back into church for her sake. What would you have said? His witness suggested that he had not continued on the road of discipleship as an adult and, perhaps, had ceased to respond to God's grace.

Whatever we reveal to others as to the nature of our lives, whether in words or deeds, is our witness. All who acknowledge that they are Christians, go to church, pray before eating their meals, or have a Bible on the desk or an *ichthus* bumper sticker are witnesses of a sort. So are those who feed the hungry, visit the imprisoned, clothe the naked, and care for widows and orphans. But it doesn't take long in today's world to notice that underneath the outward manifestations of religious faith can dwell a good deal of unfaithfulness that detracts from helping people entrust their whole lives and futures to the lordship of Jesus. Examples of both the positive and the negative dimensions of our witness come readily to mind. In fact, they are as close as today's news or last Sunday's gathering of Christians at any church.

The primary goal of training or equipping Christians as witnesses is to help them become more aware of how to live in and for Christ (Col. 1:27-29), to recognize the impact of their lives on others (Philem. 6), and to prayerfully trust the Holy Spirit to lead them (Rom. 8:14) in all of their daily choices of words and deeds. Perhaps the best single passage of scripture that clarifies this task is found in 1 Peter 3:15-16: "In your hearts sanctify Christ as Lord. Always be ready to make your defense to anyone who demands from you an accounting for the hope that is in you; yet do it with gentleness and reverence." In our witness we must be prepared to respond, but always with a gentle and respectful attitude toward others.

Witnessing is no small matter, and it is a central task in every Christian. It is, in fact, inherent in the name "Christians," which means Christ's people. John Wesley understood that the goal of the Spirit's sanctifying work in us is holiness and perfect love. Even though we must grow into perfect love throughout our lifetimes, he also believed that every truly converted person has "the mind that was in Christ."[3] The task of helping Christ's people become better witnesses is in large part about helping them to think and live in a manner that represents the mind of Christ and not their own.

Research to Inform Today's Witnesses

God has a way of reaching out to us through others who, as witnesses, become part of our own story and challenge us to ever greater faithfulness on behalf of those who still have not really heard or experienced the power of God's redeeming love. Robin Wainwright has developed a basic interview outline for his students to determine how God works in the lives of people to bring them to faith. I began to use this inductive-discovery approach with my classes, asking every student to interview five people who have confessed Christ, so we might discern how God's Spirit and our witness enabled others to come to faith. We tinkered with the outline and the questions for three or four years and then began to put the data into a computer program. Over the next twelve years we compiled data from more than ten thousand interviews and, with reasonable confidence, can make claims about how persons come to faith and whose witness most helped them. Other versions of this interview approach have been used elsewhere in the world,[4] and similar results gave us confidence to publish what we had learned in 1999 as *The Contagious Witness: Exploring Christian Conversion*.[5] A couple lessons are worth citing here because they inform our larger task of equipping church members for more effective witness.

The agents of Christian influence and Christian decision are not always the same people. That is to say, all kinds of Christian witnesses contribute to stirring in people's imagination a desire to experience a real relationship with God and become followers of Christ. These are, however, almost without exception trusted family members, friends, and clergy. This should not surprise us, but it should encourage us to remind those we serve in the church how important their day-to-day relationships are as part of God's great design to "seek out and to save the lost" (Luke 19:10). Note the chart below that shows the results of about four thousand randomly selected interviews from the study.

Most Important Persons Influencing Your Decision
4,016 Cases

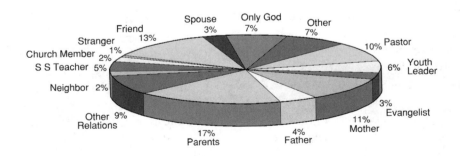

The pie chart is read from "pastor" on the right side of the pie (top left on the legend) clockwise to "youth leader" (6 percent), "evangelist" (3 percent), "mother" (11 percent), "father" (4 percent), "both parents" (17 percent), "other relative" (9 percent), and so on. Notice that "stranger" accounts for only 1 percent while "friend" accounts for 13 percent of the total sample. The influence of a "friend" increases to 23 percent for those who come to a faith decision for Christ as teenagers between ages 15 and 19 and 24.5 percent for young adults 20 to 24. It is important for every-day Christians to realize how critical their influence is on others with whom they have daily contact.

We also asked what about these witnesses had the greatest impact on those who were interviewed. The pie chart and the percentages reveal that, more than anything else, what influences other people to come to Christ is the obvious relationship of witnesses with God. Persons variously referred to this as "showed me Jesus," "loved God," and "seemed to know God." In second place, and close behind in third, the data indicate something about the character and personality of the witnesses and how they manifested special care for the persons they influenced.

What Characteristic Most Influenced Your Decision?
3,811 Cases

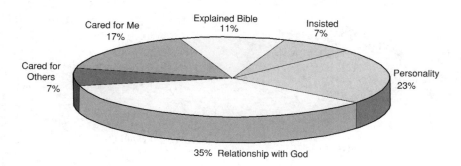

Cared for Me 17%

Explained Bible 11%

Insisted 7%

Cared for Others 7%

Personality 23%

35% Relationship with God

Many of our church members today would probably say that they don't mind being thought of as "influencers" when it comes to their witness; they just don't want to have to "talk." But how do people actually come to Christian decisions? Paul reminded the Christians in Rome, "How are they to call on one in whom they have not believed? And how are they to believe in one of whom they have never heard? And how are they to hear without someone to proclaim him? And how are they to proclaim him unless they are sent? As it is written, 'How beautiful are the feet of those who bring good news!' " (Rom. 10:14-15). The first part of being a faithful witness is manifesting our own relationship with God and having "beautiful feet." It is about moving those feet toward others in faith-filled and caring love. But the next part is being able to "tell" good news.

The data from our interviews indicate that even though "explaining" the Bible or the gospel was not critically important in the first phase of our witness as influencers, when it comes to helping people find their own faith experience with God through Christ, "explaining" becomes more important.

What Characteristic of the Person Led You to Decide 3,571 Cases

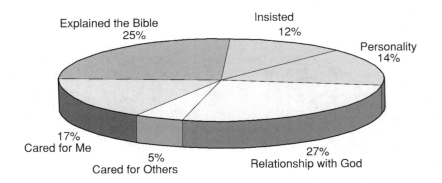

Again, the most important characteristic of witnesses who help others come to a Christian faith decision is the manifestation of a personal relationship with God. But at this stage, when people are readied by the Spirit to entrust their lives to Christ, helping them understand the gospel message and how to find their way to saving faith is the second most important contribution we can make. Witnesses reveal their faith by their deeds *and* by their words.

This information leads us to ask: Who are those most frequently named as the ones who helped bring people to a decision for Christ? Here we notice a few more shifts.

Most Important Persons Leading You to a Decision
3,975 Cases

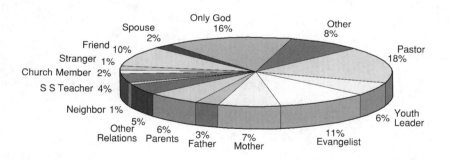

Reading clockwise from the "pastor" (18 percent), we move next to "youth leader" (6 percent and increasing among younger generations), "evangelist" (11 percent and declining for younger generations), "parents" (all together 16 percent), and around to "friend" (10 percent and only half that in older generations), and "God alone" (16 percent). Pastors, evangelists, and youth leaders now account for 35 percent of the most helpful agents at the time of decision. Parents account for another 16 percent, friends for 10 percent, and God alone for 16 percent. This last figure might require a bit of explanation. All of us would probably acknowledge that God reached out to us and led us to our faith decision.

But those who were often alone when they committed themselves to Christ or had a deep encounter with God report that although many influenced their faith journey, they couldn't name anyone in particular who helped them make the actual decision. It was entirely between themselves and God.

Perhaps, in summary, it can be said that Christians help others come to faith in Christ, first, by their own example of living out their faith relationship on a daily basis. Second, they help persons come to faith by being able to help clarify how others can find what they have found. Third, they need to be able to demonstrate that their love for God and understanding of the gospel inform how they live their lives in caring intentionally for others. Probably no real surprises here. So what's the problem? The problem is only that too many of our members still think this task belongs to someone else. True, pastors, evangelists, youth leaders, and others are important, especially at "decision time." Those of us in one of these categories need to take seriously our roles in clarifying and calling for decisions. But without the witnessing contribution of parents and friends, we are losing the battle. *Witness: Exploring and Sharing Your Christian Faith* helps us to realize that we are all witnesses and assists everyone to become a better witness for the glory of God.

Helping Today's Christians Become Better Witnesses

If we want to be better witnesses, then a logical place to begin is with Jesus. How did the followers of Jesus become his witnesses? For one thing they spent a great deal of time with him. They "witnessed" the way he thought, prayed, talked, and acted. A witness is not expected to be an expert on everything, only on what he or she really "knows" by experience. A good witness remembers. One of the things Jesus told his disciples the Holy Spirit would do was to help them remember all that Jesus had taught them (John 14:26). Part of the Spirit's empowerment of Christ's witnesses is this gift of expanding their understanding of the things of God. Thus, part of our task in preparing more Christians to be effective witnesses is to help them pay attention to the way of Jesus and listen together to the Spirit's teaching.

In addition, Jesus prepared his disciples to be his witnesses by giving them practical assignments for growing in their confidence that God would act through them. They were really apprentices of the Master

Teacher. Some of the tasks he gave them were quite simple: "stay here and pray" or "give them something to eat." But each task increased their confidence that they could, indeed, participate in the work of the Kingdom. So when they were sent out on larger assignments of announcing the Kingdom and offering God's healing, they were ready. Yet after Jesus' arrest and crucifixion, these disciples still denied that they knew him, and they huddled in fear. What happened? In part, it became more costly to be a witness. In fact, the word "witness" is our translation of the Greek word "martyr." The ultimate witness is one's willingness to lay down one's life for the truth one knows and cannot deny. This life-surrendering witness by Christian disciples is still happening around the world today, and it is never easy. Many of us are ignorant of this reality, but the facts are that being a true witness for Christ is not just about easy living. It is about living and dying in confident assurance that Jesus is truly "the resurrection and the life" (John 11:25-26). Thus again, the power to be a true witness is a spiritual power that frees us from fear and from desperately clinging to the things that are less than God and enables us to be bold in deeds and words of agape love (2 Tim. 1:7-8).

Welcome to *Witness*

Witness: Exploring and Sharing Your Christian Faith is a twenty-five-week adventure in Christian living, not unlike the highly successful DISCIPLE Bible study series. Together with others in a small band of brothers and sisters, Christians learn how to walk closer to Jesus, to let the Spirit remind them of what they believe and know, and to reach out as individuals and as congregations bearing witness to the world around them. Some think this process should be able to take place in two, four, or six training sessions. But becoming better witnesses is not merely about short-term dips into training events (as helpful as they can be); it is more about being steeped in the life of Jesus who offers long drinks of living water to those who listen to him and become members of his Body (John 4:1-42; 7:37-39). The goal is a new life perspective that transforms us by helping us experience with others what it feels like to belong to a culture of being Christian witnesses. This kind of change and empowerment takes time and is more like a journey to be taken than an event to attend. It is fleshed out in *Witness* through the metaphor of hiking or "thru-hiking the Appalachian Trail."

Millions of hikers take short treks on the trail each year, but only a small percentage set out to "stay the course" for the whole pilgrimage. Undertaking such a journey is life changing for the thru-hikers; they cannot return to living in their old habitats quite the same way as they did before. They have seen too much and learned too much about themselves and about others. They will forever be different. *Witness* hopes to make this kind of difference in those who join on the trail metaphorically. There are many such transforming experiences in life, and such transformation should also be the case in the work of bearing witness.

Over the twenty-five weeks of the program, the journey is divided into five "trails":

1. Trail One (4 weeks): Exploring Vistas of God's Purpose for the World. Themes examined include Shalom, Salvation, Eternal Life, New Covenant, God's Glory, The Kingdom, The Sin Problem, Sin's Solution, God as the Evangelist, Evangelism, and Witnesses.
2. Trail Two (4 weeks): Up the Mountain with Jesus. Themes examined include Jesus as Prophet-Teacher, Son of Man, Son of God, Messiah, King, God Incarnate, Savior, Lord, and Friend.
3. Trail Three (4 weeks): Into Life in the Holy Spirit. Themes examined include Who Is the Holy Spirit?; The Spirit of the Holy Trinity; The Spirit of Creation-Creativity-New Creation; The Spirit of Amazing Grace; and The Spirit of Ministry and Witness.

These three trails constitute the first half of the journey. An introductory session explains the program and orients participants. During this session a six-minute clip of the Witness video is shown depicting the "thru-hiker" metaphor and the overall purpose and concept of *Witness*. Those who choose to begin the journey are reminded they will need only a Bible, a copy of the *Workbook* and the *Journal*, an open attitude, and a cooperative spirit.

Each week's assignments include (1) six daily scripture passages related to the theme of the week that they are to read and reflect on in their *Journals*, (2) a chapter in the *Workbook* (five or six pages) to read and interact with, (3) an action assignment designed to help them discover progressively how to live out and talk about their witness for Christ, and (4) a weekly group session for prayer and sharing insights from each week on the trail. A "Trail Guide for Leaders" is located in the back of the *Workbook*, giving general guidance for facilitating each meeting and specific suggestions for each week.[6] No special training is required for the group leader, whose primary job is to guide the discussion and help the participants discover insights from their readings and witness action assignments. *Witness* groups typically consist of four to twelve people, but as few as two and even some large Sunday school classes have successfully used the material. Although the group dynamics spelled out for the leader are designed for a time frame of sixty to ninety minutes, some have streamlined their conversations to fifty minutes, and others have expanded to more than two hours.

The first three trails are designed to explore the content and meaning of our biblical and Wesleyan heritage. Participants discover or rediscover the bedrock of our faith through reading and reflecting on the scripture passages and the weekly themes examined in the *Workbook*. Conversations held "out on the trail" during the week and around the "campfire" at week's end give new significance to the importance and power of personal witness. Daily prayer for persons encountered along the trail and for fellow hikers in the group help us stay in touch with the Spirit's leading. At the beginning of each new trail another video clip is shown to remind the group of their progress so far and to orient them to the next stage of their journey. Over these first several weeks on the *Witness* trail a life pattern begins to develop, and hikers discover a new joy in living with more intentionality and boldness as witnesses for Christ.

Pressing On

The overall intent of the first twelve weeks is to help those who participate become more aware of how our witness as Christians is tied to the biblical story of (1) God's purpose for us, (2) the human problem of sin, and (3) God's provision for us in the gift of Christ and the Holy Spirit. Action assignments lead to conversations with family, friends, and other church members to learn how to listen to what others think about these matters of life and faith. In addition, the weekly group meetings expand our individual insights into a broadening array of perspectives and experiences and provide a deepening sense of purposeful Christian community.

This process leads into the last twelve weeks on the trail. The ultimate goal of *Witness* is to engender a new climate or a new culture of Christian witness in our congregations as well as in individual lives. Trail Four, The

Church and Its Witness, explores the biblical meaning and purpose of being the church and asks, "How are we doing?" Trail Five, My Life as Christ's Witness, focuses on each individual's growing ability to live out a life of intentional, daily sensitivity to the Spirit's leading as Christ's witness. As before, each trail opens with a short video clip of how far we have traveled and the new vistas ahead. During these last two trails the hikers are expected to assume more and more responsibility for the content of the group sessions. The *Workbook* becomes background material to establish a context for examining our current faithfulness as witnessing congregations and individuals. On Trail Four they interview church members, community leaders, and missionaries, and become acquainted with the languages and cultures around them in their own "Jerusalem." They begin an analysis of the current effectiveness of their own church to reach out to the community with a meaningful witness to children and youth, to troubled persons, to seekers, and across the usual ethnic and cultural barriers. They must assume more of the task of recognizing where to find certain key Bible verses and passages that relate to their lives as Christ's witnesses. The incline of the trail becomes a bit steeper over the last twelve weeks.

Trail Five is designed mostly around three key responsibilities found in the passage mentioned earlier from 1 Peter 3:15-16. First, there is the critical primary relationship. How are we to be contagious witnesses to the reality of the presence of God for other people's lives unless we maintain our own intimacy with Christ? In Jesus' words: "I am the vine, you are the branches. Those who abide in me and I in them bear much fruit, because apart from me you can do nothing" (John 15:5). Henri Nouwen offered a powerful summary of this reality when he wrote, "When we no longer walk in the presence of the Lord, we cannot be living reminders of his divine presence in our lives. We then quickly become strangers in an alien land who have forgotten where we come from and where we are going. Then we are no longer the way to the experience of God, but rather *in* the way of the experience of God."[7]

The second emphasis in Trail Five is on being prepared to give an answer to anyone who might ask for the reason that you have hope. Again and again people are amazed at how unprepared they are to talk about their faith and the reason they have hope in Christ. The whole journey of *Witness* is designed to provide background information for people to use in such conversations and to give them opportunities to grow in their ability and confidence to express their faith. Recent information from the Barna Research Group[8] indicates that United Methodists and other mainline Protestant denominations rank close to the bottom of the chart on percentage of members giving any verbal witness to their faith over the course of a year. Only about one in five said they did so. We would not have to examine Barna's study in great detail to recognize that the denominations that are growing and reaching new people for Christ are at the top end of the chart (40 to 60 percent indicating they have had such conversations). Our Methodist/Wesleyan heritage is filled with admonitions and examples of just this kind of contagious personal witnessing. *Witness* is designed to help our people "be prepared to give an answer."

The third item of instruction from Peter is *how* Christians are to give this witness, that is, "with gentleness and reverence." Over the course of the whole *Witness* journey there is an emphasis on learning how to reveal that it is "the love of Christ [that] urges us on" (2 Cor. 5:14). Manifesting gentleness and respect equates not with timidity but with sensitive and attentive love and concern for the other. A key ingredient in this style of living out the Christian witness is learning how to listen deeply into the life stories of others. If we alienate others through our insistence, we have not manifested gentleness and reverence, or respect. This is a special effort in the prayerful and practical action assignments of Trail Five.

For many persons, Trail Five is the steepest trail of the journey. Yet it is a primary reason we are on this journey. On Trail Five the members of the group are expected to look intentionally for opportunities to engage in such conversations and invite people to respond to God's offer of love, forgiveness, grace, and purposeful life. Memorizing key passages of scripture or at least knowing where to find them becomes a challenge for some who have never thought they needed to actually know "where in the Bible it says that."

Nevertheless, the primary emphasis is not only on memorizing, but also on looking for opportunities to be helpful to others as they become open to sharing their deepest longings for faith, hope, and love. Indeed, a simple expression of our deep feeling that, in Christ, we are blessed can be a powerful witness. This is the reason that 1 Peter 3:15-16 becomes such a helpful foundation for the *Witness* material. It is designed not to make an "evangelist" out of every Christian, but to enable every Christian to become a better "witness."

Suggestions for Further Study

Fox, H. Eddie, and George Morris. *Faith-Sharing: Dynamic Christian Witnessing by Invitation*. Nashville: Discipleship Resources, 1986.

Hunter, George. *The Celtic Way of Evangelism*. Nashville: Abingdon Press, 2000.

————. *Radical Outreach*. Nashville: Abingdon Press, 2003.

Kraft, Charles H. *Communication Theory for Christian Witness*. Rev. ed. Maryknoll, N.Y.: Orbis, 2002.

McLaren, Brian. *The Story We Find Ourselves In*. San Francisco: Josey-Bass, 2003.

————. *More Ready Than You Realize*. Grand Rapids: Zondervan, 2002.

Pippert, Rebecca. *Out of the Salt Shaker & Into the World*. Downers Grove, Ill.: InterVarsity Press, 1999.

Poe, Harry Lee. *Christian Witness in a Postmodern World*. Nashville: Abingdon Press, 2001.

Richardson, Rick. *Evangelism Outside the Box: New Ways to Help People Experience the Good News*. Downers Grove, Ill.: InterVarsity Press, 2000.

CHAPTER 17

Three Types of Faith Sharing

Scott J. Jones

D aniel T. Niles, a Methodist evangelist from Sri Lanka, defines "evangelism" in this way: "It is one beggar telling another beggar where to get food."[1] This rich image avoids many negative associations that often are attributed to the ministry of evangelism and evokes the idea of sharing something special. Evangelism may be well conceived as helping persons find the spiritual food that will nourish their lives. When one has found a feast in a starving world, love requires sharing it with those who are hungry.

Persons witness to the love of God in Jesus Christ in a wide variety of ways. Deeds of mercy, acts of self-sacrifice, the writing of books and pamphlets, and many other forms can helpfully embody one's witness for Christ. But the verbal sharing of the good news is another equally valid way of bearing witness to Christ. Faith sharing is the verbal communication of the gospel with non-Christians that includes an indication of one's personal faith in Christ. It can occur with a large audience, but most often happens in one-on-one or small group settings. It can be done through digital media, but its personal quality is enhanced when it is done face-to-face. Other verbal forms of communicating the gospel, such as preaching and teaching, may include faith sharing if they have this personal aspect. Faith sharing is one type of verbal witness to the faith, and in at least one of its three types, it is the responsibility of all Christians.

Importance

Such verbal communication is an important part of the ministry of evangelism for three reasons. First, Christ commanded all his followers to be witnesses to the gospel. Jesus said that his disciples are to be his witnesses to the ends of the earth (Acts 1:8). Christian discipleship means that we are to live our lives so that the love of God in Christ Jesus motivates all that we do. At its deepest level, the life of each disciple is to be lived in Christ, bearing witness to what God has done. Thus, when we speak of the various aspects of Christian discipleship, faith sharing is one of the essential aspects.[2] Sometimes bearing witness is done through our deeds, as when we feed the hungry or clothe the naked (Matt. 25:31-46). Witness by deeds is an essential part of discipleship.

But our deeds can easily be misunderstood without the words that give our deeds an explanatory context. We can feed hungry people for many different reasons. For example, giving a Thanksgiving basket of food to a poor family could be motivated by at least three different purposes. One purpose could be to fulfill a requirement for some type of award in an organization that requires social service projects. Or it could be done as a condescending way of demonstrating one's social and economic superiority. Or it could be done as an expression of love and solidarity with those for whom Christ died. Persons receiving such aid are fully entitled to speculate on why it is being given. Verbal witness added to such actions clarifies the situation. Even then, the tests of honesty and sincerity in the verbal witness will take time. Over time one sees the complex interaction between words and deeds. The point being made here is that it is essential that such verbal witness be given so that the purpose of the deeds might be known.

There is no substitute for a verbal sharing of the gospel. Who God is, what God has done in Christ, and what God is now doing through the Holy Spirit are all part of a story that must be shared with others. Verbal witness does more than explain our actions. It is an inescapable part of evangelism. Walter Brueggemann says, "Evangelism means inviting people into these stories as the definitional story of our life, and thereby authorizing people to give up, abandon, and renounce other stories that have shaped their lives in false or distorting ways."³ To invite persons in to the story in this way requires verbally telling the story to them.

Second, verbal communication of the gospel is important because it clarifies a significant role for laypersons in the ministry of the church. Too often a congregation will claim that its lay members are the ministers of the congregation. They are invited to teach Sunday school classes, lead committees, participate in mission trips, and fulfill other volunteer functions related to the institutional life. Far too often congregations don't help laypersons understand how they are to relate to their non-Christian neighbors. It is the job of every layperson to share the gospel with others. To love non-Christians well is to evangelize them. To evangelize them well is to do it lovingly.⁴ A ministry of faith sharing clarifies how everyone can do that.

Third, faith sharing is one of the most effective ways in which non-Christians become disciples. In many parts of Europe and North America, a majority of the persons do not have an active relationship with a congregation. Although they may identify themselves as Christians, they are not practicing their faith. One of the most effective ways in which persons become Christians or reactivate their discipleship is by the invitation of someone with whom they have a relationship. It is often through the witness of a relative, neighbor, coworker, or friend that a person begins to investigate the possibility of a relationship with Christ and membership in his church. Many laypersons will suggest that verbal witnessing is the pastor's job. That is true in the sense that it is part of what an ordained clergyperson is supposed to do: preach the Word. At the same time, however, many non-Christian persons will hear a minister and suggest that the message is being given because it is part of her job to do so. Authentic faith sharing from a trusted friend is often more effective than anything a clergyperson could say.

In part this relates to the history of Christianity in Europe and North America. The church has been an active part of our culture for centuries, and outsiders sometimes mistrust the salaried institutional representatives of the movement. When outsiders perceive faith sharing as inviting them to join an institution, then they suggest that the pastor is simply a salesperson trying to get his numbers higher or make his organization more successful. The laity does not appear to have the same self-interested motive as the clergy often do. Another factor is the sheer numerical reality that there are hundreds of laypersons for every clergyperson. If a congregation can get its laity to share the faith, their efforts will be multiplied many times more than if the job is left to the clergy. Thus, for at least these three reasons, faith sharing is important.

Characteristics of the Faith Sharer

The other six aspects of Christian discipleship give us an outline of the characteristics of a faith sharer. While this by no means summarizes Christian discipleship, it shows the ways in which all of the aspects of discipleship are mutually interdependent, and how the other six shape the ministry of faith sharing. One does not have to be far advanced in any one or all of these in order to share one's faith. Beginners can often be very effective, precisely by sharing their struggles in these areas. But just as discipleship means being initiated into each of the areas, some beginning is necessary in each one for the disciple to share her faith with integrity.

With regard to morality, the faith sharer has to walk the walk as well as talk the talk. As noted above, we live in a culture where there is a long history of people doing evangelism. Many times non-Christian people have had experiences they regard as negative with people who call themselves Christians. One part of evangelism is the telling of God's amazing love for the world in Christ Jesus. When that love is shown by deeds and by high moral standards of one's life, then one's words are credible. The person who talks about God's love while practicing hatred cannot be believed. The person who sacrificially gives of himself to others while talking about God's love is believable.

Many times faith sharing can be effective only when the sharer has earned the right to be heard. In a world bombarded by many different messages and many different religions and ideologies, Christians should stand out for the quality of their lives. An early Christian apologist was trying to explain the Christians to Emperor Hadrian in the second century. He said, Christians

> love one another. And from the widows they do not turn away their countenance; and they rescue the orphan from him who does him violence; and he who has gives to him who has not, without grudging. And when they see the stranger they bring him to their dwellings, and rejoice over him as over a true brother; for they do not call brothers those who are after the flesh, but those who are in the spirit and in God. But when one of their poor passes away from the world, and any of them sees him, then he pro-

vides for his burial according to his ability; and if they hear that any of their number is imprisoned or oppressed for the name of their Messiah, all of them provide for his needs, and if it is possible that he may be delivered, they deliver him.[5]

When John Wesley was talking about the spread of Christianity, he claimed that the greatest "stumbling-block" to the spread of the gospel was "the lives of the Christians."[6]

Christian evangelism should be motivated by love because the greatest commandment is not to make disciples. It is to love God and neighbor (Matt. 22:34-40). Because of this, it should also have love as the criterion of its effectiveness. The faith sharer should be a loving person and be seen by others as motivated by love for those being evangelized.

With regard to conversion, the faith sharer should have an experience of God's grace to share with others. Every disciple has a story about how she came to believe in Christ. Some of them might be quite dramatic, involving changes such as leaving a life in a gang to becoming a Christian evangelist, or leaving the life of power and corruption in government to becoming a Christian leader. The stories of most Christians are much more ordinary and thus much more powerful for other people who are considering the Christian faith. Being able to communicate one's own faith journey is an important part of faith sharing. But there is another aspect as well. If one is inviting another person to become a Christian, one must know one's own answer to the question *why*. What is the Christian life doing for you right now? Why should anyone undertake it? Why are *you* a Christian? This may involve telling the story of why one originally decided for Christ, but it may also involve new reasons that have evolved over the years of one's Christian journey.

With regard to cognitive commitments, the faith sharer has to know the basics of the story. While sharing one's personal story is part of the process, one also has to know the basics of the biblical witness to the gospel. As already stated, this does not require advanced knowledge. The more one knows about Christian teaching and the meaning of the Bible, the better it would be. But some minimal knowledge is necessary. For example, one should be able to point to certain key biblical texts that would talk about God and Christ, such as John 1 and John 3:16. One might use the Apostles' Creed or the Nicene Creed as basic summaries of the faith. To the extent that one's Bible study would lead to an ability to summarize the whole Bible in a few short sentences, one has gained the ability to begin teaching the non-Christian person what the faith is all about. John Wesley, for example, often noted that the whole "marrow" of scripture is salvation by faith through what Christ has done for us.

The faith sharer needs to be an active member of a Christian congregation. New Christians are taught, inculturated, loved, and baptized by communities of faith. Thus, to share the faith with a non-Christian requires that she be introduced to such a community. Indeed, the matching of words and deeds discussed above means that the non-Christian person is going to ask about the faith sharer's practice. However, this does not mean that the faith sharer must initiate a new believer into his or her congregation. There may be many reasons for helping a non-Christian person become a member of another community of faith. Even then, that will be in imitation of or in reaction to what the faith sharer's community is like. The most frequently followed course is for the faith sharer to welcome the new believer into her own community.

Spiritual gifts are given to every believer. With regard to faith sharing, the way in which one's faith is shared will differ from person to person. I have made the mistake of giving examples of faith sharing that presumed the person is an extrovert who is comfortable talking with strangers in public settings. For many persons, this is never going to happen because they are more introverted. However, such persons may well have a gift for talking with persons on the telephone where they may feel more comfortable. Others may build deep friendships through work or neighborhood relationships. All persons have ways in which they relate to others based on their personalities and patterns of interaction. Learning how God can use those patterns to share faith is an important discovery, and we should celebrate the varieties of spiritual gifts, including different patterns of relationships.

The category of spiritual disciplines involves the many practices by which Christians receive God's grace; what John Wesley referred to as the means of grace. Prayer, Bible study, the Lord's Supper, worship, Sunday school, mission trips, activities supporting social justice, and feeding the poor are all ways in which we may experience the grace of God in our lives. Christians do these things. At the same time, non-Christians often come to the faith by exploring one or more of these disciplines to see what Christianity is all about. Thus, faith sharers should participate in worship, for example, knowing that some non-Christian persons may be sitting near them and sharing, in some way, their worship experience.

But the most important spiritual discipline undergirding faith sharing is prayer. William Abraham in his *Logic of Evangelism* made it clear that there are four agents in the evangelistic process: God, the evangelist, the church, and the person being evangelized. Abraham argues clearly that the priority is with God.[7] Too often Christians believe that evangelism is something we are doing for God. Rather, we should always understand that it is God who is seeking all persons, and that we are simply instruments by which God's love is communicated to others. Thus, we should be praying for God's guidance in this ministry, and for God to include us in what God is doing. There is a deep humility engendered by this ministry of prayer, as we acknowledge that it is not our work alone. It is something God has been doing long before we were involved, and God has multiple instruments that can be used to accomplish those purposes.

Three Types of Faith Sharing

Faith sharing is often construed very narrowly as the confrontational approach made to strangers inviting them to become Christians. The negative stereotype of knocking on doors and asking strangers, "Are you saved?" has led many persons to believe that they do not want to participate in this ministry. Without ruling out this approach (it might be appropriate in some situations) we do well to think more broadly and systematically about this ministry. Faith sharing may take many different forms. All of them, however, can be grouped into three types. Each type can be used with different audiences in different ways, but they have varying levels of intensity and different functions. They will be used by different groups of Christians. Invitation is to be done by all Christians. Testimony is done by those who have a gift for telling their own stories and requires some level of practice and perhaps even training. Mentoring requires the time and the ability to walk with another person on the spiritual journey and usually requires having been mentored in some way.

Invitation

All Christians should invite their non-Christian friends into a relationship with Jesus Christ. The loving motivation for this is to introduce one's friends to the Lord who is most important in one's life. It is a way of sharing one's life and meaning with others. Invitation is a gentle offer of a relationship. It should never be coercive or manipulative. It should respect the right of the other person to decline the invitation with no negative repercussions. It makes clear what is being offered, transmits the offer with genuine warmth, and then awaits the person's response.[8] An invitation into a relationship with Christ can come in a variety of ways. For example, inviting someone to a worship service at one's congregation is a primary way to do this. One presumes that Christ will be present through the power of the Holy Spirit in that service, and that a non-Christian person can encounter Christ there. The encounter may be quite superficial. It may be so vague that the person may not even name the experience as "encountering Christ." It may be named as experiencing warm fellowship, stimulating one's thinking, having the mystical experience of spiritual values, or enjoying a good time. An invitation to worship could be especially powerful if the congregation is prepared to welcome non-Christians and to help them experience the presence of Christ. That should include follow-up that will show genuine hospitality and will eventually help them name their spiritual awakening as the prevenient grace of Christ wooing them into a real relationship.

Invitations to other kinds of things can also work this way. An invitation to participate in Alpha, Beginnings, or some other small group experience designed especially for seekers would serve the same purpose. For others, the invitation to work a Saturday on a mission project might be the best way. For example, if a congregation is working for four consecutive Saturdays on a Habitat for Humanity project, and a Christian invites a non-Christian to come and work for a day, that could be the start of a relationship with the church and through it, a deepening of the relationship with Christ. Invitations to men's sports teams can work in this way so long as the presence of Christ in the group can be discerned by the non-Christian person.

The crucial element here is that the faith sharer is looking for the right time and place to invite the non-Christian into a situation where she might take steps toward a deeper relationship with Christ. An evangelistically effective congregation will have many such opportunities in its program. But its members must be constantly looking for the right match between the non-Christian's self-perceived needs and interests and the ways in which God is using the congregation to touch them.

The most crucial point to help persons take on this basic Christian responsibility is to show them how easily it is done. First, remind them that we are never to proselytize persons who are active in another Christian congregation. Getting persons to change from one denomination to another is not a "net gain" for the reign of God. Second, help them think of persons they already have a relationship with who might appreciate an invitation. Ask them to think about friends, relatives, neighbors, or associates at work. Third, show them how to ask something like, "Do you have a church home?" If the answer is yes, then rejoice. If the answer is no, then follow up with a gentle invitation like, "My church is having a special event that I think might interest you. Would you like to come with me? Maybe we could go out to lunch afterward." Modeling a gentle, invitational approach gives the disciples an idea of how they might be inviting too.

As an illustration, consider the story of George and Susan.[9] They were raised in the church and participated in its ministries as children and youths. During their college years they dropped out, in part because their denomination had no effective campus ministry at their school. They met in college, married, and had three children. When the children were in elementary school, they began thinking about church, but it never seemed to be the right time to start. They thought of themselves as being too busy to add one more activity. However, a local church was having a "Bring a Friend Sunday," and two families they knew invited them to come. They knew these families through the school and community activities in which the children were involved. It just so happened that the people who invited them attended the same denomination in which George and Susan had been raised. On that Sunday they felt right at home, and their children attended Sunday school with friends. The church followed up with genuine hospitality, and they came back the next week. The third week was Easter, and it felt very right for them to be in church as a family. They recommitted their lives to Christ after twenty years of inactivity. Years later they are deeply involved in the music and youth programs of the congregation. A simple invitation led to committed discipleship.

The problem with special events to which visitors are invited is that they come so infrequently. In an evangelistically effective congregation, every Sunday is "Bring a Friend Sunday," and the members are inviting people to worship, small group ministries, and other entry points on a regular basis throughout the year.

Testimony

One text that reminds us of the importance of telling our story is 1 Peter 3:15-16: "Always be ready to make your defense to anyone who demands from you an accounting for the hope that is in you; yet do it with gentleness and reverence." Two key points are made that are often taken as separate realities. On the one hand, Christians should always be ready to talk about their faith in Christ. They need to be ready to give a testimony about what God has done and to point to the hope they have in the Lord. On the other hand, Christians must not be overbearing or aggressive. They should give their testimony in a loving, respectful, and gentle manner.

Too often Christians are uncomfortable talking about what God has done in their lives. Some have never had to formulate an account of what God has done. Perhaps God has always been there, and we think that we don't have a story to tell. Others regard religion as a private matter that should not be discussed. Others may think no one would be interested in their stories. These hesitations need to be overcome to be effective evangelists. Persons can become comfortable by practicing testimony and seeing it done by others. Every Christian should be encouraged to formulate a personal account in written form. Each person's story should be affirmed as important. And the concern that religion is private should be dealt with in two ways. First, we must be respectful and tolerant of others' beliefs or refusal to believe. Second, we should acknowledge that religion is shared among communities of people and that the Christian community is always ready to invite others to join. Hence, genuine Christianity is never private.

Timing is significant in testimony. We must select an appropriate time and place in which to tell the story so that we are "gentle and reverent" toward others. However, it helps if we have rehearsed our story ahead of time. We also have to give ourselves permission to tell the story when a genuine opportunity arises. In many Christian denominations there is a heritage of telling such stories to build up the church. Roman Catholics tell stories about the faith of their saints. Many Protestant Latinos/as give *testimonios* about their conversion experiences. Methodist love feasts from the eighteenth and nineteenth centuries encouraged persons to tell about their encounters with God. Baptist revivals would often allow persons to recount their experiences. In all these cases, ordinary persons are lifted up as models of what the Christian life might be like.

Ordinary persons should be given a chance to share their stories precisely because they encourage other ordinary persons. When hearing the story, people get the idea that God might do something similar in their lives, whether that is to enter into the Christian faith or to take the next step in their discipleship. Many times it is the power of a realistic story well told that will open up a person to the possibilities of a relationship with Christ. Such testimony can be given before large groups of people. That way many can hear and relate to the experience of one person. But sometimes the most effective testimony comes in a one-on-one conversation where a specific question is asked. Sometimes the question is not specifically religious.

Consider the following hypothetical situation. Two men are having lunch in the company lunchroom. They are alone. One says to the other, "My wife asked me for a divorce last night. I am really broken up by this—it is totally unexpected and I don't know what to do. You seem happily married. How do you do it? What should I do?" When asked of a Christian, this is what 1 Peter calls a request for an accounting of the "hope that is in you." Sometimes persons are too uncomfortable talking about their faith or even about personal matters like marriage and divorce, and especially men will sometimes pass off such a comment with a joke. But what if the Christian man said, "Well, you know, I'm no expert on marriage, but my wife and I went through some really hard times a few years back. It was my Sunday school class that brought us through, plus some counseling with my pastor. Do you have a church home?" In a very brief and gentle way, the man has offered part of his Christian testimony, a short and relevant account of what God has done in his life that might well connect with the other man's need. By asking if he has a church home and a Sunday school class, he is indicating one aspect of how he solved his marital difficulties.

Many people look at Christians and wish to have some quality that they exemplify. They will be looking for clues about how to get the same things in their lives. When Christians testify how God has helped them grow, solve problems, cope with tragedy, or find happiness, they are invited into the Christian life. Consider the case of Joann. She was new in a particular community and not finding any friends. She tried a number of solutions including happy hour at the local bars and involvement with a young women's club. She was successful in her career, but finding herself more and more unhappy. While she was accumulating material goods and prestige, her life was not going the direction she wanted.

When she went back home for a holiday, she ran into a high school class-mate who told her about her conversion experience and the difference it had made. She was involved in a Bible study group and was tutoring children in an inner-city mission. For her, life had become full and rich without having to change jobs or give up her career. Joann went back to her city and began looking for a relationship with Christ by attending an Alpha class at a church near her home. A year later she committed her life to Christ and became the coordinator for the youth group's spring mission trip. Life was much more fulfilling. Testimonies can provide persons with models of how they might find the fullness of the Christian life.

Mentoring

Not all non-Christians are seeking a relationship with Christ. Nor are all of them seeking some way of life for which Christianity might be the answer. But when non-Christians do begin to seek, it is often a difficult journey. They need guides. Mentors are the spiritual guides to help seekers move toward their goal. Christians often underestimate how daunting it is for non-Christians to even begin asking about relationships with Christ. We assume that everyone knows the basics of the faith, that the basics are noncontroversial, or that entry into Christian discipleship comes at relatively little cost. For some, all of those might be true. But for others, there is a high cost of discipleship, and the journey is long and arduous.

The other metaphor for this way of faith sharing is that of the midwife. If the person is in labor, seeking to be born again as a child of God, there is need for an experienced person to explain the various things that are going on and to give encouragement. A midwife is a trusted and experienced person who is not doing the hard work, but accompanies the person through the process of the new birth. It is so much easier to have a friend at times like that. The mentor is a spiritual friend.

We might think of five types of difficulties that the mentor can help the seeker overcome. First, there are the social difficulties. Becoming a Christian usually involves participation in a Christian community. Entry into the community means finding friends and guides who will explain the customs and practices of the community and help the newcomer feel at home. Strange things often happen in a church; that is, they appear strange to the outsider who has never experienced them before. The mentor can be one's friend helping the new person fit into the group.

Second, the seeker may have intellectual questions about the faith. Questions about what the Bible says, how one can begin reading it without getting bogged down in some of the more obscure sections, and what certain key words like "Trinity" mean are important. Sometimes there are questions arising out of personal experience like, "Why did God let my father die when we were praying so hard for him to live?" The mentor does not have to be a professional theologian to answer these questions. Indeed, some perennial questions are so hard, there is no consensus in the church about how best to answer them. What is needed from the mentor is honesty about how she understands these things, to help orient the seeker to a Christian worldview in dealing with difficult issues. In some cases, referring the seeker to a pastor or more knowledgeable person may be helpful.

Third, there are sometimes past experiences with Christianity or with other religions that need attention. Most of us have had experiences with Christians who did not act in ways that truly shared God's love, offered inadequate expressions of the faith, or failed us at key times in our lives. Often, entry into the Christian faith means learning to focus on Christ rather than on Christians. It may take a mentor to acknowledge that others have had bad experiences as well without their losing their faith. It may mean coming to terms with the differences and similarities between Christianity and other religions. It may mean acknowledging that Christianity, even one's denomination or congregation, is imperfect. But without a mentor to acknowledge these things, the seeker may never learn about them.

Fourth, there can be moral issues that prevent persons from becoming Christians. They may be addicted to alcohol or engaged in illegal activities or doing things harmful to themselves and others that they refuse to give up. They know that becoming a Christian means resisting those behaviors and eventually (if not immediately) giving them up. It may mean leaving an immoral group like a gang to become part of the church. Such a step requires the support of a mentor.

Fifth, there are sometimes relational issues that need a mentor. If the seeker is married to a non-Christian or is part of an extended family that is very hostile to Christianity, there may be significant personal costs in becoming a Christian. Learning how to navigate these difficulties requires advice, support, and encouragement. A mentor might help to ease these relational realities.

One way in which mentors are being trained in many churches today is through the small groups that train persons to become leaders. These persons often gain sensitivity to the spiritual struggles of persons in their groups and are able to find ways of supporting and guiding them through the process. In all of these situations, mentoring is a way of sharing one's faith. One helps the other by sharing the spiritual struggles that one has encountered personally, or that one has studied or heard about from others.

Just Do It

In any given congregation, there should be an expectation that all persons participate in the invitational type of faith sharing. For many congregations, simply naming that expectation will increase the percentage of persons who do so, and that will contribute to the congregation's evangelistic effectiveness.[10] A much smaller number will be able to tell their story to others. This is especially true of giving one's testimony in front of a group of persons. But many will learn how to tell their story in more private settings. The number of persons who will learn how to mentor seekers and others entering into Christian discipleship will be much smaller. In part this will be because of limited time for many, but also limited training opportunities and the fact that some will have the personality gifts and relational skills that make mentorship more natural than it is for others. Nonetheless, in small ways and larger ways, we are called just to do it; as Christians, sharing our faith should become as constant as our praying and as natural as our breathing.

CHAPTER 18

The Alpha Course[1]

Philip R. Meadows

From its modest beginnings as a simple homegrown program of cate-chesis for new Christians at Holy Trinity Brompton (HTB)—a charismatic-evangelical Anglican church in central London—the Alpha Course has grown to become a worldwide "movement" of evangelism and church renewal. In Britain, a recent poll showed that 20 percent of the adult population can now identify Alpha as a Christian course.[2] And as a result of advertising campaigns at the local and the national levels, the Alpha logo—a man wrestling with a question mark—is widely recognized as its "trademark." Alpha has been publicly recommended by theologians and church leaders from most major denominations: Anglican, Baptist, Methodist, Pentecostal, Presbyterian, Salvation Army, and Roman Catholic. Today, there are more than seven thousand courses running in Britain; and the influence of Alpha has extended into 85 percent of the prisons, 74 percent of the universities, and even the armed forces.[3] In 2001, a British television company, ITV, broadcast a documentary series of ten one-hour programs on the Alpha Course, hosted by Sir David Frost, titled *Alpha: Will It Change Their Lives?* It is estimated that about one million viewers tuned in each week to hear excerpts from the talks and follow the progress of a small group.[4]

Having outgrown the administrative capacities of HTB itself, the movement is now coordinated by a closely related charitable organization called Alpha International, which currently facilitates the work of nearly 30,000 courses worldwide, through 30 nationally based offices and 23 country-specific Web sites. Of these courses, there are 7,070 in the USA, and a total of about 6,000 in the former Commonwealth countries of Australia, Canada, New Zealand, and South Africa. Beyond this, Alpha is being offered on every continent, among 147 different countries, and in 49 languages, including 4 different dialects of Chinese. The latest statistics claim that 6 million people have attended an Alpha Course worldwide.[5]

In Britain, numerous surveys have been undertaken to assess the impact of this impressive record.[6] Notwithstanding the difficulties of measuring the "effectiveness" of courses like Alpha, it seems safe to say that (on average) around a sixth of the participants "come to faith" for the first time, and more than half of those with some sort of Christian commitment find themselves "moved forward" in the faith.[7] At least as significant, however, is the overall impact that running the course has upon the renewal of congregational life in the local church. When the course is reused over an extended period of time, churches report not only an arrest of their decline in membership, but also a deepening of Christian fellowship, an enlivening of worship, a new commitment to service, and a more missionally oriented church culture.[8] We wait to see whether such findings are reproduced in other contexts around the world.

The purpose of this essay is neither to confirm nor to dispute these claims, but to offer theological reflection upon the Alpha Course as a model of evangelism. In order to do this, we will (1) examine what constitutes the course itself; (2) identify evangelistic principles that it seems to embody; and (3) deal with some of the serious criticisms that it has raised.

1. The Character of Alpha

Alpha was started in 1977 by Charles Marnham, then curate of HTB, as a four-session course aimed at "presenting the basic principles of the Christian faith to new Christians in a relaxed and informal setting."[9] Each session began with a meal, followed by a talk, and concluded with discussion in small groups. Successive leaders continued to develop the course—expanding the material and including a weekend retreat—yet the basic pattern of meeting has remained the same to date. When Nicky Gumbel took up leadership of Alpha in 1990, it had already become a central feature of church life at HTB, attracting around one hundred people for each course, including a large proportion of nonchurchgoers. Although the course was originally designed to offer *instruction about the Christian life* for new converts, it had also become an *introduction to the Christian faith* for inquirers.[10]

Observing this trend, Gumbel revised the elements of Alpha into an intentionally evangelistic program. The whole church environment, the sharing of meals, the style of the talks, and the leadership of small groups would be made hospitable to nonchurchgoers; and the weekend away became a time during which many participants would experience evangelical conversion and a filling of the Spirit. The success of Alpha led to requests from other churches for copies of the curriculum and the eventual publication of Gumbel's best-selling book *Questions of Life* (1993), which contains transcripts of the talks upon which the course sessions are founded.[11] Alpha International now describes the course as "a 15-session practical introduction to the Christian faith . . . aimed especially at people who don't go to church."[12]

Figure 1. A Typical Alpha Session

7:00 p.m. Evening Meal
7:40 p.m. Welcome
7:50 p.m. Worship
8:00 p.m. Video or Talk (see below)
8:45 p.m. Coffee

1.1. An Introduction to Christianity

The first session of Alpha is a "celebration" in which those who have been invited to "come and see" what the course is about are made to feel welcome by the hospitality, then presented with testimonials from previous participants, and finally treated to a talk asking the rhetorical question, "Christianity: Boring, Untrue, and Irrelevant?" Subsequent sessions, which compose the Alpha Course proper, include small group discussion after the talk (see figure 1).

Those whose interest has been piqued by the celebration are invited to sign up for the whole course and to return the following week to begin a fifteen-session cycle over eleven weeks (see figure 2). The cycle concludes (or begins) with another celebration at which some of the current participants offer their testimonies and a new cohort is recruited.

Figure 2: Alpha Course Sessions

CELEBRATION
1. Christianity: Boring, Untrue and Irrelevant?

WEEKLY SESSIONS
12. How Can I Resist Evil?
13. Why and How Should We Tell Others?
14. Does God Heal Today?
15. What about the Church?

WEEKLY SESSIONS
2. Who Is Jesus?
3. Why Did Jesus Die?
4. How Can I Be Sure of My Faith?
5. Why and How Should I Read the Bible?
6. Why and How Do I Pray?
7. How Does God Guide Us?

WEEKEND AWAY
8. Who Is the Holy Spirit?
9. What Does the Holy Spirit Do?
10. How Can I Be Filled with the Spirit?
11. How Can I Make the Most of the Rest of My Life?

Questions of Life. Alpha claims to answer the great questions of life, like "What is the purpose of life?" and "What happens when we die?" Given that neither of these questions is explicitly dealt with in the sessions themselves, it would be reasonable to ask, "What kind of life raises the questions actually tackled in the Alpha Course?" It may be true that there is a certain curiosity about the Christian faith among nonchurchgoers, but it is unlikely that truly secular people are daily haunted by questions like "Why did Jesus die?" or "Why and how should I read the Bible?" The fact is that such questions are raised only by an encounter with the gospel itself or by those already striving after the Christian life. In other words, Alpha tells inquirers what sorts of questions they should ask when confronted with the gospel story, if they are to understand the promises and claims it makes upon them. By answering its own questions, then, Alpha narrates the gospel through a series of formal talks and small group discussions; constantly inviting people to reread their lives in light of the good news about Jesus Christ and what it means to follow him.

Christian Apologetics. Apart from the session on "Who is Jesus?" and some prefatory comments in the session on reading the Bible, there is little about the Alpha talks that would count as "classical apologetics," such as defending the reliability of scripture or seeking to persuade unbelievers about the truth of the gospel by rational argumentation from publicly available evidence for the life, death, and resurrection of Jesus. Rather, the apologetic force of these "homilies" lies in making the gospel *intelligible* through the plain exposition of Christian doctrine; *credible* through its power to make sense of people's lives; and *compelling* through the actual witness of those whose lives have been transformed by it. The talks are narrative and parabolic in style, each seeking to make contact between gospel and hearer through an extensive use of familiar illustrations, affective stories, and inspiring testimonies. This approach also sets up the discursive tone of the small groups as a context for faith sharing, during which leaders and helpers may engage an inquirer's questions through the naturally persuasive form of personal witness. In this way, Alpha as an introduction to *Christianity* comes primarily through an introduction to *Christians!*

Searching Issues. The purpose of the talks is clearly to "proclaim" the gospel with confidence, but in such a way that questions and objections to the Christian faith are stirred up. It is among the small groups, then, that a real defense of this confident gospel takes place: not in the form of disembodied arguments or assertions, but in the discursively open-ended environment of dialogue between believers and inquirers. Under the conditions of postmodernity, there is wisdom in Alpha's claim that the problem of suffering, the challenge of religious pluralism, and the skepticism of a scientific culture, and so forth, cannot be resolved satisfactorily through the presentation of knock-down arguments and an appeal to "common sense." Of course, Christian arguments deal with objections like these, and Gumbel outlines some of them in a separate book, *Searching Issues* (1994), which is used in the training of small group leaders rather than the course itself.[13] Studying this material, then, is meant not to provide pat answers to big questions, but to educate real people who can embody such arguments over the long haul of personal witness with others.

Relational Theology. Although much can be (and has been) said about the actual content of the talks, we can already see why merely focusing on textual details will not give us access to the much broader evangelistic strengths of the Alpha Course. There are, however, two strongly theological commitments that shape Alpha as a whole. First, Gumbel claims that "at the heart of Christianity is a relationship with God."[14] Jonathan Bayes traces this thread through *Questions of Life* in the following way:

> To have a relationship with God is the reason for which we were created; the relationship is one in which we are God's sons and daughters; it is very intimate, the most exciting relationship, and to live within it is the most satisfying and meaningful way to live—it is a life of an eternal quality; it is God's own desire that we should have this relationship; the breaking of the relationship was both the root and the result of sin . . . ; without it we suffer such feelings as inner hunger, emptiness, and meaninglessness; the main point of the Bible is to show how we can have this relationship; the way into this relationship with God is through what Jesus Christ has done for us on the cross, through his righteousness and through our relationship with him; it is the work of the Spirit to bring us into, to maintain, to develop, and to assure us of, our relationship with God . . . ; the relationship is developed by prayer . . . ; it is the spring from which our guidance and our witness come.[15]

Although Gumbel does situate this intensely personal relationship with God in the context of Christian community, it seems to come as something of an afterthought.[16] Arguably, this deficiency is made up in the otherwise broadly ecclesial setting of the Alpha Course as a whole.

Charismatic Influence. The second theological emphasis is a distinctively charismatic dimension to the way this life of relationship with God, in Christ, is accomplished through the life-transforming presence and power of the Holy Spirit. HTB has long been a center for the charismatic movement in Britain. The ministries of John Wimber and other leaders of the Vineyard Christian Fellowship have been particularly influential in shaping its approach to the person and work of the Holy Spirit in evangelism. Wimber frequently visited HTB with his ministry teams during the 1980s, and Gumbel attributes his own sense of calling as an evangelist to a dramatic life-changing experience of the Spirit on one of those occasions in 1982. During the early 1990s, HTB was to become a main "carrier" of the so-called Toronto Blessing—having originated at the Toronto Airport Vineyard—notable for its unusual manifestations like falling over, uncontrollable shaking, and "holy laughter." Although there is no explicit reference to the Toronto Blessing in the Alpha materials, the course gently introduces its participants to many familiar emphases of the charismatic movement, especially through its extensive teaching on the Holy Spirit and its "ministry time" during the weekend away, when the filling and gifting of the Spirit are sought, and speaking in tongues is encouraged.[17] Within a few weeks of the "Holy Spirit weekend" there is a session on miraculous healing in the regular course curriculum.

Small Groups. We have identified how small groups connect the course material with personal witness as a form of Christian apologetics. To suggest that these small groups really lie at the heart of Alpha, however, means that the "course" is not merely an *introduction* to Christianity but also an *initiation* into the Christian life. We are told that "the overall purpose of the small group, along with the course as a whole, is to help to bring people into a relationship with Jesus Christ."[18] This is accomplished not by adopting special techniques in group dynamics, but by modeling Bible study, discovering prayer, and forming Christian friendships. In other words, coming to Christ through learning about the Christian life is, in part, accomplished by a form of "apprenticeship" in the means of grace. In addition, the small groups provide a context of intimacy and accountability in which Christian ministry can be exercised. For the leaders of Alpha, this means participating in the ministry of the Spirit, who leads people to Christ, bestows spiritual gifts, and empowers the growth of a new life, built on biblical claims and promises.

1.2. A Renewal of Church Life

It is not surprising that Alpha has made as much, if not more, of an impact on renewing the life of local churches as the evangelizing of nonchurchgoers. The fact is that many of our churches are plagued with a doctrinal amnesia and a spiritual aridity that have impoverished their Christian life and witness in an unbelieving world.[19] Insofar as Alpha has rekindled a love of the gospel and a spiritual vitality among church members, it reminds us that a truly evangelistic church is itself constantly being reevangelized.

Core Commitment. When we consider Alpha as a means of church renewal, we are once again alerted to the weakness of speaking about it as a "course." Given the limited resources of most local churches, running a course is not likely to be one program among many, but a "core commitment" that shapes the whole culture of a congregation's life together: drawing upon its practices of hospitality, doing church administration, conducting worship, delivering talks, and leading small groups. Where these gifts are not already in place, they must be cultivated through the prayerful training of leaders and helpers. So, when the Evangelical Alliance (UK) refers to Alpha as a "model" of church,[20] it means the way in which the course can renew a congregational sense of missionary purpose centered on evangelism and discipleship. Clearly, Alpha does not fully address the requirements of any missional ecclesiology, but it has often inspired a churchwide recovery of intimate fellowship, Bible study, corporate prayer, pastoral care, lay ministry, and lively worship. Perhaps more important, however, is that Alpha offers a pattern for how all these practices can be combined in the life of a local church as a means for making disciples of Jesus Christ. This is one fruit of Alpha's insistence upon repeating the course with the kind of constancy necessary for habituating good practices of personal and corporate witness.

Christian Initiation. Alpha claims that there is need for "three conversions: to Christ, to his church, to his cause."[21] These are not three separate conversions, but a single conversion with three inseparable dimensions. We should not think of Alpha as first leading people to Christ, then passing them on to the church, so that they can be equipped for his cause. This would reduce the course to another parachurch activity within, or appended to, the church itself. Insofar as Alpha is a self-consciously ecclesial activity, however, we might say that it is only through the Christian community that people are introduced to Christ and taught how to follow him. So, when pressed with the question, "What sort of church are we bringing them into?" those proposing to run a course are really being asked to reflect upon the character of their life together. Alpha must not be reduced to a programmatic technique because the people who run it *are* the church! Neither can it be an end in itself because Alpha does not exhaust what it means to *be* the church! To participate in a course is a form of Christian initiation that can be completed only through incorporation into the core practices of discipleship that characterize a particular ecclesial community. Any church considering Alpha should also be pressed to examine whether it actually has a form of Christian life worth being initiated into or how running the course could help to cultivate it.

1.3. The Dynamics of a Movement

Over the last decade, Alpha has taken on many qualities of a renewal movement, with an ecumenical flavor, and on an international scale.

Basic Christianity. Historically speaking, it is a common feature of renewal movements to claim that they are recovering a kind of scriptural Christianity essential to any form of church life. Alpha is no exception, and claims that the teaching found in *Questions of Life* and the simple practices that constitute the course as a whole are common to (or at least compatible with) the more distinctive commitments of any historic tradition. If the test of this were simply the range of denominations that have endorsed Alpha—from Evangelical Free to Roman Catholic—then it would seem the course does indeed have that sort of ecumenical appeal. It is not surprising, therefore, that teaching on tradition-specific doctrines concerning the nature of church, sacraments, and so forth is absent from the course. Alpha leaders point out that the course is not intended to exhaust the catechesis necessary for full participation in the life of any particular ecclesial tradition. Hence, the strategy employed by *Alpha for Catholics* is to supplement the standard Alpha Course with additional follow-up sessions covering Catholic ecclesiology and sacramental theology.[22] As we will see, however, much of the controversy about the course, from Protestants and Catholics, has centered on the depth of Alpha's particular commitments to the evangelical-charismatic tradition. The claim to basic Christianity turns out to be deceptively simple, even if these charismatic emphases are found across the denominations or actively sought by churches within them.

Alpha Churches. We live in a time when mainstream denominations are suffering from a crisis of identity. On the one hand, this has resulted from a failure to catechize members in the distinctive doctrines and practices associated with their historic traditions. On the other hand, an increasingly privatized and consumerist approach to the Christian life has meant that churchgoing is more likely to be influenced by personal preference than denominational loyalty. In the midst of this, the kind of "core commitment" that Alpha requires, and the extensive influence it can have upon a congregation's life together, has led to the new identity of an "Alpha church." It is not unusual for a renewal movement to become an *ecclesiola in ecclesia* (i.e., a "church within a church"); but Alpha could even be described as a quasi-denominational organization in the midst of the church catholic. The tension arises when being an "Alpha church" communicates more about the life of a congregation than being Methodist, Baptist, or Roman Catholic.

Authorized Texts. The quasi-denominational "feel" of Alpha is strengthened by the politics of the movement itself. The talks published in *Questions of Life* have become the "authorized text" upon which every Alpha Course must be based, together with a whole host of other resource materials on the practicalities of running it.[23] If a congregation is to run an Alpha Course and be recognized as an Alpha church, then it must abide by the copyright protection of these Alpha materials: "Use of Alpha International publications is permitted only when in conjunction with the running or promotion of Alpha International courses."[24] Although one is permitted to make minor adaptations to the course, "these should only concern the length of the talks or the number of sessions." In such case, however, "the essential character of the course must be retained" and "the person responsible must . . . not publish or promote such a course." The reason for these limitations is precisely to "ensure the uniformity" and "integrity of the courses," regardless of the denominational context in which they are run, a strategy that can seem more like "colonization" than ecumenical "cooperation." The uniformity of Alpha Courses does have the distinct advantage of enabling people to recommend courses with confidence to distant friends and family.

Apostolic Leadership. The movement is also identified with the "apostolic" leadership of Gumbel and his HTB team, especially through the gathering of regional conferences around the world (and now simulcast via satellite) in which the Alpha vision is cast, its materials are promoted, training is offered, and the movement is defended against its critics.[25] This pattern of itinerancy, together with the regular publication of *Alpha News*,[26] brings a sense of corporate connection and common purpose to the entire movement.

2. Some Principles Behind Alpha

A typical Alpha conference will open with a discussion of the "six new testament principles of evangelism" that the course is supposed to embody: (1) evangelism is most effective through the local church; (2) evangelism is a process; (3) evangelism involves the whole person; (4) models of evangelism include classical, holistic, and power evangelism; (5) evangelism in the power of the Holy Spirit is both dynamic and effective; and (6) "effective evangelism" requires the filling and refilling of the Holy Spirit.[27] In the following sections, we will examine these principles in the context of current trends in the study of evangelism.

2.1. The Church as Evangelist

When I ask my students what kinds of people and practices they associate with evangelism, they typically think of "crusaders" like Billy Graham and Luis Palau proclaiming the gospel to packed football stadiums; the visit of a revival preacher at a church's annual camp meeting; the charismatic appeal of television evangelists broadcasting their message from a megachurch; or the "lone ranger" clothed in a sandwich board who announces some version of the gospel to passersby on the sidewalk. As an alternative to such activities, they might speak about the evangelistic work of various nondenominational parachurch organizations, especially among young people and college students, such as Young Life (U.S.), Youth With A Mission (international), InterVarsity Christian Fellowship (U.S.), or the Christian Union Movement (UK). Finally, they might think of those who have been appointed to the "office" of evangelist by an institutional church, those reluctantly appointed to an "evangelism committee" in a local church, or perhaps those bold individuals for whom it seems second nature to share their faith with strangers whether inside or outside the church.

The Gift of Evangelist. What crusades, revivals, parachurch organizations, institutional offices, and itinerant individuals have in common is that they tend to detach the practice of evangelism from the life of the church itself. Over the long term, this has meant that Christian education, spiritual formation, and social activism have tended to supplant a vision for, commitment to, and skill in evangelism among our local churches. Contemporary scholars have sought to address this by encouraging something of a paradigm shift toward the idea of a "missional ecclesiology."[28] We have been reminded that evangelism is to be situated within the *missio Dei* (i.e., the mission of the triune God, whose primary witness to the world is the church's life together in Christ, gathered and indwelled by the Spirit). Among the diversity of spiritual gifts bestowed upon the church, that of evangelist is given "to equip the saints for the work of ministry, for building up the body of Christ" (Eph. 4:11-12). So, the charism of an evangelist is not only for personally leading people to Christ, but also for cultivating the evangelistic ministry of making disciples throughout the whole life of the church. Evangelism, then, is not so much a *program* of the church, but a *description* of its very life and vocation in a world of unbelief. Some speak of "the church as evangelist," or an evangelistic community in which every member plays a part in bringing people to Christ and fulfilling the Great Commission.

Beyond Proclamation. In a broad sense, we might think of Alpha as the gift of "the charism of" evangelism to the local church rather than strictly a program of evangelism. In other words, the charism of Alpha is not merely for bringing people to Christ, but for bringing a new sense of evangelistic purpose to the whole life of the church. The question facing every church member, then, is not *whether* one should be involved in evangelism, but *what* part one has to play because evangelism requires the giftedness of every member in the Body. Alpha has the virtue of enabling those with the gifts of administration, hospitality, encouraging, and helping, for example, to see that the task of communicating the gospel is not the sole province of teachers, preachers, and pastors. Considered from this starting point, Alpha's claim that "evangelism is most effective through the local Church" recognizes that introducing people to Jesus Christ cannot be reduced to a disembodied proclamation of the gospel. Rather, an inquirer is just as likely to encounter Christ through the gift of a meal or the peculiar flavor of Christian friendship, as through persuasive talks and apologetic arguments. Unbelievers are also brought to Christ as they taste and see Christians who truly follow him: by "eavesdropping" on their worship, sharing in their prayers, listening to their stories, and receiving their service.

2.2. Evangelism as a Process

Again, when I ask my students to define the nature of Christian conversion, they typically begin with a revivalistic pattern of proclamation and decision common to the evangelists and evangelical organizations described above. Conversion happens in a datable moment, occasioned by an appeal to give one's life to Christ and a personal decision to follow him, often marked by an invitation to kneel, stand, or "come forward" for a prayer of commitment. Whether this occurs at a crusade, a revival meeting, or faith sharing in the street, the "decisionism" associated with these practices tends to detach the work of conversion from the ministry of the local church. Moreover, there is also a subtle temptation to think of evangelism as a "technique" that produces converts, if only the "effectiveness" of an appeal can be assured.[29]

The Nature of Conversion. To begin with, the idea of the church as evangelist does not deny that there is a need for making a *decision* to follow Christ or that there is or can be a single *moment* of Christian conversion. Rather, it is to suggest that the conditions that make such a *momentous decision* possible typically include an extended period of cate-chesis in which the claims of Christ and the cost of discipleship can be considered. It also presumes that a life-changing encounter with Christ, together with the gifts of repentance and faith, can come at any time, not just those moments "engineered" by an evangelist. There has been much debate among contemporary scholars about whether conversion is an event or a process: whether regeneration, the new birth, or new life in Christ is given in a moment or occurs over time.[30] It is common for Wesleyans to hold a view of conversion that includes a moment of for-giveness and new birth (i.e., justification) *and* a process of growth in grace (i.e., the seeking after justification and the subsequent work of sanctification). I think Alpha is wise in speaking about *evangelism* as a process rather than *conversion* itself, because this helps to locate the nec-essary moment of repentance and faith in the ongoing practices of a church that leads people to Christ and nurtures them as his disciples.

Belonging before Believing. In an increasingly post-Christian and post-modern society, where the accidental catechism of a wider Christendom culture is waning and skepticism about any claim to truth is rising, it is unlikely that revivalistic forms of evangelism have much of a future. Under these conditions, it has been observed that most people come to faith through Christian friendships and gradual inclusion into the life of a local church.[31] It has been said that "belonging precedes believing" because convincing the head and heart about the truth of the gospel is seeing it proven in the lives of Christians and gradually discovering that it makes a claim on one's own life as well. Postmoderns are likely to call this "authenticity," or an experience of the gospel made "real" among those whose lives make sense only if what they believe is actually true.[32]

2.3. Evangelizing the Whole Person

The ecclesial context of evangelism as a process also helps to make sense of Alpha's claim that it involves the whole person: with an appeal to the head, the heart, the conscience, and the will. It matters that all these are addressed and that they are mutually dependent aspects of authentic conversion and Christian life.

Faith and Reason. Making the distinction between faith and fideism is important since Christian faith does not begin where secular reason stops. The gospel story, which we live by faith, makes complete sense of our lives. Faith is not pitted against reason, but shapes and directs it in a manner consistent with the truth about God in Christ by the illuminating power of the Spirit and through the means of grace. The postmodern mind, however, knows that many stories invite our trust, many powers lie behind them, and many possible reasons exist for giving them our allegiance. Merely demonstrating the reasons for believing is unlikely to turn skeptics into believers; postmodernity makes it possible to affirm the rationality of Christian faith with a resounding, "Whatever!" Rather, the "reasonableness" of our faith is demonstrated as the gospel is rendered intelligible (and compelling) by people who think, speak, and act in ways that truly embody what they profess.

Experimental Christianity. Alpha is right, therefore, that an appeal to the head is insufficient and requires the more experimental dimensions of heart, conscience, and will. Wesleyans have no difficulty in affirming that the work of the Spirit in conversion includes being *convinced* of God's love, being *convicted* of sin, and being *called* to yield one's life in repentance and faith. The Spirit's influence comes by persuasion, not coercion, preveniently inspiring those restless "drawings" and "desires" after God upon which our evangelism depends. In a postmodern culture that tends to thrive upon the narcissistic excess of pursuing one's private spiritual journey, however, Alpha needs to take care that its charismatic emphasis upon spiritual experience does not become a substitute for true conversion and growth in discipleship. Christian experience is not a purely inward or private matter. First, it is the experience of a whole way of life shaped by obedience to Jesus Christ. Second, it is also a participation in the experience of Christian community: as we encounter the presence of God through the ministry of one to another, and as we depend upon the testimony of others to the grace of God even when personal experience eludes us.

2.4. The Spirit in Evangelism

Three of the six principles of evangelism presumed by Alpha relate to its dependence on the person and power of the Holy Spirit. Having affirmed what is referred to as *classical evangelism* (i.e., "proclaiming the unchanging message of Jesus Christ and him crucified") and what is known in some circles as *holistic evangelism* (i.e., the interpenetration of faith sharing and social action),[33] we are introduced to the idea of *power evangelism* (i.e., "proclamation of the gospel combined with a demonstration of the Spirit's power"). In short: words, works, and wonders!

Although Gumbel has been influenced by many writers and thinkers on the person and activity of the Spirit, Alpha's emphasis on "power evangelism" is clearly indebted to the work of John Wimber.[34] Although a full analysis of his teaching on power evangelism lies outside the scope of this essay, we can identify a few key features.

Signs of the Kingdom. Wimber defines evangelism as a proclamation of the kingdom of God accompanied by seven "signs of the Kingdom," or public demonstrations of the present-yet-future reign of God. The first sign is Jesus himself, God breaking into human history, in whom and through whom the Kingdom is made present among us. The second sign is that the gospel of the Kingdom is now preached by the followers of Jesus.[35] The third sign is exorcism or the confrontation and expulsion of evil principalities and powers. Although Wimber is willing to include demonic ideologies and social structures in this, he certainly reasserts the reality of "power encounters" with demonic spirits and the need for ministries of deliverance. The fourth sign is healing miracles, which Wimber also takes to be a present anticipation of the final Kingdom in which disorder, disease, and death will be no more. The fifth sign is the miracle of conversion and new birth, which is experienced as a foretaste "of the powers of the age to come" (Heb. 6:5). The sixth sign is the people of the Kingdom, among whom the gifts and the fruit of the Spirit are made manifest, especially that of love, which issues in good works and social responsibility. The seventh sign is suffering, or the willingness to live a cruciform life as a sign that we have entered the salvation of God, the promise of the Kingdom.

Kingdom Evangelism. The basic premise behind power evangelism is that the same Spirit who empowered the earthly ministry of Jesus is given to his disciples so that they may continue to bear the signs of the Kingdom until it fully comes. In particular, the authority with which Jesus healed the sick is now delegated to his followers and remains a most convincing sign of God's manifest presence and power to save. The Alpha Course emphasizes all of these. Whether or not one is willing to accept Wimber's emphasis on signs and wonders, contemporary scholars would agree that announcing the eschatological kingdom of God certainly lies at the heart of the gospel, as a present-yet-future reality in which the powers and principalities of this world are overthrown and a foretaste of eternal life is made known.[36] Indeed, William Abraham's influential work has made initiation into the kingdom of God a primary definition of evangelism;[37] and others have made strong ecclesiological claims for the church itself to become a sign, foretaste, and herald of the Kingdom.[38]

The Power of the Spirit. Whether one is convinced by the arguments for power evangelism, an emphasis on the work of the Holy Spirit is a key to understanding evangelism in the context of the *missio Dei*. We must remember that bringing people into a saving relationship with Jesus Christ is God's own work, in which we are invited to participate as coworkers in the gospel.[39] Discerning the Spirit in evangelism, then, will require an adventurous posture that is liable to scandalize approaches to church growth shaped by the managerial sciences, especially insofar as they seek to predict and secure the future through various bureaucratic and technological means.[40] When Alpha uses the language of "effectiveness" in evangelism, I take it to mean a basic confidence in the effective-yet-unpredictable presence and power of the Spirit to change lives, rather than the ability to deploy a strategic plan for church growth, complete with measurable goals against which the success of our operations can be calculated.[41] Alpha's charismatic emphasis on the "filling and refilling of the Holy Spirit," however, must not be sought as some ecstatic or privatized end in itself, but an openness to the fruit and gifts of the Spirit for shaping the evangelistic life of the whole church.

3. Taking Issue with Alpha

It is not surprising that a movement of such influence should also be the subject of much critique. Apart from the publication of significant scholarly analyses in the form of books, articles, essays, and conference presentations, Alpha has received a good deal of attention from the news media, Christian magazines, and other independent publishers, especially through the Internet. Although the organization is very effective at promoting itself—through its Web sites, conferences, and the publication of *Alpha News*—one supposes that the worldwide level of support for Alpha among the churches, as noted at the beginning of this essay, speaks for itself. Criticisms of Alpha, however, are quite wide ranging, from questions of style and delivery to more substantive issues of course content, and the ethos of the movement as a whole.

3.1. Issues about Content

Many critiques of the Alpha Course are based upon theological analyses of Gumbel's book *Questions of Life,* and the adequacy of the curriculum as an introduction to the Christian faith for nonchurchgoers. Although this curriculum may well describe its nature as a "course," we have noted that it certainly does not describe the significance of Alpha as a whole pattern of evangelism. Nevertheless, it is in many ways foundational for the rest and warrants careful attention, together with a critique of its critics.

Theologically Ambiguous? One frequently raised issue concerns the lack of clarity about exactly who is being addressed by the course material. On the one hand, much of the curriculum seems to assume participants are already Christian, and this is, in part, a historical accident rooted in the origins of Alpha as a program of catechesis for new believers. The course certainly has appealed to existing church members as an opportunity for spiritual recommitment and renewal, if not a form of initial evangelization. On the other hand, HTB also discovered by historical accident that nonchurchgoers were coming to faith for the first time by participating in the same catechetical environment. What are we to learn from this? At the very least, it suggests that the Spirit works in the lives of seekers and believers, to convert and confirm in the faith, as they find themselves on a common spiritual journey. However, Gumbel does conclude the session "Why Did Jesus Die?" with an invitation to give one's life to Christ and leads us through a sinner's prayer. It makes sense, then, to follow with a session on "How Can I Be Sure of My Faith?" Although it is not anticipated that every unbeliever will be converted in that moment, the logic of the material itself clearly assumes that it will be the case for some. What troubles many commentators is the uncertainty with which the course proceeds to the weekend away and the indiscriminate invitation for all to be filled with the Spirit and speak in tongues. There is a fear that true conversion to Christ may be substituted by a thirst for spiritual experience that does not amount to real Christian discipleship. The test, then, is whether Alpha's emphasis on the work of the Holy Spirit actually leads people to Jesus Christ and enables them to bear the fruit of a Christlike life over the long haul.

Theologically Inadequate? Although many commentators have pointed out certain weaknesses or omissions in the course material, there is certainly no consensus against Alpha. By and large, the various criticisms are offered by people who would typically argue with each other over their own particular theological commitments and ecclesial practices, whether evangelical or liberal, Calvinist or Arminian, Protestant or Catholic. Depending upon whom one listens to, there could be too much or too little attention paid to the doctrine of sin, the holiness and wrath of God, the Atonement and Resurrection, the kingdom of God, church and sacraments, or social ethics. Although trinitarian thinking runs through the entire course, the doctrine of the Trinity is not itself taken up as a specific question in the formal curriculum. It is, however, dealt with in *Searching Issues* as part of the leadership training and, therefore, is open for discussion in the small groups. An appeal to the open-endedness of small group discussion could be used as a catchall for any limitations in the talks themselves, yet there is a sense in which the pre-scribed order of questions defines what is essential or basic in Christian faith and life. Given this fact, leaving specific questions about doctrines like the Trinity to small group discussion on purely apologetic grounds could run the danger of implying that these are merely peripheral, albeit searching, issues.[42] Despite the inevitable limitations of a course like Alpha, Gumbel has done a fine job of weaving in key material about suffering and sexual purity—specifically dealt with in *Searching Issues*—throughout the talks themselves.

Theologically Inflexible? We have already suggested that Alpha's appeal to basic Christianity is a deceptively simple claim that obscures the particular theological commitments of the movement. It is not that Alpha intends to deceive; it is simply that there really can be no theologically neutral embodiment of the gospel. Again, this is highlighted by the approved adaptation of *Alpha for Catholics*. In an essay titled "Is 'Alpha for Catholics'?" William Cork argues that "this is not a Catholic adaptation of the Protestant program, but is the Protestant program with Catholic teaching presented afterwards as a supplement."[43] So, he asks, "Can Catholic evangelization really be done in such a way that certain items distinctive to Catholicism can somehow be detached from what Evangelical Protestants believe to be 'the basic Christian truths'?" His conclusion is that it "does not offer simply 'basic Christian truths' common to all, but presents specific teachings on the Church, the Sacraments, and the gifts of the Holy Spirit that constitute the theology of the Charismatic Protestantism which gave birth to Alpha."[44] Any church, Protestant or Catholic, must consider whether Alpha is consistent with its historic traditions and whether its distinctive commitments can be treated as a mere appendix to the course itself. These questions will persist as long as Alpha's copyright prohibits more or less substantial adaptations of the course materials themselves. The issue facing Alpha is whether it is willing to give up the quasi-denominational uniformity demanded by its marketing strategy for the sake of a theological freedom in which the Spirit might actually bring people to Christ through the particular commitments of different ecclesial traditions.

Theologically Dangerous? For others, Alpha is not merely inadequate or inflexible but simply unbiblical and even heretical. Such assessments, of course, presuppose a "sound" reading of the Scriptures founded upon theological commitments (often of a more Reformed or Calvinist nature) that the Alpha movement does not share. Chris Hand's oft-quoted article asks, "Is the popular Alpha Course leading people astray?";[45] Wendy Howard asks, "Alpha Course—Friend or Foe?";[46] Paul Fitton asks, "Is It Bible-Based or Hell-Inspired?";[47] and Richard Fisher asks, "The Alpha Course, Final Answer or Fatal Attraction?"[48] In answering each of these rhetorical questions, we are not surprised to find that Alpha is seriously hazardous to our spiritual health, if not a weapon in the hands of the Enemy against Christianity itself. William Horsburgh warns that through Alpha, you may be "Coursing Your Way to a Cult,"[49] noting the way that the movement operates under the umbrella of orthodoxy, while instilling its alleged errors by manipulating people's emotions, especially after removing them to unfamiliar territory during a weekend away. One thing that many adversaries have in common is a concern about the influence of John Wimber, who is seen as the last link in a long chain of spiritual deception with roots in the New Age movement, the Freemasons, and a wide range of other cults. Some of these commentators, however, also espouse a form of premillennialist anti-Catholicism that rejects the "Kingdom now" eschatology of the charismatic movement, and associates the ecumenical commitments of Alpha with a global conspiracy striving for a one world church, led by the pope, and the New Age, New World order. Make of this what you will.

3.2. Issues with Ethos

I will now try to summarize and engage with some of the more significant criticisms of Alpha that relate to the distinctive character of the movement as a whole.

Individualism? It cannot be denied that the influence of evangelical piety has often resulted in an emphasis upon personal experience at the expense of Christian community and the concern for wider social issues. It also cannot be denied, however, that evangelicals throughout church history have often led the way in confronting social evils and ameliorating the plight of the poor. In light of this, three things can be said about the charge of individualism. First, the impact of Alpha simply cannot be assessed on the extent to which the curriculum addresses questions of social justice. Again, the real test will be whether those who come to faith through Alpha end up actually doing the good works of the Kingdom or not. Second, simply being involved in programs of social action does not guard against the problem of individualism. It is quite possible for people to be doing good deeds for entirely selfish reasons or adopting methods that further ensconce their beneficiaries in the mores of a deeply individualistic culture. Third, it seems to me that given the ecclesiological commitments we have discussed, any purely individualistic outcome of the Alpha Course would have to be judged a failure simply on its own terms.

Consumerism? When asked why Alpha insists on its copyright-protected uniformity, we are presented with an argument that seems self-evidently reasonable to anyone raised on the principles of consumerism. Gumbel claims that, just like the McDonald's hamburger, wherever people choose to participate in an Alpha Course, they should know exactly what they are going to get! In an article titled "Alpha—The McDonaldization of Religion?" Pete Ward identifies this as an approach to "brand recognition" that makes Alpha a vendor of evangelistic products in a marketplace of spiritual experiences, competing to meet the "felt-needs" of private consumers.[50] Drawing on the work of George Ritzer,[51] he argues that Alpha appeals to the technological rationalization of efficiency, calculability, predictability, and control as a means to this end. Ward concludes, however, that McDonaldization is a "not entirely unwelcome aspect of cultural life in late capitalism" and that Alpha can be seen as "a significant contextualization of the methods of evangelism and maybe the gospel itself."[52] Whether or not this is true of Alpha, the movement certainly needs to face a clear and present danger that the totalizing narrative of our Western free-market economics has the power to shape the future of the church in a manner inconsistent with the gospel of Jesus Christ. Indeed, it seems important to ask, "Why is the evangelistic potential of the Alpha Course dependent upon this kind of brand recognition?" In part, the answer must lie in the kind of marketing strategy it has adopted, namely, the widespread use of advertising on billboards and public transport to elicit the response of a target population that has no existing contact with the church. This, of course, simply alerts us to the danger that Alpha poses of short-circuiting the need for church members to engage in the hard work of personal witness and building relationships with nonchurchgoers.

Pragmatism? There are great benefits and dangers for a local church using a fully packaged program like the Alpha Course. On the one hand, it may provide a way for churches that lack experience in evangelism to cultivate good evangelistic habits and renew a sense of missional vocation. On the other hand, Ward concludes that the downside of this approach is that it teaches people how to use a product rather than how to do evangelism.[53] If this is true, then the sense of satisfaction at having accomplished something evangelistic by running an Alpha Course may turn out to be little more than a simulacrum of real evangelism. In a similar vein, Martyn Percy criticizes Alpha as encouraging a form of "join-the-dots Christianity."[54] He warns us against an oversimplified approach to the complexities of wrestling with the Christian faith and urges us to resist those mechanistic approaches to evangelism that diminish the real struggle required to live the gospel in a world such as ours. This must be remembered by charismatics as well, insofar as the gifts and fruit of the Spirit are to be sought in the rigors of daily life and not simply the rarefied atmosphere of a weekend away.

Emotivism? One thing that liberals and conservative evangelicals have in common is their suspicion of Alpha's charismatic emphasis upon spiritual experience. From a liberal perspective, Percy concludes that Alpha reflects the therapeutic felt-needs of a largely middle-class constituency that has little interest in confronting the issues of peace and justice required by a true commitment to the gospel. The widespread appeal of Alpha, however, seems to belie this claim.[55] Stephen Hunt's research also suggests that Alpha can become a "tool for helping people with emotional or psychological problems, rather than a means of evangelism."[56] From an evangelical perspective, there is a related concern that satisfying the postmodern thirst for spiritual experience is a quality more typical of the New Age movement than plain old Christianity. Indeed, it does seem unlikely that those attending an Alpha Course with the hope of meeting some "felt need" for spiritual power or inner healing are going to be challenged with the radical claims of Jesus, that anyone who would follow him must deny themselves and take up their cross daily. Hence, the question being asked by some is to what extent Alpha is promoting "new life" (i.e., conversion, new birth, and a cruciform pattern of discipleship) or just a "new lifestyle" (i.e., a new form of nominalism that merely supplies certain social and psychological needs generated by our secular culture).[57] This also returns us to the sense of doctrinal deficiency expressed by some who claim that Alpha's overly "relational" theology has turned the God of the Bible into a kind of divine therapist and that the radical claims of the Christian faith have been emasculated for the sake of relevancy. Since others have seen Alpha as a model of orthodoxy, such critique is likely to reflect the deep differences between various schools of thought and practice.

4. The End of Alpha

By addressing the criticisms of Alpha toward the conclusion of the essay, I have run the risk of giving them the final word. Let me say, therefore, that the strengths of the course highlighted in the first two sections are reason enough to be thankful for all its accomplishments, and to commend it for use in the local church. Alpha's self-proclaimed "end" or goal is to bring people into relationship with Jesus Christ. I suggest that Alpha is best adopted as a "mentor" in evangelism rather than a "tool" for church growth. The question is, How are we to understand it as a means to this end? As a "mentor," it is certainly hoped that running a course will help nonchurchgoers come to faith, but its most important purpose is to apprentice a church in the necessary skills and lasting habits of evangelism. The true end of Alpha, then, lies in renewing a sense of missionary vocation throughout the life of a Christian community so that it may participate in the *missio Dei*, through the gifting and guidance of the Holy Spirit. If this is not the case, and a church resorts merely to the technological appropriation of an evangelistic "tool," then it becomes vulnerable to the dangers of a consumerist and pragmatic Christianity. It is also likely to remain inept at engaging the long-term challenges of evangelism in its own particular context.

If I am right, the goal of Alpha must also quite literally be the "end" of Alpha, since its purpose as a mentor would be to work itself out of a job, even if such an end seems a long way off. Indeed, a helpful outcome of the Alpha Course has been the development of various new "process evangelism" courses: some tailor-made by local churches for their own use, and others made available as a resource for the wider Christian community.[58] Unless the Alpha movement is really intent upon forming Alpha churches, the organization should think seriously about what it might mean to act more like a mentor than a "guru," that is, to intentionally form others as evangelists with their own peculiar gifts to the church catholic, rather than simply reproducing carbon copies of itself. Such nonidentical repetition of skills and habits is more likely to extend the work of the gospel through the widely different and constantly changing circumstances of local church mission and ministry.

The Future of the Great Commission

Jesus came and said to them, "All authority in heaven and on earth has been given to me. Go therefore and make disciples of all nations, baptizing them in the name of the Father and of the Son and of the Holy Spirit, and teaching them to obey everything that I have commanded you. And remember, I am with you always, to the end of the age."

—Matt. 28:18-20

I n this volume, scholars from a range of backgrounds and social locations have come together to consider the Great Commission and its meaning for the church in the twenty-first century. We have sought to initiate a conversation about evangelism and mission in a rapidly changing world, in light of new and previously neglected contexts, and in recognition of the need for a larger vision of their theory and practice. Even so, these essays have barely scratched the surface of the meaning and future of the Great Commission. In conclusion, then, we will highlight significant themes emerging from our conversation and offer an assessment of some issues and concerns left to be addressed by other scholars and practitioners in the future.

Reconsidering the Conversation

The authors in Part One point us toward a redefinition of the Great Commission. No longer conceptualizing mission and evangelism in terms of mere "conversion" to the Christian faith, the Great Commission is viewed as a lifetime process involving *baptizing* and *teaching*. As Elaine Robinson indicates, the mission of The United Methodist Church has increasingly evolved from a sense of mission as outreach to that of mission as the overarching process of making disciples of Jesus Christ. From a Wesleyan theological perspective, this process of making disciples can be understood as representing the hallmarks of Wesleyan faith: justification and sanctification grounded in the prevenient, convincing, justifying, sanctifying, and glorifying grace of God. With clear theological vision, Stephen Gunter connects the Great Commission to John Wesley's *via salutis*. He reminds us that Jesus Christ must be the center of any evangelistic practice, but the Christ who is known by the total narrative of his life and work. This theological basis suggests not only the need to recognize the two natures of Christ, but also the offices of Priest, Prophet, and King as fundamental to a Wesleyan soteriology. Dana Robert deepens our theological grounding as she argues that, because the gospel of Jesus Christ is timeless, the Great Commission—much like the individual disciple—is to be conceived not so much as a product to be finished, but as a process to be pursued across changing historical circumstances. Today, to reconceptualize the Great Commission, we must negotiate the historical process of globalization without neglecting the normativity of the life and work of Jesus Christ.

In Part Two, we moved from the theological and theoretical understanding of the Great Commission to examine a few (though too few) particular contexts in which evangelism and mission take place. In the context of barrio evangelization, Harold Recinos illustrates the gospel demand to ameliorate the suffering of other persons. For Latinos/as, "evangelization means the good news proclaimed by Jesus questions the basic alienation of human beings from God and the structures of sin that negate the kingdom of God is at hand" (p. 112). Evangelism and mission are thus a process of conversion of the center to the margins—a process in which the gospel message transforms unjust social, political, and economic institutions and offers the fullness of life to the disenfranchised. In a similar vein, Laceye Warner argues that women's contributions to the Great Commission have been substantial, though largely unrecognized due to discursive practices that have limited the meaning and practice of evangelism. She brings to light how women have a long and successful history of practices, even "networks," of compassion toward those who suffer. Implicit in Warner's argument is the need to utilize and learn from the gifts and graces of countless marginalized persons who have practiced the Great Commission despite institutional barriers. Moving beyond the United States to a global perspective, we find two widely divergent contexts: John Wesley Kurewa's African context, in which the church is being planted and watered and is growing, and Achim Härtner's European context, where a renewal and a revitalization of Christian faith are urgently needed. Taken together, these essays demonstrate a reality too often neglected in the past: context matters. In the twenty-first century, the Great Commission requires sensitive contextualization if it is to bear faithful witness to God in Christ in the Holy Spirit.

Finally, in Part Three, the essays broaden our understanding of the art and practice of evangelism and mission. The ongoing formation of Christians and Christian communities—in the various contexts and situations encountered in our world today—requires us to learn and participate in a variety of practices. We are introduced to programs that evangelize congregations and individuals, such as DISCIPLE and Alpha. We are reminded that Christian practices such as hospitality, singing, preaching, and faith sharing contribute to living out the Great Commission. Growing in grace from the first awareness of God's presence to the fullest expression of God's love means more than simply having faith in Christ; it suggests the need for participating in and sharing with others a wide range of practices.

Furthering the Conversation

As suggested in the essays, the relationship among theology, context, and practices can lead us to a deepened and widened sense of the Great Commission today. Yet this volume has only begun to consider the meaning of and possibilities for expressing the Great Commission in the decades to come. To stretch our thinking and to conceptualize and practice evangelism and mission in new and imaginative ways, we conclude with several issues and concerns for ongoing consideration in light of the gospel. In true Wesleyan fashion, no one text—not even the Great Commission of Matthew 28:18-20—should be considered apart from the overarching message of scripture, the "marrow" of salvation by faith, and the interplay of various texts. The areas for further consideration arise out of this conversation among biblical texts and the Wesleyan theological tradition.

First, the creation narratives in Genesis 1:1–2:4*a* and 2:4*b*–3:24 raise the question of the relationship between the Great Commission and the whole of God's creation. In the beginning, God created the cosmos with an intimate connection between the human being and the rest of creation. Humanity was commanded to serve as cocaretaker with God of the earth and its many forms of life (Gen. 1:28), and the redemption of fallen humanity will include the reconciliation of the whole created order: "See, I am making all things new" (Rev. 21:5). In a world where economic "development" has often accompanied the spread of Christianity and led to environmental degradation, and where traditional relationships to the earth are often viewed as vestiges of primitive, indigenous religions, the relationship between the Great Commission and the care of the earth requires careful consideration. Should the work of the evangelist be oriented not only toward the transformation of human life, but also toward the flourishing of other forms of life and the nonrenewable natural resources for which we are accountable? The stories and context of John Wesley Kurewa's essay remind us that many Africans continue to live connected to the earth in a manner that has become foreign to many North Americans and Europeans. Christian faith and life are premised upon the eschatological vision of the new creation; as this world groans toward completion, our role as cocaretakers of the earth remains important, even as we seek to offer Christ to all the nations and peoples.

In light of the interconnectedness of the whole of creation and our recognition of the ongoing process of globalization, we are led to consider Harold Recinos's call to attend to the poor and marginalized peoples of the world and, in particular, the role that evangelization can and should play in the alleviation of suffering. The biblical witnesses that command us to care for the poor, the stranger, the widow, and the orphan are found in the Hebrew Scriptures and the New Testament. Joon-Sik Park highlights the importance of biblical hospitality and "boundary crossing." He suggests that "hospitality to the stranger, particularly to the marginalized, is then both intrinsic to the gospel and crucial to its proclamation" (p. 149). Such prescriptions become increasingly important as Christianity loses ground in North America and Western Europe, but continues to flourish and grow in the Two-thirds World. Indeed, Philip Jenkins has provocatively argued that the Christianity in the Southern Hemisphere will become dominant in this century, and "members of a Southern-dominated church are likely to be among the poorer people on the planet."[1] Certainly, the evangelistic practice of hospitality on the part of Western peoples will have to consider John Wesley's oft-repeated admonition to earn, save, and give all we can. In an age of economic interconnectedness, the church will have to consider what it means to counter the ongoing concentration of the world's wealth in the hands of the few. The early Christian communities "would sell their possessions and goods and distribute the proceeds to all, as any had need" (Acts 2:45). Evangelism in the twenty-first century is called to accountability for the poor and marginalized and the overwhelming needs of all of God's people throughout the world.

The growth of Southern Christianity raises the question, once more, of the decline of Western Christianity and the need to renew and revitalize it. Although the situation in the United States is not yet as critical as that of Western Europe, it is nonetheless evident that the renewal of Christianity is of concern for evangelism and mission in the twenty-first century. Many Western Christians today are what John Wesley referred to as "almost Christians," or those persons who have the form of religion without the power or perhaps take the name of Christian without the identity and formation as followers of God in Christ in the Holy Spirit. The means of grace or spiritual disciplines, as Harold Knight contends, are central to the vitality of Christian faith and life. Christianity without a spiritual depth cannot expect to thrive, as was demonstrated so clearly in the Anglican Church and the Methodist movement of eighteenth-century England. The conversation in this volume has only begun to consider the importance of context and practices in relation to the potential for a new Great Awakening across the West.

Finally, in the twenty-first century, evangelism and mission cannot ignore the presence of other religious traditions and, indeed, must continually consider the Great Commission in this light. Having above pointed toward the concerns of globalization, the growth of Southern Christianity, and a global economic disequilibrium, respect toward other faith traditions looms as an undeniable feature of our life on this earth. In recognition of the many global conflicts in which religion plays a lesser or greater role, the need for sensitive explorations of the Great Commission in relation to other religious traditions looms large. Wesleyans have a long and vibrant ecumenical tradition, a "Catholic

Spirit," which must be held in creative tension with our evangelical heritage of "spreading scriptural holiness."

In the final estimation, there is much work left to be done in the academic and the ecclesial settings. As Christians, we live with an eschatological vision in which the new creation is breaking into our world, yet awaits completion. Two thousand years ago, the followers of Jesus Christ believed the completion of all things was imminent; there was not a moment to lose. Over the centuries, with the delayed parousia and the many peaks and valleys of the institutional church, our sense of heightened expectation and urgency to love and to share that love has diminished. We cannot recapture the experience and mission of the first Christians, but we can reshape and renew the experience and mission of twenty-first-century Christians. The process and practice of discipleship, in light of our eschatological horizon, demand that we continue to conceptualize, contextualize, and practice the Great Commission of Jesus Christ now and to the end of the age.

CONTRIBUTING AUTHORS

Dean G. Blevins served local churches as youth minister and associate minister of Christian Education. Dean earned his Ph.D. at Claremont School of Theology and is currently the J. B. Elizer Chair of Christian Ministry in the school of Religion at Trevecca Nazarene University. He has published a number of articles, including contributions to the *Journal for the Academy of Evangelism in Theological Education, Christian Education Journal, Wesleyan Theological Journal,* and serves as Senior Editor of *Didache: Faithful Teaching,* an online journal dedicated to Wesleyan global higher education.

Candy Gunther Brown is an assistant professor of American Studies at Saint Louis University. She received her Ph.D. from Harvard University. Her publications include *The Word in the World: Evangelical Writing, Publishing, and Reading in America, 1789-1880* (2004).

Ron Crandall has served as a missionary in Vietnam, as well as a pastor of churches in the USA. Formerly a Director of Local Church Evangelism for the General Board of Discipleship, he is currently is the McCreless Professor of Evangelism and Associate Dean of the School of World Mission and Evangelism at Asbury Theological Seminary. His earned doctorate (DTh.P) is in Pastoral Theology from Fuller Theological Seminary. In addition to a variety of articles on church growth and evangelism, his recent publications include: *Turnaround Strategies for the Small Church* (1995); *The Contagious Witness: Exploring Christian Conversion* (1999), and *Witness: Exploring and Sharing Your Christian Faith* (2001).

W. Stephen Gunter is the president of Young Harris College in Young Harris, Georgia. He has served the church as a parish pastor and was previously the Arthur J. Moore Associate Professor of Evangelism in The

Candler School of Theology at Emory University. He earned his Ph.D. at the University of Leiden, The Netherlands. His publications include *Resurrection Knowledge* (1999), *The Quotable Mr. Wesley* (1999, 2003) and *John Wesley and The Netherlands* (2003). He is the past president of the Wesleyan Theological Society, past chair of the Wesleyan Studies Group in the American Academy of Religion, and a founding member of the editorial board for Kingswood Books, Abingdon Press.

Achim Härtner, M.A. in Religious Communications, has served as parish pastor and is currently E. Stanley Jones Professor of Evangelism at Reutlingen Theological Seminary, Germany. He is author of several articles in theological magazines and anthologies; his homiletics textbook *Prediigen lernen: Ein Lehrbuch für die Praxis* (2001, co-authored by Dr. Holger Eschmann), also appeared as a Bulgarian (2003) and English edition, *Learning to Preach* (2004).

Scott J. Jones is the resident bishop of the Kansas East and Kansas West conferences of The United Mthodist Church. Formerly, he served as the McCreless Associate Professor of Evangelism at Perkins School of Theology, Southern Methodist University. His most recent books are *United Methodist Doctrine: The Extreme Center* (2002) and *The Evangelistic Love of God and Neighbor: A Theology of Witness and Discipleship* (2003).

Henry H. Knight III is Donald and Pearl Wright Professor of Wesleyan Studies at Saint Paul School of Theology, Kansas City, Missouri. For eleven years he occupied the E. Stanley Jones Chair of Evangelism at Saint Paul. His Ph.D. is from Emory University. He is the author of *The Presence of God in the Christian Life: John Wesley and the Means of Grace; A Future for Truth: Evangelical Theology in a Postmodern Age; Eight Life-Enriching Practices of United Methodists,* and, with Don E. Saliers, *The Conversation Matters: Why United Methodists Should Talk With One Another.* He has served as Editor of the *Journal of the Academy for Evangelism in Theological Education* and President of the Wesleyan Theological Society.

John Wesley Zwomunondiita Kurewa has served the church as a pastor, a lecturer in theology, and as Administrative Assistant to Bishop Muzorewa. He also served as Secretary for Evangelism with the

World Council of Churches, first African Secretary to the Parliament of Zimbabwe (soon after Independence), founding Vice Chancellor (President) of Africa University, and is currently E. Stanley Jones Associate Professor of Evangelism in the Faculty of Theology at Africa University. He earned his Ph.D. at Northwestern University. His publications include *Biblical Proclamation for Africa Today* (1995), *The Church in Mission* (1997), and *Preaching and Cultural Identity* (2000). He was presented with awards of distinguished service by Asbury College and Garrett Evangelical-Theological Seminary, and is also recipient of the Honarary Doctor of Sacred Theology from MacMurry College.

Philip R. Meadows is an ordained presbyter in the British Methodist Church. He worked for three years as lecturer in theology and religious studies at Westminster College, Oxford; six years as E. Stanley Jones Professor of Evangelism at Garrett-Evangelical Theological Seminary, near Chicago; and now serves as Director of Postgraduate Studies, Cliff College, England. He specializes in Wesley studies, missiology and the theology of evangelism; and is past president of the Wesleyan Theological Society. His research and publication interests seek to combine theology and discipleship in the Wesleyan tradition with the missionary challenges of contemporary culture.

Joon-Sik Park is the E. Stanley Jones Associate Professor of World Evangelism at the Methodist Theological School in Ohio, Delaware, Ohio. Earlier he served as pastor of multicultural United Methodist congregations in Ohio and Kentucky. His publications have appeared in the *International Bulletin of Missionary Research*, the *International Review of Mission*, *Mennonite Quarterly Review*, and *Missiology*, including the articles: "Ecclesiologies in Creative Tension: The Church as Ethical and Missional Reality in H. Richard Niebuhr and John H. Yoder" and "'As You Go': John Howard Yoder as a Mission Theologian."

Stephen W. Rankin spent fifteen years in parish ministry both as a youth leader and a pastor before moving to Southwestern College. He holds the Kirk Chair in Religious Studies and serves as campus minister and director of Discipleship Southwestern. He earned his Ph.D. from Northwestern University through the Joint Program in Religious Studies with Garrett-Evangelical Theological Seminary. He has published articles in scholarly journals and church-related publications and is editing a collection of essays on evangelism to be published by Haworth Press.

Harold J. Recinos, an ordained elder and member of the Baltimore-Washington Annual Conference of The United Methodist Church, is Professor of Church and Society at Perkins School of Theology, Southern Methodist University. He has also taught on the faculty of Wesley Theological Seminary in Washington, D.C. His Ph.D. in Cultural Anthropology (with Honors) is from the American University in Washington, D.C. An author of articles in English and Spanish, his books include *Hear the Cry! A Latino Pastor Challenges the Church* (1989), *Jesus Weeps: Global Encounters on Our Doorstep* (1992), and *Who Comes in the Name of the Lord? Jesus at the Margins* (1997).

Dana L. Robert is the Truman Collins Professor of World Mission at the Boston University School of Theology. Her books include *American Women in Mission: A Social History of Their Thought and Practice* (1997), *'Occupy Until I Come': A.T. Pierson and the Evangelization of the World* (2003), and coauthorship of *Christianity: A Social and Cultural History* (1997). With her husband M. L. Daneel, she edits the series "African Initiatives in Christian Mission" (University of South Africa Press).

Elaine A. Robinson is Assistant Professor of Theology and Methodist Studies at Brite Divinity School, Texas Christian University. An ordained elder in the Rocky Mountain Conference of The United Methodist Church, she earned her Ph.D. from Emory University and her M.T.S. from Perkins School of Theology. She served as pastor of Nazareth UMC in Winder, Georgia and now affiliates with La Trinidad Iglesia Methodista Unida in Forth Worth, Texas. She is the author of *These Three: The Theological Virtues of Faith, Hope, and Love* (2004).

Bryan Stone has a background in urban and multicultural ministry, church planting, and faith-based non-profit development. He is the E. Stanley Jones Professor of Evangelism at Boston University School of Theology and earned his Ph.D. from Southern Methodist University. His publications include *Compassionate Ministry: Theological Foundations* (1996) and *Faith and Film: Theological Themes at the Cinema* (2000).

Andrew F. Walls, a graduate of the Universities of Oxford and Aberdeen, served in West Africa at Fourah Bay College, Sierra Leone, and at the University of Nigeria, Nsukka, where he was Head of the Department of Religion. For many years he was Professor of Religious Studies and Riddoch Lecturer in Comparative Religion at the University of Aberdeen, Scotland, before becoming Director of the Centre for the Study of Christianity in the Non-Western World at the University of Edinburgh, Scotland. He has been Visiting Professor of World Christianity at Yale and at Harvard Universities, and Guest Professor of Ecumenics and Mission at Princeton Theological Seminary. He is a past General Secretary of the International Association of Mission Studies. Recent publications include *The Missionary Movement in Christian History* (Orbis, 1996), and *The Cross-Cultural Process in Christian History* (Orbis, 2002). Currently he serves as Honorary Professor in the University of Edinburgh, Director of the Scottish Institute of Missionary Studies at the University of Aberdeen, and Professor at the Akrofi-Christaller Memorial Centre in Ghana.

Laceye Warner, an ordained elder in The United Methodist Church, is currently Assistant Professor of the Practice of Evangelism and Methodist Studies and the Royce and Jane Reynolds Teaching Fellow at Duke Divinity School. She earned her Ph.D. at Trinity College, University of Bristol. The author of several articles examining the historical context and theological motivations of women in evangelistic ministries, she is working on a book entitled *Saving Women: Re-visioning Evangelism* that is supported by a grant from the Association of Theological Schools and Lilly Foundation.

Rob Weber is a native of Atlanta, Georgia, who attended Millsaps College in Jackson, Mississippi, earning a degree in Theater and Philosophy, received his M. Div. from the Iliff School of Theology in Denver, Colorado, and earned a D.Min. from United Theological Seminary in Communication and Leadership. He is a parish pastor, church planter and elder in the Louisiana Annual Conference, where he has served since 1987. His publications include *ReConnecting*, which is designed to help churches develop a shared memory and identity that emerged from the origins of the Methodist movement; and *Visual Leadership: The Church Leader As Imagesmith*, which shows pastors how to develop multigenerational leadership in an image-oriented culture. He is featured in the video segments for *Beginnings: An Introduction to the Christian Faith*, and most recently, he has written *ReConnecting Worship: Where Tradition and Innovation Converge*.

NOTES

1. The Great Commission 1910–2010

1. The idea is pursued further in Andrew F. Walls, "Mission and Migration: The Diaspora in Christian History," *Journal of African Christian Thought* 5, no. 2 (2002): 3-11.

2. On the conference see W. Richey Hogg, *Ecumenical Foundations: A History of the International Missionary Council and Its Nineteenth Century Background* (New York: Harper, 1952), chap. 3; Andrew F. Walls, *The Cross-Cultural Process in Christian History* (Maryknoll, N.Y.: Orbis, 2002), chap. 3.

3. Edited by Harlan P. Beach and James S. Dennis (New York, 1910).

4. See, for example, J. Stanley Friesen, *Missionary Responses to Tribal Religions at Edinburgh 1910* (New York: Peter Lang, 1996).

5. On Mott, see Charles Howard Hopkins, *John R. Mott, 1865–1955: A Biography* (Grand Rapids: Eerdmans, 1979).

6. World Missionary Conference 1910. Report of Commission I: *Carrying the Gospel to all the Non-Christian World* (Edinburgh: Oliphant, Anderson and Ferrier, 1910), 5. Hereafter referred to as "Report."

7. Report, 281-82.

8. Ibid., 342.

9. Ibid., 360-61.

10. The effects of this are noted in the Report, where the point is made that since missions arrived by sea, they tended to concentrate on coastal areas and move inland by ports and waterways. Islam had traveled by the great overland trading routes. Report, 284-85.

11. Ibid., 33.

12. Ibid., 364.

13. Ibid., 96.

14. Cf., ibid., 298-316.

15. Ibid., 434-36. Warneck does make strategic as well as theological observations.

16. A volume similar to the Report of Commission I was published for each of the other commissions; a ninth volume, titled *History and Records*, contains an account of the conference.

17. W. H. Temple Gairdner, *"Edinburgh 1910": an account and interpretation of the World Missionary Conference* (Edinburgh: Oliphant, Anderson and Ferrier, 1910).

2. The Great Commission in an Age of Globalization

1. Luis Bush, "Where Are We Now? Evaluating Progress on the Great Commission," *Mission Frontiers* (June 2000): 15.

2. Ibid., 16.

3. Ralph Winter quoted in ibid., 13.

4. While less widely known than his evangelistic "crusades," Billy Graham's sponsorship of the Lausanne Movement and of global meetings of non-Western evangelists has been extremely important for evangelical missions.

5. See Robert Schreiter's works on reconciliation as a model for mission, including *Reconciliation: Mission and Ministry in a Changing Social Order* (Maryknoll, N.Y.: Orbis, 1992), and *The Ministry of Reconciliation: Spirituality and Strategies* (Maryknoll, N.Y.: Orbis, 1998). See also William R. Burrows, "Reconciling All in Christ: The Oldest New Paradigm for Mission," *Mission Studies* 15-1, no. 29 (1998): 79-98.

6. Michael Ryan, "Wondering What's Next," *Boston Globe Magazine*, December 30, 2001, 27.

7. The roots of this New Age position with its skepticism about Christian mission to the world can be found in modern theologians such as Dietrich Bonhoeffer, for example, who claimed that in a "world come of age," mature humanity no longer needs to resort to God as a working hypothesis or *deus ex machina*.

8. Roland Robertson, *Globalization: Social Theory and Global Culture* (London: Sage, 1992), 8.

9. Richard H. Bliese, "Globalization," in *Dictionary of Mission: Theology, History, Perspectives*, ed. Karl Müller, Theo Sundermeier, Stephen B. Bevans, and Richard H. Bliese (Maryknoll, N.Y.: Orbis, 1997), 172.

10. Other arguments can be made for Catholicism as globalizing force, but I am concerned with the modern period and the Protestant era.

11. The kingdom of God metaphor in no way implies that the dominant Western forms of government, culture, and economics are embedded in this vision of God's reign, as today's critics sometimes charge and earlier generations of missionaries, at times, might have believed.

12. See Dana L. Robert, "The First Globalization: The Internationalization of the Protestant Missionary Movement Between the World Wars," *International Bulletin of Missionary Research* 26, no. 2 (April 2002): 50-66.

13. Because of the heavy loss of life, critics of the early missionary movement attacked it as wasteful. In response, missionary supporters interpreted missionary losses not as failures, but as spiritual successes because of the profound witness of martyrdom. For the process by which missionary death was transformed into spiritual victory, see the case of the first U.S. missionary martyr, Harriet Newell. Dana L. Robert, *American Women in Mission: A Social History of Their Thought and Practice* (Macon, Ga.: Mercer Univ. Press, 1997), 40-42.

14. See the volume by David Hempton, *Methodism: Empire of the Spirit* (Yale Univ. Press, 2004).

15. Daniel H. Bays, "The Growth of Independent Christianity in China, 1900–1937," in *Christianity in China: From the Eighteenth Century to the Present*, ed. Bays (Stanford: Stanford Univ. Press, 1996), 310.

16. Dana L. Robert, "Shifting Southward: Global Christianity Since 1945," *International Bulletin of Missionary Research* 24, no. 2 (April 2000): 53.

17. See Andrew Walls's analysis of mission-state relations in Africa since independence, in "Africa in Christian History: Retrospect and Prospect," *Journal of African Christian Thought* 1, no. 1 (1998): 2-16.

18. The Russia Initiatives were the first major example of the new flexible approach by the General Board of Global Ministries.

19. Larry Keyes, "Non-Western Mission Boards and Societies," in *Evangelical Dictionary of World Missions*, ed. Scott Moreau (Grand Rapids: Baker, 2000), 696.

20. Bliese, "Globalization," 176-77.

21. Max Warren was head of the Church Missionary Society during the mid-twentieth century, when the mission movement was grappling with the effects of nationalism and decolonization. His edited "Christian Presence" series reflected missionary attempts to take a postcolonial stance toward non-Christian faiths. Dutch missiologist Hendrik Kraemer's *The Christian Message in a Non-Christian World* (1938) remains the classic text of a missionary theology of "biblical realism." On the missiological context of the mid-twentieth century, see Timothy Yates, *Christian Mission in the Twentieth Century* (Cambridge: Cambridge Univ. Press, 1994), 105-17, 138-43.

22. J. Dudley Woodberry, "Terror, Islam and Mission: Reflections of a Guest in Muslim Lands," *International Bulletin of Missionary Research* 26, no. 1 (January 2002): 2-7.

23. Robert, *American Women in Mission*, 3.

24. See, e.g., Max Warren's discussion of the Great Commission in *I Believe in the Great Commission* (Grand Rapids: Eerdmans, 1976), and *The Christian Imperative* (London: SCM Press, 1955).

25. "Making Disciples Means Changing Hearts, Bishop Says," United Methodist News Service, no. 121, March 21, 2002.

3. The Global Mission of The United Methodist Church

1. *The Book of Discipline of The United Methodist Church* (Nashville: United Methodist Publishing House, 2004), ¶120, p. 87.

2. The task of The United Methodist Church is integrally related to the nature of the church; however, in this essay, our analysis will focus primarily on the task, dealing with the nature of the UMC only as necessary to further our understanding.

3. The sense of "missional outreach" is most clearly articulated in chapter 5, section VII, which deals with the General Board of Global Ministries. However, the narrower sense is used elsewhere as in chapter 4, section VIII: "The purpose of a mission is to provide ministry with a particular group or region whose needs cannot be fully met with the existing structures and resources of the annual conference(s)." *BOD*, ¶590, p. 348.

4. Albert Outler, "The Mission Fair," in *Albert Outler: The Churchman*, ed. Bob W. Parrott (Anderson, Ind.: Bristol House, 1995), 213.

5. *BOD*, ¶101, p. 47.

6. Ibid.

7. Ibid.

8. Ibid., ¶101, p. 48.

9. This understanding of the "two dimensions of Christian discipleship" is also articulated in terms of the "privilege and obligation" of Christian ministry: "The privilege is a relationship with God that is deeply spiritual. The obligation is to respond to God's call to holy living in the world." *BOD*, ¶133, p. 91.

10. Ibid., ¶121, p. 87.

11. Ibid., ¶121, pp. 87-88.

12. Ibid., ¶121, p. 88.

13. Ibid., ¶124, pp. 88-89.

14. Ibid., ¶125, p. 89.

15. Ibid.

16. *BOD*, ¶131, p. 90.

17. Ibid.

18. Ibid., ¶130, p. 90.

19. Note that the spelling of this word is disputed, sometimes written as "itineracy" and other times as "itinerancy."

20. *BOD*, ¶430, p. 289.

21. Richard P. Heitzenrater, "Connectionalism and Itinerancy: Wesleyan Principles and Practice," in *Connectionalism: Ecclesiology, Mission and Identity*, ed. Russell E. Richey, Dennis M. Campbell, and William B. Lawrence (Nashville: Abingdon Press, 1997), 35.

22. Thomas Edward Frank, *Polity, Practice, and the Mission of The United Methodist Church* (Nashville: Abingdon Press, 2002), 118f. We should understand this democratic system as a representative democracy rather than a pure form.

23. *BOD*, ¶338, p. 236. It should be noted that the newest order of ordained ministry, the deacon, is not itinerant.

24. *BOD*, ¶430, p. 307.

25. Frank, *Polity, Practice, and the Mission*, 67.

26. Heitzenrater, "Connectionalism and Itinerancy," 35.

27. Ibid.

28. *BOD*, ¶120, p. 87. We should note the ambiguity in terms of whether this is to be applied to the church universal or The United Methodist Church, in particular.

29. Frank, *Polity, Practice, and the Mission*, 163.

30. Ibid., p. 174.

31. *BOD*, ¶103, pp. 62, 67f.

32. Ibid., ¶122, p. 87-88.

33. Ibid., ¶123, p. 88.

34. Ibid., ¶124, pp. 88-89.

35. Ibid., ¶1301, p. 549.

36. Ibid.

37. Ibid., ¶1302, pp. 549-50.

38. Ibid., ¶103, pp. 72-74. Although the General Rules remain an important part of the doctrinal standards of the UMC and normative by discipline, there is generally little awareness of these Rules within the local congregations.

39. Ibid., ¶101, p. 47.

40. Ibid.

41. Ibid., ¶104, p. 84.

42. Ibid.

43. Ibid., ¶104, p. 85.

44. Ibid., ¶124, p. 89.

45. Ted A. Campbell, "John Wesley on the Mission of the Church," in *The Mission of the Church in Methodist Perspective*, ed. Alan G. Padgett (Lewiston, N.Y.: Edwin Mellen Press, 1992), 56. Although Wesley did go to Georgia as a missionary, his work there was largely a failure, and he recognized his primary work lay in the British Isles.

46. Ibid.

47. Randy L. Maddox, "Wesley's Prescription for 'Making Disciples of Jesus Christ': Insights for the Twenty-First-Century Church," *Quarterly Review* 23, no. 1 (Spring 2003): 15-28. The full text of his presentation to the bishops can be found online at http://www.pulpitandpew.duke.edu/maddox%20paper 9-23-02.pdf.

48. The United Brethren had allowed for the ordination of women as early as 1889. At the formation of the EUB in 1946, the ordination of women ceased, though those holding credentials were permitted to continue their ministry, at least in a limited or local sense.

49. Frank, *Polity, Practice, and the Mission*, 97.

50. *The Book of Discipline of The United Methodist Church* (Nashville: United Methodist Publishing House, 1968), ¶113, p. 70.

51. "The Commission on the Mission of The United Methodist Church, 'Grace Upon Grace': God's Mission and Ours," in *Daily Christian Advocate*, advance ed. (Nashville: United Methodist Publishing House, February 25, 1988), E-19.

52. Ibid., C-15-C-23.

53. L. Gregory Jones and Michael G. Cartwright, "Vital Congregations: Toward a Wesleyan Vision for The United Methodist Church's Identity and Mission," in *The Mission of the Church in Methodist Perspective*, 90-91.

54. Bishop Melvin G. Talbert (San Francisco Area), secretary of the Council of Bishops, quoted in *The United Methodist Newscope: The National Weekly Newsletter for United Methodist Leaders* 19, no. 55 (November 29, 1991): 1.

55. *The Book of Discipline of The United Methodist Church* (Nashville: United Methodist Publishing House, 1996), ¶202, p. 114.

56. 1968 *BOD*, ¶105, p. 68.

57. 1996 *BOD*, ¶204, p. 116; cf. 2000 *BOD*, "Care of Members," ¶204, p. 124.

58. Methodist scholars such as Russell Richey have been making the case for renewing discussions related to the ecclesiology of the UMC. Clearly, while the democratic polity has distinct advantages, our theological reflection is often done piecemeal and the theological work done by quadrennial commissions is often revised on the floor of the General Conference.

59. Frederick A. Norwood, *The Story of American Methodism* (Nashville: Abingdon Press, 1971), 132.

60. Russell E. Richey, "Understandings of Ecclesiology in Methodism," unpublished paper, originally presented in abbreviated form to the national dialogue between The United Methodist and Episcopalian Churches.

61. Outler, "The Mission Fair," 215.

62. Richey, "Understandings of Ecclesiology in Methodism," 25-26 n. 53.

63. This essay was prepared initially for the national Roman Catholic–United Methodist dialogue in April 2003, and has been revised for inclusion in this volume. I am particularly grateful to Bruce Robbins for his background information on the "Grace Upon Grace" statement, and to Page Thomas of the Methodist Center at the Bridwell Library, Perkins School of Theology, for his assistance with some of the archival research.

4. Jesus Christ: The Heart of the Great Commission

1. *The Book of Discipline of The United Methodist Church* (Nashville: United Methodist Publishing House, 2000), ¶104, p. 85.

2. Ibid., ¶101, p. 41.

3. Ibid., ¶102, p. 51

4. Ibid., ¶101, p. 48.

5. Cf. Alister McGrath, *The Genesis of Doctrine* (Grand Rapids: Eerdmans, 1997), 1-13.

6. For a discussion of this complex religious expectation, see J. Neusner, W. S. Green, and J. Z. Smith, eds., *Judaism and Their Messiahs at the Turn of the Christian Era* (Cambridge: Cambridge Univ. Press, 1998).

7. *The Bicentennial Edition of the Works of John Wesley* (Nashville: Abingdon Press, 1984–), 3:204. Hereafter cited as *Bicentennial Works*.

8. Letter to Charles Wesley (28 December 1774), *The Letters of the Rev. John Wesley, A.M.*, ed. John Telford (London: Epworth Press, 1931), 6:134.

9. Wesley would have learned this from, among other places, his reading and frequent use of John Pearson, *An Exposition of the Creed* (London: Printed by J. M. for John Williams, 1676), 93ff.

10. Randy L. Maddox, *Responsible Grace: John Wesley's Practical Theology* (Nashville: Kingswood, 1994), 109-16.

11. *Minutes of the Methodist Conferences, from the First, held in London, by the Late Rev.*

John Wesley, A.M. in the Year 1744, vol. 1 (London: John Mason, 1862). These "Minutes" may also be found in the various editions of the *Works of John Wesley*, 1872 and following reprints.

12. *Explanatory Notes on the New Testament* (London: Bowyer, 1755). Wesley finished these *Notes* and wrote the Preface to the 1st edition in January 1754. Hereafter cited as *Notes*.

13. Augustine, "Answer to the Two Letters of the Pelagians," 2:8, 18, in *The Works of Saint Augustine, Answer to the Pelagians II*, trans. Roland J. Teske (Hyde Park, N.Y.: New City Press, 1998), 1/24:155. Augustine frequently refers to the verse from John 15:5 throughout his writings and sermons.

14. See especially the longest theological tract that Wesley wrote, the 1757 piece, "The Doctrine of Original Sin: According to Scripture, Reason, and Experience," in *Bicentennial Works*, vol. 12, and the 1759 sermon, "Original Sin," in *Sermons*, 2:170-85.

15. *Works*, ed. Jackson, 10:284-98.

16. *Bicentennial Works*, 1:447-65. The ¶ references that follow are from this sermon.

17. *Bicentennial Works*, 2:37-38.

18. *Notes on the New Testament*, Hebrews 7:25.

19. Ibid., Matthew 1:16.

20. "Upon our Lord's Sermon on the Mount, Discourse the Fourth," in *Bicentennial Works*, 1:531.

21. *Journal* (17 October 1771), in *Bicentennial Works*, 22:293.

22. *Bicentennial Works*, 2:33-43.

23. Ibid., 2:38.

24. Ibid., 2:34.

25. Galatians 3:24.

26. *Bicentennial Works*, 2:41.

27. Ibid., 2:43.

28. Richard P. Heitzenrater, *Wesley and the People Called Methodists* (Nashville: Abingdon Press, 1995), 242.

5. Megatrends That Challenge an Evangelizing Church

1. Unless otherwise noted, all translations of German texts are by the author of this essay.

2. Cited from the German weekly news magazine *Focus*, May 2002, titled "Angst" (fear), 105.

3. Cf. Achim Härtner and Holger Eschmann, *Predigen lernen: Ein Lehrbuch für die Praxis* (Stuttgart: Edition Anker, 2001), 35-40. An English edition of this volume is available: *Learning to Preach: Fundamentals—Practical Guide—Consolidation*, Cliff College Academic Series (Calver, Hope Valley, UK: Cliff College Publishing, 2004).

4. Cf. Howard A. Snyder, *Earth Currents: The Struggle for the World's Soul* (Nashville: Abingdon Press, 1995).

5. New York: Anchor Press/Doubleday, 1979.

6. In his latest volume he even speaks of "The End of Humankind"!

7. On postmodernism cf. Leonard Sweet, *Aqua Church: Essential Leadership Arts for Piloting Your Church in Today's Fluid Culture* (Loveland, Colo.: Group Publishing, 1999). For an overview of the historical background of post-Enlightenment understanding of life and faith, see W. Stephen Gunter, *Resurrection Knowledge: Recovering the Gospel for a Postmodern World* (Nashville: Abingdon Press, 1999), 15-29; and the fundamental philosophical work of Wolfgang Welsch, *Unsere postmoderne Moderne*, 5th ed. (Berlin: Akademie-Verlag, 1997).

8. This assessment originates from the late German Roman Catholic theologian Karl Rahner (1904–84) who had considered Germany to be a "heidnisches Land mit christlicher Vergangenheit und christlichen Restbeständen," quoted in *Der Spiegel*, no. 25, 1992, 44.

9. On the critical issue of re-traditioning a church and society, see Gunter, *Resurrection Knowledge*, 13ff.

10. Beginning with Descartes' principle *cogito, ergo sum*, the individual reasoning subject increasingly became the center of the interpretation of the world.

11 See the classic work of Colin Morris, *Start Your Own Religion* (London: BBC Books, 1992).

12. Cf. Peter L. Berger, *A Far Glory: The Quest of Faith in an Age of Credulity* (New York: Free Press, 1992). The quote was taken from the German edition *Sehnsucht nach Sinn* (Frankfurt: Campus Verlag, 1995), 45.

13. Paul Tillich, *Systematic Theology*, vol. 1 (Chicago: Univ. of Chicago Press, 1951), 12.

14. Gerhard Schulze, *Kulissen des Glücks* (Frankfurt: 1999), 12ff.

15. Quote taken from the weekly political magazine *Die Zeit*, January 13, 1989, 48.

16. Lutz Friedrich, *Autobiografie und Religion in der Spätmoderne: Biografische Suchbewegungen im Zeitalter transzendenter Obdachlosigkeit* (Stuttgart: Kohlhammer Verlag, 1999), 220.

17. Cf. Viktor E. Frankl, . . . *trotzdem Ja zum Leben sagen: Ein Psychologe erlebt das Konzentrationslager*, 18th ed. (Munich: Deutscher Taschenbuch Verlag, 1999); *Man's Search for Meaning*, 78th ed. (New York: Simon & Schuster, 1988); and *The Unheard Cry for Meaning*, 10th ed. (New York: Simon & Schuster, 1985).

18. Odo Marquard, *Zur Diätetik der Sinnerwartungen: Philosophische Bemerkungen*, in *Apologie des Zufälligen: Philosophische Studien* (Stuttgart: Philipp Reclam Verlag, 1986), 33-53.

19. Deutscher Evangelischer Kirchentag, Stuttgart, June 17, 1999.

20. Published in New York by Pantheon (1999).

21. Robert Levine, *A Geography of Time* (New York: Basic Books, 1997).

22. Ibid., 165.

23. Florian Illies, *Generation Golf* (Frankfurt: Fischer Taschenbuch Verlag, 2001), 59.

24. Jugendwerk der Deutschen Shell, ed., *Jugend 2000*, 2 vols. (Opladen, 2000).

25. For example, see "Data-Concept Studie: *Jugend 2000*," *Focus*, March 20, 2000, 62ff.

26. Cf. Gerhard Schulze, *Die Erlebnisgesellschaft: Kultursoziologie der Gegenwart*, 8th ed. (Frankfurt: Campus Verlag, 2000).

27. See the instructive comments by George G. Hunter III, *How to Reach Secular People* (Nashville: Abingdon Press, 1992).

28. Cf. Alfred Duhbach and Roland J. Campiche, eds., *Jede(r) ein Sonderfall? Religion in der Schweiz* (Zürich: NZN Buchverlag/Friedrich Reinhardt Verlag, 1993), 186, 307f.

29. Such as the study of Klaus-Peter Jörns, *Die neuen Gesichter Gottes* (Munich: C. H. Beck, 1997). Cf. George G. Hunter, *Radical Outreach: The Recovery of Apostolic Ministry and Evangelism* (Nashville: Abingdon Press, 2003), 43ff.

30. Cf. Lesslie Newbigin, *Foolishness to the Greeks: The Gospel and Western Culture* (Nashville: Abingdon Press, 1986), 18ff; and Michael Nüchtern, *Kirche in Konkurrenz* (Stuttgart: Quell Verlag, 1997), 17f.

31. Berger, *Sehnsucht nach Sinn*, 92.

32. Cf. Achim Härtner, "What Shape Should Evangelism and Mission Take in Our Multicultural, Pluralistic World?" *Quarterly Review,* Winter 2002, 411, 415-17.

33. George Morris and H. E. Fox, *Faith Sharing* (Nashville: Abingdon Press, 1986), 79ff. Also see G. Howard Mellor, "Evangelism and Religious Pluralism in the Wesleyan Heritage," in *Theology and Evangelism in the Wesleyan Heritage,* ed. James C. Logan (Nashville: Kingswood, 1994), 109-26.

34. Cf. Richard Sennett, *The Fall of Public Man* (New York: Vintage Books, 1978; Norton, 1992).

35. Cf. John B. Cobb Jr., *Grace & Responsibility: A Wesleyan Theology for Today* (Nashville: Abingdon Press, 1995), 26f, who names and unfolds the issue of "Broadening 'Salvation.' "

36. "We should construe evangelism as primary initiation into the kingdom of God" is the general thesis of William J. Abraham in his book *The Logic of Evangelism* (Grand Rapids: Eerdmans, 1989), 13.

37. Cf. Achim Härtner, *Kommunikationswissenschaft und Verkündigung des Evangeliums: Homiletische Ein und Aussichten,* in *Das Evangelium, eine Kraft Gottes: Reden—Hören—Tun,* ed. J. Barthel and M. Marquardt (Stuttgart: Medienwerk der Evangelisch-methodistischen Kirche, 2002), 106f.

38. The original quote is "Ego evangelio non crederem, nisi me catholicae ecclesiae commoveret auctoritas," found in Augustin's tract *Contra epistulam, quam vocant fundamenti 5,* 6 (dated 405–6 CE), cited by Alfred Schindler, "Augustin/Augustinismus," in *Theologische Realenzyklopädie* (TRE), vol. 4 (Berlin: Walter de Gruyter, 1979), 664.

39. Peter L. Berger, *The Heretical Imperative* (Garden City: Anchor Books, 1980), esp. 25ff.

40. The first two steps in Mark Mittelberg's program unfolded in *How to Build a Contagious Congregation* (Grand Rapids: Eerdmans, 1995) deal with the fundamental role of modeling leadership for effective evangelism. In part 3 of his book Mittelberg provides numerous examples of faith sharing and growing congregations. For further examples of holistic evangelistic outreach, see George G. Hunter III, *Church for the Unchurched* (Nashville: Abingdon Press, 1996), and Achim Härtner, *Herz und Mund und Tat und Leben—Ermutigung zu einer Gemeindepraxis aus dem Evangelium,* in *Das Evangelium, eine Kraft Gottes: Reden—Hören—Tun,* ed. J. Barthel and M. Marquardt (Stuttgart: Medienwerk der Evangelisch-methodistischen Kirche, 2001), 214-21.

41. *The Book of Discipline of The United Methodist Church* (Nashville: United Methodist Publishing House, 1996), ¶245, p. 136.

42. Cf. Theodore W. Runyon, *The New Creation: John Wesley's Theology Today* (Nashville: Abingdon Pres, 1998), 207ff.

43. Cf. Walter Klaiber, "Gemeinsam gesandt—Ökumene in der Perspektive des gemeinsamen Zeugnisses," *Una Sancta,* March 2001, 208-19. Bishop Klaiber is interpreting the second paragraph of the "Charta Oecumenica," an ecumenical agreement of "Guidelines for the Growing Cooperation among the Churches in Europe," approved by the Conference of European Churches (CEC) and the Council of European Bishops' Conferences (CCEE) in Strasbourg (2001), following the Ecumenical Assemblies of Basel (1989) and Graz (1997).

44. Bundesministerium für Familie, Senioren, Frauen und Jugend, ed., *9. Jugendbericht* (Bonn, 1994).

45. In a youth survey for Germany, published in August 2002 (Jugendwerk der Deutschen Shell, ed., *Jugend 2002* [Opladen, 2002]), 34 percent of the 2,500 interviewees (12 to 25 years of age) call themselves "politically interested"; in 1991 it was 57 percent.

46. Florian Illies, *Generation Golf,* 194f.

47. Amitai Etzioni, *The New Golden Rule: Community and Morality in a Democratic Society* (New York: Basic Books/HarperCollins, 1996).

48. Allensbacher Institut für Demoskopie (annual survey, Spring 2002), *Christsein heute*, August 2002, 16.

49. Newbigin, *Foolishness to the Greeks*; George W. Hunter, *How to Reach Secular People*, and *The Celtic Way of Evangelism: How to Reach the West . . . Again* (Nashville: Abingdon Press, 2000). Hunter speaks of a "New Apostolic Age."

50. The term goes back to Jean-Jacques Rousseau's expression "religion civile" and was profiled sociologically by Robert N. Bellah. See Robert N. Bellah, *Beyond Belief: Essays on Religion in a Post-traditional World* (New York: Harper & Row, 1970), *The Broken Covenant: American Civil Religion in Time of Trial* (New York: Seabury Press, 1975), and *Habits of the Heart: Individualism and Commitment in America*, updated ed. (Berkeley: Univ. of California Press, 1996).

51. Gerhard Lohfink, *Wie hat Jesus Gemeinde gewollt?*, new ed. (Freiburg: Herder Verlag, 1993), esp. 142ff.

52. That is what the biblical terms for sin originally indicate: the Hebrew *'awon* and the Greek word *hamartia*. On the whole issue of sin and salvation in a Methodist perspective cf. Randy L. Maddox, *Responsible Grace: John Wesley's Practical Theology* (Nashville: Kingswood, 1994), chap. 3, "Humanity's Need and God's Initial Restoring Grace," 65-93. Also see Walter Klaiber and Manfred Marquardt, *Living Grace: An Outline of United Methodist Theology* (Nashville: Abingdon Press, 2001), chap. 2, "Universal Salvation, or God's Love for God's World," 93-215; and Scott J. Jones, *United Methodist Doctrine: The Extreme Center* (Nashville: Abingdon Press, 2002), chap. 5, "Creation, Sin, Grace, and Repentance," 145-64.

53. Chorus of Jon Bon Jovi's first song of his album *Crush*, titled "It's My Life," Island Mercury Records (Berlin: Polydor Island Group, 2000).

54. The eschatological aspect of the gospel message needs to be reemphasized in today's Christian communication. Cf. Maddox, *Responsible Grace*, 230-53.

55. On centrality of love in John Wesley's theology see Cobb, *Grace & Responsibility*, 57f.

56. Cf. Henry H. Knight, *Eight Life-enriching Practices of United Methodists* (Nashville: Abingdon Press, 2001), 118.

6. Building the Church in Africa:
Church Planting as an Inclusive Praxis

1. "Turn to God—Rejoice in Hope!" An Approach to the Theme of the Eighth Assembly of the WCC (1998).

2. Richard A. Kaufman, "Scholars Uncovering Church's Hidden History," *Christianity Today* 42, no. 8 (July13, 1998): 22.

3. "Urban and Rural Christians and Populations on Eight Continents," Part 8, "Statistics," Global Table 21, in *World Christian Encyclopedia: A Comparative Study of Churches and Religions in the Modern World 1900–2000*, ed. David Barrett (Oxford: Oxford Univ. Press, 1982), 780.

4. C. K. Barrett, *The First Epistle to the Corinthians* (London: Adam & Charles Black, 1968), 85.

5. Ibid.

6. Ibid.

7. Hans Conzelmann, *1 Corinthians* (Philadelphia: Fortress, 1981), 73.

8. J. Robert Nelson, *The Realm of Redemption* (London: Epworth Press, 1964), 4.

9. George Abbott-Smith, *A Manual Greek Lexicon of the New Testament* (Edinburgh: T. & T. Clark, 1954), 249.

10. Gustaf Aulen, *The Faith of the Christian Church*, trans. Eric H. Wahlstrom (Philadelphia: Muhlenberg Press, 1960), 293.

11. *The United Methodist Hymnal* (Nashville: The United Methodist Publishing House, 1989), Hymn 368.

12. Aulen, *The Faith of the Christian Church*, 293f.

13. Nelson, *The Realm of Redemption*, 6.

14. F. F. Bruce, *Commentary on the Book of the Acts* (Grand Rapids: Eerdmans, 1966), 194.

15. Ibid., 57.

16. Tracey K. Jones Jr., *Our Mission Today* (New York: World Outlook Press, 1963), 57.

17. David Bosch, "The Question of Mission Today," *Journal of Theology for Southern Africa* 1 (December 1972): 14.

18. "Steward," in *A Dictionary of the Bible*, ed. W. R. F. Browning (Oxford: Oxford Univ. Press, 1996), 355.

19. "Stewardship," in *Christian Word Book*, ed. J. Sherrell Hendricks et al. (Nashville: Abingdon Press, 1968), 289.

20. C. Umhau Wolf, "Steward, Stewardship," in *The Interpreter's Dictionary of the Bible*, vol. 4, ed. George Buttrick (Nashville: Abingdon Press, 1962), 443.

21. David W. Shenk and Ervin R. Stutzman, *Creating Communities of the Kingdom: New Testament Models of Church Planting* (Scottdale, Pa.: Herald Press, 1988), 201.

22. Official Journal of the Rhodesia Annual Conference of The United Methodist Church, December 31–January 6, 1974, 116.

23. The 2001 Reports of the Zimbabwe East Annual Conference of The United Methodist Church, December 6-9, 2001, 25.

7. Evangelization and Church Growth: A Lesson from the Barrio

1. See especially Michael Warren's essay "Decisions That Inscribe Life's Patterns," in *The Church as Countercultural*, ed. Michael L. Budde and Robert W. Brimlow (New York: SUNY, 2000), 127-51. Warren notes that the social and cultural horrors of the twentieth century produced by wars, massacres, human rights violations, and structural arrangements challenge Christian congregations to ask themselves what difference they have made toward preventing human unjust suffering and evil. How do we recognize the risen Lord in a world where human beings create unjust suffering?

2. Orlando Costas, *Christ Outside the Gate* (Maryknoll, N.Y.: Orbis, 1982), 80.

3. Interview with Chicho, Washington, D.C., 1993.

4. Harvey Cox, *Fire from Heaven* (Reading, Mass.: Addison-Wesley, 1994).

5. See Robert A. Horsley and Neil Asher Silberman, *The Message and the Kingdom* (Minneapolis: Fortress, 1997).

6. As quoted by Norman E. Thomas, "Evangelism and Liberation Theology," *Missiology: An International Review* 9, no. 4 (October 1981): 479.

7. Liberation theology is equated with an interest in politics and ethics; however, it has always been deeply interested in evangelization. See especially Thomas, "Evangelism and Liberation Theology." Also see, for instance, Guillermo Cook, "Seeing, Judging and Acting: Evangelism in Jesus' Way," *International Review of Mission* 86, no. 36: 388-96; Mortimer Arias, *The Cry of My People* (New York: Friendship Press, 1980) and *Announcing the Reign of God: Evangelization and the Subversive Memory of Jesus* (Philadelphia: Fortress,

1984); Gustavo Guitérrez, A Theology of Liberation (Maryknoll, N.Y.: Orbis, 1973); Orlando Costas, Christ Outside the Church (Maryknoll, N.Y.: Orbis, 1982); and Juan Luis Segundo, The Community Called Church (Maryknoll, N.Y.: Orbis, 1973).

8. For discussion of these themes see John Dominic Crossan, "Jesus and the Kingdom: Itinerants and Householders in Earliest Christianity," in Jesus at 2000, ed. Marcus J. Borg (Boulder, Colo.: Westview Press, 1998), 21-53. Also see Jon Sobrino, "Evangelization as Mission of the Church," in The True Church and the Poor (Maryknoll, N.Y.: Orbis, 1984), 253-301.

9. The practical consequences of the good news preached by Jesus included dispensing forgiveness and acts of compassion toward the weak, the defenseless poor, women, the sick, converted members of economic and symbolic power groups, members of other ethnic groups, hungry peasants, and landless laborers. The good news of Jesus, in word and deed, was intended to change people, their world, and the context of their relationships in light of the saving reality of God.

10. See especially Harold J. Recinos, Who Comes in the Name of the Lord? Jesus at the Margins (Nashville: Abingdon Press, 1997). This section briefly summarizes the barrio Christology outlined in the book.

11. See Orlando Costas, "The Whole World for the Whole Gospel: Recovering a Holistic Legacy for the 1980s," in Christ Outside the Gate, 168.

8. Saving Women: Re-visioning Contemporary Concepts of Evangelism

1. This research was made possible through the Lilly Theological Research Grants program.

2. Ann Braude, "Women's History Is American Religious History," in Retelling U.S. Religious History, ed. Thomas Tweed (Berkeley: Univ. of California Press, 1997), 88-92.

3. See Dana Robert, Gospel Bearers, Gender Barriers (Maryknoll, N.Y.: Orbis, 2002), introduction, 20.

4. See Jean Miller Schmidt, "Reexamining the Public/Private Split: Reforming the Continent and Spreading Scriptural Holiness," in Perspectives on American Methodism, ed. Russell Richey et al. (Nashville: Abingdon Press, 1993).

5. Donald W. Dayton, Discovering an Evangelical Heritage (New York: Harper & Row, 1976), chaps. 8–10. See also Doug Strong's nuanced argument building on Dayton and others in "The Crusade for Women's Rights and the Formative Antecedents of the Holiness Movement," Wesleyan Theological Journal 27, nos. 1–2 (1992): 132-60.

6. William Abraham, The Logic of Evangelism (Grand Rapids: Eerdmans, 1989), 92. Walter Klaiber, for example, argues for an understanding of evangelism that emphasizes the kerygma as distinct from ministries of diakonia or koinonia. See Call and Response (Nashville: Abingdon Press, 1997), 26.

7. See Abraham, The Logic of Evangelism, 13; Mortimer Arias, Announcing the Reign of God (Philadelphia: Fortress, 1984); Mortimer Arias and Alan Johnson, The Great Commission (Nashville: Abingdon Press, 1992); David Bosch, Transforming Mission (Maryknoll, N.Y.: Orbis, 1991); Walter Brueggemann, Biblical Perspectives on Evangelism (Nashville: Abingdon Press, 1993); Orlando Costas, Liberating News (Grand Rapids: Eerdmans, 1989); Darrell Guder, ed., Missional Church (Grand Rapids: Eerdmans, 1999); Scott Jones, The Evangelistic Love of God and Neighbor (Nashville: Abingdon Press, 2003); Ronald Sider, One-Sided Christianity (Grand Rapids: Zondervan, 1993).

8. Bosch, Transforming Mission, 409. According to Bosch, terms related to evangelism fell into almost complete disuse during the Middle Ages. Even today they are seldom used

in English Bible translations; alternatives include "good news," "gospel," and "preach the gospel." Since the early nineteenth century the verb "evangelize" and its derivatives "evangelism" and "evangelization" have been rehabilitated in church and mission circles. They became particularly prominent around the turn of the century because of the slogan "The evangelization of the world in this generation."

9. Catherine Brekus, *Strangers and Pilgrims* (Chapel Hill: Univ. of North Carolina Press, 1998), 284.

10. Richard Heitzenrater, *Wesley and the People Called Methodists* (Nashville: Abingdon Press, 1995), 312-13.

11. Deborah Valenze, *Prophetic Sons and Daughters* (Princeton: Princeton Univ. Press, 1985), 92; Dorothy Graham, "Chosen by God" (Ph.D. diss., Univ. of Birmingham, 1986), chap. 3.

12. Kenneth Rowe, "The Ordination of Women," in *Perspectives on American Methodism*, ed. Russell Richey et al. (Nashville: Kingswood, 1993), 298-308; *Journal of the General Conference*, MEC (1920): 517.

13. James Logan, "Offering Christ: Wesleyan Evangelism Today," in *Rethinking Wesley's Theology for Contemporary Methodism*, ed. Randy Maddox (Nashville: Kingswood, 1998), 118.

14. Nancy Hardesty, *Women Called to Witness* (Knoxville: Univ. of Tennessee Press, 1999), 84.

15. For example, see Bettye Collier-Thomas, *Daughters of Thunder* (San Francisco: Jossey-Bass, 1998), 21; and Hardesty, *Women Called to Witness*, 82, 85.

16. Brekus, *Strangers and Pilgrims*, 294. See also Catherine Brekus, "Female Evangelism in the Early Methodist Movement, 1784–1845," in *Methodism and the Shaping of American Culture*, ed. Nathan Hatch and John Wigger (Nashville: Kingswood, 2001), chap. 4.

17. Jean Miller Schmidt, *Grace Sufficient* (Nashville: Abingdon Press, 1999), 142.

18. Paul Chilcote, *John Wesley and the Women Preachers of Early Methodism* (Metuchen, N.J.: Scarecrow Press, 1991), 117.

19. Ibid., 119, 126-28.

20. Ibid., 129-31.

21. Schmidt, *Grace Sufficient*, 142.

22. Hardesty, *Women Called to Witness*, 112.

23. Susie Stanley, "Empowered Foremothers: Wesleyan/Holiness Women Speak to Today's Christian Feminists," *Wesleyan Theological Journal* 24 (1989): 104, 106, 108.

24. Hardesty, *Women Called to Witness*, 113.

25. Stanley, "Empowered Foremothers," 108.

26. Chilcote, *John Wesley and the Women Preachers of Early Methodism*, 48; Schmidt, *Grace Sufficient*, 52-53. See also John Wigger, *Taking Heaven by Storm: Methodism and the Rise of Popular Christianity in America* (Chicago: Univ. of Illinois Press, 2001), chap. 7.

27. Chilcote, *John Wesley and the Women Preachers of Early Methodism*, 68.

28. Ibid., 69.

29. See Earl Kent Brown, *Women of Mr. Wesley's Methodism* (New York: Edwin Mellen Press, 1983), for one of the earliest and comprehensive studies of women in early British Methodism. Brown examines the overlapping roles of sixty-five women. Paul Chilcote's most recent text continues his research on early Methodist women reflecting upon their writings, which shed light on their evangelistic ministries. See also Paul Chilcote, *Her Own Story: Autobiographical Portraits of Early Methodist Women* (Nashville: Kingswood, 2001).

30. Chilcote, *Her Own Story*, 132.

31. Ibid., 130-34.

32. Ibid., 134.

33. Ibid., 141.

34. Ibid.

35. Ibid., 142.

36. Dana Robert, *American Women in Mission* (Macon: Mercer Univ. Press, 1997), 129.

37. Ibid., 132.

38. Ibid., 133.

39. Ibid., 134.

40. Ibid., 167. "The first money raised by the Woman's Foreign Missionary Society for direct evangelistic work in 1869 was given to a native Bible woman, not to a western missionary with the title of 'evangelist.'"

41. Brekus, *Strangers and Pilgrims*, 299.

42. Robert, *American Women in Mission*, 162.

43. Ibid., 164.

44. "Deaconesses and Methodist Hospitals," *The Message and Deaconess Advocate*, May 1900, 8.

45. Florence Parker, "History of Nurses' Class," *The Message*, June 1891, 5.

46. Hardesty, *Women Called to Witness*, 4; Hardesty quotes Stephen Olin Garrison, ed., *Forty Witnesses* (New York: Hunt and Eaton, 1888; rpt Freeport, Pa.: Fountain Press, 1955), 69-71.

47. Hardesty, *Women Called to Witness*, 4.

48. However, Susie Stanley argues that Willard perceived the Woman's Crusade against alcohol as a modern Pentecost with such language permeating the WCTU's rhetoric. Stanley, "Empowered Foremothers," 105, 108-9.

49. Hardesty, *Women Called to Witness*, 4-5. Willard was invited to serve as president of the newly founded Evanston College for Ladies. In 1871 she became the first woman college president in America to confer degrees.

50. Ibid., 8, quoting Frances Willard, *Glimpses of Fifty Years: The Autobiography of an American Woman* (Chicago: Woman's Temperance Publication Association, H. J. Smith, 1889), 360; letter to Mrs. D. L. Moody, 5 September 1877.

51. Hardesty, *Women Called to Witness*, 10, quoting the NWCTU Minutes (1880), and Willard, *Glimpses of Fifty Years*, 370.

52. Hardesty, *Women Called to Witness*, 10.

53. Ibid.

54. WCTU Minutes (1874), 27.

55. WCTU Minutes (1877), 143.

56. Ibid.

57. Hardesty, *Women Called to Witness*, 11.

9. The Means of Grace and the Promise of New Life in the Evangelism of John Wesley

1. John Wesley, "The General Spread of the Gospel," para. 27, in *Sermons II*, ed. Albert C. Outler (Nashville: Abingdon Press, 1985), 499.

2. Ibid.

3. John Wesley, "The End of Christ's Coming," para. III.5, in *Sermons II*, 482-83.

4. Ibid.

5. This is my language, as first proposed in Henry H. Knight III, *The Presence of God in the Christian Life: John Wesley and the Means of Grace* (Lanham, Md.: Scarecrow Press, 1992), 2.

6. Wesley, "The General Spread of the Gospel," para. 11, in *Sermons II*, 489.

7. Ibid.

8. John Wesley, "On Working Out Our Own Salvation," para. III.4, in *Sermons III*, ed. Albert C. Outler (Nashville: Abingdon Press, 1986), 207.

9. See the extensive survey of the history and usage of "evangelism" and related terms in David B. Barrett, *Evangelize!: A Historical Survey of the Concept* (Birmingham: New Hope, 1987).

10. See John Wesley's comments in "The New Birth," para. IV, in *Sermons II*, 196-98.

11. On the emergence of the altar call in revivalism see David Bennett, *The Altar Call: Its Origins and Present Usage* (Lanham, Md.: University Press of America, 2000).

12. For an account of the variety of small and large group structures in early Methodism see Thomas R. Albin, " 'Inwardly Persuaded': Religion of the Heart in Early British Methodism," in *"Heart Religion" in the Methodist Tradition and Related Movements*, ed. Richard B. Steele (Lanham, Md.: Scarecrow Press, 2001), 33-66.

13. John Wesley, "The Means of Grace," para. II.1, in *Sermons I*, ed. Albert C. Outler (Nashville: Abingdon Press, 1984), 381.

14. John Wesley, "On Dissipation," para. 6, in *Sermons III*, 118.

15. John Wesley, "Walking by Sight and Walking by Faith," para. 20, in *Sermons IV*, ed. Albert C. Outler (Nashville: Abingdon Press, 1987), 58.

16. Wesley, "On Dissipation," para. 12, in *Sermons III*, 120.

17. See John Wesley, "The Nature, Design, and General Rules of the United Societies," in *The Methodist Societies*, ed. Rupert E. Davis (Nashville: Abingdon Press, 1989), 67-73.

18. John Wesley, Journal, August 25, 1763, in *Journals and Diaries IV (1755–1765)*, ed. W. Reginald Ward and Richard P. Heitzenrater (Nashville: Abingdon Press, 1992), 424.

19. William J. Abraham, *The Logic of Evangelism* (Grand Rapids: Eerdmans, 1989). The six activities are baptism, conversion, commitment to love God and neighbor, a basic understanding of the Christian creed, discovering spiritual gifts, and beginning to participate in spiritual disciplines (95, 118, 142).

20. Scott J. Jones, *The Evangelistic Love of God and Neighbor: A Theology of Discipleship and Witness* (Nashville: Abingdon Press, 2003). Jones adds faith sharing as a seventh activity.

21. George G. Hunter III, *The Celtic Way of Evangelism* (Nashville: Abingdon Press, 2000).

22. Robert E. Webber, *Journey to Jesus* (Nashville: Abingdon Press, 2001), and Daniel T. Benedict, *Come to the Waters* (Nashville: Discipleship Resources, 1996).

23. Richard V. Peace, *Conversion in the New Testament: Paul and the Twelve* (Grand Rapids: Eerdmans, 1999).

24. The centrality of affections and tempers to Wesley's understanding of the Christian life has been shown by Gregory S. Clapper, *John Wesley on Religious Affections* (Metuchen, N.J.: Scarecrow Press, 1989), and Richard B. Steele, *"Gracious Affections" and "True Virtue" According to Jonathan Edwards and John Wesley* (Metuchen, N.J.: Scarecrow Press, 1994). Significant articles include Randy L. Maddox, "Reconnecting the Means to the End: A Wesleyan Prescription for the Holiness Movement," *Wesleyan Theological Journal* 33, no. 2 (Fall 1998); and Kenneth J. Collins, "John Wesley's Topography of the Heart: Dispositions, Tempers, and Affections," *Methodist History* 36, no. 3 (April 1998). Collins has shown that Wesley uses "tempers" to describe abiding affections. For a discussion of the relation of faith, holy tempers, and the means of grace see Henry H. Knight III, "The Role of Faith and the Means of Grace in the Heart Religion of John Wesley," in *"Heart Religion,"* 273-90.

25. John Wesley, "On Charity," para. III.12, in *Sermons III*, 306.

26. See John Wesley, "On Faith," paras. 10-11, in *Sermons III*, 497.

27. Lesslie Newbigin, *The Gospel in a Pluralist Society* (Grand Rapids: Eerdmans, 1989), 222-33.

10. Evangelism and the Practice of Hospitality

1. A version of this essay was previously published in *Missiology: An International Review* 30, no. 3 (2002): 385-95, under the title of "Hospitality as Context for Evangelism." Originally, it was presented as an E. Stanley Jones Chair of Evangelism inaugural lecture at the Methodist Theological School in Ohio in April 2001.

2. Lesslie Newbigin, "Can the West Be Converted?" *Princeton Seminary Review* 6 (1985): 36. Newbigin also stresses that "the most aggressive paganism" with which the church has "to engage is the ideology that now controls the 'developed' world." *The Open Secret: An Introduction to the Theology of Mission*, rev. ed. (Grand Rapids: Eerdmans, 1995), 10.

3. Douglas John Hall, *Confessing the Faith: Christian Theology in a North American Context* (Minneapolis: Fortress, 1996), 368.

4. D. T. Niles, *That They May Have Life* (New York: Harper and Bros., 1951), 96.

5. Christine D. Pohl, *Making Room: Recovering Hospitality as a Christian Tradition* (Grand Rapids: Eerdmans, 1999), xi.

6. Ibid., 29.

7. John Koenig, *New Testament Hospitality: Partnership with Strangers as Promise and Mission* (Philadelphia: Fortress, 1985), 11. Koenig also states in his recent study on the missionary dimensions of the church's eucharistic rituals: "Answering the command to join Christ's mission becomes possible only when we can savor the eager and compassionate welcome that he extends to each of us personally (Matthew 11:28f.; Romans 15:7ff.)." *The Feast of the World's Redemption: Eucharistic Origins and Christian Mission* (Harrisburg, Pa.: Trinity Press International, 2000), 220.

8. Scripture quoted in the essay comes from the New Revised Standard Version.

9. Pohl, *Making Room*, 172.

10. Ibid., 158.

11. Niles, *That They May Have Life*, 96. In biblical hospitality, the roles of host and guest are far from being predictable, as well illustrated in the story of Zacchaeus in which Jesus invited him to be his host; host and guest roles are often exchanged or reversed. See Pohl, *Making Room*, 121. Stephen Bevans rightly stresses the missionary's role as guest: "It seems to me that if there is one basic attitude that missionaries must cultivate as part of their missionary activity and spirituality, it is this attitude of being a guest." In "Seeing Mission Through Images," *Missiology: An International Review* 19 (1991): 51.

12. Koenig, *New Testament Hospitality*, 100.

13. Niles, *That They May Have Life*, 57. According to Robert C. Tannehill, "these parables help to define the character of God and the mission of Jesus." *The Narrative Unity of Luke–Acts: A Literary Interpretation*, vol. 1, *The Gospel according to Luke* (Minneapolis: Fortress, 1986), 239.

14. Koenig, *New Testament Hospitality*, 125.

15. Pohl, *Making Room*, 33, 5.

16. Tannehill, *Narrative Unity of Luke-Acts*, 1:64.

17. Joel B. Green, *The Theology of the Gospel of Luke* (Cambridge, UK: Cambridge Univ. Press, 1995), 84.

18. David Bosch, *Transforming Mission: Paradigm Shifts in Theology of Mission* (Maryknoll, N.Y.: Orbis, 1991), 436. Gustavo Gutiérrez also writes: "The very word 'preference' denies all exclusiveness and seeks rather to call attention to those who are the

first—though not the only ones—with whom we should be in solidarity." *A Theology of Liberation*, 15th anniversary ed. (Maryknoll, N.Y.: Orbis, 1988), xxv-xxvi.

19. Bosch, *Transforming Mission*, 437.

20. Orlando E. Costas, *Liberating News: A Theology of Contextual Evangelization* (Grand Rapids: Eerdmans, 1989), 31.

21. Robert C. Tannehill, *The Narrative Unity of Luke-Acts: A Literary Interpretation*, vol. 2, *The Acts of the Apostles* (Minneapolis: Fortress, 1989), 135.

22. Beverly Roberts Gaventa, *From Darkness to Light: Aspects of Conversion in the New Testament* (Philadelphia: Fortress, 1986), 121.

23. Ibid., 109.

24. Darrell L. Guder, *The Incarnation and the Church's Witness* (Harrisburg, Pa.: Trinity Press International), 48.

25. Bosch, *Transforming Mission*, 390.

26. Hall, *Confessing the Faith*, 367.

27. John H. Yoder, "A People in the World," in *The Royal Priesthood: Essays Ecclesiological and Ecumenical*, ed. Michael G. Cartwright (Grand Rapids: Eerdmans, 1994), 75. Yoder continues: "But this congruence between the free visible existence of the believers' church and the possibility of valid missionary proclamation is not a merely pragmatic or instrumental one. It is found deeply in the nature of the gospel itself. If it is not the case that there are in a given place people of various characters and origins who have been brought together in Jesus Christ, then there is not in that place the new humanity and in that place the gospel is not true."

28. Pohl, *Making Room*, 9.

29. Ibid., 159. Stanley P. Saunders also criticizes the social and spatial arrangements of most congregations in North America: "[They] direct their expressions of solidarity or hospitality primarily at their own membership, or at potential members (usually 'people like us'). Engagement with poor or homeless people is usually understood as a form of benevolence, that is, as an act of charity rather than an opportunity to build a relationship. Thus, even congregations that provide services and financial support for poor and homeless people tend to resist actually including such persons in their fellowship." Stanley P. Saunders and Charles L. Campbell, *The Word on the Street: Performing the Scriptures in the Urban Context* (Grand Rapids: Eerdmans, 2000), 161-62.

30. Charles R. Foster and Theodore Brelsford, *We Are the Church Together: Cultural Diversity in Congregational Life* (Valley Forge, Pa.: Trinity Press International, 1996), 109.

31. Ibid., 159.

32. J. Andrew Kirk, *What Is Mission?: Theological Explorations* (Minneapolis: Fortress, 2000), 73.

33. Saunders writes that "the practices of hospitality . . . blur the boundaries between two disciplines we usually separate, spirituality and mission." *Word on the Street*, 166.

34. Roberto Escamilla, *Come to the Feast: Invitational Evangelism* (Nashville: Discipleship Resources, 1998), 39.

35. Hendrikus Berkhof, *The Doctrine of the Holy Spirit* (Richmond, Va.: John Knox, 1964), 33. According to Newbigin, "The active agent of mission is a power that rules, guides, and goes before the church: the free, sovereign, living power of the Spirit of God"; and "The church's witness is secondary and derivative. The church is witness insofar as it follows obediently where the Spirit leads." *Open Secret*, 56, 61.

36. Berkhof, *The Holy Spirit*, 36.

37. Darrell L. Guder, *The Continuing Conversion of the Church* (Grand Rapids: Eerdmans, 2000), 65.

38. Thomas R. Hawkins, *Sharing the Search: A Theology of Christian Hospitality* (Nashville: Upper Room, 1987), 84.

39. Pohl, *Making Room*, 13.
40. Guder, *Incarnation and Witness*, 29.
41. I want to express my profound appreciation to the lay members who started the Over-the-Rhine ministry with me and continue to be involved in it with their faithfulness and commitment to the gospel.
42. Pohl, *Making Room*, 131-32.
43. Guder, *Continuing Conversion*, 55.
44. Niles, *That They May Have Life*, 33, 82.
45. Costas, *Liberating News*, 18.

11. Evangelistic Hospitality in Preaching: Welcoming Everyone to the Story

1. For more information on this generation see Craig Miller and Mary Jane Pierce Norton, *Making God Real for a New Generation* (Nashville: Discipleship Resources, 2003).
2. There are many resources on the technical aspects of using video and digital imagery in worship; one of the most complete and helpful is by Tim Eason, *Media Ministry Made Easy* (Nashville: Abingdon Press, 2003).
3. For a comprehensive description of this service as well as some of the images used in projection, see *Igniting Worship Series: Communion*, by SpiritFilms and Grace Community Church (Nashville: Abingdon Press, 2003).
4. For more information on communicating and leading through media and community building, see Rob Weber, *Visual Leadership* (Nashville: Abingdon Press, 2002).

12. New Church Development

1. Cf. 1 Corinthians 4:14-15; 2 Corinthians 12:14-15; 1 Thessalonians 2:7-12.
2. It is beyond the scope of this essay to ask and answer the question of whether there are gender associations at work here whereby church "planting" would tend to resonate with males while church "birthing" would tend to resonate with females. One must also consider the fact that, globally, women produce anywhere from half to 90 percent of the world's food supply and are, therefore, not only primarily "birthers" but also "planters."
3. See for example, David Shenk and Ervin Stutzman, *Creating Communities of the Kingdom* (Scottdale, Pa.: Herald Press, 1988), 58ff.
4. C. Peter Wagner, *Church Planting for a Greater Harvest* (Ventura: Regal, 1990), 11.
5. Stuart Murray, *Church Planting: Laying Foundations* (Carlisle, UK: Paternoster Press, 1998), 179.
6. See Philip D. Kenneson and James L. Street, *Selling Out the Church: The Dangers of Church Marketing* (Nashville: Abingdon Press, 1997).
7. Ibid., 136.
8. John Howard Yoder, *The Royal Priesthood: Essays Ecumenical and Ecclesiological* (Scottdale, Pa.: Herald Press, 1998), 126.
9. Aubrey Malphurs, *Planting Growing Churches for the 21st Century*, 2d ed. (Grand Rapids: Baker, 1998), 108-9.
10. Charles Ridley, *How to Select Church Planters: A Self-study Manual for Recruiting, Screening, Interviewing and Evaluating Qualified Church Planters* (Pasadena: Fuller Evangelistic Association, 1988). In brief, Ridley's list includes (1) visioning capacity, (2) intrinsic motivation, (3) ownership of ministry, (4) reaches the unchurched,

(5) spousal cooperation, (6) effectively builds relationships, (7) committed to church growth, (8) responsive to the community, (9) utilizes giftedness of others, (10) flexible and adaptable, (11) builds group cohesiveness, (12) demonstrates resilience, and (13) exercises faith.

11. Yoder, *The Royal Priesthood*, 70-71. Yoder is here claiming this about Zwingli.

12. Murray, *Church Planting*, 121. See also the criticism of the parish model in *The Church for Others* (Geneva: World Council of Churches, 1967), 29.

13. Donald McGavran, *Understanding Church Growth* (Grand Rapids: Eerdmans, 1980), 223.

14. Murray, *Church Planting*, 145.

15. Ibid.

16. Ibid., 146.

17. For information on the cell church movement, see Michael Green, ed., *Church Without Walls: A Global Examination of the Cell Church* (Grand Rapids: Eerdmans, 2002), and Brian Sauder and Larry Kreider, *Helping You Build Cell Churches: A Comprehensive Training Manual for Pastors, Cell Leaders, and Church Planters* (House to House Press, 2002). In addition, numerous networks of cell churches can be located on the Internet.

18. James O'Halloran, *Signs of Hope: Developing Small Christian Communities* (Maryknoll, N.Y.: Orbis, 1991), 7-8.

19. Ibid.

20. See, for example, his *Familiaris Consortio* (1981).

21. Murray, *Church Planting*, 151.

22. Roger Ellis and Roger Mitchell, *Radical Church Planting* (Cambridge: Crossway, 1992), 73.

23. Walt Kallestad, *Entertainment Evangelism: Taking the Church Public* (Nashville: Abingdon Press, 1996), 16-17.

24. See Lynne and Bill Hybels, *Rediscovering Church* (Grand Rapids: Zondervan, 1995); Gregory A. Pritchard, *Willow Creek Seeker Services: Evaluating a New Way of Doing Church* (Grand Rapids: Baker, 1996); and Kimon Howland Sargeant, *Seeker Churches: Promoting Traditional Religion in a Nontraditional Way* (Rutgers Univ. Press, 2000).

25. Kenneson and Street, *Selling Out the Church*, 67.

26. Shenk and Stutzman, *Creating Communities of the Kingdom*, 44-50.

27. Ibid., 263.

28. A "rigid and inflexible attitude towards the *morphe* or structure of the congregation similar to the attitude prevalent in biblical fundamentalism." *The Church for Others*, 19.

13. Faithful Discipleship: A Conjoined Catechesis of Truth and Love

1. Sharon J. Hels, ed., *Methodism and Education: From Roots to Fulfillment* (Nashville: General Board of Higher Education and Ministry, The United Methodist Church, 2000).

2. See Beth Adams Bowser, *Living the Vision: The University Senate of The Methodist Episcopal Church, The Methodist Church, and The United Methodist Church, 1892–1991* (Nashville: Board of Higher Education, The United Methodist Church, 1992); Michael G. Cartwright, "Looking Both Ways: A 'Holy Experiment' in American Education," in *Schooling Christians: "Holy Experiments" in American Education*, ed. Stanley Hauerwas and John Westerhoff (Grand Rapids: Eerdmans, 1992); Russell E. Richey, "Connectionalism and College," in *Methodism and Education*, 57-75; John Q. Schisler, *Christian Education in Local Methodist Churches* (Nashville: Abingdon Press, 1969); John T. Smith, *Methodism*

and Education, 1849–1902: J. H. Rigg, Romanism, and Wesleyan Schools (New York: Oxford Univ. Press, 1998). See also Church of the Nazarene, "Christian, Holiness, Missional: Core Values Statement," available online (December 21, 2003), http://www.nazarene.org/welcome/values/index.html. The Church of the Nazarene locates Christian Higher Education under its commitment to mission.

3. Charles Wesley, "Hymn 461, For Children," in *The Works of John Wesley*, vol. 7, *A Collection of Hymns for the Use of the People Called Methodists*, ed. Franz Hildebrandt and Oliver A. Beckerlegge (New York: Oxford Univ. Press, 1983; Nashville: Abingdon Press, 1989), 7:643-44.

4. Ibid.

5. Richard Heitzenrater, "John Wesley and the Historian's Task," in *Mirror and Memory: Reflections on Early Methodism* (Nashville: Kingswood, 1989), 205-18; Maddox, "Reclaiming an Inheritance: Wesley as Theologian in the History of Methodist Theology," in *Rethinking Wesley's Theology for Contemporary Methodism*, ed. Randy L. Maddox (Nashville: Kingswood, 1998), 213-26.

6. Paul Sangster, *Pity My Simplicity: The Evangelical Revival and the Religious Education of Children, 1738–1800* (London: Epworth Press, 1963), 28.

7. Sondra Higgins Matthaei, *Making Disciples: Faith Formation in the Wesleyan Tradition* (Nashville: Abingdon Press, 2000); John Wesley Prince, *Wesley on Religious Education: A Study of John Wesley's Theories and Methods of the Education of Children in Religion* (New York: Methodist Book Concern, 1926). See also Alfred H. Body, *John Wesley and Education* (London: Epworth Press, 1936); John Gross, *John Wesley: Christian Educator* (Nashville: The Methodist Church, 1954); David Michael Henderson, *John Wesley's Instructional Groups*, Ph.D. diss., Indiana University, 1980 (Ann Arbor, Mich.: UMI, 1981).

8. Matthaei, *Making Disciples*, 34.

9. Body, *John Wesley and Education*, 33-68; Richard E. Brantley, *Locke, Wesley and the Method of English Romanticism* (Gainesville: University Presses of Florida, 1984); Gross, *John Wesley: Christian Educator*, 11-12; Prince, *Wesley on Religious Education*, 103; Joseph Seaborn, *John Wesley's Use of History as a Ministerial and Educational Tool*, Th.D. diss., Boston University School of Theology, 1984 (Ann Arbor, Mich.: UMI, 1985), 59-67; Martin Schmidt, *John Wesley: A Theological Biography*, 2 vols., trans. Norman Goldhawk (Nashville: Abingdon Press, 1962–72), 1:52-63, 2:175-76, 184-86; Elmer Towns, "John Wesley," in *A History of Religious Educators*, ed. Elmer Towns (Grand Rapids: Baker, 1975), 212-25.

10. James Riley Estep Jr., "John Wesley's Philosophy of Formal Childhood Education," *Christian Education Journal* 1, no. 2 (Fall 1997): 43-52, 45-46; Towns, "John Wesley," 216; Reginald A. Ward and Richard P. Heitzenrater, eds., *The Works of John Wesley: Journal and Diaries*, vols. 18–23, *The Works of John Wesley*, Bicentennial ed. (Nashville: Abingdon Press, 1988–95), 20:66; Wesley, "Remarks Upon Locke's 'Essay of Human Understanding,' " in *Works*, ed. Jackson, 13:455-64.

11. John Lawson and Harold Silver, *A Social History of Education in England* (London: Methuen, 1973), 175.

12. Body, *John Wesley and Education*, 33, 65; Estep, "John Wesley's Philosophy of Formal Childhood Education," 43-47; Prince, *Wesley on Religious Education*, 94-95, 121-23; Frank C. Pritchard, *Methodist Secondary Education: A History of the Contribution of Methodism to Secondary Education in the United Kingdom* (London: Epworth Press, 1949), 40-42; Sangster, *Pity My Simplicity*, 29.

13. John English, "John Wesley's Indebtedness to John Norris," *Church History* 67 (March 1991): 55-69, esp. 58-60; Estep, "John Wesley's Philosophy of Formal Childhood Education," 46; Frederick J. Powicke, *The Cambridge Platonists: A Study* (London: Dent, 1926; Hamden: Archon Books, 1971), 19.

14. Gregory S. Clapper, *John Wesley on Religious Affections: His Views on Experience*

and Emotions and Their Role in the Christian Life and Theology (Metuchen, N.J.: Scarecrow Press, 1989), 2-3, 148-49, 154-69.

15. Wesley, "The Means of Grace," in *Works*, ed. Outler, 1:381.

16. Wesley, "A Roman Catechism with a Reply," in *Works*, ed. Jackson, 10:113.

17. Ibid.

18. Heitzenrater, "Wesley and Education," 11.

19. Dean G. Blevins, *John Wesley and the Means of Grace: An Approach to Christian Religious Education*, Ph.D. diss., Claremont School of Theology, 1999 (Ann Arbor, Mich.: UMI, 1999), 132-34.

20. Seaborn, *John Wesley's Use of History*, 28-80; Susan Etheridge Willhauck, *John Wesley's View of Children: Foundations for Contemporary Christian Education*, Ph.D. diss., Catholic University of America, 1992 (Ann Arbor, Mich.: UMI, 1992), 17-96, 174-242.

21. Wesley, "On the Education of Children," in *Sermons*, ed. Outler, 3:354.

22. Ibid., 3:349-60. Wesley also fashioned parental countermeasures against these diseases. To fulfill the biblical injunction to "train up the child" Wesley recommended the following: (1) having regular conversation concerning God, (2) breaking the will, (3) refusing to praise children (and teaching them that they were fallen spirits), (4) teaching plainness and modesty in diet, dress, and possessions, (5) refusing to take revenge, (6) teaching veracity, sincerity, simplicity, and openness, and (7) modeling both justice and mercy.

23. Ibid., 3:349. Wesley writes, "And is it not reasonable to suppose that a Christian education should have no other end but to teach them how to think, and judge, and act according to the strictest rules of Christianity?"

24. Robert Monk, *John Wesley: His Puritan Heritage* (Nashville: Abingdon Press, 1966), 20-21.

25. Wesley, *Letters*, ed. Baker, 25:330-31; Wesley's Journal, in *Works*, ed. Ward and Heitzenrater, 19:286-91; Wesley, "On Obedience to Parents," in *Sermons*, ed. Outler, 3:361-72.

26. Steven J. Harper, *Devotional Life of John Wesley: 1703–1738*, Ph.D. diss., Duke University, 1981 (Ann Arbor, Mich.: UMI, 1982), 64.

27. Edwards, 31.

28. Monk, *John Wesley: His Puritan Heritage*, 23, 139-254; Schmidt, *John Wesley: A Theological Biography*, 1:47-63. Schmidt notes that the combined Puritan and Anglican factors gave Wesley's parents' faith "intensity and depth" (47). Schmidt, however, does not develop Susanna's interest in the Anglican tradition, choosing instead to continue his introduction with Susanna's interest in Roman Catholic mysticism through the writings of Lorenzo Scupoli and Juan de Castaniza (48).

29. Seaborn, *John Wesley's Use of History*, 34-36; Prince, *Wesley on Religious Education*, 116. Prince, like Seaborn, emphasizes Susanna's terms "conquer" and "submit" as more appropriate expressions than John Wesley's use of the term "break."

30. Wesley, "On Family Religion," in *Sermons*, ed. Outler, 3:334-46.

31. Ibid., 3:337.

32. Ibid., 3:337-40. Wesley writes, "Use such words as little children may understand, just such as they use themselves. Carefully observe the few ideas which they have already, and endeavour to graft what you say upon them" (340). Wesley proceeds to illustrate plain teaching with an example of teaching by association for the reader.

33. Ibid., 3:345.

34. Seaborn, *John Wesley's Use of History*, 32; see also Schmidt, *John Wesley: A Theological Biography*, 1:60-63.

35. Leslie F. Church, *Knight of the Burning Heart* (New York: Abingdon-Cokesbury Press, 1938), 23-30; Schmidt, *John Wesley: A Theological Biography*, 1:65-66; Seaborn, *John Wesley's Use of History*, 41-44; H. F. Mathews, *Methodism and the Education of the*

People: 1791–1851 (London: Epworth Press, 1949), 25; John Telford, *The Life of John Wesley* (1899; repr., London: Epworth Press, 1960), 21-27.

36. Body, *John Wesley and Education*, 69-71.

37. Donald Tranter, "John Wesley and the Education of Children," in *Issues in Education: Some Methodist Perspectives*, ed. Tim Macquiban (Oxford: Applied Theology Press, 1996), 30.

38. Henderson, *John Wesley's Instructional Groups*, 82.

39. Michael Bishop, "Wesley's Four Schools at Kingswood," in *Issues in Education*, 42-61; Body, *John Wesley and Education*, 71-77. Bishop gives an inaugural date of 1741 for Kingswood (49).

40. Body, *John Wesley and Education*, 76-77, 87, 139. Kingswood's original site, the "Old House," included day classes for the colliers' children, as well as evening and early morning classes for adults (139).

41. Ibid., 94-98.

42. Mathews, *Methodism and the Education of the People*, 27.

43. Body, *John Wesley and Education*, 98; Wesley, "A Plain Account of Kingswood School," in *Works*, ed. Jackson, 13:296-99. Kingswood academy became an alternative college for Methodists, one that Wesley felt rivaled any program offered by Oxford.

44. Body, *John Wesley and Education*, 77-78; Victor E. Neuburg, *Popular Education in Eighteenth Century England* (London: Woburn Press, 1971), 31. Students began at five o'clock in the morning (with preaching) and stayed until five that evening.

45. Body, *John Wesley and Education*, 139.

46. Gayle Carlton Felton, "John Wesley and the Teaching Ministry: Ramifications for Education in the Church Today," *Religious Education* 92, no. 1 (Winter 1997): 98; Prince, *Wesley on Religious Education*, 125-32.

47. Wesley, *Lessons for Children*, 3-4, cited in Prince, *Wesley on Religious Education*, 126 (emphasis in Prince).

48. John Wesley, *A Christian Library, Consisting of Extracts from and Abridgements of the Choicest Pieces of Practical Divinity which has been published in the English Tongue*, 30 vols. (London: T. Blanshard, 1819–27); Wesley, *Works*, ed. Jackson, 8:314; Wesley, Preface to the 3rd ed., *Works*, ed. Jackson, 1:ii. See also Body, *John Wesley and Education*, 99-101.

49. Willhauck, *John Wesley's View of Children*, 179-82. Willhauck argues that Wesley had regular contact with and an honest concern for children.

50. Prince, *Wesley on Religious Education*, 82-85.

51. Felton, "John Wesley and the Teaching Ministry," 97-98; Mathews, *Methodism and the Education of the People*, 36-38; Addie Grace Wardle, *History of the Sunday School in The Methodist Episcopal Church* (New York: Methodist Book Concern, 1918), 11-35; Willhauck, *John Wesley's View of Children*, 234. Mathews notes that Wesley encouraged and supported the efforts of Hannah Ball in High Wycombe who began a form of Sunday school in 1869, eleven years before Robert Raikes. Wesley did secure a Methodist Sunday school in Bolton in 1785; by 1788 the Bolton Sunday schools greeted Wesley with close to a thousand pupils (36-38).

52. Prince, *Wesley on Religious Education*, 132-37. Wesley records one famed confrontation with a Methodist minister who did not feel called to work with children. Wesley's straightforward response is that perhaps the man is also not to be a Methodist minister (135).

53. Felton, "John Wesley and the Teaching Ministry," 96; Prince, *Wesley on Religious Education*, 82-87.

54. Lee, 25-38; Seaborn, *John Wesley's Use of History*, 45-51.

55. Stanley J. Curtis, *History of Education in Great Britain*, 3rd ed. (Westport, Conn.: Greenwood Press, 1954), 134-35; Lawson and Silver, *A Social History of Education in England*, 177-78, 210-18.

56. Harper, *Devotional Life of John Wesley*, 107-8; Richard P. Heitzenrater, *Wesley and the*

People Called Methodists (Nashville: Abingdon Press, 1995), 33-95. Heitzenrater identifies three separate "beginnings" or rises of Methodism: the Oxford group (33-58), Georgia and the Frederica Society (58-73), and London with the Fetter Lane Society (73-95).

57. Harper, *Devotional Life of John Wesley*, 32-42.

58. Ibid., 76-77. Kirkham was also a lady of whom Wesley held more than casual interest.

59. Ibid., 110-11.

60. Wesley D. Tracy, "The Wesleyan Way to Spiritual Formation: Christian Spirituality in the Letters of John Wesley" (St.D. diss., San Francisco Theological Seminary, 1987), 58-61. See also Tracy, "John Wesley, Spiritual Director: Spiritual Guidance in John Wesley's Letters," *Wesley Theological Journal* 23, nos. 1–2 (Spring-Fall 1988): 148-62.

61. Henry H. Knight III, *The Presence of God in the Christian Life: John Wesley and the Means of Grace* (Metuchen, N.J.: Scarecrow Press, 1992), 95-103.

62. Harper, *Devotional Life of John Wesley,* 107.

63. John S. Simon, *John Wesley and the Religious Societies* (London: Epworth Press, 1921); Watson, 68

64. Henderson, *John Wesley's Instructional Groups*, 42-53.

65. Rupert Davies, introduction, *The Methodist Societies: History, Nature and Design*, ed. Rupert Davies, vol. 9, *The Works of John Wesley*, Bicentennial ed. (Oxford: Clarendon Press, 1980; Nashville: Abingdon Press, 1989), 9:10-12. See also Wesley's Journal, in *Works*, ed. Ward and Heitzenrater, 19:78-79.

66. Heitzenrater, *Wesley and the People Called Methodist*, 103-6. See also Wesley, "Short History of People Called Methodist," in *Works*, ed. Rupert Davies, 9:430. Wesley notes that there were three "rises" of Methodism: 1729 in Oxford, 1736 in Savannah, and May 1, 1738, in London.

67. Henderson, *John Wesley's Instructional Groups*, 91.

68. Rupert Davies, introduction, *The Methodist Societies: History, Nature and Design*, in *Works*, 9:12; Watson, 93.

69. Watson, 93-95.

70. David Michael Henderson, *John Wesley's Class Meeting: A Model of Making Disciples* (Nappanee, Ind.: Evangel Publishing House, 1997).

71. John Drakeford, *People to People Therapy* (San Francisco: Harper and Row, 1978), 17; Henderson, *John Wesley's Instructional Groups*, 98.

72. Henderson, *John Wesley's Instructional Groups*, 140; Jerry Sproull, "The Methodist Class Meeting, A Study of Its Development, Dynamics, Distinctions, Demise and Denouement" (Th.M. thesis, Asbury Theological Seminary, 1967), 87-89, 383.

73. Drakeford, *People to People Therapy,* 15.

74. Manfred Marquardt, *John Wesley's Social Ethics: Praxis and Principles*, trans. John E. Steely and W. Stephen Gunter (Nashville: Abingdon Press, 1992), 15.

75. William Walter Dean, *Disciplined Fellowship: The Rise and Decline of Cell Groups in British Methodism*, Ph.D. diss., University of Iowa, 1985 (Ann Arbor, Mich.: UMI, 1986), 365. Dean asserts this movement away from societies resulted in a generic or "diffusive Christianity" rather than a distinctive theology.

76. Henry Abelove, *The Evangelist of Desire: John Wesley and the Methodists* (Stanford: Stanford Univ. Press, 1990), 104-5; Douglas Hay and Nicholas Rogers, *Eighteenth-Century English Society: Shuttles and Swords* (Oxford: Oxford Univ. Press, 1997), 170.

77. David Hempton, *Methodism and Politics in British Society, 1750–1850* (Stanford: Stanford Univ. Press, 1984), 13-14; John Wesley, "A Short History of People Called Methodists," in *Works*, ed. Davies, 9:438.

78. John Lawson, "The People Called Methodists—Our Discipline," in *A History of*

the *Methodist Church in Great Britain*, vol. 1, ed. Rupert Davies and Gordon Rupp (London: Epworth Press, 1965), 183-209.

79. Hempton, *Methodism and Politics in British Society*, 14.

80. Leslie F. Church, *The Early Methodist People* (London: Epworth Press, 1948), 3, 184-221; Hempton, *Methodism and Politics in British Society*, 12-14; John Munsey Turner, *Conflict and Reconciliation: Studies in Methodism and Ecumenism in England: 1740–1982* (London: Epworth Press, 1985), 31; Robert Wearmouth, *Methodism and the Common People of the Eighteenth Century* (London: Epworth Press, 1945), 239-68.

81. Dean G. Blevins, "Practicing the New Creation: Wesley's Eschatalogical Community Formed by the Means of Grace," *Asbury Theological Journal* 57, no. 2; 58, no. 1 (Fall 2002/Spring 2003): 81-104.

82. Ted A. Campbell, *John Wesley and Christian Antiquity: Religious Vision and Cultural Change* (Nashville: Kingswood, 1991), 14-15; Wesley, *Works*, ed. Jackson, 8:314. As noted, his fifty-volume collection of outside works and abridgments, *A Christian Library*, was required reading for Methodist ministers as well as those attending Kingswood.

83. Wesley's Journal, in *Journal*, ed. Ward and Heitzenrater, 18:93.

84. Marquardt, *John Wesley's Social Ethics*, 59.

85. Neuberg, 134.

86. Ibid.

87. Ibid., 132-33.

88. Wesley, "Advice to the People Called Methodists," in *Writings*, ed. Davies, 9:123, 125; Wesley, "Thoughts upon Methodism," in *Writings*, ed. Davies, 9:529; Wesley, *Journal*, ed. Ward and Heitzenrater, 21:51. In 1786 Wesley states that holiness of heart and life is the essence of Methodism (9:123, 529). See also Wesley, "Letters to Samuel Sparrow, Esq.," in *Works*, ed. Jackson, 12:477.

89. Wesley, "The Righteousness of Faith," in *Sermons*, ed. Outler, 1:205; see also "The Witness of the Spirit II," 1:290; "Sermon on the Mount, III," 1:527; "The Law Established Through Faith, II," 2:38; "The Signs of the Times," 2:527; "On Perfection," 3:79; "On God's Vineyard," 3:507; "Dives and Lazarus," 4:16; "Hypocrisy in Oxford [English]," 4:396. See also Wesley, "A Farther Appeal to Men of Reason and Religion, Part I," in *Writings*, ed. Cragg, 11:132; "A Farther Appeal, Part III," 11:281, 320. See also Wesley, "The Doctrine of Original Sin, Part II," in *Works*, ed. Jackson, 9:312; "A Word to a Condemned Malefactor," 11:179.

90. Wesley, "The Character of a Methodist," in *Works*, ed. Davies, 9:35; Wesley's Journal, in *Works*, ed. Ward and Heitzenrater, 21:456. The term "holiness of heart and life" first appears in Wesley's Journal in a letter John received on April 26, 1756. Wesley, as early as 1742, states that holiness of heart and life is a comprehensive definition of salvation that includes faith (9:35).

91. Albert C. Outler, *Theology in the Wesleyan Spirit* (Nashville: Discipleship Resources, 1975), 69-88; see also Steve Harper, *Devotional Life in the Wesleyan Tradition* (Nashville: Upper Room, 1983), 65. Harper writes that the "wedding of piety and mercy forged a more effective instrument in God's hand than they could ever have been if they had opted for one form of spirituality to the exclusion of the other. Holiness of heart and life remain the twin peaks of vital spirituality."

92. Matthaei, *Making Disciples*, 25-26; see also Ruth A. Daugherty and Charles Yrigoyen Jr., *John Wesley: Holiness of Heart and Life* (Nashville: Abingdon Press, 1999).

93. Theodore Runyon, *The New Creation: John Wesley's Theology Today* (Nashville: Abingdon Press, 1998), 7-12.

94. Wesley, 2 John 1:2, *Explanatory Notes on the New Testament*, 2 vols. (London: Wesleyan Methodist Book Room, 1780; Hendrickson Publishers, 1986), n.p.

95. Wesley, 2 John 1:3, *Explanatory Notes on the New Testament*, n.p.

96. Wesley, Ephesians 4:20-21, *Explanatory Notes on the New Testament*, n.p.

97. Wesley, Ephesians 4:13, *Explanatory Notes on the New Testament*, n.p.

98. Aaron Milavec, *The Didache: Text, Translation, Analysis, and Commentary* (Collegeville, Minn.: Liturgical Press, 2003), 39-93.

99. Wesley, "The Witness of our Own Spirit," 1:308-10; "On Patience," 3:173; "Sermon on the Mount, I," 1:481, in *Works*, ed. Outler.

100. Wesley, "Christian Perfection," in *Works*, ed. Jackson, 11:444.

101. Albert C. Outler, "Methodists in Search of Consensus," in *What Should Methodists Teach? Wesleyan Tradition and Modern Diversity*, ed. M. Douglas Meeks (Nashville: Kingswood, 1990), 37.

102. Heitzenrater, "Wesley and Education," see 161 n. 29.

103. Wesley, "The Lord Our Righteousness," in *Works*, ed. Outler, 1:458.

104. Randy L. Maddox, *Responsible Grace: John Wesley's Practical Theology* (Nashville: Kingswood, 1994), 219.

105. John Westerhoff III, "The Challenge: Understanding the Problem of Faithfulness," in *A Faithful Church: Issues in the History of Catechesis*, ed. John H. Westerhoff III and O. C. Edwards Jr. (Wilton, Conn.: Morehouse-Barlow, 1981), 2.

106. Ibid.

107. Wesley, "Forms of Prayer for Every Day of the Week," in *Works*, ed. Jackson, 11:222.

14. Sanctified Singing: The Role of Hymnody in Shaping Wesleyan Evangelism, 1735–1915

1. The classic articulation of the centrality of entire sanctification to Methodism is John Leland Peters, *Christian Perfection and American Methodism* (New York: Abingdon Press, 1956). For a fuller discussion of the themes addressed in this essay, see Candy Gunther Brown, *The Word in the World: Evangelical Writing, Publishing, and Reading in America, 1789–1880* (Chapel Hill: Univ. of North Carolina Press, 2004); portions of this essay are reprinted from the book by permission.

2. Brian Stock, *Listening for the Text: On the Uses of the Past* (Baltimore: Johns Hopkins Univ. Press, 1990), 146.

3. John Wesley's clearest articulation of the doctrine of entire sanctification may be found in *A Plain Account of Christian Perfection: As Believed and Taught by the Reverend Mr. John Wesley, from the Year 1725, to the Year 1777* (New York: G. Lane, 1844).

4. See John Julian, ed., *A Dictionary of Hymnology: Setting Forth the Origin and History of Christian Hymns of All Ages and Nations* (1892; rev. ed., with new supplement, London: John Murray, 1907), 57, 332.

5. Ibid.; H. Wiley Hitchcock and Stanley Sadie, *The New Grove Dictionary of American Music*, vol. 2 (New York: Grove's Dictionaries of Music, 1986), 446-55; Emory Stevens Bucke et al., eds., *History of American Methodism* (New York: Abingdon Press, 1964), 1:285-86; Jon Michael Spencer, *Black Hymnody: A Hymnological History of the African-American Church* (Knoxville: Univ. of Tennessee Press, 1992), 8.

6. Committee to the Bishops, *The Revision of the Hymn Book of the Methodist Episcopal Church . . .* (New York: Nelson & Phillips; Cincinnati: Hitchcock & Walden, 1878), 6-7, 14; George John Stevenson, *The Methodist Hymn Book: Illustrated with Biography, History, Incident, and Anecdote* (London: S. W. Partridge, [1883?]), 6.

7. Committee to the Bishops, *Revision*, 6.

8. G. W. Henry, *The Golden Harp: A Supplement to the First Edition of Camp-Meeting*

Hymns, to Which is Added the Opinion of 12 of the Early Fathers of Methodism on the Subject of Devotional Singing . . . (Oneida: G. W. Henry, 1857), 15-16.

9. G. W. Henry, *The Golden Harp; Or, Camp-Meeting Hymns, Old and New, Set to Music* (Oneida: G. W. Henry, 1857), 10.

10. S. W. Christophers, *The Epworth Singers and Other Poets of Methodism* (New York: A. D. F. Randolph, 1874), 12.

11. Ibid.

12. James O. Murray, *Christian Hymnology: A Sermon Preached in the Brick Church, New York, December 12, 1869* (New York: Charles Scribner, 1870), 28-29.

13. William H. Parker, *The Psalmody of the Church: Its Authors, Singers and Uses* (New York and Chicago: Revell, 1889), 254.

14. Stevenson, *Methodist Hymn Book*, 54; E. O. P., *Gleams of Interest Across Hymns Ancient and Modern* (London: W. R. Russell, 1898).

15. "From *The Boys' Scrap Book*, A Work Lately Published by the American Sunday School Union," *Youth's Magazine* 1 (March 1839): 393-94.

16. Stephen A. Marini, "Hymnody in American Protestantism Project Database," Institute for the Study of American Evangelicals, Wheaton College, Wheaton, Ill., 1999, and Marini, "Hymnody as History: Early Evangelical Hymns and the Recovery of American Popular Religion," *Church History* 7 (June 2002): 273-306.

17. John Cennick, *Sacred Hymns for the Children of God* (London: John Lewis, 1742), 3.

18. Marini, "Hymnody in American Protestantism Database."

19. Index to *Hymnal of the Methodist Episcopal Church, with Tunes* (Cincinnati: Jennings & Pye; New York: Eaton & Mains, 1878); the biblical references are Malachi 3:1 (prophecy of Jesus' arrival in his temple)—stanza 1, line 2, and stanza 3, line 4; Matthew 14:14 (Jesus' compassion)—stanza 1, line 5; 2 Corinthians 3:18 (the Holy Spirit transforms Christians from one degree of glory to another)—stanza 2, lines 1 and 2, and stanza 4, line 5; Revelation 4:10 (crowns cast down in worship)—stanza 4, line 7; Revelation 21:5 (God makes all things new)—stanza 4, line 1; and Revelation 21:6 (God is Alpha and Omega)—stanza 2, line 6.

20. Julian, *Dictionary of Hymnology*, 971; Stevenson, *Methodist Hymn Book*, 415.

21. Ibid.

22. Fanny Crosby [Mrs. Alexander Van Alstyne], *Memories of Eighty Years* (Boston: James H. Earle, 1906), 127, 166-69; Bernard Ruffin, *Fanny Crosby: The Hymn Writer* (Uhrichsville, Ohio: Barbour, 1945), 7, 129.

23. Fanny Crosby, *The Silver Spray* (Cincinnati: John Church, 1868), 191.

15. Disciple Bible Study and Changed Lives

1. Information about Disciple Bible study can be found online at www.Cokesbury.com/services.aspt and can be ordered through Cokesbury Seminars at (800) 672-1789 or (800) 251-8591.

2. Among them, Spanish, Korean, German, Russian, and Chinese.

3. Mary A. Jacobs, "Disciple Grows Far Beyond Originators' Dreams," *Arkansas United Methodist*, January 2, 2004, 14. This article was reprinted from the *Dallas Morning News*, October 11, 2003, 2G.

4. The source for this comment comes from a conversation with Bishop Richard Wilke, in which he shared his memories of the events preceding the development of Disciple.

5. This summary of key events comes largely from an interview by the author with Bishop Wilke.

6. The Foundation for Evangelism has produced a CD, in which Bishop Wilke enumerates the principles that make DISCIPLE work in a local church, as well as what causes it to fail. One point made is that teachers who want to lecture and focus on content fail to understand the transformative, formational aim of the study, not to mention its emphasis not on lecture but on communal conversation.

7. In addition to small group Bible study, Wilke had been leading small home groups for marriage therapy, based on his best-selling book at the time, *Tell Me Again, I'm Listening*. The group sharing and interaction were transformative for people putting their marriages back together or otherwise strengthening them. This experience reinforced for Wilke the power of small groups gathered for a common purpose.

8. See the proceedings for May 12, 1984, in *Daily Christian Advocate*, vol. 6, no. 13, 809.

9. See the proceedings for April 27, 1988, in the *Daily Christian Advocate*, vol. 7, no. 2, 82.

10. Richard B. Wilke, *And Are We Yet Alive? The Future of The United Methodist Church* (Nashville: Abingdon Press, 1986).

11. Ibid., 17. A chart included in chapter 1 ("Sick Unto Death") shows membership at 9.2 million. Today that figure is slightly less than 8.3 million. A report—"The Denomination's Financial Mission Statement: The Recommended Funding Plan for Mission and Ministry"—from the General Conference on Finance and Administration projects an average annual *decline* of forty thousand members per year for the next several years, so the trend of membership loss continues. At the time of writing this information came from a report made by representatives of the GCFA to General Conference delegates as part of proposed legislation for 2004 General Conference.

12. See Earl G. Hunt, *A Bishop Speaks His Mind: A Candid View of United Methodism*; William H. Hinson, *A Place to Dig In: Doing Evangelism in the Local Church*; Douglas W. Johnson and Alan K. Waltz, *Facts & Possibilities: An Agenda for The United Methodist Church*; William H. Willimon and Robert L. Wilson, *Rekindling the Flame: Strategies for a Vital United Methodism*. In 1989 Abingdon published *Awaken the Giant: 28 Prescriptions for Reviving The United Methodist Church* by James W. Holsinger and Evelyn Laycock. Taken together, these books provide a substantial body of thought. For people concerned with the same issues in 2005, it is insightful to reflect on the perspectives in these books and the time that has transpired in between.

13. Bishop Wilke credits the input of Dick Murray for the interactive emphasis of DISCIPLE. In fact, one of the supplementary texts for group leaders was Murray's *Teaching the Bible to Adults and Youth* (Nashville: Abingdon Press, 1986; revised and updated, 1993).

14. Besides the Wilkes who wrote the manual, two other people should be mentioned for having a significant hand in the shaping of the DISCIPLE experience. Nellie Moser, mentioned above, gave editorial guidance to the development of the manual, and Wini Grizzle designed and oversaw the DISCIPLE leader training seminars. See Nancy Kruh, *The DISCIPLE Story: The Transforming Power of Scripture* (Nashville: Abingdon Press, 2003), esp. chap., "Feeding the Hunger," 31-46.

15. For the purposes of this discussion, I will limit references to DISCIPLE: BECOMING DISCIPLES THROUGH BIBLE STUDY, although the same plan is followed throughout all four parts.

16. This verse is from the Today's English Version (TEV). Most references are from the New Revised Standard Version.

17. DISCIPLE: BECOMING DISCIPLES THROUGH BIBLE STUDY, 12, hereafter referred to as "Study Manual."

18, Study Manual, 54-55.

19. Ibid., 97.

20. Ibid., 135. The same sort of self-reflection is encouraged in the study of the book of Romans: "Write in your own words what you think it means to be justified by faith" (196).

21. Ibid., 204.

22. Ibid., 227.

23. Session 33, "Gifts of Each Disciple," 244-49. "Veterans" of DISCIPLE commonly mention the impact of this chapter on their sense of Christian vocation, regardless of whether they pursue ordained ministry or serve as lay leaders.

24. Study Manual, 249.

25. The influence of the Dick Murray book, *Teaching the Bible to Adults and Youth*, is especially prominent in this section of the study.

26. For a person interested in some of the "human interest" stories associated with Disciple, I recommend Kruh, *The DISCIPLE Story*.

27. See chap. 4, "Transformed Lives," in Kruh, *The DISCIPLE Story*.

28. This point also illustrates a potential danger in DISCIPLE. If the group leader turns the content of critical questions into a lecture and the participatory nature of group discussion becomes minimized, DISCIPLE quickly loses its appeal.

29. See Hebrews 4:16.

30. Henry H. Knight III, *The Presence of God in the Christian Life: John Wesley and the Means of Grace*, Pietist and Wesleyan Studies, no. 3 (Lanham, Md.: Scarecrow Press). See p. 5, for example, for a typology of the means of grace.

31. We have a "quiet crisis" in the church with regard to the almost complete lack of disciplined theological reflection by pastors. The demands of the parish drive them toward practical matters, and the book market offers a steady stream of resources heavy on activity and light on theology. As a "professional academic," I feel some responsibility for this situation, because the academic guild has made the study of theology so jargon-laden and esoteric as to make it inaccessible to pastor and parishioner.

32. I am aware of the negative sound and implication of the term "non-Christian." I mean nothing by the term other than it denotes someone who has not yet consciously responded to the grace of Christ in becoming a disciple.

33. The reader may suspect that my sketch of DISCIPLE is unnecessarily complimentary, therefore naïve. To be sure, DISCIPLE can and should be subjected to scrutiny and critique, and it has its weaknesses. For example, it seems to speak most forcefully to a fairly narrow slice of the age spectrum. It does not work well with youth and college-age young adults, for example. The youth version of DISCIPLE has had very limited impact. The video presentations also seem quite dated, in the age of CD-ROM and Web-based interaction. It is not uncommon to hear of DISCIPLE groups that skip using the videos altogether because of this "talking head" quality.

34. My thanks to Mr. Chip Sprouse at Iliff School of Theology for helping put me in touch with these students.

35. Here we find a bit of gender difference. Male students who speak of an early call to ministry to which they did not respond express a wider range of reasons for not responding. For women, however, there is a common (though not exclusive) thread: they felt a call to ministry, but had no female role models to help them see that such a ministry was viable for them, or they self-eliminated because of cultural messages about women in ministry.

36. The Walk to Emmaus and the Academy for Spiritual Formation are other avenues through which people experience God's call.

37. Study Manual, 228-35.

16. Forming Christian Witnesses Through the *Witness* Adventure

1. The following essay introduces the reader to the program *Witness: Exploring and Sharing Your Christian Faith*, a joint venture of the General Board of Discipleship of The United Methodist Church and the Foundation for Evangelism. Information is available online at www.gbod.org/witness/ and materials are available through Discipleship Resources and Cokesbury.

2. See Jeremiah 31:31-34 for an example of how the new covenant will be one in which God's people will "know the Lord" and live according to God's law, for it will be written on their hearts. Paul picks up this image in 2 Corinthians 3 as he describes the nature of the new covenant. Hebrews also draws heavily on this image (8:7-13). Likewise, Ezekiel announces (36:16-36) that the new covenant of the Spirit will create a transformed people of God able to reveal God's holiness and honor his name rather than profane it among the nations.

3. A reference to 1 Corinthians 3:16 and found in *The Works of John Wesley*, vol. 11, *The Appeals to Men of Reason and Religion and Certain Related Open Letters*, ed. Gerald R. Cragg (Nashville: Abingdon Press, 1992), 107.

4. See, for example, the study done in Great Britain by John Finney, *Finding Faith Today: How Does It Happen?* published in 1992 by the British Bible Society; and James Wesley Griffin, "Christian Conversion in Post-communist Estonia" (D.Min. diss., Asbury Theological Seminary, 1995).

5. Ron Crandall (Nashville: Abingdon Press, 1999). This study includes American citizens from more than forty states, international citizens from more than thirty countries, and a host of denominational backgrounds with 45 percent being United Methodists.

6. Additional assistance including a PowerPoint presentation, lesson plans, and discussion opportunities are available on the Internet at www.evangelismwitness.org/ or www.gbod.org/witness.

7. Henri J. M. Nouwen, *The Living Reminder: Service and Prayer in Memory of Jesus Christ* (Seabury Press, HarperCollins, 1977), 29.

8. See Barna Research Online, http://www.barna.org/, July 9, 2001, for the report *Protestants, Catholics and Mormons Reflect Diverse Levels of Religious Activity*.

17. Three Types of Faith Sharing

1. Daniel T. Niles, *That They May Have Life* (New York: Harper and Bros., 1951), 96. Also attributed to C. H. Spurgeon by Michael Green in *Evangelism Through the Local Church* (London: Hodder and Stoughton, 1990), 8.

2. For a discussion of the seven aspects of Christian discipleship, see my *Evangelistic Love of God and Neighbor* (Nashville: Abingdon Press, 2003), 76-98. The seven aspects are baptism, cognitive commitments, spiritual disciplines, conversion, morality, spiritual gifts, and faith sharing.

3. Walter Brueggemann, *Biblical Perspectives on Evangelism: Living in a Three-Storied Universe* (Nashville: Abingdon Press, 1993), 10.

4. See *Evangelistic Love*, 21.

5. Aristides, "The Apology of Aristides," trans. J. Rendel Harris, in vol. 1 of *Texts and Studies: Contributions to Biblical and Patristic Literature*, ed. J. Armitage Robinson (Cambridge: Cambridge Univ. Press, 1893), 49.

6. John Wesley, "The General Spread of the Gospel," §21, in *The Works of John Wesley*, Bicentennial ed. (Nashville: Abingdon Press, 1985), 2:495.

7. William J. Abraham, *The Logic of Evangelism* (Grand Rapids: Eerdmans, 1989), 103-4.

8. There is something in invitation that is similar to hospitality. See Marjorie Thompson, *Soul Feast: An Invitation to the Christian Spiritual Life* (Louisville, Ky.: Westminster John Knox, 1995), 119-36.

9. In this and the other illustrations, I have combined the true stories of several individuals. This protects the persons I have known and makes more general the point of the illustrations.

10. See the appendix in *The Evangelistic Love of God and Neighbor,* 197. Verbal faith sharing by the laity is component number 6 in the list of 20 components of an evangelistically effective congregation.

18. The Alpha Course

1. I am very grateful for the extensive feedback that Nicky Gumbel has made on the content and argument of this essay. The essay does, of course, represent the author's assessment of the Alpha Course. Editor's Note: The Wesleyan tradition has recently developed a similar course, though less well known than Alpha, by Andy Langford, Mark Ralls, and Rob Weber, *Beginnings* (Abingdon Press, 2003). Information on *Beginnings* is available at www.Cokesbury.com or from Abingdon Press. Another program similar to Alpha, developed by two progressive United Methodist pastors and featuring presenters such as Stanley Hauerwaus, Tex Sample, Leslie Griffiths, John Cobb, and Minerva Carcaño, can be found at www.livingthequestions.com. Finally, the Christian Believer introduces the basic Christian beliefs, like DISCIPLE, and is available through Cokesbury.

2. *Alpha News,* November 2003.

3. For published statistics, see the Alpha International Web site http://alpha course.org/world/; and the latest edition of *Alpha News* at http://alphacourse.org/ runningacourse/news/.

4. See http://alphacourse.org/itv/.

5. Data in this paragraph supplied by Nicky Gumbel in March 2004.

6. For a helpful analysis of the surveys to date, see Charles Freebury, *Alpha or Emmaus? Assessing Today's Top Evangelistic Courses* (Charles Freebury, 2002). Available from Higher Severalls House, 89 Hermitage St, Crewkerne, Somerset TA18 8EX. This is a revision of an M.A. dissertation submitted to Cliff College, 2001.

7. Freebury, *Alpha or Emmaus?,* 25f. Freebury also draws upon the research of Stephen Hunt, *Anyone for Alpha? Evangelism in a Post-Christian Society* (Darton, Longman & Todd, 2001); and Mark Ireland, *A Study of the Effectiveness of Process Evangelism Courses in the Diocese of Lichfield, with Special Reference to Alpha* (M.A. thesis, Cliff College, 2000).

8. Freebury, *Alpha or Emmaus?,* 63.

9. "Origins of Alpha," http://alphacourse.org, January 2004.

10. Alpha and other (so-called) process evangelism courses have been compared to the evangelistic process of Christian initiation in the early church, but in a compressed form. Robert Webber provides us with a helpful analysis of the early church catechumenate, and how it might be more fully recovered, in *Journey to Jesus: The Worship, Evangelism and Nurture Mission of the Church* (Nashville: Abingdon Press, 2001).

11. Nicky Gumbel, *Questions of Life* (Cook Ministry Resources, 1996).

12. "About the Alpha Course," http://alphacourse.org, January 2004.

13. Nicky Gumbel, *Searching Issues* (Cook Ministry Resources, 1996).

14. Gumbel, *Questions of Life,* 101.

15. Jonathan Bayes, "Questioning 'Questions of Life': A Theological Assessment of the Alpha Course," www.diakrisis.org/alpha_course.htm.

16. See the penultimate chapter in *Questions of Life,* 217f. Apart from this, there are some reflections on the church as the family of God in the chapter on the work of the Spirit (217f.).

17. Gumbel, *Questions of Life,* 135-60. Although the course makes it clear that speaking in tongues is not the only sign of being filled with the Spirit, it is clearly the eminent sign, available to everyone, and details some ways in which it may be received. Although the material also suggests that being filled with the Spirit may occur imperceptibly, the availability of some intense charismatic experience is anticipated as an ordinary sign of it. However one evaluates these assumptions, Alpha certainly cannot be criticized for making them explicit.

18. "Leading Small Groups," *Alpha Conference, Delegate Notes,* April 2002, 13.

19. In The United Methodist Church, see William Abraham, *Waking from Doctrinal Amnesia* (Nashville: Abingdon Press, 1995).

20. See Freebury, *Alpha or Emmaus?,* 63f.

21. "Integrating Alpha into the Local Church," *Alpha Conference, Delegate Notes,* April 2002, 21. This is a talk given by Sandy Millar, vicar of HTB.

22. See http://www.christlife.org/alpha/alpha.html.

23. These include the following Alpha International publications: the *Alpha Administrator's Handbook;* an *Alpha Cookbook; Introducing Worship to Alpha and the Alpha Worship Pack; Prayer on Alpha; Maximising the Potential of Your Alpha Course;* and various other resources aimed at training leaders and helpers.

24. "Copyright," http://alphacourse.org, January 2004.

25. See Nicky Gumbel, *Telling Others: The Alpha Initiative* (Kingsway, 1995).

26. *Alpha News* and *Alpha News (International Edition)* are published in order to communicate "the spread of The Alpha Course worldwide." It contains the latest statistics on the number of countries, languages, courses, and attendees associated with Alpha. It also contains news about other Alpha initiatives, stories about church growth, commendations from notable persons, and testimonies from individuals about the life-changing effects of attending the course.

27. "The Principles of Alpha," *Alpha Conference, Delegate Notes,* April 2002, 5f.

28. See, for example, Darrell Guder et al., eds., *Missional Church: A Vision for the Sending of the Church in North America* (Grand Rapids: Eerdmans, 1998).

29. See, for example, Charles Finney, *Lectures on Revivals of Religion* (Cambridge: Harvard Univ. Press, 1960). Finney turned the revival meeting into a science by offering various "measures" that could be employed for successfully bringing sinners to repentance.

30. See Kenneth Collins and John Tyson, eds., *Conversion in the Wesleyan Tradition* (Nashville: Abingdon Press, 2001). To speak of justification and the new birth as an event does not necessitate its being a datable moment. For many, the truth of that moment is experienced only as it unfolds over time in the lifelong commitment of discipleship.

31. See George Hunter, *Church for the Unchurched* (Nashville: Abingdon Press, 1996).

32. See Kimberly Thacker, "The Value of Authenticity in Postmodern Evangelism," *Journal of the Academy for Evangelism in Theological Education* 17 (2001–2): 34-50.

33. See Ronald Sider, *Good News and Good Works: A Theology for the Whole Gospel* (Baker, 1999).

34. John Wimber and Keith Springer, *Power Evangelism* (HarperCollins, 1986). Among others, Gumbel has personally cited the special influence of Gordon Fee and Father Raneiro Cantalamessa.

35. Lesslie Newbigin reminds us, however, that whereas Jesus proclaimed the Kingdom, the early Christians proclaimed Jesus, because following Jesus is how God's reign is extended in the world. See Newbigin, *The Open Secret* (Grand Rapids: Eerdmans, 1995), 40f.

36. See, for example, Mortimar Arias, *Announcing the Reign of God* (Fortress, 1984).

37. William Abraham, *The Logic of Evangelism* (Grand Rapids: Eerdmans, 1989).

38. See Howard Snyder, *Models of the Kingdom* (Nashville: Abingdon Press, 1991).

39. See David Wells, *God the Evangelist: How the Holy Spirit Works to Bring Men and Women to Faith* (Grand Rapids: Eerdmans, 1987).

40. For a helpful critique, see Philip Kenneson and James Street, *Selling Out the Church: The Dangers of Church Marketing* (Nashville: Abingdon Press, 1997); and Douglas Webster, *Selling Jesus: What's Wrong with Marketing the Church* (IVP, 1992).

41. There is, however, a certain ambiguity in the way that Alpha uses statistics to measure its own growth, success, and portability as a tool of, or package for, "effective evangelism." See comments under section 3.2 below.

42. Michael Green has published a book/study material for those who have completed a course titled *After Alpha?* (Kingsway, 2001). The material not only defends and extends some of the themes covered in the Alpha Course, but also supplements it with additional teaching on church and sacraments, etc.

43. William Cork, "Is 'Alpha for Catholics'?" http://www.wquercus.com/alpha.htm.

44. Ibid.

45. See http://www.banner.org.uk/misc/alpha.html. See also Chris Hand, *Falling Short? The Alpha Course Examined* (Day One Publications, 1998).

46. See http://www.despatch.cth.com.au.

47. See http://www.ianpaisley.org.

48. See http://www.pfo.org/alpha-cr.htm.

49. William Horsburgh, "Making Alpha Waves," http://www.diakrisis.org/alpha_course.htm.

50. Pete Ward, "Alpha—The McDonaldization of Religion?" *Anvil* 15, no. 4 (1998): 279-86.

51. George Ritzer, *The McDonaldization of Society* (Thousand Oaks, Ca.: Pine Forge Press, 1996).

52. Ibid., 285.

53. Ibid., 286.

54. Martyn Percy, "'Join-the-Dots' Christianity—Assessing Alpha," *Reviews in Religion and Theology* 3 (1997): 14-18. See also Marcus Bockmuehl, "'Dotty' Christianity—Assessing Percy on Alpha," *Reviews in Religion and Theology* 1 (1998): 10-12.

55. Gumbel refers to the many thousands of people who have done Alpha in prisons around the world, and that the course runs in some of the poorest parts of Africa, India, and Southeast Asia, as well as inner-city churches worldwide.

56. Hunt, *Anyone for Alpha?*, 69.

57. See Elizabeth McDonald, *Alpha: New Life or New Lifestyle?* (St. Matthews Publications, 1996).

58. Booker and Ireland, *Evangelism— Which Way Now?*, chap.4. In Britain, one can find Emmaus Nurture, Credo, Christianity Explored, the Y Course, and Start! Course. From a U.S. perspective, see Andrew Kinsey, "Unfinished Evangelism: Christian Believer and Alpha as Forms of Catechetical Training for the Ancient-Future Church," *Journal of the Academy for Evangelism in Theological Education* 17 (2001–2): 51-65.

Conclusion: The Future of the Great Commission

1. Philip Jenkins, *The Next Christendom* (Oxford: Oxford Univ. Press, 2002), 7.